P9-DGS-473

The New Handbook of the Christian Year

Based on the Revised Common Lectionary

HOYT L. HICKMAN
DON E. SALIERS
LAURENCE HULL STOOKEY
JAMES F. WHITE

Abingdon Press
Nashville

THE NEW HANDBOOK OF THE CHRISTIAN YEAR

Copyright © 1986, 1992 by Abingdon Press

All rights reserved.
No part of this work may be reproduced or transmitted in any form or by any means, electronic or mechanical, including photocopying and recording, or by any information storage or retrieval system, except as may be expressly permitted by the 1976 Copyright Act or in writing from the publisher. Requests for permission should be addressed in writing to Abingdon Press, 201 Eighth Avenue South, Nashville, TN 37203.

Library of Congress Cataloging-in-Publication Data

The New handbook of the Christian year / Hoyt L. Hickman . . . [et al.].
    p.   cm.
    Previous ed. published under title: Handbook of the Christian
year.
    Includes bibliographical references and index.
    ISBN 0-687-27760-4 (alk. paper)
    1. Church year.   2. United Methodist Church (U.S.)—Liturgy—Texts.
3. Methodist Church—Liturgy—Texts.   4. Worship services.
5. Common lectionary.   I. Hickman, Hoyt L. (Hoyt Leon), 1927–
II. Handbook of the Christian year.
BV30.H35   1992
264'.076—dc20

   92-18473
   CIP

You are free to reproduce these worship services for use within your local church provided you include the following credit line and copyright notice: Reprinted from *The New Handbook of the Christian Year*, copyright © 1986, 1992 by Abingdon Press. Used by permission.

New material in this edition includes completely revised compilations of hymn titles, and scripture references and the Index of Scripture Readings updated to agree with the Revised Common Lectionary.

Unless otherwise indicated all Scripture quotations are from the Revised Standard Version of the Bible, copyrighted 1946, 1952, © 1971, 1973 by the Division of Christian Education of the National Council of the Churches of Christ in the U.S.A., and are used by permission. There are some minor adaptations.

Those noted NEB are from The New English Bible. © the Delegates of the Oxford University Press and the Syndics of the Cambridge University Press 1961, 1970. Reprinted by permission.

Symbol drawings by William Duncan from *Symbols of the Church* edited by Carroll E. Whittemore. Copyright © 1959 by Carroll E. Whittemore. Used by permission of the publisher, Abingdon Press.

See other acknowledgments on page 304.

MANUFACTURED IN THE UNITED STATES OF AMERICA

98 99 00 01 02 03 04 05 06 07 — 15 14 13 12 11 10 9 8 7 6

The New Handbook of the Christian Year

CONTENTS

PART TWO: RESOURCES FOR THE CHRISTIAN YEAR

PART THREE: APPENDICES

PREFACE TO
The New Handbook of the Christian Year

*T*he *New Handbook of the Christian Year* incorporates two major revisions of the original *Handbook of the Christian Year*.

    1. The Revised Common Lectionary (1992) has been substituted for the original Common Lectionary that was in trial use for nine years beginning in Advent 1983.

    2. The lists of suggested hymns have been completely revised so as to a) fit the Revised Common Lectionary and b) include hymns that have only recently appeared in major hymnals.

These revisions should make this handbook much more useful in the coming years.

PREFACE

T he main purpose of this book is both simple and far-reaching. Here we present for local church study and use an integrated series of services of worship for the Christian Year, with introductions, pastoral commentary, and additional resources. These resources are intended to be an invitation and guide for renewing and deepening our corporate worship. The movement of worship through the Christian Year emphasizes participation in the Lord's saving acts. Although this emphasis may be unfamiliar to many in our churches today, it is not a new idea. In fact, these gospel themes are the very essence of the faith lived and celebrated by the church in its earliest times.

It is our conviction that the reform and renewal of our worship depends upon the proclamation and celebration of the gospel in its fullness. In this we join our sisters and brothers in the great family of Christian communities who also are seeking a more faithful and authentic participation in God's redemptive action in Christ. The reality and power of the gospel can never be confined to particular days and seasons, but it is given a special intensity when celebrated through these hallowed days and seasons. The recovery of this living reality is essential to the renewal of Christian worship and life. For this reason we regard the recent widespread recovery of the Christian Year among Christians of many denominations as a sign of great hope.

The patterns, services, and texts presented in this book are rooted in Christian tradition and are ecumenical in spirit. They are also attuned to the contemporary needs and pastoral situation of a wide range of churches. Much of the material in this book appeared earlier in three books in the United Methodist Supplemental Worship Resources series: *Seasons of the Gospel* (SWR 6), *From Ashes to Fire* (SWR 8), and *From Hope to Joy* (SWR 15), which were written and edited by three of us with the sponsorship and assistance of the Section on Worship of the General Board of Discipleship of The United Methodist Church and published by Abingdon Press. In rewriting these earlier books and developing this one comprehensive resource for the entire Christian Year, we were guided by two basic principles: (1) We have tried to present these resources in ways that will make them usable in a wide range of Christian congregations; and (2) we have thoroughly updated the earlier resources, taking into account both the many suggestions received from those who have read and used them and the recent developments in the understanding and practice of the Christian Year. Foremost among the latter have been the appearance and the widespread adoption of the common calendar and *Common Lectionary* on which this book is based.

In the writing and editing of this book the three of us who were involved with the earlier books (Hoyt L. Hickman of the staff of the General Board of Discipleship, Don E. Saliers of Emory University, and James F. White of the University of Notre Dame) have been joined by Laurence Hull Stookey of Wesley Theological Seminary. Hoyt Hickman was named general editor. The following assignments were made in the preparation of first drafts. Don Saliers drafted the revisions of *From Ashes to Fire* and *From Hope to Joy* (of which he had been the original writer and compiler) and the Glossary of Christian Symbols. Laurence Stookey drafted chapters 3 and 8 and the Glossary of Liturgical Terms. James White drafted chapter 4. Hoyt Hickman drafted the revisions of *Seasons of the Gospel* (the historical and introductory parts of which had originally been written by James White) and the Annotated Bibliography. As these first drafts were revised by our joint efforts and compiled into final form, the contributions of the four of us have been so blended that it would be impossible to identify one of us as the sole author of a given chapter. We have tried to produce a book that reflects a consensus of our viewpoints, but of course it would have been in some respects a different book if one of us had written it alone.

We have benefited from the advice and assistance of many persons in the development of this book whom we wish to thank corporately. In particular we thank Sally Rhodes Ahner for her extensive research and advice in the recommendation of hymns. We thank John Brooks-Leonard for his contribution of Easter Vesper resources. We thank Susan J. White for reading portions of the manuscript and making many helpful suggestions. We thank James M. Schellman and the Consultation on Common Texts (CCT) for permission to reproduce the Common Lectionary, Index of Scripture Readings, and Index of Psalms from the CCT book *Common Lectionary*, published by the Church Hymnal Corporation. We thank Ezra Earl Jones, general secretary, Noé E. Gonzales, associate general secretary, and the General Board of Discipleship for their permission and cooperation in allowing us to use materials from the SWR books developed under their sponsorship. And we thank our families for their loving patience as we spent long hours on this book that we might have spent with them.

PART ONE

INTRODUCTION TO THE CHRISTIAN YEAR

THE CHRISTIAN YEAR

A. The Common Calendar

ADVENT SEASON

First Sunday of Advent to Fourth Sunday of Advent

CHRISTMAS SEASON

Christmas Eve/Day
First Sunday After Christmas
New Year's Eve/Day or Holy Name of Jesus
Second Sunday After Christmas
Epiphany

SEASON AFTER EPIPHANY*

First Sunday After Epiphany (Baptism of the Lord)
Second Sunday After Epiphany to Eighth Sunday After Epiphany
Last Sunday After Epiphany (Transfiguration Sunday)

LENTEN SEASON

Ash Wednesday
First Sunday of Lent to Fifth Sunday of Lent
Holy Week
   Passion/Palm Sunday
   Monday in Holy Week
   Tuesday in Holy Week

*In some churches this is called Epiphany Season and begins with Epiphany. Some churches refer to the time after Epiphany and after Pentecost as ordinary time and to the Sundays as _____ Sunday in ordinary time.

    Wednesday in Holy Week
    Holy Thursday
    Good Friday
    Holy Saturday

EASTER SEASON

    Easter Vigil
    Easter
    Easter Evening
    Second Sunday of Easter to Sixth Sunday of Easter
    Ascension (Sixth Thursday of Easter)
    Seventh Sunday of Easter
    Pentecost

SEASON AFTER PENTECOST†

    Trinity Sunday (First Sunday After Pentecost)
    Sundays After Pentecost‡
    Christ the King (Last Sunday After Pentecost)

SPECIAL DAYS

    Presentation (February 2)
    Annunciation (March 25)
    Visitation (May 31)
    Holy Cross (September 14)
    All Saints (November 1 or
      First Sunday in November)
    Thanksgiving Day

B. Dates in the Easter Cycle**

Year of Our Lord	Ash Wednesday	Easter Day	Pentecost
1986	February 12	March 30	May 18
1987	March 4	April 19	June 7
1988	February 17	April 3	May 22
1989	February 8	March 26	May 14
1990	February 28	April 15	June 3
1991	February 13	March 31	May 19
1992	March 4	April 19	June 7
1993	February 24	April 11	May 30

†United Methodists have the option of referring to this as Kingdomtide.
‡These Sundays may be referred to as _____ Sunday After Pentecost or _____ Sunday in ordinary time. Lectionary readings on these Sundays are determined not by which Sunday it is after Pentecost but by the dates within which a Sunday falls.
**Easter is observed by Protestant and Roman Catholic churches on the Sunday after the first full moon on or after March 21. This full moon may occur on any date between March 21 and April 18. Easter cannot be ealier than March 22 or later than April 25. Eastern Orthodox Christians use a somewhat different formula for calculating the date of Easter; hence their observance often does not coincide with the above dates.

Year of Our Lord	*Ash Wednesday*	*Easter Day*	*Pentecost*
1994	February 16	April 3	May 22
1995	March 1	April 16	June 4
1996	February 21	April 7	May 26
1997	February 12	March 30	May 18
1998	February 25	April 12	May 31
1999	February 17	April 4	May 23
2000	March 8	April 23	June 11
2001	February 28	April 15	June 3
2002	February 13	March 31	May 19
2003	March 5	April 20	June 8
2004	February 25	April 11	May 30
2005	February 9	March 27	May 15
2006	March 1	April 16	June 4
2007	February 21	April 8	May 27
2008	February 6	March 23	May 11
2009	February 25	April 12	May 31
2010	February 17	April 4	May 23
2011	March 9	April 24	June 12
2012	February 22	April 8	May 27
2013	February 13	March 31	May 19
2014	March 5	April 20	June 8
2015	February 18	April 5	May 24
2016	February 10	March 27	May 15
2017	March 1	April 16	June 4
2018	February 14	April 1	May 20
2019	March 6	April 21	June 9
2020	February 26	April 12	May 31

THE ORIGIN OF THE CHRISTIAN YEAR

A. Time Is Important

Christianity takes time seriously. History is where God is made known. Christians have no knowledge of God without time, for it is through actual events happening in historical time that God is revealed. God chooses to make the divine nature and will known through events that take place within the same calendar that measures the daily lives of men and women. God's self-disclosures take place within the same course of time as political events: "In the days of Herod king of Judaea" (Luke 1:5 NEB), or "it took place when Quirinius was governor of Syria" (Luke 2:2 NEB). God's time is our time, too, marked by a temporal order called a calendar.

When we encounter one of the Eastern religions in which historical time may be insignificant, we realize just how crucial time is to Christian faith. Christianity talks not of salvation in general but of salvation accomplished by specific actions of God at definite times and places. It speaks of climactic events and a finale. For Christianity, the ultimate meanings of life are revealed not by universal, timeless statements but by concrete acts of God. In the fullness of time, God invades our history, assumes our flesh, heals, teaches, and eats with sinners. There is a specific historical and spatial setting to it all: "It was winter, and the festival of the Dedication was being held in Jerusalem. Jesus was walking in the temple precincts, in Solomon's Portico" (John 10:22-23 NEB). Christ is put to death on a specific day related to the Passover festival of that year, and he rises on the third day. It is the same time we inhabit, the time in which we give birth, earn a living, grow older, and face death.

The centrality of time in Christianity is reflected in Christian worship. This worship, like the rest of life, is structured on recurring rhythms of the day, the week, and the year. Far from trying to escape time, Christian worship uses time as one of its basic structures. Our present time becomes the occasion of encounter with God's acts in time past and future. Salvation, as we experience it in worship, is a reality based on temporal events through which God comes to us. How we structure time enables us to commemorate and reexperience those very acts on which salvation is grounded. Christian worship is built on the foundation of time.

The way we use our time in daily life is one of the best indications of what is really important to us. We can always be counted on to find time for those things we consider most important, though we may not always be willing to admit to others, or even to ourselves, what our real priorities are. Whether it is financial gain, political action, or family activities, we find time for putting first those things that matter most to us. Time talks. When we give it to others, we are really giving ourselves. Time, then, inevitably expresses our priorities. How we allocate this limited resource reveals what we value most.

The church also shows what is most important to its life by the way it keeps time. Here again the use of time reveals priorities of faith and practice. One answer to "What do Christians profess?" could be "Look how they keep time!" This will become clear as we examine how Christians have kept time, beginning with the New Testament church.

The earliest portions of the New Testament are imbued with a sense of time as *kairos*, the right or proper time present, in which God has brought a new dimension to reality. "The time has come; the kingdom of God is upon you" (Mark 1:15 NEB).

Yet already within the New Testament itself—when, for instance, Luke writes his Gospel and church history begins with the book of Acts—we see the beginning of a tendency to look back, to recall the time past in which things had happened. Remembering the past comes to be almost as important as anticipating the future before the first century is ended.

The priorities of the early church's faith are disclosed by the way Christians of the second, third, and fourth centuries organized time. This was not by a systematic or planned method but was, rather, the church's spontaneous response to "the events that have happened among us" (Luke 1:1 NEB). The same type of response, the keeping memories alive, also prompted the writing of the Gospels that others might be able to follow "the traditions handed down to us by the original eyewitnesses and servants of the Gospel" (Luke 1:2 NEB). The use of time was not as systematic as the Evangelist's efforts "to write a connected narrative" (Luke 1:3 NEB), but the practice of organizing time was already present in Judaism and has had almost as persistent an influence in shaping Christian memories as have the written Gospels. Thus, for Christians, Easter is an annual *event* just as much as it is a narrative in writing. Even today, Christmas is for most people far more a yearly *occurrence* than a nativity story.

What was the faith of the early church as witnessed to by the church's use of time? It was, above all else, faith in the death and resurrection of Jesus Christ. Second, it was trust in the abiding presence of the Holy Spirit, known and experienced in the holy church. And third, it was belief that witnessed to those signs by which God had become manifest among us in Jesus Christ. While this is not a systematic summation of Christian belief, it gives a clear indication of the heart of the faith of the early church, revealed by how the church kept time.

The early church's calendar shows an implicitly trinitarian structure: belief in the Father made manifest, the Son risen, and the Holy Spirit indwelling the church. It will be helpful to probe more deeply into the history of how the early church kept time so that we may compare its practices with ours. We may find reasons to readjust our priorities in the light of those of the heroic age of Christianity. Observation of early practices provides important insights into Christian faith. We are, in fact, doing liturgical theology, using practice as our data for theological reflection.

B. The Lord's Day

The foundation of the Christian calendar is what the New Testament calls "the Lord's day" (Rev. 1:10 NEB), the first day of each week. The earliest Christians received from ancient Israel the pattern of the seven-day week. As Jews they had observed the seventh day of the week (sunset Friday to sunset Saturday) as the Sabbath, in remembrance that God rested on the seventh day after the six days of creation (Gen. 2:2; Exod. 20:8-11; 31:12-17).

The New Testament points to the first day of the week as a special time for worship. Paul told the Christians in Corinth to set aside money for the collection on the first day of the week (I Cor. 16:2). At Troas, after talking until midnight on Saturday, Paul broke bread (presumably the Eucharist) and remained in conversation with Christians there until Sunday dawned (Acts 20:7, 11). The writer of Revelation relates, "It was on the Lord's day, and I was caught up by the Spirit" (1:10 NEB). *The Lord's Day* had become a familiar Christian term for the first day of the week by the end of the first century.

The celebration of the Lord's Day has from the beginning been a way in which the church has witnessed to its faith. On the first day of creation, "God said, 'Let there be light,' and there was light; and God saw that the light was good, and he separated light from darkness. He called the light day, and the darkness night. So evening came, and morning came, the first day" (Gen. 1:3-5 NEB). All four

Gospels are careful to state that it was on the morning of the first day—the day on which creation had begun and the moment God had "separated light from darkness"—that the empty tomb was discovered (Matt. 28:1-6; Mark 16:2-6; Luke 24:1-3; John 20:1-8). The Gospels go on to state that the risen Christ appeared to the disciples on that first day of the week (Matt. 28:9 ff.; Luke 24:13 ff.; John 20:14 ff.) and also on the eighth day—that is, the next Sunday (John 20:26).

About A.D. 115 Ignatius wrote to the Christians in Magnesia and spoke of those who "ceased to keep the Sabbath [Jewish seventh-day] and lived by the Lord's Day, on which our life as well as theirs shone forth, thanks to him and his death."[1]

The *Didache*, written sometime in the late first or early second century, reminds Christians: "On the Lord's day of the Lord, come together, break bread and hold eucharist."[2]

Even pagans noticed that "on an appointed day they [Christians] had been accustomed to meet before daybreak," though Pliny, the Roman administrator who wrote these words, hardly understood this to mean a meeting for the Lord's Supper.[3]

Another term, *Sunday*, appeared by the middle of the second century. Justin Martyr told his pagan audience in about A.D. 155 that "we all hold this common gathering on Sunday, since it is the first day, on which God transforming darkness and matter made the universe, and Jesus Christ our Saviour rose from the dead on the same day."[4] Christians soon adopted the newly coined pagan term and compared Christ's rising from the dead to the rising of the sun. Even today, the English and German word is *Sunday*, while those who speak French, Spanish, and Italian refer to the *Lord's Day*.

The *Epistle of Barnabas* called Sunday "an eighth day, that is the beginning of another world . . . in which Jesus also rose from the dead."[5] Early Christians saw the Lord's Day as the eighth day of creation, when, having rested on the seventh day, God began to create anew. Anyone who is in Christ is also "a new creation" (II Cor. 5:17).

Sunday was a day of worship but not of rest until an edict by the Emperor Constantine in A.D. 321: "All judges, city people, and craftsmen shall rest on the venerable day of the Sun. But countrymen may without hindrance attend to agriculture."[6]

Sunday stood out above all other days because it was the weekly anniversary of the resurrection. In the early church, Sunday commemorated the Lord's passion, death, and resurrection; but it was, above all else, the day on which the Savior rose from the dead. As the Lord's Day, the day of the sun risen from darkness, the start of the new creation, every Sunday witnessed to the risen Lord. Tertullian tells us that Christians did not kneel on Sunday, "the day of the Lord's resurrection." Even today, Sunday takes precedence over all other occasions. Sundays of Lent remain days of joy, though within a penitential season. Each Sunday testifies to the resurrection faith. Sunday may be regarded as a weekly little Easter; even more, Easter is a yearly great Sunday.

There were other events that gave the week even more contour for the early church. Luke tells of the Pharisee who said, "I fast twice a week" (18:12 NEB). But the *Didache*, in all seriousness, told Christians: "Your fasts must not be identical with those of the hypocrites. They fast on Mondays and Thursdays; but you should fast on Wednesdays and Fridays."[7] Commemorative reasons for this had appeared by the time of a late fourth-century document, *The Apostolic Constitutions:* "Fast . . . on the fourth day of the week, . . . Judas then promising to betray Him [Jesus] for money; and . . . on [Friday] because on that day the Lord suffered the death of the cross."[8] There is evidence that some early Christians also held a certain regard for Saturday as "the memorial of the creation," from which work God rested on the seventh day. Tertullian tells us there were "some few who abstain from kneeling on the Sabbath." But these other days were decidedly inferior in importance compared with Sunday.

C. The Hours of the Day

Even the day itself became a structure of praise for the early church. The *Didache* instructed Christians to pray the Lord's Prayer three times a day. Psalm 55:17 spoke of calling upon God "evening and morning and at noon" (NEB). Another psalm declared: "Seven times a day I praise thee for the justice of thy decrees" (119:164 NEB), and "at midnight I rise to give thee thanks" (119:62 NEB). By the early third century, Tertullian could speak of the third, sixth, and ninth hours of the day as times of "special solemnity in divine prayers" because of actions of the apostles at those times.

Hippolytus, an early third-century Roman Christian, spoke of seven daily occasions for prayer. For him, nine o'clock in the morning, noon, and three in the afternoon, respectively, recalled the hours at which Jesus was nailed to the cross, "there was a great darkness," and Jesus died. Each day memorialized the crucifixion in this way. Hippolytus saw midnight as a time of prayer, for the bridegroom comes at midnight (Matt. 25:6), and each Christian must be prepared to meet him. Prayer is needed at cockcrow, for at this moment Christ was denied (Matt. 26:75). Prayer was also advocated upon rising and retiring. Monasticism later developed the hours of the day into a daily eightfold cycle of prayer. Late in the fourth century, Chrysostom urged newly baptized Christians to begin each day's work with prayer for strength to do God's will, and to end the day by rendering "an account to the Master of his whole day, and beg forgiveness for his falls."[9] Very early, then, the Christian day became a cycle of remembering Christ throughout one's daily labors in the midst of worldly concerns.

Christians adopted the Jewish sense of the liturgical day as beginning at nightfall. Hence, the *eve* of a festival such as Christmas or Easter is a part of the same day that continues at daybreak.

D. The Easter Cycle

Just as the week and the day witnessed to Jesus Christ, so too did the year serve the early church as a structure for commemoration. We read in the Old and New Testaments how the people of ancient Israel observed a variety of yearly festivals related both to the agriculture that structured their lives and to the events in their history that constituted their story as a people.

It was very significant to Jesus and his first disciples that he was crucified at Passover time, when Jews were commemorating how God had delivered their ancestors from slavery in Egypt, brought them safely through the Red Sea, and made them a free people. These earliest Christians realized that they too had been delivered by God and were no longer slaves to sin and death. They had been made a free people through the suffering, death, and resurrection of Christ. Referring to the lamb that was sacrificed at Passover, Paul wrote:

> Cleanse out the old leaven that you may be a new lump, as you really are unleavened. For Christ, our paschal lamb, has been sacrificed. Let us, therefore, celebrate the festival, not with the old leaven, the leaven of malice and evil, but with the unleavened bread of sincerity and truth (I Cor. 5:7-8 RSV).

The old Jewish event of deliverance was now made completely new in Jesus Christ. Slavery and redemption were rehearsed, but in a new sense through release from sin and death by what Christ had done.

Thus, although the early Christians celebrated God's saving work in Christ every Lord's Day, it seemed fitting when Passover time came around each year that there be a great yearly Lord's Day. Just as the week focused on the Lord's Day, so the year focused on the *Pascha* (Passover). Christians observed this Pascha at least as early as the second century, and the passage just quoted suggests that they might have observed it in New Testament times.

The second- and third-century church kept the Pascha with services signifying the making of new Christians through the acts of baptism, laying on of hands, and first communion. Just as the Pascha commemorated the escape from slavery by passage through the Red Sea, so the church saw baptism as burial with Christ in which "we were buried with him, and lay dead, in order that, as Christ was raised from the dead . . . we shall also be one with him in a resurrection like his" (Rom. 6:4-5 NEB). In the first three centuries, Christ's passion, death, and resurrection were commemorated together at the Pascha. Tertullian tells us that "the Passover affords a more than usually solemn day for baptism; when, withal, the Lord's passion, in which we are baptized, was completed."[10]

There had to be preparation for such a solemn act. Hippolytus, writing in the third century, tells us that those to be baptized fasted on Friday and Saturday and then began an all-night vigil Saturday evening. At cockcrow at the hour of the resurrection on Easter morning, they were baptized in the waters and rose with Christ as from the dead.

Early Christians engaged in a long debate, known as the Quartodeciman (fourteenth day) controversy, over whether the Christian Pascha should or should not follow the Jewish dating of Passover. The sacrifice of the Passover lamb took place on the fourteenth day of the month of Nisan in the Jewish calendar and could fall on any day of the week. Since the Jewish calendar is based on the phases of the moon, this meant that Passover commenced at full moon.

Early in the fourth century, the church finally agreed that the Pascha, unlike the Jewish Passover, must always be celebrated on a Sunday. This decision clearly recognized the symbolic meaning of Sunday. "Never on any day other than the Lord's Day should the mystery of the Lord's resurrection from the dead be celebrated, . . . on that day alone we should observe the end of the Paschal fast."[11] Thus, the weekly and yearly cycles of celebrating the resurrection reinforced each other.

Later, in western Europe, the date was fixed on the Sunday after the first full moon on or after March 21. Roman Catholics and Protestants still date Easter in this way, which is why Easter falls on a different date each year, as early as March 22 or as late as April 25.

In the course of the fourth century, the Pascha, which had previously commemorated all the events of the last days of Jesus in Jerusalem, was divided into several distinct observances spread over several days. The dissolution apparently first occurred in Jerusalem, where time and space came together at the sites of Jesus' life and ministry. A need was felt to hold separate services for each event at the holy places to serve the throngs of pilgrims who were arriving from all over the world. Scripture itself was mined for evidence as to the time and place of all the events of Christ's last week in Jerusalem. We have a good example of what had developed by about A.D. 384, chronicled in the writings of a Spanish woman named Egeria. Her notes, apparently written down so she could give talks when she got back home, have survived, and they give us a clear insight into how Jerusalem had developed its way of keeping time. These fourth-century developments have shaped the Christian practice of Holy Week ever since.

Egeria tells us that Passion/Palm Sunday, or the beginning of Holy Week, is "the beginning of the Easter Week or, as they call it here, 'The Great Week.' . . . All the people go before him [the bishop] with psalms and antiphons, all the time repeating, 'Blessed is he that cometh in the name of the Lord.' "[12] There are minor services on the next three days, except that on Wednesday the presbyter reads about Judas' plot to betray Jesus, and the "people groan and lament at this reading." On Thursday, after everyone has received communion, all "conduct the bishop to Gethsemane." And on Friday, services occur on Golgotha, where fragments of the wood of the cross are adored by all the people, who march past the cross and kiss it.

By the end of the fourth century, this way of commemorating Holy Week was complete, and Augustine stated as accepted fact that "it is clear from the Gospel on what days the Lord was crucified and rested in the tomb and rose again" and that the church has "a requirement of retaining those same days."[13] The ancient Pascha had been broken into separate commemorations: Holy Thursday, Good Friday, Holy Saturday, and Easter Eve and Day, preceded by Passion/Palm Sunday and the three lesser days of Holy Week. This is how Christians have kept Holy Week ever since. It consists of Passion/Palm Sunday, Monday in Holy Week, Tuesday in Holy Week, Wednesday in Holy Week, Holy Thursday, Good Friday, Holy Saturday, and Easter (Eve and Day). The origin of the English term *Easter* is disputed but may be derived from an Anglo-Saxon spring goddess named Eastre and her festival. Other languages such as French, Spanish, and Italian still use words derived from *Pascha*, which make it evident that we are celebrating the Christian Passover.

Second in importance to the Pascha was the celebration of another event—Pentecost. Like the Pascha, it was also a Jewish feast. It was the name Greek-speaking Jews gave to the Day of First Fruits or Feast of Weeks (*Shabuoth*), the harvest festival commanded in Leviticus 23:16: "The day after the seventh sabbath will make fifty days, and then you shall present to the LORD a grain-offering from the new crop" (NEB). Sometime during the first century A.D., Pentecost came to reflect for Jews the giving of the Torah (teaching, instruction, law) at Mount Sinai.

For Christians, Pentecost commemorated the birthday of the church when, with the noise of a wind, tongues of flame rested on the disciples, and they began to talk in other languages to be understood (Acts 2:1-41). It was significant for Christians that it was on the Jewish Pentecost that the Holy Spirit came upon the Apostles with power in order that the Christian church might be born. Christians soon began to draw the parallel between the giving of the Torah and the giving of the Holy Spirit. Possibly even Paul may be relating the two Pentecosts when he writes: "The law, then, engraved letter by letter upon stone, dispensed death, and yet it was inaugurated with divine splendour. . . . Must not even greater splendour rest upon the divine dispensation of the Spirit?" (II Cor. 3:7-8 NEB). Just as God brought covenant with Israel to fulfillment on Mount Sinai, so God brought covenant with the disciples of Christ to fulfillment at Pentecost.

Pentecost, at least as early as the second century, was a time when the church baptized candidates who had not been ready on Easter Day. Pentecost has always been regarded as an appropriate day for baptisms. We read in Acts 2:41 that on Pentecost about three thousand persons were baptized. The day we celebrate the birth of the church is surely a fitting time to celebrate the spiritual birth of new Christians.

For almost four centuries, Pentecost commemorated not only the descent of the Holy Spirit (Acts 2) but also the ascension of Christ (Acts 1:1-11). Tertullian suggests that Christ ascended into heaven at Pentecost.[14] And, in the first half of the fourth century, the historian Eusebius speaks of "the august and holy solemnity of Pentecost [i.e., the fifty days], which is distinguished by a period of seven weeks, and sealed with that one day on which the holy Scriptures attest the ascension of our common Savior into heaven, and the descent of the Holy Spirit."[15]

By the end of the fourth century, these two commemorations had been separated. *The Apostolic Constitutions* describes forty days after Easter as the proper time to "celebrate the feast of ascension of the Lord." Once again, the biblical witness has been turned into literal history by being interpreted as a means of dating past events in time. In this case, Acts 1:3 and its mention of "a period of forty days" during which the risen Jesus taught his disciples seems to have been the source for pinpointing the date of the ascension as the sixth Thursday after Easter. Where there had been one feast, by the late fourth century there were two: Ascension and Pentecost. Christ was in heaven, and the Holy Spirit dwelt in the holy church on earth. These two feasts pointed to daily realities the church could experience.

The Pascha (Easter) and Pentecost became even more than two great days; they became the first and the last days, respectively, of the oldest and most important season in the Christian year—the Great Fifty Days. While we have been using the term *Pentecost* to refer only to the fiftieth day, the matter is more complicated than that. Historically, the term was used to refer to the entire fifty-day cycle was well as the final day.

In the Jewish calendar, the Day of First Fruits (Pentecost) was seen as the conclusion of the cycle that began with Passover. In it were celebrated the Exodus and the events surrounding it. It was also the grain harvest season, beginning with the consecration of the harvest and of the harvest season. The term *Pentecost* was used to indicate both the last day of that cycle and the fifty-day cycle as a whole.

Christians such as Eusebius, quoted earlier, also used the term *Pentecost* to refer not only to the *day* of Pentecost but also to the Great Fifty Days that began with the Pascha (Easter) and extended through the fiftieth day (seventh Sunday) following. It commemorated the period of fifty days that began when Jesus rose from the dead and ended when the disciples received the Holy Spirit and the

Christian church was born. This season, already well established by the third century, was like a continuous fifty-day Lord's Day. The early Christians saw it as being to the year what the Lord's Day was to the week—the prime one-seventh of the time, when we celebrate what God has done through Christ. Augustine tells us: "These days after the Lord's resurrection form a period, not of labor, but of peace and joy. That is why there is no fasting and we pray standing, which is a sign of resurrection. This practice is observed at the altar on all Sundays, and the Alleluia is sung, to indicate that our future occupation is to be no other than the praise of God."[16] Readings from the book of Acts, the chronicle of the work of the Spirit-filled church is its earliest years, soon became an important feature of this season.

The resurrection, then, was (and still is) commemorated by a day of the week, a day of the year, and a season. There can be no doubt as to the centrality of the resurrection in the life and faith of the early church.

At the same time, the Great Fifty Days, like the Lord's Day, was and is a fully trinitarian celebration. Resurrection life and faith are the gifts of the Holy Spirit, through whom alone the risen Christ is known. Underlying it all is God's original creation and new creation. The gathering in of converts is like a harvest (Matt. 9:37-38; Luke 10:2; John 4:35), and the Great Fifty Days, with its harvest origins in Israel, is the great spiritual harvest season.

The Great Fifty Days soon came to be seen as requiring a season of preparation. This season, known as Lent, began as a period of final preparation and examination for those who were to be baptized at the Paschal (Easter) Vigil. They had already undergone a long period of instruction and preparation—similar to an apprenticeship rather than a course of study—and were now ready for the final examinations or "scrutinies," as they were called.

The Council of Nicaea (A.D. 325) provides our first recorded reference to Lent as "the forty days." About A.D. 348 Bishop Cyril of Jerusalem told those about to be baptized, "You have a long period of grace, forty days for repentance."[17] The forty days came to be seen as comparable to Jesus' forty days in the wilderness, when he fasted and prepared himself for his ministry.

By Augustine's time, Lent had become a time of preparation not only for those preparing for baptism but for all Christians, in that "part of the year . . . adjoining . . . and touching on the Lord's passion."[18] It was a time of penitence. Fasting, as a means to the spiritual discipline needed by Christians, was an important part of Lent.

Even in Lent, however, every Lord's Day was a celebration of Christ's resurrection. The fact that it was the Lord's Day was more important than the fact that it was in the Season of Lent. For this reason, the six Sundays of Lent were not counted as part of the forty days. Lent thus eventually came to have a total of forty-six days, beginning with Ash Wednesday (the seventh Wednesday before Easter) and concluding the day before Easter.

This whole time from Ash Wednesday through Pentecost—the seasons of Lent and Easter—constitutes what we call "the Easter cycle" and is the central focus of the Christian Year. It is meant to be a great time of renewal each year when the church and its members are challenged in their journey from ashes to fire.

E. The Christmas Cycle

The other great period of the Christian Year is the time organized around Christmas—the Christmas cycle. Its origins in Christian history are not quite so early as those of the Easter cycle, nor is it rooted in a festival of ancient Israel. But so meaningful have Christmas and all that surrounds it become to Christian people that Christmas has joined Easter as one of the two high points of the Christian Year.

The feast of Epiphany (January 6) is not as well known today as is Christmas, but it is older and has an even more important place in early Christian history. It was the third chief event, after the Pascha and Pentecost, in the calendar of the early church. Its origins are obscure, but the Christian feast of Epiphany may have begun in Egypt as early as the late second century.

The word *epiphany* means "manifestation." In Christian use it refers particularly to the manifestation of God in Jesus Christ. Epiphany signified several things, all of which had to do with the beginnings of Jesus Christ's work of manifesting God. This feast celebrated the birth of Christ, the baptism of Jesus, and the first miracle—of which John's Gospel says: "This deed at Cana-in-Galilee is the first of the signs by which Jesus revealed [*ephanerosen*] his glory and led his disciples to believe in him" (2:11 NEB). The common theme of all these events is Jesus Christ manifesting God to humans. Appropriately, the early church often called this day "The Theophany" (manifestation of God), and some Eastern Orthodox churches continue to use this name. The prologue to John's Gospel sets the theme: "God's only Son, he who is nearest to the Father's heart, he has made him known" (1:18 NEB).

Epiphany, like the Pascha, underwent a split in the fourth century. The earliest mention of the new feast, Christmas, occurs in a document from A.D. 354, which lists December 25 as *natus Christus in Betleem Iudeae* (Christ born in Bethlehem of Judea). There is evidence that this date may have been observed by Christians in Africa prior to 312 and in Rome about 336. Gradually, the new festival of Christmas took over part of the commemorations of Epiphany. Chrysostom told a congregation in Antioch on Christmas Day, A.D. 386: "This day . . . has now been brought to us, not many years ago, has developed so quickly and borne such fruit."[19] The following Epiphany he explained: "For this is the day on which he was baptized and made holy the nature of the waters. . . . Why then is this the day called Epiphany? Because it was not when he was born that he became manifest to all, but when he was baptized; for up to this day he was unknown to the multitudes."[20] Epiphany, which continued to be celebrated on January 6, remained in the East the celebration of Jesus' baptism, while in western Europe it became the celebration of the visit of the wise men, who represented the manifestation of God in Jesus Christ to the Gentiles.

The separated feasts of Christmas and Epiphany represent, as do developments in the Easter cycle at the same time, a growing desire of the early Christians to celebrate the anniversaries of specific events in the life of Christ. The Bible says nothing to indicate the day of the year on which Jesus was either born or baptized, or on which the wise men visited him. It is possible that the dates of January 6 and December 25 may have originated in winter solstice celebrations according to the ancient Egyptian and Julian (Roman) calendars, respectively. As Christianity became the established religion of the Roman Empire, Christmas served as the replacement for the existing pagan Festival of the Unconquered Sun which had marked the winter solstice. The theme of light conquering darkness has always been prominent in both Christmas and Epiphany. On the other hand, these dates may have been calculated using traditions regarding the date of Jesus' death and identifying the day of his death with that of his conception.

Christians came to see that Christmas and Epiphany needed a preparatory season comparable to Lent in the Easter cycle. A council in Spain in A.D. 380 decreed that "from December 17 until the day of Epiphany which is January 6 no one is permitted to be absent from Church."[21] This was a precedent for Advent at a time when Christmas itself was as yet unknown in Spain. By the fifth century a forty-day season of preparation for Epiphany was being practiced in Gaul. This paralleled Lent and began about when Advent now begins. Rome eventually adopted a season that began the fourth Sunday prior to December 25.

The desire to celebrate specific events in the life of Christ, which had splintered the Pascha into a series of commemorations and separated Christmas from Epiphany, also operated with Christmas. As a Jewish boy, Jesus would likely have been circumcised and named on the eighth day after his birth. Luke tells us: "Eight days later the time came to circumcise him, and he was given the name Jesus" (2:21 NEB). Accordingly, the commemoration on January 1 became known as the Feast of the Circumcision or the Holy Name of Jesus. Luke 2:22-40 gives the story of the Presentation in the Temple, an event that would have occurred forty days after his birth, or February 2. It was calculated that the Annunciation mentioned in Luke 1:26-38 would have occurred nine months before Christmas, or March 25. Or, as already mentioned, the date of Christmas may have been calculated from an existing celebration of the Annunciation (conception). Elizabeth was then six months pregnant, and Mary's subsequent Visitation to Elizabeth (Luke 1:39-56) was fixed on May 31, or just before the birth of John the Baptist, identified as June 24 (three months after the Annunciation). John's birth came at the summer solstice, when the sun wanes until the birth of Christ. "As he grows greater, I must grow less" (John 3:30 NEB). The Christmas cycle helps Christians relive the journey from hope to joy.

F. Through the Year

The Christian Year, especially the temporal cycle (the Easter and Christmas cycles), was basically complete by the end of the fourth century.

The subsequent history is that of the development of the sanctoral cycle (those fixed dates commemorating the deaths of saints aside from dates based on Christmas). These commemorations began early; the *Martyrdom of Polycarp* mentions that of a second-century martyr. Basically these were commemorations of local heroes and heroines of the faith. Tertullian tells us: "As often as the anniversary comes round, we make offerings for the dead as birthday honors."[22] After all, one's birth into eternity (death) was far more important than one's birth into time. Especially after relics of saints began to be moved from place to place, local saints were supplanted by saints from other regions who came to be celebrated universally. Thus the calendar became increasingly cluttered through an intermixing of the temporal and sanctoral cycles.

Only two significant additions occurred after the fourth century: Trinity Sunday and All Saints. Trinity Sunday, the Sunday After Pentecost, was introduced about A.D. 1000. Unlike other feasts, it represents a theological doctrine unrelated to a historical event. The ninth century saw the designation of November 1 as All Saints, commemorating the whole company of saints. The day had earlier springtime precedents, but the Gallican placement of All Saints in the harvest season was accepted by Rome about A.D. 835.

Let us recapitulate. John Chrysostom, in a sermon preached in A.D. 386, effectively summed up the liturgical year: "For if Christ had not been born into flesh he would not have been baptized, which is the Theophany [Epiphany], he would not have been crucified [some texts add: and risen], which is the Pascha, he would not have sent down the Spirit, which is the Pentecost."[23] During the fourth century, the three great primitive feasts—Epiphany, Pascha, and Pentecost—had split from them related days—Christmas, Good Friday, and Ascension, plus some lesser days.

What happened in the fourth century was that the church developed a more dramatic way of expressing the central realities it experienced—manifestation, resurrection, and the indwelling Spirit. The imagination of Christians directed backward in time was fruitful, intensifying their perception of the incarnation. The success of these fourth-century changes is evident by their presence among us even today. Obviously, they have rung true to both Christian faith and human experience.

All in all, the Christian Year is a remarkable reflection of the life and faith of the early church that has remained in use ever since. Modern efforts to systematize it and tidy it up have never been satisfactory. Granted, the ancient Christian calendar leaves large gaps in the year, especially after Pentecost. But its strength lies in its proclamation of the core of the Christian experience and its ability to reflect vividly that Christ has made God manifest, that Christ has risen from the dead, and that Christ has sent the Holy Spirit to dwell in the holy church.

G. Lectionaries

Closely related to the Christian Year are lectionaries. The word *lectionary*, "in the wider sense . . . denotes an ordered system of selected readings ('pericopes') appointed for liturgical use on specific occasions in the church year, thus presupposing a calendar."[24] In the narrower sense, it denotes a book or manuscript with the pericopes thus used printed or written out in full. It is in the wider sense that the term *lectionary* is used in this handbook.

Since ancient times, synagogues have had fixed scripture readings appointed for the Jewish feasts and readings for ordinary Sabbaths chosen on the principle of *lectio continua*—that is, continuous reading through the books of scripture. Such a practice may have been in use when Jesus in the synagogue at Nazareth "stood up to read the lesson and was handed the scroll of the prophet Isaiah" (Luke 4:16-17 NEB).

Although the origins of the Christian use of lectionaries are not clear, Exodus 12, which was used at the Jewish Passover, was also used for the Christian Pascha about A.D. 200 in Rome and about 180 among the Quartodecimans (observers of the fourteenth of Nisan).[25] Prior to 325, specially selected lessons were appointed for the major feast days, and the scriptures were read in *lectio continua* fashion on ordinary Sundays.

In western Europe various local lectionaries developed. Early in the ninth century, these were standardized into the traditional Sunday lectionary that was used until recent years by Roman Catholics, Anglicans, and Lutherans.

NOTES

1. Cyril Richardson, ed., *Early Christian Fathers* (Philadelphia: Westminster Press, 1953), p. 96.
2. Kirsopp Lake, trans., *The Apostolic Fathers* (Cambridge: Harvard University Press, 1965), I, 331.
3. Henry Bettenson, ed., *Documents of the Christian Church* (New York: Oxford University Press, 1952), p. 6.
4. *Early Christian Fathers*, p. 287.
5. *The Apostolic Fathers*, I, 397.
6. *Documents of the Christian Church*, p. 27.
7. *Early Christian Fathers*, p. 174.
8. James Donaldson, ed., *Ante-Nicene Fathers* (New York: Charles Scribners, 1899), VII, 469.
9. Paul W. Harkins, trans., *Baptismal Instructions*, 17 (Westminster, Md.: Newman Press, 1963), p. 127.
10. "On Baptism," 19, S. Thelwall, trans. *Ante-Nicene Fathers*, III, 678.
11. Eusebius, *The History of the Church*, V, 23, trans. G. A. Williamson (Baltimore: Penguin Books, 1965), p. 230.
12. John Wilkinson, trans., *Egeria's Travels*, xxx, 1; xxxi, 2, (London: SPCK, 1971), pp. 132-33.
13. Wilfrid Parsons, trans., *Letters* (New York: Fathers of the Church, 1951), p. 283.
14. "On Baptism," *Ante-Nicene Fathers*, III, 678.
15. E. C. Richardson, trans., "Life of Constantine the Great," in *Nicene and Post-Nicene Fathers*, 2d ser. (New York: Christian Literature Co., 1890), I, 557.
16. *Letters*, pp. 284-85.
17. William Teller, trans., *Cyril of Jerusalem and Nemesius of Emesa* (Philadelphia: Westminster Press, 1955), p. 68.
18. Wilfrid Parsons trans., *Letters*, "Letter 55 to Januarius" (New York: Fathers of the Church, 1951), p. 284.
19. John Chrysostom, *Opera Omnia*, ed. Bernard de Montfaucon (Paris: Gaume, 1834), II, 418.
20. Ibid., II, p. 436.
21. Cited by L. Duchesne, *Christian Worship*, 5th ed., (London: SPCK, 1923), p. 260 n. 3.
22. "De Corona," 3, *Ante-Nicene Fathers*, III, 94.
23. *Opera Omnia*, I, 608.
24. R. H. Fuller, "Lectionary," in *The Westminster Dictionary of Worship*, ed. J. G. Davies (Philadelphia: Westminster Press, 1979), p. 211.
25. Ibid.

THE RECOVERY OF THE CHRISTIAN YEAR

A. Protestants and the Christian Year

*T*he sixteenth-century Reformers took various approaches to the calendar. Luther removed the saints' days, seeking "to celebrate only on Lord's Days and on festivals of the Lord, abrogating completely the festivals of all the saints. . . . We regard the Festivals of the Purification [Presentation] and of the Annunciation as Festivals of Christ, like the Epiphany and the Circumcision."[1] The Church of England originally retained only commemorations of those saints mentioned in the Bible, plus All Saints. The Church of Scotland was more radical. Its 1560 *Book of Discipline* condemned all "feasts (as they term them) of apostles, martyrs, virgins, of Christmas, circumcision, epiphany, purification, and other fond feasts of our Lady. Which things, because in God's Scriptures they neither have commandment nor assurance, we judge utterly to be abolished from this realm; affirming further, that the obstinate maintainers and teachers of such abominations ought not to escape the punishment of the Civil Magistrate."[2]

In 1784 John Wesley, always the pragmatist, sent a calendar to the Methodists in America that abolished "most of the holy-days . . . as at present answering no valuable end."[3] His calendar included the four Sundays of Advent, Christmas Day, up to fifteen Sundays after Christmas, the Sunday before Easter, Good Friday, Easter Day, five Sundays after Easter, Ascension Day, the Sunday After Ascension day, Whitsunday (Pentecost), Trinity Sunday, and up to twenty-five Sundays after Trinity. His journals reveal a personal fondness for All Saints (cf. p. 259-67). Wesley's calendar was soon abandoned by American Methodists.

Most American Protestants strongly emphasized the Lord's Day, but otherwise their observance of the Christian Year was largely limited to Easter and Christmas until the twentieth century. Even Christmas was not observed in most American Protestant churches until the nineteenth century.

The Protestant Reformers sought to recover the practice of the early church; but, given what we now know about the early church, the results were mixed.

1. Although they recovered the primacy of the Lord's Day, they tended to interpret it as a Sabbath, solemn with prohibitions both of work and of pleasures, rather than as a joyous celebration of the risen Lord.

2. While they retained the primacy of Easter in the yearly calendar, they reduced it to an isolated day that tended to become a one-dimensional celebration of Jesus' resurrection and of life after death rather than an event including the whole message of the early Christian Pascha.

3. When Christmas was reintroduced into most American Protestant churches, it was in a highly secularized form that ignored Epiphany (except for including the wise men as part of the Christmas story), often gave more prominence to Santa Claus and Christmas trees than to Christ, and gradually pushed Christmas back from December 25 to a month-long "Christmas Season" which usually ended, as far as congregational celebrations were concerned, on "Christmas Sunday"—the Sunday *before* Christmas.

4. The Reformers removed some of the cluttered medieval Christian calendar that was incompatible with Protestant Christianity, but other thoroughly evangelical observances were lost and Protestants were impoverished in the process.

5. Because a weekly rhythm is not enough and the rhythms of the year are fundamental in people's lives, new observances were introduced to fill the void in the calendar. Some of these were observances in the civil year or related to the cycles of nature, such as New Year's, Memorial Day, and Thanksgiving. Others were introduced to recognize and honor groups or categories of persons, such as Children's Day, Mother's Day, and Father's Day. Still others were designated by the churches to promote certain causes, such as Rally Day (Christian Education Sunday), World Communion Sunday, and One Great Hour of Sharing.

As Protestants reflected on what had happened to the calendar of observances by which they indicated their priorities, there arose a growing movement to restore the ancient Christian Year. Although this movement began in the nineteenth century, it did not affect the practices of most American Protestants until well into the twentieth century. Lenten and Holy Week observances were gradually restored, the season before Christmas began to be observed as Advent, services were more widely held on Christmas Eve and Christmas Day, and Pentecost began to be celebrated again.

During roughly the middle third of the twentieth century, some Protestant denominations went further and promoted the observance of the whole Christian Year, but in a form that differed significantly from the ancient pattern. The differences derived partly from copying the then-current Roman Catholic and Anglican calendars and partly from attempting to rationalize and adapt the calendar to what were perceived as modern needs.

It was generally agreed that the first half of the Christian Year was divided into the seasons of Advent, Christmas(tide), Epiphany, Lent, and Easter(tide). This sequence of seasons was commonly interpreted as following the life of Christ.

There was some confusion about the second half of the Christian Year. In some denominational versions of the calendar there was a half-year Pentecost Season, beginning with the Day of Pentecost. In other versions there was a one-week Pentecost Season, followed by a long Trinity Season. This half-year was commonly interpreted as focusing on the church, which was born on the Day of Pentecost, and as complementing the other half-year focus on the life of Christ.

In 1937 the Federal Council of Churches (one of the predecessors of the National Council of Churches) produced a book, *The Christian Year*,[4] in which it was suggested that the half-year beginning with Trinity Sunday be renamed Kingdomtide. In 1940 a second edition of this book proposed dividing this half of the year into a summer season of Whitsuntide beginning with the Day of Pentecost and a fall season of Kingdomtide beginning with the last Sunday in August. When The Methodist Church first adopted a liturgical calendar with the publication of *The Book of Worship for Church and Home* (1944), it included these seasons of Whitsuntide and Kingdomtide. The revised *Book of Worship* (1965) continued the use of the Kingdomtide Season but changed Whitsuntide to Pentecost. A few other Protestants experimented briefly with this proposal and then abandoned it.

Another experiment was tried briefly by American Presbyterians, following a suggestion made in 1956 by Allan McArthur, a Scottish pastor. This involved a trinitarian conception of the year in which there was a fall season of "God the Father,"[5] the Christ-centered half of the year from Advent through the Easter Season, and a Spirit-centered summer Pentecost Season. After four years of trial use, this experiment was abandoned.

Whatever the variations in these calendars, every Sunday in the year was identified by its place in relation to a season. The sequence of seasons was made graphic for teaching purposes in "pie charts" that made each season a wedge whose size was determined by the length of the season. Since these wedges were color coded, and since the churches that observed the Christian Year commonly bought chancel paraments in the seasonal colors and changed them with the seasons, each season became popularly identified with a certain color. The question became not "What *day* is it?" but "What *season* is it?"

Although this interpretation of the Christian Year became widely popular, serious difficulties were inherent in it.

1. By being primarily a calendar of seasons rather than of days, it obscured the centrality of the Lord's Day (Sunday) as the primary Christian festival, worthy of observance for its own sake apart from any other identification.

2. The pie-chart image of the year obscured the priorities inherent in the Christian Year. It obscured the fact that Easter and its related observances have both historical and theological priority over Christmas and its related observances. It did not make clear the subsidiary character of Lent and Advent with respect to the times of Easter and Christmas for which they are but the preparation; therefore, Easter Day and Christmas Day often seemed to be climactic occasions to what preceded rather than inaugural occasions for the Great Fifty Days and the days from Christmas to Epiphany. The season or seasons in the latter half of the year looked so important on the pie chart that much effort was expended in a futile attempt to make the year a continual succession of highly significant promoted seasons.

3. The pie-chart mentality also seemed to make the year a sequential following of the life of Jesus from cradle and before to grave and beyond rather than a theological ordering of the church's living commemoration. Thus, Advent was robbed of its eschatalogical character and Easter of its connection with the formation of the church by the power of the Holy Spirit.

These patterns from the recent past are important because they represent what many persons today consider "traditional," having learned them in their formative years. To appreciate the reforms in the last third of the twentieth century that have produced the common calendar and *Common Lectionary*, it is helpful to know what was reformed and why. Nevertheless, it is important to remember that these reforms are not innovations but are *restorations* of what had become misunderstood, corrupted, or even lost across the centuries. So what seems new really is the oldest of Christian practices.

B. The Ecumenical Reform of the Christian Year

While many Protestants were rediscovering the Christian Year, scholars were making important new discoveries regarding its early history. These discoveries were part of a larger blossoming of biblical and historical studies in which scholars of all faiths were learning from one another. Protestant and Catholic liturgical scholars were increasingly seeing beyond their immediate denominational heritages and looking at our common Christian origins and heritage from an ecumenical perspective. In their respective denominations they began to advocate reforms that would recover this ancient Christian heritage for our own day.

When the Roman Catholic church held the Second Vatican Council in the early 1960s, one of its many achievements was the reform of the calendar and lectionary in the light of these new perspectives.

In 1963 the second Vatican Council in its *Constitution on the Sacred Liturgy* (Article 51) declared that "the treasures of the Bible should be opened up more lavishly so that richer fare might be provided for the faithful at the table of God's Word. In this way a more representative portion of sacred Scripture will be read to the people over a set cycle of years." This decision led to six years of compressed biblical and lectionary studies, experimentation, and revisions with a thoroughness unequaled in Christian history. During these years the Concilium for the Implementation of the Constitution on the Sacred Liturgy sought and heeded the advice of hundreds of biblical and liturgical experts from the whole range of Christian denominations. This effort bore fruit at the beginning of the 1970 Christian Year, when the new lectionary was put into effect for the Roman Catholic Church. Though the historic Catholic lectionary and most modern Protestant lectionaries had been based on a one-year cycle, the new lectionary was based on a three-year cycle. Though the traditional lectionary had two readings each Sunday, the new lectionary had three. As a result, the new lectionary had a far greater coverage of the Bible than older lectionaries, and soon scholars and worship leaders of many denominations acknowledged it as the most carefully prepared, most comprehensive, and probably finest lectionary in Christian history.

This new calendar and lectionary immediately caught the interest of American Protestants. Many of them had been consulted in its preparation and were impressed with it.

Since the Episcopal Church was in the process of revising *The Book of Common Prayer*, it was natural that it should consider this new calendar and lectionary. Several hundred consultants, both inside and outside the Episcopal Church, were contacted during the revision stage. In that process, a number of changes were made in the calendar and lectionary. The results of their efforts went into trial use among Episcopalians in 1970. A further revision was made in October 1973. This calendar and lectionary were then incorporated into *The Book of Common Prayer* that was given final approval in 1979.

In the fall of 1970 the Joint Committee on Worship for the Cumberland Presbyterian Church, the Presbyterian Church in the United States, and the United Presbyterian Church in the United States of America published *The Worshipbook*, containing still another version of this calendar and lectionary. Though following the basic pattern, it contained numerous changes, especially regarding the verses at which lessons began and ended. This version of the calendar and lectionary was later included in *The Hymnal of the United Church of Christ* (1974) and recommended by the Christian Church (Disciples of Christ).

In 1973 the Inter-Lutheran Commission on Worship, representing the Lutheran Church in America, the American Lutheran Church, the Evangelical Lutheran Church of Canada, and the Lutheran Church—Missouri Synod, published yet another version of this lectionary. Again, although the same basic pattern was followed, there were numerous changes. After trial use and further revision, this calendar and lectionary were incorporated into the new *Lutheran Book of Worship* (1978).

In the fall of 1972 the Commission on Worship of the Consultation on Church Union (COCU), meeting in Washington, D.C., began work on a version of this calendar and lectionary that would be both a means of contributing to church unity and a service to those churches that did not yet have a version of this new calendar and lectionary. The resulting calendar and lectionary were approved by COCU and published in 1974 as *A Lectionary*.

The Section on Worship of the General Board of Discipleship of The United Methodist Church, after actively cooperating in the development of the COCU version of the calendar and lectionary, voted to recommend it for study and optional use by United Methodists and then included it in their own book *Word and Table: A Basic Pattern of Sunday Worship for United Methodists* (1976). The Section on Worship worked with COCU on a further revised calendar and lectionary, which COCU was not in a position to publish but which was published in the United Methodist book *Seasons of the Gospel* (1979) and commended to United Methodists for optional use.

As the use of the new calendar and lectionary spread rapidly from one denomination to another, particularly in North America, and included a great many congregations who had never before used a lectionary, related forms of ecumenical sharing were taking place. Both denominational and commercial publishers started to produce preaching, liturgical, and musical resources based on this ecumenical calendar and lectionary. Persons wishing such resources freely purchased and used them regardless of denominational or commercial origin, and most of the publishers involved tried to make their resources suitable for use across denominational lines. Also, in many communities interdenominational clergy groups started to meet for the purpose of sharing ideas and plans for lectionary-based preaching and worship.

With such ecumenical sharing taking place, the proliferation of denominational versions of what was basically one calendar and lectionary caused much confusion and frustration. There were differences in the names of the days and seasons. During the half of the year after Pentecost, differences in dating caused some denominations to be a week or two ahead of others in the listing of a given set of lessons. On some days one or more of the lessons would differ from one denomination to another, and even when the lessons were basically the same, they might begin or end at different verses. Not only did this make it more difficult to use resources not produced by one's own denomination and to plan together in ecumenical clergy groups, it made the calendar and lectionary less a symbol of Christian unity.

Fortunately, representatives of the worship offices of a number of North American Christian denominations had been meeting together since the mid-1960s as the Consultation on Common Texts (CCT). In its first ten years the CCT had enabled these denominations to do several joint worship projects, and these denominations again worked through the CCT to produce what has become the *Common Lectionary*.

The CCT first convened a conference on the calendar and lectionary, which was held March 29–31, 1978, in Washington, D.C., and was attended by representatives of thirteen denominations in the United States and Canada as well as by several invited experts who had been prominent in calendar and lectionary reform. The conference agreed on a calendar, on the need for a consensus lectionary that would include a schedule of psalms and a more adequate coverage of the Old Testament, and on certain terminology. They recommended to the CCT that it set up a small working body to produce a consensus lectionary.

The CCT responded by setting up the North American Committee on Calendar and Lectionary (NACCL), which after several years of intensive work submitted the *Common Lectionary* to the CCT in 1982. The CCT commended this *Common Lectionary* to the participating denominations for trial use, study, and review over the liturgical years encompassed by 1983 through 1986, a period later extended to 1989. Participating denominations included the Christian (Disciples of Christ), Episcopal, Lutheran, Presbyterian, Reformed, Roman Catholic, United Church of Christ, and United Methodist in the United States and Anglican, Roman Catholic, and United Church in Canada.[6]

The use of the *Common Lectionary* has spread rapidly since 1983. In some denominations such as the United Methodist and Presbyterian in which use of a lectionary is promoted chiefly by calendars published annually, it is the one lectionary recommended during the years of trial use. In other denominations such as the Episcopal and Lutheran which have recent worship books containing their denomination's version of the three-year lectionary, many congregations have official approval to give trial use to the *Common Lectionary*. Many congregations in denominations that have never adopted a lectionary are now using the *Common Lectionary*. The study and testing of the *Common Lectionary* have now spread beyond North America to other continents, and a worldwide consultative process is being set up for the further refinement of the *Common Lectionary* after 1989. It is anticipated in the light of the very favorable response to date that the *Common Lectionary* will, with minor improvements from time to time, enter into increasingly widespread use in the years to come.

C. The Shape of the Reformed Calendar

The common calendar that has emerged from this ecumenical process of reform is outlined in chapter 1. What is the shape of the Christian Year as it is now being observed by such a wide ecumenical consensus? How do the recent denominational calendars differ from one another and from the common calendar?

All these calendars agree that the Lord's Day is of primary importance among the observances of the year and that the Christian Year contains two central cycles—the Easter cycle and the Christmas cycle. Each cycle includes a festival season (Easter and Christmas), preceded by a season of preparation and anticipation (Lent and Advent). In most denominational versions and in the *Common Lectionary*, Lent and Advent are immediately preceded by a transitional Sunday (Transfiguration and Christ the King), and the Easter and Christmas Seasons are immediately followed by a transitional Sunday (Trinity and Baptism of the Lord).

An ordering of importance is implied. Easter and the events in the history of salvation it celebrates are more important than Christmas and the events it celebrates. The festival seasons of Easter and Christmas are more important than the preparatory seasons of Lent and Advent. The time within each of these cycles takes precedence over the transitional Sundays at either end, lest minor festivals be seen as major ones. Such an ordering of time clashes with the priorities of popular piety and cannot readily be drawn as a chart. Whatever difficulties this may present in terms of teaching, it quite properly makes the year a vehicle for liturgical celebration rather than for didactic convenience.

The two cycles "float" to a limited degree in relation to each other, since the Easter cycle is calculated on a lunar cycle dependent upon the spring equinox and the Christmas cycle is based on the solar cycle. The number of Sundays outside these cycles is relatively constant from year to year. (This number is not absolute, since some years have fifty-two Sundays and some fifty-three, and since in some years the Christmas Season will embrace one Sunday but in others two.) The number of Sundays between Baptism of the Lord and Transfiguration will differ relative to those between Trinity Sunday and Christ the King, as Easter floats between March 22 and April 25.

There is general agreement on the basic form of the calendar, but there are disparities in the way in which the Sundays between the two cycles are identified.

In the Roman Catholic calendar, those Sundays outside the cycles are called "Sundays of the Year" or "Sundays in Ordinary Time." The first Sunday of the Year (i.e., that following Epiphany) is designated as "Baptism of the Lord." The last Sunday of the Year (i.e., the Sunday before Advent) is "Christ the King." The Sunday After Pentecost is considered a Sunday of the Year but has its own title ("Trinity Sunday") and propers. All other Sundays of the Year are designated simply by number (e.g., "Twentieth Sunday of the Year").

Texts are provided to cover the maximum number of Sundays of the Year (thirty-four) in those rare calendar years when there are fifty-three Sundays and Christmas Day falls on a Monday (so that only one Sunday falls within the Christmas Season). When there are five Sundays After Epiphany in such years, for example, the sixth and successive sets of readings are taken up after Trinity Sunday; but if there are eight Sundays After Epiphany, Trinity Sunday is followed by the ninth set of propers. Thus, everything is used. In those years that do not have the full complement of Sundays of the Year, unneeded propers are dropped out when the counting resumes after Trinity Sunday.

Not only is the system economical in eliminating as many superfluous sets of texts as possible, but it emphasizes the integrity of ordinary time in that the "Sundays After" do not constitute actual seasons with clearly defined themes.

Anglicans and Protestants, in adapting the calendar, chose to consider the times between the two cycles as seasons, and the common calendar does likewise.

There is either the Season After Epiphany or the Epiphany Season, and there is as yet no agreement as to which term to use. The designation "Season After Epiphany," agreed upon at the 1978 CCT conference and followed by United Methodists and Presbyterians in their use of the *Common Lectionary*, keeps Epiphany in the Christmas Season and treats the Sundays After Epiphany as comparable to the Sundays After Pentecost. The designation "Epiphany Season"—found in *The Book of Common Prayer, Lutheran Book of Worship,* and *Common Lectionary*—detaches Epiphany from the Christmas Season and makes it the first day of an Epiphany Season, which is different in kind from the Season After Pentecost. In both cases, Sundays during this season are referred to as "____ Sunday *After* Epiphany." It is significant that those calendars using "Season After Epiphany" all provide that Epiphany may be celebrated either on January 6 or on the first Sunday in January, which usually occurs before January 6 and is therefore part of the Christmas Season in any case. Few United Methodists or Presbyterians celebrate Epiphany on January 6 if it does not fall on Sunday.

There is also the Season After Pentecost, which is what these calendars call that half of the year between Pentecost and Advent. The Lutheran calendar also calls it "The Time of the Church," and the United Methodist version of the common calendar permits use of "Kingdomtide" as an alternative to "Season After Pentecost."

The *Common Lectionary* is designed to be used with any of these calendar variations.

In all versions of the three-year lectionary, including the Roman Catholic, there are clear echoes of Epiphany in the readings for the Sundays that follow. Some of the Gospels for the Sundays After Epiphany are traditionally associated with Epiphany (baptism of the Lord, the wedding at Cana) or deal with what can be considered epiphanies (manifestations) of Christ. The Transfiguration, which is clearly an epiphany, is celebrated on the Last Sunday After Epiphany by many Protestants, although Roman Catholics and Episcopalians celebrate it on August 6 and also commemorate it on the Second Sunday of Lent. The *Common Lectionary* provides for both options.

After Pentecost, the second lessons (Epistles) and Gospels in all these lectionaries, and also the first lesson (Old Testament) in the *Common Lectionary*, go in a continuous or semicontinuous cycle through books of the Bible (*lectio continua*). Thus, they are neither thematic nor are the lessons on a given Sunday necessarily related to one another. It is clearly *not* a Pentecost season, since the readings have no special relationship to Pentecost or the Holy Spirit and since the Great Fifty Days of Easter *are* the Pentecost Season.

There is, however, a discrepancy between the various versions of the lectionary after Pentecost, which has resulted in much confusion and frustration. Several of the earlier Protestant versions of the lectionary, with the *Lutheran Book of Worship*, assigned the readings according to what numbered Sunday it was *after Pentecost*. The Roman Catholic lectionary, followed by the Episcopal and Common lectionaries, on the other hand, assigns readings to Sundays that fall *within given seven-day periods on the civil calendar*. This has meant in practice that persons using resources (or working with persons) from other denominations would often find that two denominations had assigned a given set of lessons to two different Sundays.

The consultants and denominational representatives who worked with the CCT to produce the *Common Lectionary* were in agreement that the Roman Catholic and Episcopal assignment of lessons after Pentecost was better. One major advantage is that the last few sets of readings after Pentecost—eschatological readings that provide a good preparation for Advent—always are used on the Sundays immediately preceding Advent instead of being "throwaway lessons" used only when Easter comes early. With the increasing use of the *Common Lectionary* it is hoped that this confusion about lessons after Pentecost will soon be a thing of the past.

In the common calendar and *Common Lectionary* upon which this book is based, the reader must choose on the basis of denominational affiliation or personal preference how to interpret these times outside Advent/Christmas and Lent/Easter. It is clear, however, that if these times are seasons, they are seasons in a much more limited sense than are Advent, Christmas, Lent, and Easter and that they have a very different character. Each Sunday stands on its own as the Lord's Day; and beyond that, its character is set by the lessons that are read on that particular day.

Interpenetrating the Sundays and seasons of the Christian Year as we have described it so far are two sets of observances that are on fixed dates and, for that reason, usually fall on weekdays. These days occur in the Roman Catholic, Episcopalian, and Lutheran calendars, but other Protestants are discovering and observing some of them. There are several commemorations of events in the life of Christ (see pp. 23-24) that are related to Christmas and Easter and are part of the temporal cycle even if their dates do not fall within the Christmas and Easter cycles. There are also the days in the sanctoral cycle, which recognizes the grace of Christ revealed in the lives of the saints. Some of these observances are included in the common calendar and *Common Lectionary* and will be discussed in the chapter on special days.

Finally, the calendar of most local congregations includes, in practice, a number of civil, promotional, and local observances. For the most part, these lie outside the scope of this book. New Year's Eve and Day and Thanksgiving, however, have sufficient liturgical importance and are so widely observed that they have been included in the *Common Lectionary* and, therefore, in this book.

Perhaps even more important than the separate facets of the calendar is the way in which these relate to one another and to our view of God in relation to time. The preeminence of the Lord's Day indicates the presence of the risen Christ in all our experience. The resurrection punctuates our perception of time by its commemoration once every seven days, regardless of what else may be occurring in the church calendar or in our own lives. During two extended periods of the year, portions of the Paschal Mystery are held before us for closer examination. By being the primary of these two, Easter reminds us that Christmas is also a paschal observance, even if under a quite different guise, for God does come to us in various ways, yet with the same sacrificing, reconciling love.

The contrast between designations within and outside the two festival complexes further reminds us of the varied and complementary character of God's activity on our behalf. We see the divine hand in those obvious events surrounding the coming of Christ, which are often called "the mighty acts of God in history." But we also find evidence of God's work in the less spectacular events of our own day, which may be called "ongoing divine providence around us"—which is the true meaning of "ordinary" in the phrase "ordinary time." All too often in our culture "ordinary" is taken to mean dull; that is an inherent disadvantage in the Roman Catholic designation.

Just as there is in the calendar an interplay of the Easter and Christmas cycles with ordinary time, so there is a more subtle interplay of weekly and annual time. The Lord's Day begins, and is one-seventh of, the week. Easter Day begins a week of weeks (the Easter Season), which period is as close to being one-seventh of a calendar year as it is possible to achieve counting full weeks. Thus, the Easter Season, like Easter Day, is a great Sunday.

There is also the interplay between parts of the temporal cycle inextricably bound to the Easter and Christmas cycles and the parts that are outside or that float. The Annunciation is usually within Lent but occasionally falls on, or a day or so after, Easter Day—yet always within the Easter cycle. The Presentation is always in ordinary time but may precede Ash Wednesday by only a few days or by more than a month. The Visitation may fall within the Easter Season or in ordinary time. Thus, again, we see God's activity intersecting and interpenetrating time.

Finally, there is the interplay between the temporal cycle, centered in God's saving work in Christ, and the sanctoral cycle, where the grace of God is seen in the lives of those who have followed Christ since his resurrection. Thus, his saving work walks in our midst.

NOTES

1. Bard Thompson, ed., "Formula Missae," in *Liturgies of the Western Church* (Cleveland: Meridian Books, 1961), p. 109.
2. "Book of Discipline," in *John Knox's History of the Reformation in Scotland* (London: Thomas Nelson, 1949), 2:281.
3. "The Sunday Service," in *Liturgies of the Western Church*, p. 417.
4. *The Christian Year: A Suggestive Guide for the Worship of the Church*, drafted and revised by Fred Winslow Adams, 2d ed. (New York: Committee on Worship, Federal Council of the Churches of Christ in America, 1937; 1940), p. 9.
5. *The Christian Year and Lectionary Reform* (London: SCM Press, 1958).
6. The history of this work is more fully given in *Common Lectionary* (New York: The Church Hymnal Corporation, 1983), pp. 7 ff.

THE
CHRISTIAN
YEAR IN PRACTICE

A. Resources and Decisions

*P*lanning and preparing for Christian worship involve making numerous decisions about what to choose and what to reject. Worship leadership demands that we seek to make the best possible decisions for a specific occasion and congregation. There is no guarantee that our decisions will be the best, but there are ways to avoid most mistakes and enhance the likelihood of good decisions.

In this chapter we shall progress from the more general considerations of decision making about worship to specific concerns that a pastor or worship committee has to face. All revolve around making appropriate use of the worship resources included in this book.

B. The Balance of Stability and Variety

Christian worship is a marriage of two opposites: stability and variety. Both are necessary, even though they operate in opposite ways. There has to be stability so that people can worship the same God in the same way over the course of time. Yet variety is necessary to convey the fullness of the gospel. Christian worship is formed by the delicate balance between the unchanging and change. Without stability, it becomes chaotic; without variety, it becomes one-sided and repetitive.

The demand for stability is apparent in many ways—the acceptance of certain conventions, the use of a familiar structure, and the retention of familiar items. We come to worship with an enormous range of assumptions and expectations. It is the same in any other social activity, whether a banquet or a baseball game; there are conventions or rules that make it possible for us to eat together or play ball. The alternative is chaos.

Essential to most Christian worship is an order of worship. For the majority of Protestant worshipers, this is provided in a Sunday bulletin. Lutherans and Episcopalians have set orders in book form as well. The order of worship is the most important theological statement pastors set before their congregations week after week. The order manifests the priorities of the Christian life and tells how individual items such as scripture and prayer relate to one another. Unfortunately, not all orders of worship are equally adequate as theological statements. But, adequate or not, they do make such statements. Congregations tend to want a stable theology; and, consequently, orders of worship remain the same over long periods of time, varying only for significant festivals within the yearly cycle.

Stability is also found in individual items that recur. Although some Puritans felt the repetition of the Lord's Prayer fell into the category of "vain repetition," most Christians use it on a weekly basis. Because the *faith* of the church tends to be stable, creeds have a remarkable durability. Hymns often become singable by long familiarity. There is always controversy when someone tries to change the tune or words of a beloved hymn. Certain kinds of prayer, especially confession and pardon, gain power by repetition and provide continuing elements of stability.

But variety is also essential in Christian worship, and variety is the chief topic of this book. Christian worship occurs in the midst of ever-flowing human time. Each worship occasion is unique. The same group of people never meet twice for worship in the context of the same world situation. Never again will they assemble for worship with exactly the same concerns they bring this week. In worship we try not to escape time but to see all history as God's time. Granted that certain assumptions, structures, and elements will remain constant, much in Christian worship relates to the changing life situations of the worshipers. Although change certainly does not guarantee relevance, change is often essential for making worship relevant. Prayer and preaching, especially, reach out to gather up the burdens of the present moment. Without variety, worship would be rigid and monotonous.

Our task is not to make worship appealing by producing variety for its own sake. While variety is necessary for relevance, variety is worthless without authenticity. The cycle of the Christian Year is a valuable means of living in communion with Christ by making a pilgrimage through the year in contact with his person and work. The Christian Year can degenerate into mere fascination with trivia, or it may grow to be a means of unfolding, deepening communion with Christ. It is this latter level of authenticity that must accompany all efforts at relevance.

Much of the variety in Christian worship is provided by what are known as "propers"—those elements that change from time to time, such as lessons, hymns, some prayers, and choral and instrumental music. These function to tie a service of worship to its location in the year. Thus, the most important decisions in planning and preparing for worship, other than shaping an order, are the choices of propers.

Paramount among the propers are the scripture lessons. Worship planning begins with careful study of the lessons for each occasion. The character of each Sunday or festival day is set by the lessons appointed for it. These locate that occasion in the cycle of the whole biblical story. Only when the specific character of the day is determined can the choice of the other propers be made responsibly. In practice, this means that scripture sets the tone for the whole service. One does not choose a topic or theme and then seek to find a text or lessons to match it. Not only does scripture indicate the theme of the sermon but usually suggests hymns, prayers, and choral music as well. Scripture is central for the service, and God's Word is the controlling factor in it. It is here that God's Word for this world is spoken to life lived in it.

C. General Aspects of Worship

Three general aspects of worship need to be described before we can analyze specific portions: (1) the order of worship, (2) the visual elements, and (3) music. Many of the specific items we shall discuss are verbal forms of expression; some are not. But all are set in the context of an order and occur in a visual and acoustical environment. It is helpful to think through the matrix in which acts of worship are embedded, especially since this context is so easily overlooked.

1. If, as has been said, the order of worship makes a significant theological statement, what theology does our order state? What does it indicate to the Christian worshiper to discover week after week that only a single brief lesson is deemed sufficient for the congregation's one weekly gathering? What is said about preaching when that lesson is isolated from the sermon by a number of intervening items? How is the Christian life depicted when the congregation joins in confession without adequate silence and pardon? What kind of faith is portrayed if the only summons is to join

the church? Is Christian life as passive as a service in which the clergy and the choir do all the praying and singing?

The order of worship, far from being a matter governed by indifference or mere convenience, as when the choir likes to slip out after the anthem, plays a major role in the formation of the laity. The minister's function as pastoral theologian is at its most obvious in preparing the order of worship. Indeed, ordering public worship is the essence of pastoral theology. Accordingly, some criteria for judging such pastoral theology are necessary.

The first criterion is *the centrality of scripture*. Since the service of the Word is focused on scripture, this should be no surprise. This does not mean that the lessons come in the middle of the service, but it should be apparent to all who gather that the center of their coming together is to hear what God has to speak to them. Scripture is read not just to provide a text for the sermon but for its own sake as God's word to God's people.

The second criterion is a *sense of progression* that is clear and easy to follow. Worship needs movement, a "flow" that moves inevitably. From gathering to going forth, there should be an obvious feeling of progression so that the worshiper feels carried along in the whole movement.

The third criterion is *clarity of function*. Is it clear to the worshiper what a certain act is meant to do? Does the psalm make sense as a commentary and response to the Old Testament lesson? Much depends on where items are located in the order. In general, elements that have similar functions work best in conjunction with one another. Reading lessons and preaching are both acts of proclamation. Offering of money and intercessory prayer are directed to others. When the connection between such acts is made clear by close proximity, the worshiper has less shifting of direction to do and less difficulty participating in the service.

2. The visual environment can significantly shape what worshipers perceive and expect in a service. The effect of the visual environment may be subtle, but it is persistent. One may preach on the priesthood of all believers, but if the building proclaims that God and clergy alone inhabit the chancel, the building will probably win. A building that flaunts the architect's virtuosity but provides a poor setting for what the community intends to do in it is a failure as liturgical architecture.

Because no two Sundays are the same, it is desirable to vary the visual environment in the course of the year. The changing of vestments, paraments, banners, and flowers heralds the changing of the days and seasons. The Advent wreath, Lenten veil, and paschal candle help worshipers to realize more fully what season it is. The choice or design of visuals for any service is based upon the scripture lessons to be read. Sometimes a simple item can pick up a key word in the Gospel for the day, as when five lamps are lighted and five are out on the day when Matthew 25:1-13 is read. Often a visual will remain in people's minds long after the sermon has been forgotten.

The simplest, and often most effective, possibility in visual design is sheer color. Sometimes all that is necessary for a good banner or hanging is color alone, if the hue or hues are carefully chosen. Color helps form general expectations for any occasion. Purples, grays, and blues have traditionally been used for seasons of a preparatory or penitential character such as Advent or Lent. White and gold have been used for joyous seasons and events with a special christological flavor such as Christmas or the Baptism of the Lord. Flame red has been used for occasions relating to the Holy Spirit such as Pentecost or ordinations, and blood red has sometimes been used in Holy Week or for commemorations of martyrs. Green, with its suggestion of growth, has been used in seasons of less distinct character, such as the Season After Epiphany or the Season After Pentecost.

Quite apart from the color chosen, texture is important. For Lent an ornate brocade is less suitable than a rough-textured material, while at Easter a finely woven fabric may be preferable to one that is coarse in appearance.

Visual elements are not mere decoration. They are used as visual proclamation of the gospel and thereby add another dimension to worship. When used with care, they can be an integral part of the service and not just an embellishment.

3. Worship occurs in an acoustical as well as a visual environment. The way sounds behave in a

space will greatly affect how worshipers experience an event. If sound is soaked up by padded pews, drapes, and carpeting, people will be less likely to sing, because they soon feel they are singing alone. Some spaces reinforce the beauty of organ music but make preaching difficult because of excessive reverberation.

Music is a major component of worship and, like visual art, should always be a servant of worship. Its purpose is to assist in worship, not to call attention to itself. There is no place in worship for art for art's sake. Music that simply calls attention to the instrument or to the performer fails as liturgical music. Indeed, the best liturgical music, like the best church architecture, may often be the least obtrusive. This often demands consummate skill and restraint.

Some liturgical music is purely instrumental, such as an organ voluntary. Important as words are in Christian worship, music without words may be an offering of worship and may aid the congregation in worship. Although a few denominations forbid the use of instruments in worship, most take it for granted. An organ represents a major investment for any congregation; but, if used appropriately, it is a major contributor to any congregation's worship.

Most liturgical music, however, consists of singing, usually with organ or other instrumental accompaniment. Our worship basically follows a call-and-response pattern involving, on the one hand, the minister and other leaders of worship and, on the other hand, the congregation. The congregation's responses of prayer and praise commonly take the form of hymns, songs, and sung refrains. Sometimes the call, or proclamation of the Word, is sung by a solo voice (cantor). A choir may function either as proclaimer of the Word or as responder on behalf of the whole congregation.

Singing can immeasurably intensify our acts of worship. Much that we now read in unison or in response would probably be felt more deeply if it were sung. If there is to be new life in our worship, it is crucial that there be new life in our singing.

Any act of worship that the congregation *can* sing it *should* sing. Hymns, songs, and sung responses may well be the most effective way in which the people participate in worship. Choirs perform a valuable function by singing acts of worship that require more skill or rehearsal time than the congregation as a whole has, but they should not take the singing of the people's responses away from the rest of the congregation. As Carlton Young has said: "We treat the choir as if it were the congregation; we ought, instead, to treat the congregation as if it were the choir."

Music can be irrelevant or even harmful as well as helpful to our worship. The problem is not as simple as good and bad music or good and bad performances. Music, however beautiful or skillfully performed, can obscure or distort the words that are sung, and the words sung may themselves be inappropriate to the occasion. Even instrumental music may have associations or express feelings that are inappropriate to a given occasion. A church musician needs careful study of worship to make music an integral part of worship. We hold too high a view of music in worship to regard it simply as pious background or embellishment.

Selecting music, therefore, is one of the most demanding tasks in preparing for worship. Some music, such as the doxology or the Gloria Patri, may be constant Sunday after Sunday, but most music changes each week. We should look at the relationship of music to the Christian Year, especially through study of the lectionary. When hymns and anthems are musical commentaries on the lessons for the day, and when psalms and canticles (scripture songs) are sung, music can participate in the proclamation of the Word in ways beyond the power of ordinary speech. The lectionary, then, is a basic tool of the church musician. No one profits more from the use of the lectionary than does the musician. Using it, the musician can plan music, order it, and rehearse it months in advance. It is the best means of making sure music will be an integral part of worship and not simply pious entertainment.

D. The Functional Analysis of Worship

Individual elements of worship can best be understood by examining their functions. This functional analysis utilizes what might be called the "liturgical circle," although it may be a spiral since it really describes a forward-moving process. This process has four stages: (1) observation of a worshiping community's practice, (2) descriptive theological analysis, (3) normative theological reflection, and (4) reform of the community's practice. Practice moves through theory back to practice. Let us look at each of these stages.

1. *Observation of a worshiping community's practice.* Observation takes some detachment. It is not easy for a pastor who has responsibility for leading worship to look critically at what is going on. Not only must pastors be aware of what they themselves are saying and doing, but they also must be concerned that the musicians, ushers, and others with worship responsibilities are functioning properly. Regular members of the congregation also have difficulty in being good observers because they are caught up in the acts of worship and because of their assumptions, based on long familiarity, as to who does what and how it is to be done. In fact, some of the most penetrating observations might be made by a pagan who came to church one Sunday just to find out what strange things Christians do.

To lead worship well, we need to learn to observe—to see and hear what the community is doing in expressing its faith whenever it assembles. As in all ethical decisions, we must ask: "What is going on?" "What is happening?" These questions involve all who are affected by an action, whether in ethics or in worship; in either case we have to be keen observers. Seemingly insignificant details may tell us much.

How much, for example, does the pastor sit down during the service? That may be an important clue to discovering whether he or she *presides over* or *dominates* the service. If the pastor stands for almost the entire service, it often means that little leadership is delegated to others. It probably indicates a one-person domination of the community's chief gathering—a dominance that would not be tolerated in a business meeting, where one would be likely to sit to preside rather than dominate. A good presider elicits participation from all present so that they can feel they are valued as important parts of the community.

Observation is a complicated matter. We need to become sensitive to the widely varied roles that different people in the congregation play. Worship is a multifaceted event. Fretting or cooing for example, is acceptable for a baby, not for a teenager. We have to grasp the complexity of any community.

2. *Descriptive theological analysis.* Observation leads to our second stage in functional analysis: that of trying to understand the faith to which the congregation's words and actions give witness. In chapter 2 we defined the faith of the early church in terms of how it organized time.

Our problem at this second stage is trying to find out what the various actions and words we have observed are actually meant to do. What does the community intend? What does it wish to express? Obviously, much happens simply by habitual repetition, but what does it mean to the participants? How does it reflect what they believe and cherish enough to give up Sunday mornings to do it together? We are, in short, trying to discover what makes the community one. What is its source of unity? At this point we must be descriptive, trying to interpret what is going on.

This leads to making faith statements out of the activities observed. Is the community's attention focused largely on itself or directed outward? Is its piety a somber penitential one or one of paschal joy? Does it relate to those things in Christian faith that have been believed "at all times and in all places," or is its faith conceived of in terms of local place and memory? Is scripture the touchstone of authenticity for it, or are those corporate memories rather vague? These and many other questions come to mind in trying to do a descriptive theological analysis of what the community expresses.

3. *Normative theological reflection.* The pastor has to bring normative judgments to the faith that she or he finds expressed in the congregation's worship. A minister has theological training and responsibilties as a pastoral theologian. Nowhere is this function more necessary than with regard to worship leadership. This is where theological training gets constant use, perhaps more use than in any other aspect of ministry. One is forced, as representative minister, to make theological judgments, and these must be *systematic, historic,* and *pastoral* to serve the congregation well.

First, one should be *systematic* in trying to find coherence in the theological statements the congregation is making. The official theology of the congregation and its actual belief may have little in common. Just as someone who tells you that you are too fat and then offers you cookies is making a self-contradictory statement, congregations often make self-contradictory statements that are highly significant and call for judgments to be made. For instance, if the official theology professes the centrality of scripture in the community's faith and life but the order of worship relegates scripture to a marginal role, a judgment is called for. Does listening for God's Word in scripture play a major role in the service or a minor one? Or if the official theology teaches the great importance of prayer but the order of worship leaves little or no opportunity for the people to pray, again a judgment is called for. Does the community gather to speak to God in prayer, or is that a minor concern?

Also, theological judgments should be *historic*. Is the faith that we have observed and described in our local church adequate in the light of the historic faith of the universal church? We have seen that historical knowledge is crucial in understanding the Christian Year. It is also important in making any judgment that relates our local church to the universal church.

Finally, our theological judgments should be *pastoral*, taking into account the actual life circumstances of the people in our congregation and its surrounding secular community. How well does the congregation's worship reflect the full richness of who these people are in the light of their particular local, ethnic, cultural, and personal histories? How well does our worship take account of both men and women, of the various age levels and levels of faith development, of the various handicapping conditions represented in the congregation and its surrounding community?

4. *Reform of the community's practice.* Having made such critical judgments, we are able to move on to the last stage, that of reforming actual practice. While worship reformation is not limited to the local congregation—witness the massive reformation of denominational liturgies in recent years—our concern here is with the local process.

This involves (1) resolving the self-contradictions and inconsistencies that may be present so the people can really do what they mean and mean what they do, (2) helping the congregation express in worship a faith that is in accord with that of the universal church, and (3) helping the congregation express in worship their actual life circumstances and those of their surrounding community.

The representative minister as pastoral theologian is a bridge builder, linking the faith of that local congregation with that of the universal church, making the local church universal and the universal church local. All worship reform must come through dialogue with those one seeks to serve. One should never try to change people's worship without knowing, accepting, and loving them as they are. But one can change their worship by taking them into one's confidence and interpreting how changes would help them express better what they believe.

Thus, our functional analysis comes full circle, from observation of a congregation's worship, to descriptive analysis, to normative reflection, and finally to reform of practice itself. It is an ongoing process that calls for self-critical awareness and continual reform.

E. The Elements of Worship Through the Year

In the light of these more general considerations we shall look at the individual elements of worship and the ways in which each of them functions during the Christian Year. Some of these elements remain the same from week to week; we call them the "ordinary" of the service, and they supply the stability needed for effective worship. Other elements change from week to week or from season to season; we call them the "propers," and they supply the variety needed for effective worship. Our primary concern in this book is, of course, with the propers.

As we have indicated, the order of worship is important. Just as in recent years there has been a remarkable recovery of the Christian Year, so there has been a remarkable recovery of the classic order of Word and table. Each of the denominations that have participated in the development of the common calendar and *Common Lectionary* has also in recent years published a reformed order of worship that reflects this classic order. In this book we shall be using this order in ways that can be adapted readily to denominational or local variations. Churches using fundamentally different orders of worship can also follow the Christian Year, adapting the resources in this book to their needs. On certain days of the year, such as the days of Holy Week, there are traditional and practical reasons for changing the order of worship from the usual weekly pattern; those special orders of worship will be explained in the chapters dealing with those days. Meanwhile, we shall now look at the individual elements of Sunday worship.

F. Entering into Worship

Gathering. The coming together of the congregation for worship is an important part of the worship service, although it is often not recognized as such. Although there are structures of gathering that probably remain constant week after week, there is much that changes in what people experience as they gather.

What do the people see as they come together? Do they see their fellow worshipers dressed for Good Friday or for Easter, for winter or for summer? Do the flowers, paraments, and banners announce that this is a festive season such as Christmas or Easter, or a somber season such as Lent? As the people enter, are they given something that reminds them what day it is—a palm branch on Passion/Palm Sunday or a candle on Christmas or Easter Eve?

What do the people hear as they come together? As they greet their neighbors, most of whom they probably have not seen for a week or more, what is happening in the community or in the world that is on everyone's lips? If there has been a recent tragedy that makes it hard to celebrate Christmas, a disaster that throws Good Friday and Easter into a new light, some great good news that is on everyone's mind at Thanksgiving, such events cannot help being part of our observance of these days. When organ or other instrumental music is played during the gathering, it is important to relate the music to the day or season and to enable the people to listen.

Announcements may be made during the gathering or later in the service; but, wherever they are placed, they vary from Sunday to Sunday and help set the tone for the day. The plea for money that comes just before Christmas so that the church can pay its year-end bills and the announcement at Easter that the pastor will be moving in June to another church are dramatic examples of what often happens more subtly—the announcements interact, for good or for ill, with the church calendar.

Greeting. The first words spoken by the minister or sung by the choir to the gathered congregation, regardless of what they are called (salutation, scripture sentences, call to worship, introit) or whether they come before or after the opening hymn, are a greeting in the name of the Lord. The greeting may reflect the season or festival of the Christian Year at hand. It may be chosen from the lessons or psalm for the day. On the other hand, there is much to be said for its being constant from Sunday to Sunday. If the greeting calls for a congregational response, a constant response will be memorized quickly and come naturally to the people's lips, while a response that is different every Sunday will have to be read from the printed page. In this book we shall occasionally suggest a special greeting for a particular day, though not for every Sunday. Persons wishing a different greeting for every Sunday, related to the lectionary, will find them in *When We Gather, Word and Witness,* and *The New Lectionary Series* (see Annotated Bibliography).

Opening Hymn. This is customarily a hymn of praise—a greeting to the God in whose name we have been (or will be) greeted. It is by no means the only praise to God in the service, and the opening hymn ought to sound a note of praise that is echoed throughout the service. Some hymns of praise are clearly well suited to particular days or seasons, and these we shall mention when we come to those days and seasons. On the other hand, there are many fine hymns of praise suited for use throughout the year and many Sundays when these general hymns are most appropriate. There is no need to try to relate the opening hymn to the lectionary week after week; if there is a hymn that has a clear relationship to one of the scriptures, it is better to sing it immediately before or after that lesson is read or preached.

Opening Prayer(s). An opening prayer may serve various functions. It can mark the end of the introductory part of the service by summing up our common purpose, as in the Collect for Purity: "That we may perfectly love you, and worthily magnify your holy name." It may be a prayer of adoration and praise. Such a prayer for every day in the three-year lectionary cycle may be found in *When We Gather* (see Annotated Bibliography).

It may be a prayer of confession, followed by an assurance of pardon, although this may come later in the service. A prayer of confession and assurance of pardon for every day in the three-year lectionary cycle may be found in *When We Gather*. In some congregations there is confession only on penitential occasions such as in Lent; on such occasions there may be a full service of reconciliation—scripture readings, examination of conscience, confession, and pardon—that focuses the experience much more intensely than does a single prayer each Sunday.

Another possibility is to see the opening prayer as initiating the proclamation of the Word by announcing a main theme to be found in the scriptures. Both historic and modern collects are frequently used in this way. *A Handbook for the Lectionary, The Book of Common Prayer, Lutheran Book of Worship,* and the Roman Catholic *Sunday Missal* (see Annotated Bibliograpy) all contain collects for each Sunday and special observances in the Christian Year. A sampling of such collects is found in this book.

Finally, there can be a prayer for illumination before the reading of the scriptures, in which we pray that the Holy Spirit may illuminate our hearts and minds as God's Word is read, sung, preached, and heard.

Many churches have a sequence of two or more opening prayers, so as to include more than one of these functions.

Acts of Praise. There is often an act of praise after the opening prayer or inserted between the prayers. There are a number of possibilities. This is the traditional place of the *Kyrie Eleison* and the *Gloria in Excelsis.* The congregation may sing a hymn or psalm or say a litany of praise, or the choir may sing an anthem.

Whether at this place or at some other place in the order of worship, there is at least one choir anthem in most Protestant services. *Reformed Liturgy and Music* and *Word and Witness* (see Annotated Bibliograhy) are among the resources that suggest an appropriate anthem for each day in the three-year lectionary cycle.

G. Proclaiming the Word

Scripture is read in worship as God's word to God's people. That in itself should guarantee it a major role in any service of Christian worship. The reading of Scripture is a form of self-giving in which the presence of Christ is made known. Jesus himself read Scripture in worship (Luke 4:16-21) and referred to it constantly in speaking of God. Christians read Scripture to hear the living God speak to us through the risen Christ in the power of the Holy Spirit. Our focus is not on the words themselves but on God's living Word (Logos), Jesus Christ speaking to us through words. Many prayers of illumination ask that we may hear Christ the Word while we listen to the words of Scripture.

This applies not just to the Gospel readings in which Jesus speaks and acts but to all the canonical Scriptures. In hearing the scriptures read, the Christian community recalls the corporate memories that make it one. We are baptized into these memories; they become our possession and give us our identity as Christians. They are recovered every time we join with the community in worship and scripture is read. The reading of scripture is a form of *anamnesis*—that is, of remembering, recalling, experiencing anew the reality of God's mighty acts in sacred history. The events themselves remain unique and unrepeatable, but remembering them helps us relive sacred history for ourselves. The reading of scripture makes these events again present in their power to save. Thereby we can appropriate them as part of our personal history. Reading the lessons becomes a way of bridging history so that the eyewitnesses of sacred events have no advantage over those who participate in them through remembering.

This is the unique function of the canonical Scriptures. No matter how edifying the great writings other than Scripture may be, they have no such function. They are not the corporate memories that unify the community. Indeed, if they are controversial, their function can be the opposite, that is, they can divide the community. Christian preaching may properly quote from many sources, but if it is not based on Scripture it loses its God-given foundation. Only the canonical Scriptures function to unify the community by rehearsing its corporate memories. The weekly recital of these memories through Word and sacrament is the chief means of building up the Christian community.

Scripture, then, is read for its own sake, as God's Word. Preaching usually follows as explication and application of what has been read. It is a serious misunderstanding to think that Scripture is read, as unfortunately sometimes happens, simply to provide a text or background for the sermon.

Christ uses human agents and talents to give himself to us through the lessons. The reader, lay or ordained, has a very important ministry and should prepare carefully. One cannot read Scripture aloud without interpreting it; no matter how it is read, it is being interpreted. The extremes of "hamming it up" are just as bad as "clamming it up" in monotone. It is a marvel that Christ would entrust the treasure of his self-giving to earthen vessels, but this is exactly what happens when the Scriptures are read in worship. There are ways, however, that leaders can prepare for this exalted task: reading the passages aloud a number of times, circling pitfalls (in pencil), and looking up difficult or unfamiliar names in a Bible that has a pronouncing dictionary. The lessons should be read from a large, attractively bound pulpit Bible. These are now available for most translations. The visual appearance of the Bible makes a statement about the importance the community places on God's Word as read in worship. A handheld book, not to mention a leaflet, undercuts this visual message. Opening and closing the Bible are also expressive acts.

Understanding how the *Common Lectionary* works is important in making the best use of it. Three lessons are read each Sunday and on certain other days over a three-year cycle. The first lesson is usually from the Old Testament, the second usually from one of the Epistles, and the third always from one of the four Gospels. There is also a three-year cycle of psalms, which has a function different from that of the lessons. The three years of the cycle are named "A," "B," and "C," with Year C being any year divisible by three, such as 1986. Each liturgical year begins on the First Sunday of Advent in the previous calendar year; thus, liturgical 1986 began on the First Sunday of Advent 1985.

Each of the three years has its own distinctive character. The reading governing that character is the Gospel, arranged to fit the sequence of the Christian Year. In Year A the Gospel lessons are mostly from Matthew, and the Old Testament lessons in the Season After Pentecost are from the Pentateuch, Ruth, and prophetic eschatology. Year B is the year of Mark's Gospel, and the Old Testament lessons after Pentecost are from the David narrative, Wisdom Literature, and the last eight Sundays from the present Roman Catholic lectionary. In Year C Luke is the predominant Gospel, and the Old Testament lessons after Pentecost are from the prophets, beginning with Elijah. John's Gospel is used throughout all three years, especially during the Easter cycle.

From the second or third Sunday prior to Advent through Easter Day, and on Pentecost and Trinity Sundays, the first lesson is usually related to the Gospel, as are alternative readings from Acts on Easter Day, Ascension, and Pentecost. The second lesson generally relates to the theme of the other two lessons from Christ the King through the Baptism of the Lord and from Transfiguration through Easter Day as well as on Ascension, Pentecost, and Trinity Sunday. On most other Sundays the second lesson is semicontinuous through the Epistles; hence, a relationship between the second lesson and the Gospel is not necessarily implied. From the Sunday after Trinity until just before Advent, Old Testament lessons are also semicontinuous, for the most part, and all three lessons go their separate ways.

While the basic pattern of three lessons and a psalm is followed throughout the year, variations occur at certain points: (1) On Passion/Palm Sunday and on Good Friday, the Gospel lesson is much longer than usual, as entire passion narratives from the Synoptics and John, respectively, are appointed then. (2) For Passion/Palm Sunday additional lessons related to Jesus' entry into Jerusalem are provided for use during the liturgy or procession of psalms. (3) At the Easter Vigil, the psalm, Epistle, and Gospel readings are preceded by ten Old Testament lessons, plus eight psalms and two canticles. (4) For Christmas Eve and Day, three separate sets of lessons are provided. More will be said about each of these days when it is discussed later in this book.

The systematic reading of three lessons through use of the lectionary has probably been the most important, the most popular, and the most successful of the recent reforms in Christian worship. It provides the best means for the Christian community to recall systematically its corporate memories. The most valid alternative seems to be a systematic policy of reading continuously through books of the Scriptures (*lectio continua*), and this is partially provided in the lectionary itself. Without a lectionary or a program of continuous reading, a congregation is likely to be subjected to a patchwork of the pastor's favorite passages and thereby restricted to the narrow measure of one person's grasp of the gospel. The lectionary can free a congregation from the limits of the pastor's private canon of Scripture and give a much more whole, balanced presentation of the whole story and teachings of the Bible.

The standard order for this part of the service is first lesson, psalm, second lesson, hymn, Gospel, and sermon. Notice the rhythm of proclamation and response, with the Gospel and sermon treated as a great unified proclamation which will be followed by a great response that we shall consider later.

The *first lesson* is from the Old Testament, except for readings from Acts during the Easter Season—about which more will be said in the chapter on that season. For most churches, the new lectionary represents a significant increase in the number of readings from the Old Testament. Seven passages appear from books of the Apocrypha (Baruch and Ecclesiasticus); canonical Old Testament alternatives are given for all but one, and that one (at the Easter Vigil) may be omitted. This provision of alternatives reflects a continuing difference among Christians as to whether these books are part of the canon of Scripture.

The *psalm* functions as a response to the first lesson. Since the first lesson is usually from the Old Testament, many of the appointed psalms declaim the same history, giving expression to human experience in response to that history. Sometimes the psalm is a commentary, often of a personal nature, on the images and events in the first lesson. Other psalms are a doxological exclamation on the first lesson, linking with themes and images in the Gospel. The sermon may refer to or be based on a passage from the psalm, but the function of the psalm as a response should not be confused with that of the lessons as proclamation. The gathered people pray the psalm—often as intimate and honest conversation with God.

There are many ways of singing or saying the psalms. Bear in mind that they were intended to be sung, since they constitute the oldest hymnbook of God's people. Psalms may be sung in hymnic form as metrical paraphrases to tunes from Scottish and French Psalters or from early American sources. This style is often easy to sing, but the texts may compromise the actual wording and expressive structure and range of the psalms. Many congregations are becoming familiar with various responsorial and antiphonal musical settings. In the former, the leader, cantor, or choir may sing (or speak) the verses of the psalm, after each section of which the congregation sings a simple response, or antiphon, which may be drawn from one of the psalm verses. In the antiphonal style, two sides of the congregation alternate the verses or sections by singing on a simple tone. In longer psalms, various sections may be sung by cantor or choir, with a mixed variety of responses by the congregation. Some settings may be "through-composed"—that is set for organ (or other accompaniment), choir, and congregation.

When singing is not attempted, the psalms may be recited in dialogue between minister and people or, better, between two or more sections of the congregation.

A wide variety of translations are available for liturgical use, and many recent musical settings are now available, such as those of Joseph Gelineau, David Isele, Michael Joncas, and the psalm tones of the *Lutheran Book of Worship* and of other communities.

While it is by no means necessary to conclude the psalm with the Gloria Patri, this is the appointed place for that acclamation when it is used.

In some of the services there are responsories. These are intended as congregational responses to scripture which give specific focus to our understanding of the implications of the lesson. Each is related to the particular lesson and is composed of scriptural phrases that express a powerful image or voice. These may be recited in either responsorial or antiphonal style. Musicians are encouraged to compose simple musical settings for them.

The *second lesson* is from the Epistles, except on several occasions in the three-year cycle when it is from Acts or Revelation. Portions are read from all the Epistles except II John, III John, and Jude. Since we read the Epistles in course through much of the year, the second lesson may not relate directly to the first lesson and the Gospel. Its distinct function is likely to be an emphasis on teaching, particularly ethical, that contrasts with the narration and dialogue in the other lessons. This gives an important balance to the readings and often to the preaching.

The *hymn* (sometimes called "the gradual hymn") which customarily follows the second lesson is a response to the lessons and a prelude to the Gospel—thus a "bridge." It may be a commentary on what precedes or what follows. It does not have to be a hymn but may be a song, a spiritual, a stanza, a brief response, or a refrain. In any case, it should be carefully chosen to relate to the lessons and to the spirit of the day or season. Except in penitential seasons, it is usually joyful. It is an old custom to avoid hymns or other acts of praise with "alleluia" during Lent and to make constant use of them during the Easter Season, so that Easter becomes all the more festive by contrast.

In the discussion of the days and seasons in the rest of this book, we shall suggest particular hymns as being appropriate to the scriptures for the day—recognizing that not all these hymns will be in the hymnal used in your church. Several understandings are important as these suggestions are considered. (1) These suggestions are meant to stimulate your own creativity. You will often think of hymns that are equally appropriate if not more so, particularly in the light of your congregation's preferences or limitations. (2) Do not introduce more than one unfamiliar hymn to a congregation at a time, and plan in most congregations to take about a month to teach them any hymn with an unfamiliar tune. (3) When possible, set unfamiliar words to a familiar tune. This requires skill and an ability to use the metrical index in your hymnal, but it will enable you to sing many texts that are set to tunes your congregation cannot sing. (4) It may often be better to sing a known, beloved hymn that has only a vague relationship to the day's scripture lessons than to come to grief with a hymn, however appropriate its words, which the people cannot or will not sing.

The *Gospel* has traditionally been accorded the place of honor by Christians in the reading of scripture, since it deals most directly with the words and actions of Jesus Christ. To be sure, we should avoid any "red letter" view of Scripture which obscures the fact that Christ speaks through *all* Scripture and that the good news resounds from Genesis through Revelation. But the Gospels deal with the climactic event of our salvation history.

In many congregations the people stand for the reading of the Gospel. If they have already been standing for the preceding hymn, they simply remain standing for the Gospel.

Since the Gospel lessons are arranged on the basis of the Christian Year, they will suggest the central character of each service. Events in the life and ministry of Jesus are central in the Christmas and Easter cycles. After Epiphany, the Gospel lessons tend to be accounts of miracles and parables. In the half of the year after Pentecost, the Gospels are read in course, concentrating more on Jesus' teaching. The Gospel, then, functions as a recalling throughout the year of what God has done in Jesus Christ.

The *Sermon* is the means by which God's Word is made contemporary and applied to the situations of modern life for society, the congregation, or the individual. It can be an interpretation of the

Gospel, another of the lessons, the psalm, or perhaps more than one of these. One certainly does not have to preach on all three lessons; it is enough to preach on one of them. On the other hand, there are days when the lessons relate to one another in such a way that it is natural and effective that the sermon deal with two or even all three of them.

There are four essential dimensions of good preaching: the power of God in preaching, the relation of preaching to Scripture, the authority of the faith of the church in what is preached, and the situation and response of a given congregation to what is heard and seen. Without the active power of God, the Word is not preached or heard. A sermon unrelated to Scripture has little to say that is specifically Christian and little to differentiate it from a lecture. Preaching is based on the faith of the whole church, not a purely private faith; therefore, sermons that are preached without the consciousness that the church has authorized us to speak for it can be divisive and tear down the body rather than build it up. And finally, the congregation has an active role to play in listening attentively to hear what Word God has for it today. The preacher, in short, preaches by the power of God, on the basis of Scripture, by the authority of the church, to a congregation listening in faith for God's Word.

H. Responding to the Word

After the sermon the service moves to a quite flexible section, one open to a variety of forms.

The service so far has focused primarily on God's Word to us, coming to a climax in the great unified proclamation of the Gospel/sermon. We Protestants seem tempted to end the service at this point or, at least, to move from the sermon directly to a brief "sending forth." The only response needed, we may tell ourselves, is to go out into the world and obey the message we have heard.

More and more, however, we are recovering the ancient wisdom that the Gospel/sermon proclamation calls for an authentic response—here and now! We preach for a response, and the long-term response of Christian faith and life scattered in the world can be patterned and empowered in a corporate response that models in the worshiping assembly the faith and life to which God is calling us in the world.

This response can vary according to the occasion in the Christian Year, the lessons, and the sermon. It is far less important to follow a routine pattern, especially if it is perceived as a tacked-on anticlimax, than it is to invite responses that are the natural, inevitable reaction to what has been heard in the Word of God.

Often an *invitation* at the conclusion of the sermon specifically calls for response. This may take various forms. It may be an invitation to Christian discipleship which calls persons forward who wish to commit or recommit their lives to Christ, to be baptized or to present children for baptism, or to affiliate with the local congregation. It may be a call for commitment to some specific ministry or for those who wish simply to come forward and kneel in prayer. A particular group may be invited—a class to be confirmed, officers or workers to be installed or recognized and thanked, an organization to be recognized.

Often a *hymn* follows the sermon. If it is in the context of an invitation, it is commonly a hymn of invitation and response; in any event, it is normally a response to the Word that has been read and preached. Such a hymn, like a hymn that follows a scripture lesson, should be carefully chosen to relate to the proclamation preceding it and to any specific commitment being called for. The specific hymn suggestions given for particular days and scriptures later in this book should be seen in the light of the understandings discussed earlier in this chapter. It is important that the people be invited to stand for this hymn; the act of standing is in itself a sign of authentic response and commitment.

The classic act of response to the proclamation of the Word is *Christian baptism*. Other acts of Christian commitment are all related to God's baptismal covenant with us. Such acts call for careful advance pastoral preparation and counseling, and the ceremonies themselves deserve to be as impressive as possible. Increasingly, these occasional services are tied to the Christian Year by observing "baptismal festivals." These occur most appropriately at the Baptism of the Lord, the Easter Vigil, Pentecost, and All Saints but can be scheduled at other times. On such occasions the whole service focuses on entrance into, and renewal of, the baptismal covenant.

Often the use of the *creed* will be an appropriate response to the Word, especially when Holy Communion is not celebrated. (An adequate prayer of thanksgiving over the bread and cup serves much the same function as a creed.)

Although some churches do not use creeds, two or possibly three creeds have been used so widely and so long that they can be called "ecumenical creeds." These ecumenical creeds function to proclaim that a congregation joins in the universal faith of the Christian church. The Apostles' Creed is the ancient baptismal creed still commonly used in Christian baptism. On Sundays when there no baptisms, its recitation can remind us of, and reaffirm, the faith in which we have been baptized. The Nicene Creed eventually was inserted into the Eucharist in both East and West. Both creeds are readily available in denominational worship resources (see Annotated Bibliography). A third creed, the so-called Athanasian Creed, has been widely used at times in the West, and an abbreviated version is included for Trinity Sunday in this book.

Modern statements or affirmations of faith serve other functions and hence are not rightly called "creeds." Some are official statements of faith adopted by a denomination and affirm denominational unity. Others are adopted by local congregations or other Christian organizations and affirm a parochial unity. Still others are the statements of individuals and serve as personal witness rather than as affirmations of unity.

A time of *prayer* that includes petitions, intercessions, and thanksgivings for specific persons, events, and causes is most appropriately a response to the Word. Members of the congregation may have the opportunity to express concerns or prayer requests, which may be done in many ways, depending on the size, character, and customs of the congregation; but this time of prayer comes to life when the prayers are as specific as possible. We are reaching out to others in the world, the wider church, the community, and the congregation.

A prayer of confession, followed by an assurance of pardon, may come at this time in the service, especially when it is an appropriate response to the Word as it has been proclaimed that day.

In recent years the *passing of the peace* has once again become a common part of Christian worship. It is a physical act of handclasp or embrace—a "kiss of peace"—mentioned in the New Testament and in the *Didache*, a Christian document from the second century. There may or may not be an exchange of words: "The peace of the Lord be with you." "And also with you." Its function is to signify reconciliation with other people as we prepare to make our offering to God, in obedience to the teaching of Matthew 5:23-24. For this reason it may follow the confession and pardon and may be followed by the offering.

The *offering*, like intercessions, is meant for others. It is a concrete way of responding to God's Word with action, to put our money where our mouth is. Frequently, a choir anthem is sung or an organ voluntary is played as an offering of music to God, or the congregation may sing a hymn of dedication. The offering may be brought forward while the congregation sings a stanza or doxology such as "Praise God, from Whom All Blessings Flow."

Recognizing how flexible and diverse the responses to the Word can be, we can now see how important it is in this part of the service to maintain a balance of stability and variety. Because of the very specific character of so many of the responses, there can be a wide range of content from one Sunday to another, often related to the days and seasons of the Christian Year. It is also important that there be structure and stability from week to week—an order that sets the responses into context, the repetition of an act of worship such as the Apostles' Creed, a litany or other structure into which specific petitions and intercessions can be placed, and the offering ceremony. If dull routine on the one hand and chaos on the other are successfully avoided, this can be a time in the service when the Spirit moves with power.

At this point we come to a major option for most Protestant traditions. If Holy Communion is to be celebrated, different things will be done beginning at this point in the service. We shall treat first the noncommunion option. In both options, though, thanksgiving is central.

On those occasions when Holy Communion is not celebrated, the responses to the Word continue with *thanksgiving*. The obvious response to good news is thanksgiving: "Thank God!" In response to the Gospel we give thanks for what God has done for us. The proclamation of the good news ought inevitably to lead to thanksgiving. Whatever else is contained in our thanksgiving, it ought to be an ample and joyful recital of God's great actions. It therefore has a creedal character and is especially important if no creed has been said earlier. It may also include specific thanksgivings for God's recent blessings, if these have not been included earlier with the petitions and intercessions. It may be prayed by the pastor, in unison, or as a litany.

The *Lord's Prayer*, as the model of all prayer, can be used anywhere in the service but is especially appropriate at the conclusion of the thanksgiving. As the summary of all prayer, it is thus the final climactic prayer in the service. It should certainly be prayed by the whole congregation, and if they can effectively sing it, so much the better. Following the Lord's Prayer, a moment of holy silence may seem fitting.

No matter what may have happened during the earlier responses to the Word—and these can sometimes remind us painfully of the suffering and sin in the world—the thanksgiving and Lord's Prayer provide a constant and very positive climax the congregation can count on, Sunday after Sunday.

The *closing hymn* may be a hymn of praise or simply a doxological stanza, or it may be a hymn of sending forth into the world.

Just as the spoken part of worship began with a greeting, so a farewell is also appropriate. A *dismissal with blessing*, often called the "benediction," accomplishes two things. It is a dismissal that sends the people out into life and work in the world, and it is a blessing—a pronouncement (not a prayer) that the triune God goes with us as we scatter into the world. The words used may vary with the day or season, but there is much to be said for their being constant from Sunday to Sunday.

The action of *scattering* into the world, like the action of gathering, is part of worship. Greetings and conversation are as important after the service as they are before the service. What we have done while assembled in worship is a modeling of the Christian life we are to lead day by day.

I. A Feast for All Seasons

When Holy Communion is celebrated, it customarily follows the offering and is followed by the closing hymn and dismissal with blessing.

The actions of Jesus in the upper room are reenacted: *taking* the bread and cup, *giving thanks* (blessing) over the bread and cup, *breaking* the bread, and *giving* the bread and cup. Since *taking* the bread and cup is preparatory to the primary action of *giving thanks* and since *breaking* the bread is preparatory to the primary action of *giving* the bread and cup, we may think of Holy Communion as consisting of two primary parts: thanksgiving (blessing) and giving (communion).

The *Great Thanksgiving*—also known as the Eucharistic Prayer, Anaphora, Canon, or (inappropriately) Prayer of Consecration—is the only one of the four actions of Holy Communion that is primarily words. It is the church's chief doxological statement of its faith. Historically, early Christianity borrowed much from both the form and the content of Jewish blessings or prayers of thanksgiving. The content was enlarged to climax in God's work in Jesus Christ, but the Jewish concept of giving thanks to God by blessing God through the recital of God's mighty acts survived.

Christians have often varied this prayer, or parts of it, during the course of the Christian Year. This enables a church in the course of the year to incorporate more content—especially more detailed recital of God's mighty acts—into the prayer than could be done on any one occasion. In the remainder of this book a number of Great Thanksgivings will be included in the resources for particular days and seasons. They follow a basic pattern that is ancient and that has been characteristic of Great Thanksgivings influenced by recent ecumenical reforms. These illustrate how the Great Thanksgiving can be varied during the course of the year. Other collections of Great Thanksgivings, including seasonal variations, can be found in the denominational worship books listed in the Annotated Bibliography.

The breaking of bread is both an important utilitarian act in preparing the bread for giving and a powerful sign of the unity of the community (I Cor. 10:16-17).

Giving the bread and cup is the climax of Holy Communion and is often referred to as the "communion." The word "communion" is a translation of the New Testament Greek word *koinonia*, which may also be translated "participation," "sharing," or "fellowship." While different churches give the bread and cup in different ways, most congregations prefer that this be done in the same way throughout the year. It is possible, however, to vary with the time of year—for instance, receiving the bread and cup kneeling during Lent, sitting at table on Holy Thursday, and standing during the Easter Season.

When we reflect on the many meanings of this supreme act of Christian worship, we shall probably find that the facets of meaning that come to mind at a Christmas Eve communion, a Holy Thursday communion, an Easter communion, and an All Saints communion will be very different from one another. Part of the reason for varying the Great Thanksgiving is to uncover more of the inexhaustible dimensions of meaning that are appropriate throughout the unfolding year. Holy Communion is indeed a feast for all seasons, and by participating in it throughout the year, we can grow in our appreciation of its immeasurable richness.

PART TWO

RESOURCES FOR THE CHRISTIAN YEAR

FROM HOPE TO JOY: ADVENT AND CHRISTMAS/EPIPHANY

A. A Theological and Pastoral Introduction

C hristians confess and proclaim that "the Word became flesh and dwelt among us" (John 1:14). This is the great message of the incarnation, that Jesus Christ was born into human history in the fullness of time for the salvation of the world. This is what we seek to celebrate, to proclaim, and to manifest to all peoples in this particular season of the church's year of grace.

In Advent we sing, "Come, thou long-expected Jesus, / Born to set thy people free." At Christmas we join with the herald angels, singing, "Glory to the newborn King!" Epiphany bids us behold the light shining in the darkness, the Root of Jesse, David's Son to whom in adoration we sing, "O Morning Star, how fair and bright / Thou beamest forth in truth and light!" The story these days have to tell upon the mountain is one of "good tidings and great joy"—for the Messiah has come. Yet such is God's advent among us that we can never fully grasp the mystery of incarnate deity, so we must continue to remember and to experience anew, year upon year, the permanent crisis of light in the midst of the world's darkness and turmoil. We relive the fear and hope and joy that Christian worship expresses in the narrative of his coming to judge the world in the form of a Child weak in infancy—the wood of whose cradle foreshadows the cross.

The theology of Advent, Christmas, and Epiphany is powerful because we cannot fully understand Jesus' birth without first understanding that he is Savior and Lord. This means that any authentic celebration of Advent and Christmas must be experienced as part of the larger story of his life, suffering, death, and resurrection. In other words, incarnation is one central aspect of the Paschal Mystery, which will be discussed in connection with the Easter cycle. The birth narratives in Matthew are themselves an expression of a saving faith in Christ. The worship patterns offered here will serve to heighten this inner connection between his birth and his redemptive passion, death, and resurrection.

Christmas is, in many respects, more popular with Western Christians than any other season of the year. The Eastern churches, from the beginning, have focused on Epiphany. Hispanic traditions have vividly portrayed the "Three Kings." While there are certainly cultural reasons for these interests, the fundamental Western images and themes of Christmas seem intimate and perhaps closest to the tenderness at the heart of humanity. Images of the holy family, the poverty and difficulty of their circumstances, the affectionate simplicity of the scenes at the manger, and the doxology on the starlit hillsides all combine to form a deep place of receptivity in the human heart for the news that heaven and earth have met, that God and humankind are reconciled. Certainly the innocence of the Child and the dramatic swirl of events in Bethlehem and Jerusalem capture our imagination. Various traditions have focused much devotional life around the crèche.

The Advent-Christmas-Epiphany cycle is both narrative and thematic, historical and theological. On one level it takes us through the narrative of hope and expectation for the coming Messiah, expressed so powerfully by the prophets, most especially by Isaiah. Then Christmas and Epiphany take us from the birth narratives to the first manifestation of Jesus' identity and divinity in the gifts of the Magi, his baptism by John in the Jordan, and his first miracle at the wedding in Cana. At the same time, we are celebrating and proclaiming more than a simple chronology of events. The whole cycle also speaks of the yearning and hope of human beings for salvation, the wonderment of God assuming human flesh, the anticipation by the wise men of Jesus' death and burial, and the solidarity with humanity that is the very way of Emmanuel, God-with-us.

Thus, to celebrate the Advent-Christmas-Epiphany cycle well we must submit to its wide range of themes and emotions: from hope to joy, from darkness to light, from yearning for deliverance to the very manifestation of God's coming in judgment and in life-giving solidarity with humanity. There is a vision in the readings of redeemed society and urgent expectancy of God's final shalom—justice, peace, righteousness, and reconciliation.

Historically, the original special day in this whole cycle was Epiphany. This day of "theophany" or of manifestation of God's light and power in Christ was, along with Easter and Pentecost, the third chief event in the Christian calendar of the early church. It speaks to the archetypal human experience of longing for the light in the midst of the shortest and darkest days of the year. In the earliest lectionaries and sermons for this day, Epiphany focused on John 1:1–2:11. The themes from its beginning included Christ as light, his advent into the world, his baptism in the Jordan, and the first miracle of turning water into wine. Common to all these is the theological claim that God was in Jesus Christ, being manifest to human beings even to the ends of the earth.

In western Europe, Christmas came to concentrate more exclusively on the birth narratives than did Epiphany and became much more prominent. We have inherited a tendency to regard Christmas as emphasizing the incarnation in a narrower sense than is appropriate to the full richness of Word made flesh and manifest in Jesus Christ.

In this book we emphasize the recovered balance of these themes, for Epiphany is the more ancient of the two festivals and includes a much richer set of theological meanings: the whole purpose and power of the incarnation shown in the beginning of Jesus' ministry.

Advent is a season of great tension. It is primarily concerned with eschatology and not, as our contemporary American commercial sense would have it, with preparing for Christmas cheer. Rather, Advent expresses hope and expectation for both the first *and* second comings of Christ. There is paradox here. The First Sunday of Advent is called the beginning of the Christian Year. Yet it plunges us immediately into the tension between the "already" of Christ having come in the flesh and the "not yet" of the consummation of all things in Christ at the end of time. Advent challenges us to rethink and confront in Word and sacramental sign-acts the revelation of Christ's time in the midst of our times. Thus, we *begin* the year reflecting and praying together about the end of all history.

Advent is both a time of thanks for the gift of Christ to us in past time and a time of anticipation of his second coming. It contains both threat and promise, and this characteristic is carried out in the lessons and in the hymnody of the season. This is why you will find a particular emphasis upon the Advent hymns throughout the season in distinction from Christmas carols and hymns. Generally speaking, most congregations have not received much exposure to and good teaching in the range of texts such as "Lo, He Comes with Clouds Descending" or "There's a Voice in the Wilderness Crying." A study of the classical collects for each Sunday from *The Book of Common Prayer* will show the theology of Advent in vivid images.

In planning services of worship during the Sundays of Advent, then, we must acknowledge that the Advent readings express not merely expectation of Christ's nativity, which has already happened, but the coming of Christ to rule, to judge, and to save. The hope in which the church participates and the expectation we share are of the kingdom come. In this sense the eschatological cry of our Lord's Prayer is surely in tune with Advent: "Thy kingdom come, thy will be done, on earth. . . ." Preaching is an exciting challenge in the light of the lessons. The prophetic element is particularly strong throughout these Sundays: We hope for the destruction of the powers of evil, for the righteousness and justice of God, for the dawning of God's shalom over all the nations and the undoing of the machines of war. For Christians, this hope has been intensified by the first coming of Christ. Thus, our preaching, praying, singing, and celebrating the gospel in these weeks should not be deprived of such rich and powerful eschatology. Only by experiencing these tensions and the expectations of the whole groaning world in travail can our participation in the dying and rising of Christ be made real. As Louis Bouyer remarked in *Liturgical Piety*, "The purpose of Advent, Christmas and Epiphany is ceaselessly to reanimate in us that hope, that expectation."*

This sheds new light on our celebrations of Christmas and the days immediately following it. Christmas is far richer and deeper than a sentimental remembrance of the birth and childhood of Jesus. We should never deny nor suppress the intimacy and tenderness of the beginning point of incarnation, but Christmas itself means much more. "Joy to the world, the Lord is come!" means precisely that the One who comes is indeed our Redeemer—the very One into whose dying and rising we are baptized, just as he is baptized in the Jordan into our human lot. If we understand Christmas this way, our worship services will be capable of addressing the deepest places of human need and touch down in our most profound experiences. This is why we must bring together resources for significant family worship while at the same time explore in new ways the historic repertoire of song, as with the service of lessons and carols.

It is significant that the period between Christmas and Epiphany became, for certain segments of the early church, a baptismal period second in importance only to the Easter Vigil and the Great Fifty Days. The Season of Christmas contains no mere secular sentiment; rather, it takes us through the witness of several martyrs and saints: December 26, Saint Stephen, Deacon and Martyr; December 27, Saint John, Apostle and Evangelist; December 28, The Holy Innocents, Martyrs; and January 1, the Holy Name of Jesus and/or the Solemnity of Mary. Although many Protestants have not observed these feasts, they serve to remind us of the powerful connection Christmas and Epiphany have with the baptismal reality of dying and rising with Christ.

The resources in this book place particular emphasis on the possibilities of baptism and/or baptismal renewal in this season. John Wesley's covenant service, which has a venerable history of use on New Year's Eve as a "watch night service," is also suitable as a full congregational act on the Sunday called "Baptism of the Lord"—the first Sunday following Epiphany. Local pastors and congregations will certainly wish to explore the possibilities of baptismal celebrations as part of the regular services between Christmas and Epiphany, with the explicit inclusion of the renewal of baptismal vows by the whole congregation.

We can approach the Christmas-Epiphany Season with a sense of excitement once we understand how the whole season initiates us into the manifestation of God in Jesus Christ. The Sundays following Epiphany take us from Christ's own baptism through the recalling of the signs and teachings and wonders he performed in his earthly ministry. It is as though Epiphany and the whole season thereafter resound with the theme in John's Gospel: "The light shines in the darkness, and the darkness has not overcome it" (1:5). We behold his glory in what he said and did—for these very things we believe Christ says and does in our own time and place. The Last Sunday After Epiphany and before the beginning of Lent is Transfiguration, a time filled with his glory in anticipation of the resurrected glory yet to come.

B. Preparing the People and the Place

The Advent-Christmas-Epiphany cycle of the Christian Year is an extraordinarily rich period. It presents Christians with a marvelous array of family and church customs, and it calls us to a deeper

---

*Bouyer, Louis, *Liturgical Piety* (University of Notre Dame Press, 1955), p. 204.

spiritual life together in Christ. At the same time, this season challenges us to create an environment of prayer and song, of Scripture, fellowship, and sacramental actions that counters the crass commercial use of Christmas carols from Thanksgiving on to sell anything and everything. Planning for Advent and Christmas-Epiphany requires a conviction about the theological realities we are called to rediscover and to celebrate. Observing these days together means making decisions about what specific events, activities, and particular worship occasions should express and about how the church as a whole community should prepare itself to enter into the rhythms and themes of Advent and Christmas-Epiphany.

One of the most widespread and popular customs in both churches and homes during this season is the Advent wreath. For many congregations this may be one of the most visible signs, along with the change to purple or deep blue paraments, of the first Sundays of the year. The Advent wreath, which was traditionally suspended from the ceiling or an arch so as to suggest the shape of a tree, consists of four candles and a larger Christ candle in the center. In some traditions three of the candles are purple or dark blue and the fourth is a rose, symbolizing the Third Sunday of Advent (Gaudete—"rejoice"). The actual color is not crucial, though we recommend that all four be purple or dark blue and be the same size.

A candle is lighted the First Sunday of Advent, usually during the very first part of the service by a family or a specially appointed layperson. Then, one more is lighted on each of the following Sundays until all four are lighted. Finally, on Christmas Eve or the first service of Christmas Day, the middle white candle is lighted.

There are several possibilities for the ceremony of lighting the candles. After having moved to the place of the wreath in the sanctuary, one member of the designated family lights the candle(s) while another member recites or reads an appropriate text immediately following the opening hymn and collect.

First Sunday:	*We light this candle as a symbol of expectation. May the light sent from God shine in the darkness to show us the way to salvation. O come, O come, Emmanuel!*
Second Sunday:	*We light this candle as a symbol of proclamation. May the Word sent from God through the prophets lead us to the way of salvation. O Come, O come, Emmanuel!*
Third Sunday:	*We light this candle as a symbol of joy. May the joyful promise of your presence, O God, make us rejoice in our hope of salvation. O Come, O come, Emmanuel!*
Fourth Sunday:	*We light this candle as a symbol of purity. May the visitation of your Holy Spirit, O God, purify us that we may be ready for the coming of Jesus, our hope and joy. O come, O come, Emmanuel!*

Then on Christmas Eve or Christmas morning, the acolytes or other ministers of the light will light all the candles, including the Christ candle, at the opening hymn or procession.

Another possibility is to use the pattern of the O Antiphons, reading a different one each Sunday, with the congregation and choir singing a refrain as their response to the lighting of the candle(s). Those who are to do the ceremony move to the place of the Advent wreath immediately following the opening prayer or collect. The text is recited while the candle is being lighted.

First Sunday:	O come, O come, Emmanuel, And ransom captive Israel, That mourns in lonely exile here Until the Son of God appear.

Refrain (sung by congregation)

Rejoice! Rejoice! Emmanuel
Shall come to thee, O Israel!

Second Sunday:	O come, thou Wisdom from on high, And order all things, far and nigh; To us the path of knowledge show, And cause us in her ways to go.

Refrain

Third Sunday:	O come, thou Dayspring, come and cheer Our spirits by thine advent here; Disperse the gloomy clouds of night, And death's dark shadows put to flight.

Refrain

Fourth Sunday:	O come, Desire of nations, bind All peoples in one heart and mind; Bid envy, strife, and quarrels cease; Fill the whole world with heaven's peace.

Refrain

In a similar way, each home may wish to have a brief reading or hymn stanza to accompany the lighting of the various candles of the Advent wreath. The wreath may be placed on a prominent table or in a central place in the house. It would be especially appropriate to use this on Sundays or for evening meals during the week when the whole household is assembled. Then during the Christmas Season the Christ candle could be lighted at each meal with a hymn and opening table grace.

Nearly every local church and home will have a Christmas tree of some sort. The Christmas tree customs have roots in the mystery plays performed in the churches as early as the eleventh century. From the so-called Paradise Play, we find the custom of the paradise tree. This tree represented the Garden of Eden but also the tree of life and, by association, the tree upon which Christ was crucified for our redemption. This is why the paradise tree contains various items: apples, oranges, small interestingly baked breads, pastry, and candy.

The custom of the Chrismon Tree is becoming widely known. This involves the use of various symbols from the genealogy of Christ and of his life, death, and resurrection. The tree is decorated during early Advent and stands as a tree of remembrance of the whole story and significance of Christ whose birth we celebrate at Christmas. Specific instructions about the creation of the symbols from various materials may be found in the *Chrismons* series of books published by The Lutheran Church of the Ascension, 314 West Main Street, Danville, Virginia 24541.

Another variation for church and for home is sometimes referred to as the Jesse Tree, which is basically a family tree of Jesus. The phrase of the prophet Isaiah, "There shall come forth a shoot from the stump of Jesse," gives us the image of this tree. As with the Chrismon, various symbols are placed on the tree that remind us of Christ's coming into human history. Some figures are types of Christ from the Old Testament—Key of David, the Scepter of Israel—while others represent various prophets and other figures in Jewish scriptures: Noah's ark, the tablets of the law given to Moses, Abraham's knife, Jacob's ladder, the shell and sandals of John the Baptist, and so on.

The planning committee should choose one of these Advent tree customs as a main focus. The actual decoration of such trees may take place informally on a Saturday or weekday evening. A brief service of prayer and song may precede or, better, follow the decorating, along with festive refreshments. Or this event may follow a Wednesday night fellowship dinner with all those attending being given a part in the tree ceremony. Careful planning is necessary if there are large numbers of people. One idea for the prayer service is to use appropriate Scripture texts from which the various symbols are drawn. Suitable Advent hymns and carols may be sung.

The following poem, adapted from *Prayers, Poems and Songs* by Huub Oosterhuis, may be used as the whole group gathers about the tree:

> At last night is ending,
> the day is drawing near.
>
> The people living in the night
> will see the long-awaited light.
> Rising in the darkness from afar,
> it shines on them, the morning star.
>
> The Son of man will come once more,
> not as a child, obscure and poor;
> only the Father knows the day,
> all we must do is watch and pray.
>
> Though sun and moon may cease to shine,
> we who believe will know his sign:
>
> This is when we will understand
> his second coming is at hand.
>
> In the winter when the tree seems dead,
> we have to hope and look ahead
> to the green branch that will appear
> when summer and new life are near.
>
> Exposed to every wind and storm,
> deprived of beauty and of form,
> but we who live in faith know well
> that branch is called Emmanuel.
>
> God with us is a living name,
> God will not put our faith to shame,
> if we are open to receive
> the Son in whom we all believe.
>
> At last night is ending,
> the day is drawing near.

The decorating of the tree and the placing of the Advent wreath may also be incorporated into a regular Sunday service simply by having the tree with the symbols higher on the tree already in place. Then, following the first reading or a hymn, a procession may be formed moving to a place where the symbols may be placed on the lower parts of the tree. In some local churches, it is possible to arrange the decorating prior to the morning service.

A related custom in many churches is the hanging of the greens. Again, this may be best done following a weeknight supper. Depending upon the number of persons involved, the size of the room, and the extent of the greenery, this may be concluded with a short service of hymns or carols, scripture readings, and prayer.

In an excellent resource we commend, *Keeping Advent* (revised edition, published by the Liturgical Conference, 806 Rhode Island Avenue, NE, Washington, D.C. 20018), the following paragraphs from page 30 remind us of a special Advent gift a local church may give to others:

> Setting up a Jesse tree, Advent wreath, or paradise tree can become a part of a liturgy celebrated in a nursing home for retired citizens. Invite parishioners to come and worship at the local nursing home during Advent. It is a good time to bring the parish church to those unable to attend the worship center for services.
> During Advent, people everywhere will find themselves with much to do in the short space of time. Shopping, baking, decorating, praying, cleaning, all fill the weeks very easily. Christians need not reject these pre-Christmas activities, but should try to keep good perspective. Parishioners can be encouraged to bring gifts for the needy and place them around the tree of Jesse or paradise tree. These gifts can be distributed by volunteers.

Further care and planning for the Advent and Christmas environment should include the possibilities of banners, textile art, and the service bulletins (the covers, the graphics, and possible calligraphy of the text). The biblical titles for Jesus in the Advent antiphons or those symbols used on the Chrismon or Jesse Tree present a wide range of design. Simplicity and focus are desirable; clutter and "busyness" are not, especially during Advent. For example, simple and somber-hued bolts of cloth hung in bold verticals may be far more effective than wordy or cluttered banners. Use imagination and restraint. Purple, blue, or gray and heavy textures are appropriate to Advent. Then the transition to Christmas Eve or Christmas Day—suddenly white, gold, yellow, with fine textures of cloth—changes the environment dramatically. Visual symbols for this season include angels, star bursts, shepherds and the manger, the holy family, and—above all—light and splendor. The Chrismon or Jesse Tree provides continuity of symbolism against this changed visual background.

For Epiphany the environment should reflect visually the great images: the Magi, their gifts of gold, frankincense, and myrrh, and their three crowns. We may also use the imagery of the baptism in the Jordan and the miracle at the wedding in Cana—colorful earthen jugs representing water-turned-wine.

C. The Sundays of Advent

The four Sundays of Advent invite special attention to the visual environment of the sanctuary. Most appropriate are purple, blue, gray, or somber hues, with rough or coarse textures in the paraments, stoles, and banners. The custom of the Advent wreath with four candles heightens the sense of anticipation and may suggest specific visual connections with the textiles used. The messianic titles of Jesus in the O Antiphons also suggest visual possibilities for banners, worship bulletins, and the entrance spaces to the sanctuary. Other visual symbols are suggested by the scripture lessons: a plumb line (Amos), trumpets of announcement, scales of justice, the Root or Tree of Jesse, and eschatological words *Maranatha*, and *Come, Lord Jesus*.

GATHERING

GREETING

> Show us your mercy, O Lord,
> **And grant us your salvation.**
> Truth shall spring up from the earth,
> **And righteousness shall look down from heaven.**
> > *or*
> I will hear what the Lord God has to say.
> **A Voice that speaks for peace.**

Peace for all people and for God's friends,
And to those who turn to God in their hearts.
Blessings on the one who comes in the name of the Lord.
Glory to God in the highest.
And peace to God's people on earth.

HYMN

"Come, Thou Long-Expected Jesus," "All Earth Is Waiting," "People, Look East," "On Jordan's Bank the Baptist's Cry," "O Come, O Come, Emmanuel," "Hail to the Lord's Anointed," and "Lift Up Your Heads" are especially suitable.

If the hymn is to be an entrance song with procession, it precedes the greeting.

OPENING PRAYER

The Lord be with you.
And also with you.
Let us pray. *A brief pause.*

God of Israel,
with expectant hearts
we your people await Christ's coming.
As once he came in humility,
so now may he come in glory,
that he may make all things perfect
in your everlasting kingdom.
For he is Lord for ever and ever. **Amen.**

LIGHTING OF THE ADVENT WREATH

Those appointed may process to the place of the wreath in the front of the sanctuary. While the candle is lighted, appropriate texts may be read, recited, or sung. In some instances, the Advent wreath ceremony may be combined with the opening hymn, as when "O Come, O Come, Emmanuel" is used.

FIRST LESSON

First Sunday	Isaiah 2:1-5	(Year A: 1995, 1998, 2001)
	Isaiah 64:1-9	(Year B: 1993, 1996, 1999)
	Jeremiah 33:14-16	(Year C: 1994, 1997, 2000)
Second Sunday	Isaiah 11:1-10	(Year A: 1995, 1998, 2001)
	Isaiah 40:1-11	(Year B: 1993, 1996, 1999)
	Baruch 5:1-9 *or*	(Year C: 1994, 1997, 2000)
	Malachi 3:1-4	
Third Sunday	Isaiah 35:1-10	(Year A: 1995, 1998, 2001)
	Isaiah 61:1-4, 8-11	(Year B: 1993, 1996, 1999)
	Zephaniah 3:14-20	(Year C: 1994, 1997, 2000)
Fourth Sunday	Isaiah 7:10-16	(Year A: 1995, 1998, 2001)
	II Samuel 7:1-11, 16	(Year B: 1993, 1996, 1999)
	Micah 5:2-5*a*	(Year C: 1994, 1997, 2000)

PSALM

First Sunday	Psalm 122	(Year A: 1995, 1998, 2001)
	Psalm 80:1-7	(Year B: 1993, 1996, 1999)
	Psalm 25:1-10	(Year C: 1994, 1997, 2000)
Second Sunday	Psalm 72:1-7, 18-19	(Year A: 1995, 1998, 2001)
	Psalm 85:1-2, 8-13	(Year B: 1993, 1996, 1999)
	Luke 1:68-79	(Year C: 1994, 1997, 2000)
Third Sunday	Psalm 146:5-10 *or* Luke 1:47-55	(Year A: 1995, 1998, 2001)
	Psalm 126 *or* Luke 1:47-55	(Year B: 1993, 1996, 1999)
	Isaiah 12:2-6	(Year C: 1994, 1997, 2000)
Fourth Sunday	Psalm 80:1-7, 17-19	(Year A: 1995, 1998, 2001)
	Luke 1:47-55 *or* Psalm 89:1-4, 19-26	(Year B: 1993, 1996, 1999)
	Luke 1:47-55 *or* Psalm 80:1-7	(Year C: 1994, 1997, 2000)

SECOND LESSON

First Sunday	Romans 13:11-14	(Year A: 1995, 1998, 2001)
	I Corinthians 1:3-9	(Year B: 1993, 1996, 1999)
	I Thessalonians 3:9-13	(Year C: 1994, 1997, 2000)
Second Sunday	Romans 15:4-13	(Year A: 1995, 1998, 2001)
	II Peter 3:8-15*a*	(Year B: 1993, 1996, 1999)
	Philippians 1:3-11	(Year C: 1994, 1997, 2000)
Third Sunday	James 5:7-10	(Year A: 1995, 1998, 2001)
	I Thessalonians 5:16-24	(Year B: 1993, 1996, 1999)
	Philippians 4:4-7	(Year C: 1994, 1997, 2000)
Fourth Sunday	Romans 1:1-7	(Year A: 1995, 1998, 2001)
	Romans 16:25-27	(Year B: 1993, 1996, 1999)
	Hebrews 10:5-10	(Year C: 1994, 1997, 2000)

HYMN OR ANTHEM

GOSPEL

First Sunday	Matthew 24:36-44	(Year A: 1995, 1998, 2001)
	Mark 13:24-37	(Year B: 1993, 1996, 1999)
	Luke 21:25-36	(Year C: 1994, 1997, 2000)
Second Sunday	Matthew 3:1-12	(Year A: 1995, 1998, 2001)
	Mark 1:1-8	(Year B: 1993, 1996, 1999)
	Luke 3:1-6	(Year C: 1994, 1997, 2000)
Third Sunday	Matthew 11:2-11	(Year A: 1995, 1998, 2001)
	John 1:6-8, 19-28	(Year B: 1993, 1996, 1999)
	Luke 3:7-18	(Year C: 1994, 1997, 2000)
Fourth Sunday	Matthew 1:18-25	(Year A: 1995, 1998, 2001)
	Luke 1:26-38	(Year B: 1993, 1996, 1999)
	Luke 1:39-55 (46-55)	(Year C: 1994, 1997, 2000)

SERMON

CREED

PRAYERS OF THE PEOPLE OR PASTORAL PRAYER

To each petition responding: **Savior of the nations, hear our prayer.**

THE PEACE

OFFERING

GREAT THANKSGIVING

The Lord be with you.

And also with you.

Lift up your hearts.

We lift them to the Lord.

Let us give thanks to the Lord our God.

It is right to give our thanks and praise.

It is right, and a good and joyful thing,
always and everywhere to give thanks to you,
Father Almighty, Creator of heaven and earth.

You formed us in your image
and breathed into us the breath of life.
When we turned away, and our love failed,
your love remained steadfast.
You delivered us from captivity,
made covenant to be our sovereign God,
and spoke to us through your prophets,
who looked for that day
when justice shall roll down like waters
and righteousness like an ever-flowing stream,
when nation shall not lift up sword against nation,
neither shall they learn war any more.

And so, with your people on earth
and all the company of heaven,
we praise your name and join their unending hymn:

**Holy, holy, holy Lord, God of power and might,
heaven and earth are full of your glory.
Hosanna in the highest.
Blessed is he who comes in the name of the Lord.
Hosanna in the highest.**

Holy are you, and blessed is your Son Jesus Christ,
whom you sent in the fullness of time
to be a light to the nations.
You scatter the proud in the imagination of their hearts
and have mercy on those who fear you

from generation to generation.
You put down the mighty from their thrones
and exalt those of low degree.
You fill the hungry with good things,
and the rich you send empty away.

Your own Son came among us as a servant,
to be Emmanuel, your presence with us.
He humbled himself in obedience to your will
and freely accepted death on a cross.
By the baptism of his suffering, death, and resurrection
you gave birth to your church,
delivered us from slavery to sin and death,
and made with us a new covenant by water and the Spirit.

On the night in which he gave himself up for us
he took bread, gave thanks to you, broke the bread,
gave it to his disciples, and said:
"Take, eat; this is my body which is given for you.
Do this in remembrance of me."

When the supper was over he took the cup,
gave thanks to you, gave it to his disciples, and said:
"Drink from this, all of you;
this is my blood of the new covenant,
poured out for you and for many for the forgiveness of sins.
Do this, as often as you drink it, in remembrance of me."

And so,
in remembrance of these your mighty acts in Jesus Christ,
we offer ourselves in praise and thanksgiving
as a holy and living sacrifice,
in union with Christ's offering for us,
as we proclaim the mystery of faith.

Christ has died, Christ is risen, Christ will come again.

Pour out your Holy Spirit on us, gathered here,
and on these gifts of bread and wine.
Make them be for us the body and blood of Christ,
that we may be for the world the body of Christ,
redeemed by his blood.
By your Spirit make us one with Christ,
one with each other,
and one in ministry to all the world,
until Christ comes in final victory
and we feast at his heavenly banquet.
Through your Son Jesus Christ,
with the Holy Spirit in your holy church
all honor and glory is yours, Almighty Father,
now and for ever.

Amen.

THE LORD'S PRAYER

BREAKING THE BREAD

COMMUNION

PRAYER AFTER COMMUNION

HYMN

DISMISSAL WITH BLESSING

Appendix: The O Antiphons

For at least nine centuries and perhaps much longer, the church has sung a solemn antiphon on each of the last seven days in preparation for Christmas. At the hour of vespers, this grave, pleading, yet confident song rises to the One so long expected. Embodying the very heart of the meaning of Advent worship, each of the prayers addresses the Lord by one of the great scriptural titles: "O Wisdom," "Adonai," "Root of Jesse," "Emmanuel." Each ends with a plea for Christ's coming now in grace and finally in glory: "Come, teach us," "Come, redeem us."

Three possible uses of these antiphons are (1) as the central congregational act in a special late afternoon or evening vespers, in the context of a simple order of Advent hymns or carols, lessons, and prayers; (2) at the beginning of any of the Sundays of Advent in relation to the lighting of the Advent wreath, with appropriate modifications; or (3) as a response to the sermon, or in place of a hymn or anthem between the second lesson and the Gospel.

Two translations follow, in contemporary and in traditional English.

O Wisdom proceeding from the mouth of the highest,
reaching from eternity to eternity
and disposing all things with strength and sweetness:
   Come, teach us the way of knowledge.
O Lord and Leader of Israel,
you appeared to Moses in the burning bush
and delivered the law to him on Sinai:
   Come, redeem us by your outstretched arm.
O Root of Jesse,
you stand as a sign of the people;
before you rulers do not open their mouths;
to you all nations shall pray:
   Come and deliver us, do not delay.
O Key of David and Scepter of Israel,
you open and no one shuts;
you shut and no one opens:
   Come and release from prison those who sit in
   darkness and in the shadow of death.
O Dayspring, Splendor of Eternal Light and Sun of Righteousness:
   Come and enlighten those who sit in darkness
   and in the shadow of death.
O King of nations,
their desire and the cornerstone that binds them in one:

Come and save those whom you formed of clay.
O Emmanuel, our King and Lawgiver,
the Expectation and Savior of the nations:
Come and save us, O Lord our God.

or

O Wisdom, who came forth from the mouth of the Most High,
reaching from end to end and ordering all things
mightily and sweetly:
Come, and teach us the way of prudence.
O Adonai and Leader of the house of Israel,
who appeared to Moses in the flames of the burning bush
and gave him the law on Sinai:
Come, and with your outstretched arm redeem us.
O Root of Jesse, who stands for an ensign of the people,
before whom kings shall keep silence
and to whom the Gentiles shall make their supplication:
Come, deliver us and tarry not.
O Key of David and Scepter of the house of Israel,
who opens and no one shuts, who shuts and no one opens:
**Come and bring forth from prison the captives who
sit in darkness and in the shadow of death.**
O Dayspring, Brightness of the Light eternal and Sun of Justice:
**Come, and enlighten them that sit in darkness
and in the shadow of death.**
O King of the Gentiles and their Desired One,
Cornerstone that makes both one:
**Come, and deliver us whom you formed
out of the dust of the earth.**
O Emmanuel, our Ruler and Lawgiver,
the Expected of the nations and their Savior:
Come to save us, O Lord our God.

D. A Service of Lessons and Carols

One of the most beloved traditions of Advent and Christmas from England is a form of worship known as the "festival of lessons and carols." There are two principal versions, the Advent carol service and the service of nine lessons and carols (Christmas Eve). The pattern in both is the same: God's Word is proclaimed and contemplated in a special sequence of readings, prayers, and both choral and congregational song. The service of nine lessons and carols was first conceived by Archbishop Benson for use in the Truro Cathedral in the late nineteenth century. It was simplified and adapted for use in King's College Chapel, Cambridge, in 1918, by Dean Eric Milner-White. Advent carol services were essentially adaptations of this basic pattern, originating in schools and colleges where it was not possible to celebrate Christmas during term-time.

Many different versions of these services may be found in local churches and universities throughout the United States and the world. The following orders are adapted from the King's College Chapel version. Suitable variations are suggested under Alternative Patterns. The beauty of this form of worship is in its flexibility and its musical dialogue based upon the Christmas (or Advent) lessons. The pattern is quite simple, but the elaborations may be as eloquent as musical resources available to a local community will permit. Yet it may be done with a very small choir, or even without a choir when the carols and hymns chosen are familiar.

In many local churches the tradition of lessons and carols during late Advent or on Christmas Eve as the family-oriented service, or as an ecumenical community event involving several chuches, is well established. Congregations and choirs find that, over several years, a marvelous range of choral and congregational music may be experienced and treasured. The following suggestions serve only to illustrate some of the many possibilities and to invite further imaginative planning by choirs, pastors, and worship committees.

The carols and anthems given in the first order are suitable for Christmas Eve. If you plan such a service for mid-December, however, specific attention should be paid to using Advent lessons and carols along with appropriate choral literature. Similarly, some churches may wish to hold the service twice: first on Christmas Eve and then again on Epiphany evening as a type of concluding vespers to the whole Christmas-Epiphany cycle. The use of specific Epiphany hymns and choral music should be used in the latter case.

Careful planning and cooperation between musicians and the pastor and/or other liturgical ministers are crucial for the integrity and depth of celebration these services may bring. A marvelous collection of choral music, carols, and anthems, espcially suited for lessons and carols, is found in *Carols for Choirs, 1, 2, and 3* (Oxford University Press, 1961, 1970, and 1978). The texts for the original nine lessons and carols are printed as an appendix to volume 1, and an order for the Advent carol service may be found in the appendix to volume 2. The *Oxford Book of Carols*, also published by Oxford University Press, is another indispensable resource.

ORGAN PRELUDE or PRESERVICE INSTRUMENTAL MUSIC

PROCESSIONAL HYMN "Once in Royal David's City"

THE BIDDING PRAYER

> Beloved in Christ, we come by this service to prepare ourselves to hear again the message of the angels, and to go in heart and mind to Bethlehem, and to see the loving-kindness of our God, and the Babe lying in a manger:

> Let us therefore open the Holy Scriptures and read the earliest tale of that disobedience to God's holy will, which is common to us all; and then the story of the birth of Jesus Christ our Lord, to save us from our sins and make us pure and happy; and let us thank him with our carols of praise:

> But first let us pray for the needs of this whole world; and especially for peace and goodwill among all people; that they may learn to love one another, as children of one God and Father of all:

> And because this would most rejoice his heart, let us remember before him the poor and helpless, the cold, the hungry, and the oppressed; the sick and them that mourn, the lonely and the unloved; the aged and the little children; and all who know not the Lord Jesus, or who love him not, or who by sins have grieved his heart:

> Lastly let us remember before God all those who rejoice with us, but upon another shore and in a greater light, that multitude no one can number, with whom, in this Lord Jesus, we evermore are one:

> These prayers and praises let us humbly offer up to the throne of heaven, in the words that Christ himself has taught us:

THE LORD'S PRAYER

BLESSING

The almighty God bless us with divine grace: Christ give us the joys of everlasting life: and unto the fellowship of the citizens above may the King of Angels bring us all. **Amen.**

| HYMN | "Of the Father's Love Begotten" | |

| FIRST LESSON | | Genesis 3:8-15 |

God announces in the Garden of Eden that the seed of woman shall bruise the serpent's head.

CAROL	"Adam Lay Ybunden"	Text: XV century, anon.
		Music: Boris Ord
		or
		Benjamin Britten

| SECOND LESSON | | Genesis 22:1-8 |

God promises to faithful Abraham that his seed shall the nations of the earth call blessed.

| HYMN | "O Come, O Come, Emmanuel" | Veni Emmanuel |

| THIRD LESSON | | Isaiah 9:2, 6-7 |

Christ's birth and kingdom are foretold by Isaiah.

| CAROL | "Lo, How a Rose E'er Blooming" | Michael Praetorius |

| FOURTH LESSON | | Isaiah 11:1-9 |

The peace that Christ will bring us is foreshown.

or   Micah 5:2-4

The prophet Micah foretells the glory of little Bethlehem.

| CAROL | "O Little Town of Bethlehem" | |

| FIFTH LESSON | | Luke 1:26-35, 38 |

The angel Gabriel salutes the blessed Virgin Mary.

| CAROL | "There Is No Rose" | Text: XV English |
| | | Music: Benjamin Britten |

| SIXTH LESSON | | Matthew 1:18-21 |

Saint Matthew tells of the birth of Jesus.

| CAROL | "The First Noel" | |

| SEVENTH LESSON | | Luke 2:8-20 |

The shepherds go to the manger.

| CAROL | "Infant Holy, Infant Lowly" | Traditional Polish |
| | *and/or* | |

CAROL	"Lullay, My Liking"	Text: XV century English
		Music: Gustav Holst
		(1874–1934)

| EIGHTH LESSON | | Matthew 2:1-11 |

The wise men are led by the star to Jesus.

CAROL	"In the Bleak Midwinter"	
	and/or	
CAROL	"On This Day Earth Shall Ring"	Personent Hodie

| NINTH LESSON | | John 1:1-14 |

Saint John unfolds the great mystery of the incarnation.

| CAROL | "Silent Night, Holy Night" | |

THE COLLECT *(or suitable free prayer, or other prayers for the season)*
The Lord be with you.
And with your spirit.
Let us pray:

Lord Jesus, Child of Bethlehem, who in love made humankind, create in us love so pure and perfect that whosoever our heart loves may be after thy will, in thy name, and for thy sake. **Amen.**

THE CHRISTMAS BLESSING *(if appropriate)*

HYMN   "O Come, All Ye Faithful"

DISMISSAL *(if a silent recessional is not preferred).*

May the One who by his incarnation gathered into one things earthly and heavenly, fill you with the sweetness of inward peace and goodwill; and the blessing of God, the love of Christ, and the fellowship of the Holy Spirit remain with you always.

Go forth in peace and joy.

Thanks be to God! Alleluia!

CLOSING VOLUNTARY *(optional)*

Alternative 1A

As a Christmas Eve candlelight service (when Holy Communion is not celebrated)

PRELUDE

OPENING SENTENCE   Luke 2:10-11

> Behold, I bring you good news of a great joy which will come to all the people; for to you is born this day in the city of David, a Savior, who is Christ the Lord.

PROCESSIONAL HYMN

HYMN   "Hail to the Lord's Anointed"
                                  (stanzas 1-3)

THE WORD OF PROMISE   Luke 2:1-7

COLLECT

> Stir up our hearts, O Lord, to make ready the way of your only Son, so that by his coming we may be enabled to serve you with pure minds; through your Son, Jesus Christ our Lord, who lives and reigns with you and the Holy Spirit, one God, world without end. **Amen.**
>
>   *(Service Book and Hymnal, 75, adapted)*

CAROL(S): Choral Settings

HYMN   "The People That in Darkness Sat"

[THE SERMON]

CAROL: Choir and Congregation

THE WORD OF ANNOUNCEMENT   Luke 2:8-13

COLLECT

CHORAL OFFERING

THE WORD OF ADORATION   Luke 2:15-20 and/or
                                                Matthew 2:1-11

COLLECT OR CONCLUDING PRAYERS

CAROL(S): Choral Settings

CONCLUDING HYMN   "Hark! the Herald Angels Sing"

BLESSING AND DISMISSAL

CHORAL RESPONSE and/or CLOSING VOLUNTARY

Alternative 1B

OPENING PRAYER (or BIDDING PRAYER)

[CHORAL INVITATORY]

LESSONS AND CAROLS INTERSPERSED

The number of lessons read may vary, concluding with John 1:1-14.

[THE APOSTLES' CREED] and/or

THE COLLECT

THE LIGHTING OF THE CANDLES

The ministers will first light their candles from the Christ candle in the Advent wreath, then in turn pass the light to acolytes and ushers, and to the congregation, each saying:

The peace of Christ be with you.
and each in response:
and also with you.

HYMN   "Silent Night, Holy Night"

BLESSING AND DISMISSAL

Let us bless the Lord.
Thanks be to God!

[SILENT RECESSION]

Alternative 2

As a Sunday afternoon or evening service, late Advent through Epiphany
Instrumental and/or choral music should be featured. In Advent, the O Antiphons may be used. In between Christmas and Epiphany, the music should not be Advent, but Christmas and Epiphany hymns, carols, and appropriate anthems.

Alternative 3

As a Sunday morning service in Advent
This may be especially suitable for the third Sunday, which is sometimes called "rejoicing (Gaudete) Sunday." The pattern may be similar to the full order or Alternative 1A. After the processional or opening hymn, the O Antiphons (see pp. 55 and 62-63) may be used. The

responses may be a set, simple repeated musical phrase. A brief sermon would follow any of the readings toward the last third of the service. Provision should be made for the offering of gifts, perhaps immediately following the sermon.

A final note: When congregational singing is emphasized rather than the choral presentations of the choir, the hymns and carols can be varied in simple yet effective ways. For example, in a five-stanza processional hymn, the first would be sung by the congregation, the second by the choir, the third by women (or solo voices), the fourth by men or the choir, and the fifth by everyone. If the congregation sings well, one stanza should be *a cappella* in four parts.

Suggested Lessons for Advent Carol Service

FIRST LESSON   Isaiah 40:1-8

   The prophet proclaims good news to a people in exile.

SECOND LESSON   Jeremiah 23:5-6

   The Lord promises to send his people a righteous King.

THIRD LESSON   Zechariah 9:9-10

   The Lord promises that the king will come to Israel in peace.

FOURTH LESSON   Haggai 2:6-9

   The Lord promises Israel more splendor than ever before.

FIFTH LESSON   Isaiah 35:1-6

   The prophet foretells the advent of the Desire of all nations.

SIXTH LESSON   Luke 1:26-35, 38

   The angel Gabriel salutes the blessed Virgin Mary.

SIXTH LESSON (*alternative*)   Romans 8:28-29

   Saint Paul declares the good purpose of God.

SEVENTH LESSON   Mark 1:1-15

Jesus proclaims the coming of the kingdom of God.

E. Christmas Eve, Christmas Day, and the Sundays After Christmas

Christmas Eve services have enjoyed great popularity. The candlelight service and the Christmas Eve Holy Communion have special appeal to Christians because of the environment of the night solemnity, the lights shining in the darkness, and the glorious range of music associated with the biblical themes. Christmas Eve focuses on the profound intimacy of tender humanity and the mystery of the nativity. Many churches celebrate the sacrament of the Lord's Supper on this evening.

In recent years, increasing numbers of churches have developed, or wish to develop, an early evening or late afternoon pattern of worship oriented especially toward families who, because of younger children, find it difficult to attend the midnight service. We have already given one example of a family-oriented liturgy designed as lessons and carols. Many variations may be developed from the simple pattern. The use of the children's choirs or of instrumental and congregational music with children's participation is particularly encouraged.

The two services for Christmas Eve that follow are designed to be flexible to allow borrowing of elements from one to the other. Some churches may not hold services on Christmas Day when it does not fall on Sunday. In this event, the scripture lessons and psalms for the First Sunday After Christmas are in continuity with those used on Christmas Eve.

The visual environment of the sanctuary or worship space and related spaces changes dramatically from the Fourth Sunday of Advent to the Christmas Season. Now white, yellow, gold, and the finest and most joyful combinations of these should be used, along with elegant textures for the paraments, stoles, banners, and other textiles.

The Christmas crèche should appear on Christmas Eve and be kept up to the Presentation in the Temple (February 2), or at least through the twelve days of Christmas. A wide range of visual symbols present themselves: manger, angels, shepherds, star of peace, as well as images in Christmas carols. These may be the design on bulletins and on special covers for the liturgical books (Bible used in procession, for example).

CHRISTMAS EVE FAMILY SERVICE

GATHERING AND GREETING

Choral or instrumental music may be offered, especially selections based upon any of the carols and hymns to be sung by the congregation during the service. Informal singing of Christmas carols may also be appropriate.

PROCESSIONAL CAROL

Especially appropriate are "Hark! the Herald Angels Sing," "It Came upon the Midnight Clear," "Joy to the World," and "O Come, All Ye Faithful."

OPENING PRAYER

The Lord be with you.
And also with you.
Let us pray: *A brief silence.*

God, Creator of all life,
you made us in your image
   and sent your Son to be our flesh.
Grant us now in this glad time of his birth,
   that we, who have been born again through his grace,
   may daily find all things made new in him.
For he lives and reigns with you and the Holy Spirit.
Amen.

[LIGHTING OF THE ADVENT AND CHRIST CANDLES]

This may occur at the conclusion of informal carol singing if there is to be no procession. While the persons who will light the candles move to the place of the wreath, or as each candle is lighted, the congregation and choir(s) may sing appropriate hymn stanzas or refrains.

RESPONSE TO LIGHTING OF THE CHRIST CANDLE

Jesus Christ is the Light of the world!
A light no darkness can extinguish.
      or
A hymn may be sung: "Break Forth, O Beauteous Heavenly Light"
                      "Light of the World" (stanza 1 or 3)
                            or
                      refrain from "Go, Tell It on the Mountain"

PRAYER FOR ILLUMINATION

Lord, open our minds and hearts
by the power of your Holy Spirit,
that we may hear and rejoice
in the gospel of our Savior's birth,
told in story and song this night.
Amen.

Alternative 1

STORY or READING

ANTHEM or CAROL
      Focusing response to the story of the scripture lesson.

STORY or READING

ANTHEM

STORY or READING

CAROL

[GOSPEL and SERMON] *(if not already incorporated into the pattern)*

OFFERING

Appropriate music by choir(s) may be offered, or a psalm by song leader and congregation responding with antiphon, especially Psalms 96, 97, or 98.

CHRISTMAS PRAYERS

Petitions may be given, the congregation responding:
In the name of Lord Jesus, hear us.

CONCLUDING COLLECT

> O God, you have caused this holy night to shine
> with the brightness of the true Light:
> Grant that we, who have known the mystery of that Light on earth,
> may also enjoy him perfectly in heaven;
> where with you and the Holy Spirit he lives and reigns,
> one God, in glory everlasting.
> **Amen.**   BCP

and/or

LORD'S PRAYER

CAROL   "Joy to the World"

DISMISSAL WITH BLESSING

> Go in peace, go in joy
>   to serve God and neighbor in all that you do.
> **We are sent in the name of the Christ child.**
> The peace of God which passes all understanding,
>   keep your hearts and minds in the knowledge and love of God
>   and of his Son Jesus Christ our Lord;
>   and the blessing of God Almighty, the Father, the Son,
>   and the Holy Spirit, be among you, and remain with you always.
> **Amen. Thanks be to God!**

Alternative 2

FIRST LESSON   Isaiah 9:2-7   (All years)

PSALM or ANTHEM   Psalm 96   (All years)

SECOND LESSON   Titus 2:11-14   (All years)

ALLELUIA (ANTHEM, HYMN, or CANTICLE)

GOSPEL   Luke 2:1-10   (All years)

SERMON
> *A short cantata may be offered as the proclamation.*

CHRISTMAS PRAYERS AND OFFERING

[LIGHTING OF THE ADVENT AND CHRIST CANDLES]

HYMN   "Joy to the World"
> *May be used as offertory song if the Lord's Supper is celebrated, in which case the gifts of bread and wine are presented along with the other gifts.*

GREAT THANKSGIVING

The Lord be with you.

And also with you.

Lift up your hearts.

We lift them to the Lord.

Let us give thanks to the Lord our God.

It is right to give our thanks and praise.

It is right, and a good and joyful thing,
always and everywhere to give thanks to you,
Father Almighty, Creator of heaven and earth.

You created light out of darkness
and brought forth life on the earth.
You formed us in your image
and breathed into us the breath of life.
When we turned away, and our love failed,
your love remained steadfast.
You delivered us from captivity,
made covenant to be our sovereign God,
and spoke to us through your prophets.
You loved the world so much
you gave your only Son Jesus Christ to be our Savior.

As the angels sang glory to you in the highest
and peace to your people on earth,
so with your people on earth
and all the company of heaven
we praise your name and join their unending hymn:

Holy, holy, holy Lord, God of power and might,
heaven and earth are full of your glory.
Hosanna in the highest.
Blessed is he who comes in the name of the Lord.
Hosanna in the highest.

Holy are you, and blessed is your Son Jesus Christ.
As Mary and Joseph went from Galilee to Bethlehem
and there found no room,
so Jesus went from Galilee to Jerusalem
and was despised and rejected.

As in the poverty of a stable Jesus was born,
so by the baptism of his suffering, death, and resurrection
you gave birth to your church,
delivered us from slavery to sin and death,
and made with us a new covenant by water and the Spirit.

As your Word became flesh, born of woman,
on that night long ago,
so on the night in which he gave himself up for us
he took bread, gave thanks to you, broke the bread,
gave it to his disciples, and said:
"Take, eat; this is my body which is given for you.
Do this in remembrance of me."

When the supper was over he took the cup,
gave thanks to you, gave it to his disciples, and said:
"Drink from this, all of you;
this is my blood of the new covenant,
poured out for you and for many
for the forgiveness of sins.
Do this, as often as you drink it, in remembrance of me."

And so,
in remembrance of these your mighty acts in Jesus Christ,
we offer ourselves in praise and thanksgiving
as a holy and living sacrifice,
in union with Christ's offering for us,
as we proclaim the mystery of faith.

Christ has died, Christ is risen, Christ will come again.

Pour out your Holy Spirit on us, gathered here,
and on these gifts of bread and wine.
Make them be for us the body and blood of Christ,
that we may be for the world the body of Christ,
redeemed by his blood.

By your Spirit make us one with Christ,
one with each other,
and one in ministry to all the world,
until Christ comes in final victory
and we feast at his heavenly banquet.

Through your Son Jesus Christ,
with the Holy Spirit in your holy church,
all honor and glory is yours, Almighty Father,
now and forever.

Amen.

THE LORD'S PRAYER

BREAKING THE BREAD

COMMUNION

Appropriate carols may be sung during communion.

PRAYER AFTER COMMUNION

We give you thanks, most gracious God,
for allowing us to share in this feast as your family
and to be fed with the bread of heaven;
give us grace that we all may grow in love,
glorifying you in all things,
through Jesus Christ our Lord.
Amen.

HYMN or CAROL

"Joy to the World" *or* "Angels We Have Heard on High"

DISMISSAL WITH BLESSING

Go in peace and joy to love and serve the Lord.
We are sent in the name of the Christ Child.
Let us bless the Lord.
Thanks be to God! Alleluia!

CHRISTMAS EVE: HOLY COMMUNION

GATHERING

Where no procession is held, following appropriate music, a simple greeting may be given:

Jesus Christ is born!
O come, let us adore him!

HYMN AND PROCESSION

Hymn   "O Come, All Ye Faithful" *or* "Hark! the Herald Angels Sing"

OPENING PRAYER

The Lord be with you.
And also with you.
Let us pray: *A brief silence.*
O Christ,
your wonderful birth is meaningless
  unless we are born again.
Your death is meaningless
  unless we die to sin.
Your resurrection is meaningless
  if you only have been raised.
Bring us now to such love for you
  that we may enjoy you for ever.
For all things in the heavens and on earth
  are yours eternally.
Amen.
                or
O God, you have caused this holy night to shine
with the brightness of the true Light:

Grant that we, who have known the mystery
of that Light on earth,
may also enjoy him perfectly in heaven;
where with you and the Holy Spirit he lives and reigns,
one God, in glory everlasting.
Amen.

ACT OF PRAISE or ANTHEM

"Glory Be to God on High" (*Gloria in Excelsis*)

[LIGHTING OF THE ADVENT AND CHRIST CANDLES]

See previous services for alternative action and texts.

PRAYER FOR ILLUMINATION

Lord, open our minds and hearts
by the power of your Holy Spirit,
that we may hear and rejoice
in the Gospel of our Savior,
Jesus Christ, the Light of the world.
Amen.

FIRST LESSON

The service may follow the pattern of Alternative 2. The lighting of the congregation's candles may take place immediately upon the lighting of the Christ candle or may follow Holy Communion, the candles being extinguished after the singing of "Silent Night" as the concluding hymn.

Commentary

If Christmas does not fall on a Sunday and a service is to be held on Christmas Day, it is appropriate to use the same pattern as for the Christmas Eve second service, omitting the lighting of the congregation's candles. Use the prayer texts that do not mention "holy night." If Christmas falls on Sunday, December 25, and the Christmas lessons have been used the preceding evening for a Christmas Eve service, either of the following sets of lessons may be used:

FIRST LESSON	Isaiah 62:6-7, 10-12
PSALM	Psalm 97
SECOND LESSON	Titus 3:4-7
GOSPEL	Luke 2:8-20

or

FIRST LESSON	Isaiah 52:7-10
PSALM	Psalm 98
SECOND LESSON	Hebrews 1:1-12
GOSPEL	John 1:1-14

In addition to plans for the environment and for visuals mentioned earlier, the use of dance in the processions or in specific congregational actions should be considered. A simple movement of adoration, with sensitivity to the space, might well highlight a Christmas crèche. Specific symbols on the Chrismon or Jesse Tree may be used in the dance or on the dancers' garments. Colors of white, yellow, and gold in fine textures are appropriate for the vestments and garments as well.

In planning music for these services, care should be taken to use a variety of instruments and musicians. Try not to do everything in a single service, but allow a cumulative unfolding of many gifts throughout these days. If both early and late evening Christmas Eve services are celebrated, design the music (choral, instrumental, and congregational) with the particular gatherings and themes of the lessons in mind. If large numbers of families with children are to be present, music suitable for children should be encouraged.

The Sundays After Christmas

There are either one or two Sundays after Christmas and before Epiphany. The First Sunday After Christmas falls between December 26 and January 1 inclusive. The Second Sunday After Christmas, if it occurs, falls between January 2 and 5 inclusive. During the entire Christmas Season, Christmas visuals should remain in place, and Christmas carols and other Christmas music are appropriate. The lessons and psalms are as follows:

FIRST LESSON

First Sunday	Isaiah 63:7-9	(Year A: 1995, 1998, 2001)
	Isaiah 61:10–62:3	(Year B: 1993, 1996, 1999)
	I Samuel 2:18-20, 26	(Year C: 1/1/1995, 1997, 2000)
Second Sunday	Jeremiah 31:7-14 *or*	(All years)
	Sirach 24:1-12	

PSALM

First Sunday	Psalm 148	(All years)
Second Sunday	Psalm 147:12-20 *or*	(All years)
	Wisdom of Solomon 10:15-21	

SECOND LESSON

First Sunday	Hebrews 2:10-18	(Year A: 1995, 1998, 2001)
	Galatians 4:4-7	(Year B: 1993, 1996, 1999)
	Colossians 3:12-17	(Year C: 1/1/1995, 1997, 2000)
Second Sunday	Ephesians 1:3-14	(All years)

GOSPEL

First Sunday	Matthew 2:13-23	(Year A: 1995, 1998, 2001)
	Luke 2:22-40	(Year B: 1993, 1996, 1999)
	Luke 2:41-52	(Year C: 1/1/1995, 1997, 2000)
Second Sunday	John 1:(1-9) 10-18	(All years)

There are other options on these Sundays. January 1 or the nearest Sunday may be observed as New Year's, using New Year's lessons and resources (see next section, "John Wesley's Covenant

Service"). The first Sunday in January may be observed as Epiphany Sunday, using Epiphany lessons and resources.

Since Jesus was circumcised and named on his eighth day (Luke 2:21), January 1 is observed as the Holy Name of Our Lord Jesus Christ in the Episcopal calendar; as the Name of Jesus in the Lutheran calendar; and as the Solemnity of Mary, Mother of God, in the Roman Catholic calendar. Some other Protestants also remember the naming of Jesus on this date. The lessons and psalm are Numbers 6:22-27, Psalm 67, Galatians 4:4-7 or Philippians 2:9-13, and Luke 2:15-21. The following opening prayer may be used:

> Eternal Father, you gave your Son the name of Jesus to be a sign of our salvation.
> Plant in every heart the love of the Savior of the world, Jesus Christ our Lord,
> who lives and reigns with you and the Holy Spirit, one God, now and for ever. **Amen.**

F. John Wesley's Covenant Service

Historical Introduction

John Wesley established covenant services as an important part of early Methodist life. His *Journal* often reveals an interest in covenanting. For example, on Christmas Day, 1747, he wrote, "Urged the wholly giving up ourselves to God and renewing in every point our covenant that the Lord should be our God." The first Methodist covenant service was held August 11, 1755. Wesley wrote in his *Journal*,

> I explained once more the nature of such an engagement and the manner of doing it acceptably to God. At six in the evening we met for that purpose at the French Church in Spitalfields. After I had recited the tenor of the covenant proposal, in the words of that blessed man, Richard Alleine, all the people stood up, in testimony of assent, to the number of about eighteen hundred persons. Such a night I scarce ever saw before. Surely the fruit of it shall remain for ever.

According to his *Journal*, covenant services were held on a variety of occasions, but toward the end of his life, they were usually celebrated on New Year's Day or on a Sunday near the beginning of the year.

Wesley drew on a number of sources for the service. His primary source was the writing of the Presbyterian minister Joseph Alleine: *An Alarm to the Unconverted* and *Directions for Believers Covenanting with God*. The Presbyterians and Baptists also had traditions of establishing covenants, but Wesley claimed that the Scriptures established the practice. He justified use of the service with passages such as Deuteronomy 26:17-18 and Jeremiah 31:31-34.

Wesley took great pains to instruct his followers in the meaning and purpose of a covenant. When he first used the service, several days were spent instructing those who would participate. Later the instruction was limited to the day of the service. Wesley allowed only those with special tickets to participate in the service, which always concluded with communion.

In Wesley's time the service consisted of reading long portions of the works of Joseph Alleine which exhorted the people to live lives completely dedicated to God. This was followed by repeating the covenant prayer which was very similar to the one used today and then in the celebration of the Lord's Supper.

Although the service depends on a written form of the covenant prayer, Wesley never prepared a practical outline for the service. He only published long sections of Joseph Alleine's writing about a covenant that included the covenant prayer. He did not insert the service in the prayer book he sent to the American Methodists in 1784, nor did he supply the early American Methodists with instructions concerning the service. Therefore, generations of American Methodists were unaware of the service. During this century, the service has been recovered by many churches. *The Book of Worship for Church and Home* (1944) included an abridged form of the service in its historical section.

Though the service was called "John Wesley's Covenant Service," Wesley would not have recognized it. The service was actually a slightly modified copy of the one being used by British Methodists at that time. Since Wesley's death, the service had been greatly revised, but the covenant prayer itself had been changed little through the years.

The service given here borrows heavily from the British Methodist covenant service. It is designed for use as the main service of worship on the First Sunday After Epiphany (Baptism of the Lord). You may wish to use the following introduction in John Wesley's own words either printed on the bulletin cover or in place of the "Greeting."

> Dearly beloved, the Christian life, to which we are called, is a life in Christ, redeemed from sin, and through him consecrated to God. Upon this life we have entered, having been admitted into that New Covenant of which our Lord Jesus Christ is mediator, and which He sealed with His own blood, that it might stand for ever.
>
> On one side the Covenant is God's promise that He will fulfill in and through us all that He declared in Christ Jesus, who is the Author and Perfecter of our faith. That His promise still stands we are sure, for we have known His goodness, and proved His grace in our lives day by day.
>
> On the other side we stand pledged to live no more unto ourselves, but to Him who loved us and gave Himself for us, and has called us to serve Him that the purpose of His coming might be fulfilled.
>
> From time to time, we renew our vows of consecration, especially when we gather at the Lord's Table: but on this day we meet expressly, as generations of our fathers* have met, that we may joyfully and solemnly renew the Covenant which bound them and binds us to God.
>
> Let us then, remembering the mercies of God, and the hope of His calling, examine ourselves by the light of His Spirit, that we may see wherein we have failed or fallen short in faith and practice, and, considering all that this Covenant means, may give ourselves anew to God.

Order of Worship

GATHERING *Suitable music may be offered.*

GREETING

> Grace and peace from God our Father
> and the Lord Jesus Christ.
> **Amen.**
> Come let us worship the Lord who established a new covenant
> through his Son Jesus Christ.
> **We come in spirit and in truth.**

HYMN "O for a Thousand Tongues to Sing"

PRAYER OF ADORATION

> Let us pray:
> Let us worship our Creator, the God of love;
> God continually preserves and sustains us;
> we have been loved with an everlasting love; through Jesus Christ
> we have been given complete knowledge of God's glory.
> **You are God; we praise you; we acknowledge you to be the Lord.**
> Let us glory in the grace of our Lord Jesus Christ.
> Though he was rich, for our sakes he became poor;

*Or "Forebears"

he was tempted in all points as we are,
but he was without sin;
he went about doing good
and preaching the gospel of the kingdom;
he accepted death, death on the cross;
he was dead and is alive for ever;
he has opened the kingdom of heaven
to all who trust in him;
he sits in glory at the right hand of God;
he will come again to be our Judge.

You, Christ, are the King of Glory.

Let us rejoice in the fellowship of the Holy Spirit,
the Lord, the Giver of Life.
Through the Spirit we are born into the family of God,
and made members of the body of Christ;
the witness of the Spirit confirms us;
the wisdom teaches us;
the power enables us;
the Spirit will do far more for us than we ask or think.

All praise to you, Holy Spirit.

SILENT PRAYER

THE LORD'S PRAYER

FIRST LESSON

    Ecclesiastes 3:1-13*   (All years)

PSALM OR ANTHEM

    Psalm 8*   (All years)

SECOND LESSON

    Revelation 21:1-6a*   (All years)

HYMN

   Appropriate hymns include:
      "Come, Let Us Use the Grace Divine"
      "God of the Ages"
      "O God, Our Help in Ages Past"

GOSPEL

    Matthew 25:31-46*   (All years)

These are New Year's Lessons. On other than New Year's Eve or Day use appropriate lessons. See Commentary on pp. 83-84.

SERMON

HYMN   "Come, Let Us See the Grace Divine"

RESPONSES AND OFFERINGS

CONFESSION OF SIN

> Let us humbly confess our sins to God.
> O God, you have shown us the way of life
> through your Son, Jesus Christ.
> We confess with shame our slowness to learn of him,
> our failure to follow him, and our reluctance to bear the cross.
>
> **Have mercy on us, Lord, and forgive us.**
>
> We confess the poverty of our worship,
> our neglect of fellowship and of the means of grace,
> our hesitating witness for Christ,
> our evasion of responsibilities in our service,
> our imperfect stewardship of your gifts.
>
> **Have mercy on us, Lord, and forgive us.**
>
> Let each of us in silence make confession to God.

SILENCE

> Have mercy on us, Lord, and forgive us.
>
> **Have mercy on me, O God, according to your steadfast love;**
> **In your abundant mercy blot out my transgressions.**
> **Wash me thoroughly from my iniquity,**
> **and cleanse me from my sin.**
> **Create in me a clean heart, O God,**
> **and put a new and right spirit within me.**
>
> Now the message that we have heard from God's Son
> and announce is this: God is light,
> and there is no darkness at all in him.
> If we live in the light—just as he is in the light—
> then we have fellowship with one another,
> and the blood of Jesus, his Son,
> purifies us from every sin.
> If we say that we have no sin, we deceive ourselves,
> and there is no truth in us.
> But if we confess our sins to God,
> he will keep his promise and do what is right;
> he will forgive us all our wrongdoing.
>
> **Amen. Thanks be to God.**

COLLECT

Let us pray:

**Father, you have appointed our Lord Jesus Christ
as Mediator of a new covenant;
give us grace to draw near with fullness of faith
and join ourselves in a perpetual covenant with you,
through Jesus Christ our Lord. Amen.**

THE COVENANT

In the old covenant, God chose Israel to be a
special people and to obey the law.
Our Lord Jesus Christ, by his death and resurrection,
has made a new covenant with all who trust in him.
We stand within this covenant and we bear his name.
On the one side, God promises in this covenant
to give us new life in Christ.
On the other side, we are pledged
to live not for ourselves but for God.
Today, therefore, we meet
to renew the covenant which binds us to God.
The people stand.
Friends, let us claim the covenant God has made with his people,
and accept the yoke of Christ.
To accept the yoke of Christ means that we
allow Christ to guide all that we do and are,
and that Christ himself is our only reward.
Christ has many services to be done;
some are easy, others are difficult;
some make others applaud us, others bring only reproach;
some we desire to do because of our own interests;
others seem unnatural.
Sometimes we please Christ and meet our own needs,
at other times we cannot please Christ
unless we deny ourselves.
Yet Christ strengthens us and gives us
the power to do all these things.
Therefore let us make this covenant of God our own.
Let us give ourselves completely to God,
trusting in his promises and relying on his grace.

**I give myself completely to you, God.
Assign me to my place in your creation.
Let me suffer for you.
Give me the work you would have me do.
Give me many tasks
or have me step aside while you call others.
Put me forward or humble me.
Give me riches or let me live in poverty.
I freely give all that I am and all that I have to you.
And now, holy God, Father, Son, and Holy Spirit,**

you are mine and I am yours. So be it.
May this covenant made on earth continue for all eternity.
Amen.

CONCERNS AND PRAYERS

THE PEACE

OFFERING

GREAT THANKSGIVING

> *The prayer text is the same as for Epiphany, found on pp. 86-88.*

BREAKING OF BREAD AND TAKING OF THE CUP

GIVING OF THE BREAD AND THE CUP

PRAYER AFTER COMMUNION

Let us give thanks to the Lord.

Lord, we give thanks for the gift of this holy meal.
We praise you that you sent your Son,
that through him we might be reconciled completely to you.
Christ sacrificed himself for us;
grant that all we are and all we do be a response to him,
in whose strong name we pray. Amen.

HYMN   "A Charge to Keep I Have"

DISMISSAL WITH BLESSING

May the God who established a covenant
with those who seek to enter the kingdom
be always present with you.

Amen.

May Jesus Christ who sealed the new covenant
with his sacrifice on the cross bring you peace.

Amen.

May the Holy Spirit of God guide your life, now and for ever.

Amen.

Go in peace to serve God and your neighbor in all that you do.

Amen. Thanks be to God!

Commentary

This covenant service may be celebrated on various days at the beginning of the calendar year. If used as a Watch Night (New Year's Eve) service, the lessons given in the order of worship are appropriate. It may be the main service on the First Sunday After Epiphany—Baptism of the Lord. If so, the lessons for that day should be used. The first Sunday of the year is also appropriate. When celebrated on the First Sunday After Epiphany, it marks a natural culmination of the Advent and Christmas/Epiphany experience.

During the year, a covenant service could mark a special anniversary such as the founding of a congregation. If it is celebrated at another time, the following lessons may be read: Jeremiah 31:31-35; Hebrews 12:22-29; John 15:1-8 or Matthew 11:27-30.

If a service of baptism and/or reaffirmation is to be incorporated, it may follow at the place indicated "Responses and Offerings." In this case the renunciation of sin and profession of faith can replace the confession of sin in the text of the order of worship just given.

In most situations it is impossible to follow Wesley's practice of having long periods of instruction precede the service. But authentically celebrated Advent and Christmas Seasons naturally prepare a congregation for the renewal of baptismal covenant. Announcements of the service should be sensitively planned to contribute to more mature and eager participation.

Although at times the Lord's Supper has been omitted from the service, the covenant service is in reality a special form of the celebration of Holy Communion which renews our personal commitment to Christ in the light of all that our baptism into Christ means.

G. Epiphany

The visual environment of the worship space should employ the finest and most joyful of textures, with white, gold, and yellow predominating. Epiphany is a day of splendor and light. Images of the Wise Men and their gifts—gold, frankincense (which may be burned as incense) and myrrh—are appropriate for banners, dancers' garments, and for use in processions. Two other primary images for this feast of Christ's manifestation are his baptism in the Jordan and the wedding at Cana (cf. John 2:11).

GREETING

> The grace of the Lord Jesus Christ be with you.
> **And also with you.**
> The splendor of Christ shines upon us.
> **Praise the Lord!**

HYMN

> "As with Gladness Men of Old," "Light of the World, We Hail Thee," "Brightest and Best," "How Brightly Shines the Morning Star," and "Christ, Whose Glory Fills the Skies" are especially suitable.
> *If this is a processional hymn, it precedes the opening greeting.*

PRAYER

> The Lord be with you.
> **And also with you.**
> Let us pray: *A brief silence.*

> God of all glory, by the guidance of a star you led the Wise Men to worship the Christ Child. By the light of faith lead us to your glory in heaven. We ask this through Christ our Lord.

> **Amen.**

ACT OF PRAISE

Here may be sung the Gloria in Excelsis, *or the* Te Deum, *or another canticle of praise.*

FIRST LESSON   Isaiah 60:1-6   (All years)

PSALM   Psalm 72:1-14   (All years)

SECOND LESSON   Ephesians 3:1-12   (All years)

ALLELUIA, HYMN, or ANTHEM

GOSPEL   Matthew 2:1-12   (All years)

PRAYERS FOR OTHERS

Here may be offered a bidding prayer, or pastoral prayer, followed by petitions from the congregation with the people responding, **Lord of light, hear our prayer.**

or

Let us pray for the church and for the world.
Grant, Almighty God, that all who confess your name may be united in your truth, live together in your love, and reveal your glory in the world.
Silence.
Lord, in your mercy,
Hear our prayer.
Guide the people of this land, and of all the nations, in the ways of justice and peace; that we may honor one another and serve the common good.
Silence.
Lord, in your mercy,
Hear our prayer.
Give us all a reverence for the earth as your own creation, that we may use its resources rightly in the service of others and to your honor and glory.
Silence.
Lord, in your mercy,
Hear our prayer.
Comfort and heal all those who suffer in body, mind, or spirit; give them courage and hope in their troubles, and bring them the joy of your salvation.
Silence.
Lord, in your mercy,
Hear our prayer, through Jesus Christ our Lord. Amen.

INVITATION TO THE TABLE AND PEACE

Christ invites to this table all who confess faith in his promises and who intend to live as reconciled people. Let us, as God's forgiven and accepted people, exchange signs of peace and reconciliation with one another.
The peace of our Lord Christ be with you all.
And also with you.
Exchange signs of peace.

OFFERING

Choral or instrumental music may be offered, or a simple dance sequence that ends with the presentation of the gifts of bread and wine along with the collection. As an alternative to the doxology, use an appropriate hymn or carol stanza such as Christ Is the World's True Light *or stanzas 1 and 3 of* As with Gladness Men of Old.

GREAT THANKSGIVING

The Lord be with you.

And also with you.

Lift up your hearts.

We lift them to the Lord.

Let us give thanks to the Lord our God.

It is right to give our thanks and praise.

It is right, and a good and joyful thing,
always and everywhere to give thanks to you,
Father Almighty, Creator of heaven and earth.

Before the mountains were brought forth
or you had formed the earth,
from everlasting to everlasting you alone are God.
You created light out of darkness
and brought forth life on the earth.
You formed us in your image
and breathed into us the breath of life.
When we turned away, and our love failed,
your love remained steadfast.
You delivered us from captivity,
made covenant to be our sovereign God,
and spoke to us through your prophets.
And so, with your people on earth
and all the company of heaven,
we praise your name and join their unending hymn:

**Holy, holy, holy Lord, God of power and might,
heaven and earth are full of your glory.
Hosanna in the highest.
Blessed is he who comes in the name of the Lord.
Hosanna in the highest.**

Holy are you, and blessed is your Son Jesus Christ,
in whom you have revealed yourself,
our light and our salvation.

You sent a star to guide the Magi
to where the Christ was born;
and your signs and witnesses
in every age and through all the world
have led your people from far places to his light.
In his baptism and in his table fellowship
he took his place with sinners.
Your Spirit anointed him to preach good news to the poor,
to proclaim release to the captives
and recovering of sight to the blind,
to set at liberty those who were oppressed,
and to announce that the time had come
when you would save your people.
By the baptism of his suffering, death, and resurrection
you gave birth to your church,
delivered us from slavery to sin and death,
and made with us a new covenant by water and the Spirit.

On the night in which he gave himself up for us
he took bread, gave thanks to you, broke the bread,
gave it to his disciples, and said:
"Take, eat; this is my body which is given for you.
Do this in remembrance of me."

When the supper was over he took the cup,
gave thanks to you, gave it to his disciples, and said:
"Drink from this, all of you;
this is my blood of the new covenant,
poured out for you and for many
for the forgiveness of sins.
Do this, as often as you drink it, in remembrance of me."

And so,
in remembrance of these your mighty acts in Jesus Christ,
we offer ourselves in praise and thanksgiving
as a holy and living sacrifice,
in union with Christ's offering for us,
as we proclaim the mystery of faith.

Christ has died, Christ is risen, Christ will come again.

Pour out your Holy Spirit on us, gathered here,
and on these gifts of bread and wine.
Make them be for us the body and blood of Christ,
that we may be for the world the body of Christ,
redeemed by his blood.

By your Spirit make us one with Christ,
one with each other,
and one in ministry to all the world,
until Christ comes in final victory
and we feast at his heavenly banquet.

Through your Son Jesus Christ,
with the Holy Spirit in your holy church,
all honor and glory is yours, Almighty Father,
now and for ever.
Amen.

THE LORD'S PRAYER

BREAKING THE BREAD

And he was known to them in the breaking of the bread.

PRESENTING THE CUP

The gifts of God for the people of God.

Here may be sung the traditional "Lamb of God," or a psalm antiphon and verse such as "O taste and see the goodness of the Lord," Psalm 34, while the ministers and people begin the communion sharing.

COMMUNION

Hymns or psalms during communion: "Go, Tell It on the Mountain," "Heralds of Christ," "Christ Is the World's True Light," or "Rise, Shine, You People," Psalm 89:1-7; Psalm 72 if not used before, perhaps ending with a meditative choral piece, followed by silence.

PRAYER AFTER COMMUNION

The Lord be with you.
And also with you.

Let us pray:
Pour out upon us
the spirit of your love, O Lord,
and unite the wills
of those whom you have fed
with one heavenly food;
through Jesus Christ our Lord.
    or
You have given yourself to us, Lord.
Now we give ourselves for others.
Your love has made us a new people;
As a people of love we will serve you with joy.
Your glory has filled our hearts.
Help us to glorify you in all things. Amen.

HYMN   "Christ Is the World's True Light"
             "Go, Tell It on the Mountain"
             "Rise, Shine, You People"

DISMISSAL WITH BLESSING

> Now may our Lord Jesus Christ himself,
> and God our Father,
> who loved us
> and gave us eternal comfort and good hope through grace,
> comfort your hearts and establish them
> in every good work and word.
> **Amen.**
> Go in peace to love and serve the Lord.
> **Amen. Thanks be to God!**

POSTLUDE OR FESTIVE MUSIC

Commentary

Epiphany is to be a day of great joy for all Christians. It completes the twelve days of Christmas; more important, this is the festival of the manifestation of God's Word made flesh, honored by the gifts from all nations and peoples. The central images of the Magi bearing gifts suggest processions, banners, and a specific emphasis upon our joining the whole world in adoration and self-giving. Another image from tradition is that of the wedding feast at Cana: "The first of the signs by which Jesus revealed his glory" (John 2:11 NEB).

Most local churches will celebrate Epiphany on the first Sunday in January and use the appropriate lessons in place of those indicated from the Second Sunday After Christmas.

Epiphany is an excellent day for baptism, which may best be celebrated following the sermon and before the prayers of the people. Many churches will also celebrate the Lord's Supper. Since this is likely to take more time than the usual Sunday service, it is helpful to announce this to the congregation ahead of time.

Planning for the music, both choral and congregational, requires a clear sense of the rhythm and focus of the service. For example, the instrumental and choral literature based on the great Epiphany hymn, "O Morning Star, How Fair and Bright," is extensive and may be found in all ranges of difficulty. If particular psalm settings are used, such as cantor or choir with psalm tones for the people, plan to introduce such music well in advance, preferably at a time in the early to mid-fall at a Wednesday evening gathering, along with the other new music for the Advent-Christmas cycle. This allows time to learn and to explore the significance and power of the texts as prayer well before the actual service.

Good pastoral imagination is called for since this service is adaptable to every situation and can be very simple or quite elaborate, depending upon the size of the church and the resources available. Remember that simple things done well are more appropriate than complex, ambitious things hastily planned and done in anxiety. Epiphany should be the welcome, joyous conclusion to the entire sweep of Advent-Christmas. Christ is the Light of the world. This is why we have a story to tell to the nations.

H. Baptism of the Lord

The festival of Epiphany presents us with a great richness of images concerning Jesus Christ, the Light of the world. It is truly a feast of plenty, proclaiming the manifestation of the Son of God incarnate in human flesh. Three primary mysteries of the Christian faith are brought together: the star leading the Magi to the cradle, the presence of Jesus at the marriage feast and the miraculous water-turned-wine, and the baptism of Jesus in the Jordan.

The Sundays after Epiphany, beginning with Baptism of the Lord and ending with

Transfiguration, do not in themselves constitute a special season. They are ordinary time, if you will. However, the Scripture readings continue to shine with the radiance and sound forth echoes of the meaning of Christmas-Epiphany. Some of the music, both choral and instrumental, associated with Epiphany may well be carried into our worship during some of the subsequent Sundays.

The basic color for the Sundays after Epiphany is green, except for Baptism of the Lord on the first Sunday following, and Transfiguration on the last Sunday following. Throughout these Sundays the visual materials should witness to the mighty signs and teachings by which God became manifest in the person and work of Jesus Christ. In particular, the scripture lessons should be studied for various possibilities.

The first Sunday following January 6 is called "Baptism of the Lord." We have suggested that Wesley's covenant service be used on this occasion. However, some congregations will prefer to use the covenant service as a watch night on New Year's Eve or New Year's Day evening. In that case, the following service is especially suitable for the first Sunday.

GATHERING

Choral or instrumental music may be offered, focusing especially on baptismal themes and texts.

GREETING
Ascribe to the Lord, O heavenly beings,
Ascribe to the Lord glory and strength.
Ascribe to the Lord the glory of his name,
Worship the Lord in holy array.
The voice of the Lord is upon the water.
The God of glory thunders, the Lord upon many waters.
The voice of the Lord is powerful.
The voice of God is full of majesty.
Let us praise the name of the Lord!

HYMN (PROCESSION)   "Blessed Jesus, at Thy Word"
                              "Christ for the World We Sing"
                              "Glorious Things of Thee Are Spoken"
                              "The Church's One Foundation"
                              "O Love, How Deep, How Broad, How High"
                              "The Word Became Flesh"

OPENING PRAYER

The Lord be with you.
And also with you.
Let us pray: *A brief silence.*

Living God,
    when the Spirit descended on Jesus
    at his baptism in Jordan's water
    you revealed him as your own beloved Son.
Keep us, your children who have been born of water and the Spirit,
    always faithful to him
    who is Lord for ever and ever.
Amen.

FIRST LESSON

    Isaiah 42:1-9   (Year A: 1993, 1996, 1999)
    Genesis 1:1-5   (Year B: 1994, 1997, 2000)
    Isaiah 43:1-7   (Year C: 1995, 1998, 2001)

PSALM   Psalm 29   (All years)

SECOND LESSON

    Acts 10:34-43   (Year A: 1993, 1996, 1999)
    Acts 19:1-7   (Year B: 1994, 1997, 2000)
    Acts 8:14-17   (Year C: 1995, 1998, 2001)

ALLELUIA (HYMN OR ANTHEM)

GOSPEL

    Matthew 3:13-17   (Year A: 1993, 1996, 1999)
    Mark 1:4-11   (Year B: 1994, 1997, 2000)
    Luke 3:15-17, 21-22   (Year C: 1995, 1998, 2001)

SERMON

SERVICE OF BAPTISM AND/OR BAPTISMAL REAFFIRMATION

THE PRAYERS

If specific petitions are offered, the people may respond: **Hear us in your mercy, Lord,** *or* **To you be thanks and praise,** *to supplications and thanksgiving, respectively.*

PEACE

The peace may be initiated by the newly baptized, confirmed, or those making special reaffirmations.
The peace of Christ be with you all.
And also with you.

OFFERING

A hymn may be sung as the table is prepared, such as "Christian People, Raise Your Song," "How Good to Offer Thanks," "We Give Thee But Thine Own," or "I Come with Joy unto the Lord."

GREAT THANKSGIVING

The text is the same as for Epiphany, found on pp. 86-88.

THE LORD'S PRAYER

BREAKING THE BREAD

COMMUNION

Suitable hymns, songs, and psalms may be sung by congregation and choir, interspersed with silence.

PRAYER AFTER COMMUNION

Let us pray:

We give you thanks, most gracious God,
that you have given us your love
in this holy gospel feast
and have refreshed us by your Holy Spirit.
Now strengthen and defend us
in joyful service to all the world;
through Jesus Christ our Lord.
Amen.

HYMN

"This Is the Spirit's Entry Now"
"Rejoice, Ye Pure in Heart"
"We Know That Christ Is Raised"
"We're Marching to Zion"
This may be a procession to a place of reception for the newly baptized; if so, the hymn may follow the blessing and dismissal.

DISMISSAL WITH BLESSING

Go in peace.
We are sent in Christ's name.
Now may the God of peace
who brought again from the dead
our Lord Jesus,
the great Shepherd of the sheep,
by the blood of the eternal covenant,
equip you with everything good
that you may do his will,
working in you
that which is pleasing in his sight,
through Jesus Christ:
to whom be glory for ever and ever.
Amen.

I. The Sundays After Epiphany

The Sundays after Epiphany, as few as four and as many as nine, depending upon the variable date of Lent and Easter, are not a special season. Beginning with Baptism of the Lord and concluding with Transfiguration, these Sundays nevertheless give witness to the ministry and mission of Jesus Christ. Worship during these ordinary Sundays of January and February provides opportunity for proclaiming and witnessing to the concrete way in which God reveals Jesus and the way Jesus as Messiah reveals God to all humanity.

These Sundays acquire their point and focus primarily from the ordering of the readings from God's Word. The Epistle lessons present First and Second Corinthians in a nearly continuous sequence over the three-year cycle, thus allowing the congregation to hear and receive Paul's messages to one specific early church; January and February are natural times to assess the year just past and plan for mission and ministry. Multiple images of the life of discipleship and witness occur in the Gospel readings to enrich such an exploration of the church's manifestation of God in Christ to the world. If this focus is given, care must be taken not to lose the sense of the whole gospel which is the essence of the Lord's Day—each Sunday a "little Easter." This may be accomplished by careful choice of hymns, prayer texts, psalmody, and choral music.

These Sundays may also concentrate on unfolding themes in the Gospel and Old Testament readings. Here we find an abundance of images and specific teachings that give witness to the manifestation of God in the ministry of Jesus. All three years place a reading from John's Gospel on the Second Sunday After Epiphany, focusing the theological and existential meanings of who Jesus is for the world. Worshiping Christians who have just celebrated the renewal of baptismal covenant in the light of Jesus' solidarity with humanity in baptism need to enter deeply into the story line of what he does and says. For what he did and said in the Gospels, Christ will do and say now—in Word and sacrament, but also in and through the salt and light of our discipleship and witness. The great prophetic images that come to us from the Jewish scriptures are especially powerful during these Sundays in directing us to serve all humanity in righteousness, justice, and peace.

Among many Protestant traditions, this period of time has focused on mission to the world. When integrated with the readings and celebrated in the light of the "manifestations" of Christmas-Epiphany, such an emphasis on preaching and liturgy provides a good opportunity to proclaim, pray, and celebrate the social implications of discipleship and mission—Christ's ongoing work in the world. Here there is no incompatibility between evangelical witness and involvement in the saving work of social justice, reconciliation, and God's reign among the nations. An indispensable resource to aid in planning preaching and worship may be found in *Social Themes of the Christian Year: A Commentary on the Lectionary,* edited by Dieter T. Hessel (Philadelphia: Geneva Press, 1983). The scripture readings also provide a solid basis for congregational Bible study and prayer on the work of the kingdom and our social witness to the world.

For the celebration of Holy Communion during these Sundays, you may wish to use either the Great Thanksgiving for Epiphany or the one found in the chapter on Trinity Sunday, which is suitable at any time of the year but especially on the Sundays after Epiphany or after Pentecost.

These Sundays also present an opportunity to learn hymns and songs from other ethnic and national traditions. Highly recommended for use by choirs and by congregations are the following recent collections that include excellent music and texts from Asian-American, black, and Hispanic traditions: *Hymns from the Four Winds* (Abingdon Press, 1983), *Celebremos II, Segunda Parte* (Discipleship Resources, 1983), and *Songs of Zion* (Abingdon Press, 1982). Careful study and selection of hymns and songs from these sources by pastors, choir directors, and organists for use in relation to the themes of the scripture lessons and the sermon and prayers will open up the sense of the manifestation of Christ in many cultures and traditions—truly an experience of the "mission to all peoples."

As with the introduction of all music that the congregation may sing, care must be taken to provide good occasions for learning the music. A congregational hymn festival or a more informal gathering for hymn learning, fellowship, and prayer during these weeks is to be encouraged. These may involve gathering two or more neighboring churches and can also be an ecumenical experience of sharing new music of faith across denominational and cultural lines.

The color for the Sundays between Baptism of the Lord and Transfiguration is green, and the scriptures for each Sunday are a rich source of visual possibilities. Some hymns related to the lessons are listed also.

SECOND SUNDAY AFTER EPIPHANY (between January 14 and 20 inclusive)

Year A: 1993, 1996, 1999

Isaiah 49:1-7; Psalm 40:1-11; I Corinthians 1:1-9; John 1:29-42
"Jesus Calls Us O'er the Tumult" (John)
"Just As I Am, Without One Plea" (John)
"On Jordan's Bank the Baptist's Cry"
"We Would See Jesus" (John)
Any musical setting of the *Agnus Dei* ("Lamb of God") (John)

Year B: 1994, 1997, 2000

I Samuel 3:1-10 (11-20); Psalm 139: 1-6, 13-18; I Corinthians 6:12-20; John 1:43-51
"Jesus Calls Us O'er the Tumult" (John)
"We Would See Jesus" (esp. v. 5) (John)

Year C: 1995, 1998, 2001

Isaiah 62:1-5; Psalm 36:5-10; I Corinthians 12:1-11; John 2:1-11
"Christ, from Whom All Blessings Flow" (I Cor.)
"Many Gifts, One Spirit" (I Cor.)
"One Bread, One Body" (I Cor.)
"As Man and Woman We Were Made" (John)

THIRD SUNDAY AFTER EPIPHANY (between January 21 and 27 inclusive)

Year A: 1993, 1996, 1999

"Isaiah 9:1-4; Psalm 27:1, 4-9; I Corinthians 1:10-18; Matthew 4:12-23
"I Want to Walk as a Child of the Light" (Isa.; Ps.)
"Blest Be the Tie that Binds" (I Cor.)
"Lord, You Have Come to the Lakeshore" (Matt.)

Year B: 1994, 1997, 2000

Jonah 3:1-5, 10; Psalm 62:5-12; I Corinthians 7:29-31; Mark 1:14-20
"Jesus Calls Us O'er the Tumult" (Mark)
"Lord, You Have Come to the Lakeshore" (Mark)

Year C: 1995, 1998, 2001

Nehemiah 8:1-3, 5-6, 8-10; Psalm 19; I Corinthians 12:12-31*a*; Luke 4:14-21
"Let's Sing unto the Lord" (Ps.)
"Christ, from Whom All Blessings Flow" (I Cor.)
"One Bread, One Body" (I Cor.)
"Hail to the Lord's Anointed" (Luke)

FOURTH SUNDAY AFTER EPIPHANY (between January 28 and February 3 inclusive)
If it is the Last Sunday After Epiphany, see Transfiguration.

Year A: 1993, 1996, 1999
Micah 6:1-8; Psalm 15; I Corinthians 1:18-31; Matthew 5:1-12
"What Does the Lord Require" (Mic.)
"The Old Rugged Cross"
"When I Survey the Wondrous Cross" (I Cor.)
"Lord, I Want to Be a Christian" (Matt.)

Year B: 1994, 1997, 2000

> Deuteronomy 18:15-20; Psalm 111; I Corinthians 8:1-13; Mark 1:21-28
> "Lord, Speak to Me" (Deut.)
> "I Want a Principle Within" (Ps.)
> "Silence, Frenzied, Unclean Spirit" *or* any hymn on healing (Mark)
> "O Young and Fearless Prophet" (Mark)

Year C: 1995, 1998, 2001

> Jeremiah 1:4-10; Psalm 71:1-6; I Corinthians 13:1-13; Luke 4:21-30
> "Are Ye Able" (Jer.)
> "Saranam, Saranam" (Ps.)
> "Morning Glory, Starlit Sky" (I Cor.)
> "The Gift of Love" (I Cor.)
> "We'll Understand It Better By and By" (I Cor. 13:12)

FIFTH SUNDAY AFTER EPIPHANY (between February 4 and 10 inclusive)
If it is the Last Sunday After Epiphany, see Transfiguration.

Year A: 1993, 1996, 1999

> Isaiah 58:3-9*a* (9*b*-12); Psalm 112:1-9 (10); I Corinthians 2:1-12 (13-16); Matthew 5:13-20
> "Hope of the World" (Isa.; Ps.)
> "Ask Ye What Great Thing I Know" (I Cor.)
> "This Little Light of Mine" (Matt.)

Year B: 1994, 1997, 2000

> Isaiah 40:21-31; Psalm 147:1-11; I Corinthians 9:16-23; Mark 1:29-39
> "All Earth Is Waiting" (Isa.)
> "Come, Ye Disconsolate" *or* any hymn on healing (Isa.; Ps.; Mark)

Year C: 1995, 1998, 2001

> Isaiah 6:1-8 (9-13); Psalm 138; I Corinthians 15:1-11; Luke 5:1-11
> "Here I Am, Lord" (Isa.)
> "Holy, Holy, Holy" (Isa.)
> "Send Me, Lord" (Isa.)
> "The Voice of God Is Calling" (Isa.)
> "Whom Shall I Send" (Isa.)
> "Amazing Grace" (I Cor.)
> "Christ Is Risen" (I Cor.)
> "Lord, You Have Come to the Lakeshore" (Luke)

SIXTH SUNDAY AFTER EPIPHANY (between February 11 and 17 inclusive)
If it is the Last Sunday After Epiphany, see Transfiguration.

Year A: 1993, 1996, 1999

> Deuteronomy 30:5-12 *or* Sirach 15:15-20; Psalm 119:1-8; I Corinthians 3:1-9; Matthew 5:21-37
> "Trust and Obey" (Deut.; Matt.)
> "A Mighty Fortress Is Our God" (Ps.)
> "Dear Jesus, in Whose Life I See" (Matt.)
> "I Want a Principle Within" (Matt.)

Year B: 1994, 1997, 2000

II Kings 5:1-14; Psalm 30; I Corinthians 9:24-27; Mark 1:40-45
"There Is a Balm in Gilead" *or* any hymn on healing (II Kings; Mark)
"He Touched Me" (Mark)

Year C: 1995, 1998, 2001

Jeremiah 17:5-10; Psalm 1; I Corinthians 15:12-20; Luke 6:17-26
"I Shall Not Be Moved" (Jer.; Ps.)
"Christ Is Risen" (I Cor.)
"Sing with All the Saints in Glory" (I Cor.)
"O Young and Fearless Prophet" (Luke)
"Are Ye Able" (Luke)

SEVENTH SUNDAY AFTER EPIPHANY (between February 18 and 24 inclusive)
If it is the Last Sunday After Epiphany, see Transfiguration.

Year A: 1993, 1996, 1999

Leviticus 19:1-2, 9-18; Psalm 119:33-40; I Corinthians 3:10-11, 16-23; Matthew 5:38-48
"Christ Is Made the Sure Foundation" (I Cor.)
"Lord, I Want to Be a Christian" (Lev.; Matt.)
"O Love, How Deep, How Broad" (Lev.; Matt.)
"O Young and Fearless Prophet" (Matt.)

Year B: 1994, 1997, 2000

Isaiah 43:18-25; Psalm 41; II Corinthians 1:18-22; Mark 2:1-12
"Come, Thou Fount of Every Blessing" (Isa.; Ps.)
"Ask Ye What Great Thing I Know" (I Cor.)
"The Old Rugged Cross" (I Cor.)
"Come, Ye Disconsolate" (Mark)
"Heal Me, Hands of Jesus" (Mark)
"When Jesus the Healer Passed through Galilee" (Mark)
"Where Cross the Crowded Ways of Life" (Mark)

Year C: 1995, 1998, 2001

Genesis 45:3-11, 15; Psalm 37:1-11, 39-40; I Corinthians 15:35-38, 42-50; Luke 6:27-38
"Depth of Mercy" (Gen.)
"God Will Take Care of You" (Ps.)
"Sing with All the Sons of Glory" (I Cor.)
"Love Divine, All Loves Excelling" (Luke)

EIGHTH SUNDAY AFTER EPIPHANY (between February 25 and 29 inclusive)

Year A: 1993, 1996, 1999

Isaiah 49:8-16*a*; Psalm 131; I Corinthians 4:1-5; Matthew 6:24-34
"I Want to Walk as a Child of the Light" (I Cor.)
"O Master, Let Me Walk with Thee" (Matt.)
"Seek Ye First" (Matt.)

Year B: 1994, 1997, 2000

Hosea 2:14-20; Psalm 103:1-13, 22; II Corinthians 3:1-6; Mark 2:13-22
"There's a Wideness in God's Mercy" (Hos.)
"Praise to the Lord, the Almighty" (Ps.)
"Praise, My Soul, the King of Heaven" (Ps.)
"Spirit of the Living God" (I Cor.)
"Jesus Calls Us O'er the Tumult" (Mark)

Year C: 1995, 1998, 2001

Isaiah 55:10-13 *or* Sirach 27:4-7; Psalm 92:1-4, 12-15; I Corinthians 15:51-58; Luke 6:39-49
"Joyful, Joyful, We Adore Thee" (Isa.; Ps.)
"O Happy Day" (Isa.; Ps.)
"My Lord, What a Morning" (I Cor.)
"If Thou But Suffer God to Guide Thee" (Luke)
"My Hope Is Built" (Luke)

J. Transfiguration (Last Sunday After Epiphany)

Having come through several Sundays whose primary color is green, we now celebrate Transfiguration—with its vision of Christ and the prophetic figures on the mountaintop. The color is white, and the visual environment should reflect the blaze of glory. The shining figures of the patriarchs and prophets suggest bold images. See also the commentary that follows the order of worship.

GATHERING

GREETING

The Lord is Sovereign; let the people tremble in awe.
God is enthroned upon the cherubim; let the earth shake.
The Lord is great in Zion, and is high above all peoples.
Proclaim the greatness of the Lord our God, and worship God upon the holy mountain.

HYMN

Appropriate hymns include:
"All Hail the Power of Jesus' Name"
"Christ Is Made the Sure Foundation"
"Christ upon the Mountain Peak" ("Jesus on the Mountain Peak")
"Christ, Whose Glory Fills the Skies"
"Fairest Lord Jesus"
"O Wondrous Sight! O Vision Fair"
"Swiftly Pass the Clouds of Glory"

If the hymn is processional, the greeting may follow. Banners, a book with a brilliant cover, and a processional cross may be used.

OPENING PRAYER

The Lord be with you.
And also with you.
Let us pray: *A brief silence.*

O God, who before the passion of your only begotten Son
revealed his glory upon the holy mountain:
Grant to us that we, beholding by faith the light of his countenance,
may be strengthened to bear our cross,
and be changed into his likeness from glory to glory;
through Jesus Christ our Lord,
who lives and reigns with you and the Holy Spirit,
one God, for ever and ever.
Amen.

or

God of glory and mercy,
before his death in shame
your Son went to the mountaintop
and you revealed his life in glory.
Where prophets witnessed to him,
you proclaimed him your Son,
but he returned to die among us.
Help us face evil with courage,
knowing that all things, even death,
are subject to your transforming power.
We ask this through Christ our Lord.
Amen.

FIRST LESSON

Exodus 24:12-18	(Year A: 1993, 1996, 1999)
II Kings 2:1-12	(Year B: 1994, 1997, 2000)
Exodus 34:29-35	(Year C: 1995, 1998, 2001)

PSALM

Psalm 2 *or* Psalm 99	(Year A: 1993, 1996, 1999)
Psalm 50:1-6	(Year B: 1994, 1997, 2000)
Psalm 99	(Year C: 1995, 1998, 2001)

Response: **Sing the glory of the Lord forever!**

SECOND LESSON

II Peter 1:16-21	(Year A: 1993, 1996, 1999)
II Corinthians 4:3-6	(Year B: 1994, 1997, 2000)
II Corinthians 3:12–4:2	(Year C: 1995, 1998, 2001)

HYMN, ANTHEM, or CANTICLE

GOSPEL

Matthew 17:1-9   (Year A: 1993, 1996, 1999)
Mark 9:2-9   (Year B: 1994, 1997, 2000)
Luke 9:28-36 (37-43)   (Year C: 1995, 1998, 2001)

SERMON

PRAYERS

The presiding minister may offer prayers and invite the petitions of the congregation, after each of which all may respond: **Christ in glory, hear our prayer** *or* **Look upon us in mercy, Lord.**

or

Gracious God, we pray for your holy church;
That we all may be one.
Grant that every member of the church may truly and humbly serve you;
That your name may be glorified by all people.
We pray for all who govern and hold authority in the nations of the world;
That there may be justice and transforming peace on the earth.
Give us grace to do your will in all that we undertake;
That our works may find favor in your sight.
Have compassion on those who suffer this day from any grief or trouble;
That they may be delivered from their distress.
Give to the departed eternal rest;
Let perpetual light shine upon them.
We praise you for your saints who have entered into joy;
May we also come to share in your heavenly kingdom.
Let us pray for our own needs:
Silence.   (BCP)

THE LORD'S PRAYER

If Holy Communion is celebrated, this prayer follows the Great Thanksgiving; if not, the service concludes with offering, hymn, and dismissal with blessing.

THE PEACE

If Holy Communion is celebrated, the following invitation is given before the peace is exchanged:

Christ invites to this table all who confess their faith in him, and who intend to lead a life of love, witness, and faithful service, seeking reconciliation, justice, and peace.
The peace of Christ be with you all.

And also with you.

All exchange signs of peace and reconciliation.

OFFERING

Choral or instrumental music carrying the scriptural themes, or a dance sequence which ends with the presentation of the gifts of bread and wine along with the offering. The image of Christ in glory with the witnesses may be used.

GREAT THANKSGIVING[1]

The Lord be with you.
And also with you.
Lift up your hearts.
We lift them to the Lord.
Let us give thanks to the Lord our God.
It is right to give our thanks and praise.

It is truly right to glorify you, Father,
and to give you thanks,
for you alone are God, living and true,
dwelling in light inaccessible
from before time and for ever.

Fountain of life
and source of all goodness,
you made all things
and fill them with your blessing;
you created them to rejoice
in the splendor of your radiance.

Countless throngs of angels
stand before you to serve you night and day;
and, beholding the glory of your presence,
they offer you unceasing praise.
Joining with them, and giving voice
to every creature under heaven,
we acclaim you, and glorify your name,
as we sing (say):

Holy, holy, holy Lord,
God of power and might,
Heaven and earth are full of your glory.
Hosanna in the highest.
Blessed is he who comes in the name of the Lord.
Hosanna in the highest.

We acclaim you, holy Lord,
glorious in power;
your mighty works reveal
your wisdom and love.
You formed us in your own image,

---

[1]The text for this prayer is *A Common Eucharistic Prayer*, adapted from the Anaphora of Saint Basil and Roman Canon IV by the Committee for a Common Eucharistic Prayer, Marion Hatchett, chairman (privately printed, 1975).

giving the whole world into our care,
so that,
in obedience to you, our Creator,
we might rule and serve all your creatures.
When our disobedience took us far from you,
you did not abandon us to the power of death.
In your mercy you came to our help
so that in seeking you we might find you.
Again and again you called us into covenant with you,
as the prophets taught us
to hope for salvation.
Father, you loved the world so much
that in the fullness of time
you sent your only Son to be our Savior.
Incarnate by the Holy Spirit,
born of the Virgin Mary,
he lived as one of us,
yet without sin.
To the poor he proclaimed
the good news of salvation;
to prisoners, freedom;
to the sorrowful, joy.
To fulfill your purpose
he gave himself up to death;
and, rising from the grave,
destroyed death
and made the whole creation new.
And that we might live
no longer for ourselves
but for him who died and rose for us,
he sent the Holy Spirit,
his own first gift for those who believe,
to complete his work in the world,
and to bring to fulfillment
the sanctification of all.

When the hour had come
for him to be glorified by you,
his Heavenly Father,
having loved his own
who were in the world,
he loved them to the end:
at supper with them he took bread,
and after giving you thanks,
he broke the bread,
gave it to his disciples, and said:
"Take, eat;
this is my body which is given for you."
When the supper was over,
he took the cup.

Again he returned thanks to you,
gave the cup to his disciples, and said:
"Drink from this, all of you;
this is the cup of the new covenant in my blood,
poured out for you and many,
for the forgiveness of sins."
When we eat this bread and drink this cup,
we experience anew
the presence of the Lord Jesus Christ
and look forward to his coming
in final victory.

Father, we now celebrate
this memorial of our redemption.
Recalling Christ's death
and his descent among the dead,
proclaiming his resurrection
and ascension to your right hand,
awaiting his coming in glory;
and offering to you
from the gifts you have given us
this bread and this cup,
we praise you and we bless you.

We praise you, we bless you,
We give thanks to you,
And we pray to you, Lord our God.

Lord, we pray
that in your goodness and mercy
your Holy Spirit may descend upon us,
and upon these gifts,
sanctifying them and showing them to be
holy gifts for your holy people,
the bread of life
and the cup of salvation,
the body and blood of your Son Jesus Christ.
Grant that all who share this bread and cup
may become one body and one spirit,
a living sacrifice in Christ
to the praise of your name.

Remember, Lord,
your one holy catholic and apostolic church,
redeemed by the blood of your Christ.
Reveal its unity, guard its faith, and preserve it in peace.
Remember (_____) and all who minister in your church.
Remember all your people,
and those who seek your truth.
Remember (_____) and all

who have died in the peace of Christ,
and those whose faith is known to you alone;
bring them into the place of eternal joy and light.

And grant that we may find our inheritance
with the blessed Virgin Mary,
with patriarchs, prophets, apostles, and martyrs,
and with all the saints who have found favor with you in ages past.
We praise you in union with them and give you glory
through your Son Jesus Christ our Lord.

Through Christ,
and with Christ, and in Christ,
all honor and glory are yours,
Almighty God and Father,
in the unity of the Holy Spirit,
for ever and ever.
Amen.

THE LORD'S PRAYER

BREAKING THE BREAD

COMMUNION

Hymns and appropriate psalms (especially 34 and 145) may be sung during the communion.

PRAYER AFTER COMMUNION

The Lord be with you.
And also with you.
Let us pray:

Lord,
we give thanks for these holy mysteries
which bring to us here on earth
a share of the transformed life to come,
through Jesus Christ our Lord.
Amen.

HYMN

"Lord, Whose Love Through Humble Service"
"O Love, How Deep, How Broad, How High"
"Behold Us, Lord, a Little Space"
"O Wondrous Type!"

DISMISSAL WITH BLESSING

Go in peace to serve God and your neighbor in all that you do.
We are sent in Christ's name.
The Lord make glory shine upon you

and be gracious to you.
The Lord look upon you with favor
and give you peace, now and in the time to come.
Amen.

Commentary

The Sundays after Epiphany have explored various signs of Christ's manifestation of God. Today we focus on the awe and wonder of Christ's glory hidden from the eyes of the world, yet revealed to eyes of faith who know his suffering, death, and resurrection. Traditionally this feast is celebrated on August 6, as is still the case with Roman Catholic and Episcopal churches. It marks the transition from Jesus' ministry of teaching and healing in Galilee to his ministry of sacrifice in Jerusalem; thus, it is also appropriately celebrated by other Protestant traditions as the last Sunday before the beginning of Lent.

The proclamation may choose to focus on the relationship between the glory of Christ's transformation with Moses and Elijah and the realities he is yet to face. This relates directly to the faith journey and experiences of God's people here and now.

The patriarchs and prophets may be pictured in the line of God's messengers. Jesus is the last of the line of biblical prophets. There are modern prophets as well who may be named in our prayers and in our hymns and songs. For example, Martin Luther King, Jr.'s, final speech with its unforgettable use of "mountaintop" imagery reminds us that Jesus had to come down to the world's sin and death and face his own obedience unto death. The service may explore this tension, focusing on God's gracious will and power to transform and transfigure all humanity. The text of this historic Great Thanksgiving, based on the ancient prayer of Saint Basil, should be studied for further images and themes that may be expressed in music and the visual environment.

6

FROM
ASHES TO FIRE:
LENT AND
EASTER/PENTECOST

A. Proclaiming the Paschal Mystery:
An Introduction to the Seasons of Lent and Easter

*A*t the heart of the Christian faith is our participation in the life, suffering, death, resurrection, and ascension of Jesus Christ as Lord. We proclaim that "the Word became flesh and dwelt among us" (John 1:14). Jesus Christ was born into human history in the fullness of time for our salvation. In time he lived and taught, suffered and was put to death; but God "raised him from the dead and made him sit at his right hand . . . and he has put all things under his feet and has made him the head over all things for the church, which is his body, the fulness of him who fills all in all" (Eph. 1:20, 22-23). Through the death and resurrection of Jesus Christ, we are delivered from sin and death, and by the Holy Spirit we are born into eternal life with God. This we confess; this we must renew continually in our worship and in our lives.

What is this Paschal Mystery that is the very heart of the Christian gospel and of all our life and worship? Most Protestants are probably unfamiliar with the expression. We are more familiar with the term *passover*, which translates the term *pesah* in various English versions of the Bible and in some hymn texts. Passover is a celebration of the ancient Hebrew agricultural spring feast and of the saving rescue and deliverance of the Israelites from bondage in Egypt which occurred during that time of year. The paschal lamb, which was sacrificed to God in memory of that night of deliverance from death, became a central symbol of redemption. This symbol appears in the New Testament, especially in John's Gospel and in the writings of Paul. "Christ, our paschal lamb, has been sacrificed. Let us, therefore, celebrate the festival" (I Cor. 5:7-8).

When we speak of the Paschal Mystery, then, we refer to the whole range of meanings associated with the saving work of Christ and the church's participation therein. It may refer specifically to those days in which we celebrate the narrative of passion-death-resurrection; it may be used to speak of the reality and power of Christ in the sacraments and his living Word; but it also refers to our continuing experience of living with the Lord. It is thus a rich, powerful concept as well as an image. In this light we may claim that a genuine recovery of the wholeness of the Paschal Mystery in our worship will bring a deeper personal commitment to the lordship of Christ in our common life and a deeper sense of what it is to be the church, the people of God.

At the very center of our worship and proclamation is the story of God's whole history with humankind, brought to focus in the passion, death, and resurrection of Christ. Since the beginning of Christian worship, these events have given shape and meaning to the week, the whole year, and even to each day of the Christian community's life. In remembering the mystery of our redemption in

Christ through the seasons of Lent and Easter, we are formed in the pattern of his death and resurrection and his life-giving Spirit.

Some Implications for Lent

Since the seasons of Lent and Easter celebrate the most definitive aspects of God's redemptive acts, we must carefully plan our worship with prayerful study of the Scriptures and the foundational themes of the feasts and seasons. Lent is a time for evangelism and for true conversion—a time for growing through repentance, fellowship, prayer, fasting, and concentration upon our baptismal covenant. We are to be signs of God's kingdom in this world. The themes of repentance and preparation for sharing in the death and resurrection of Christ are basic to those preparing for baptism and confirmation and to the whole body of Christians who will renew their baptismal faith during the Easter Season. Lent is thus not giving up something but rather taking upon ourselves the intention and the receptivity to God's grace so that we may worthily participate in the mystery of God-with-us.

In preparing to worship during these seasons, we do well to explore the meaning of Christian initiation as a lifelong process of being transformed into the life and holiness of our Lord. All this, as the New Testament and the early church plainly taught and experienced, is not an individual's private experience. It is a communal reality that is the heartbeat of the church's worship and mission in human history. Thus, the whole pattern of practical Christian evangelism and conversion is inherent in the meaning of this season: encounter with Christ, instruction, initiation, and growth together in common life and ministry. Lent thereby gives a meaning and depth to Christian conversion and to following through so that the seeds of God's Word may fall on fertile soil.

Essential to the most effective use of these services and liturgical resources is the intention of each local church to prepare new converts and members for initiation at Easter. In so doing, the whole church is to be engaged in a common process of renewal and reliving conversion. This itself is basic to authentic worship: the process of praying, of searching the Scriptures, of renewing the meaning of witness and discipleship, of taking seriously penance and reconciliation, and of participating in the rhythm of celebrations, in Word and sacrament, culminating in Easter and the Great Fifty Days.

Ash Wednesday developed as a day of penitence to mark the beginning of Lent—the forty days of preparation for the paschal celebrations of Easter. Ash Wednesday is a particular time for new beginnings in the faith, a time for returning to the Lord. On this day we recall our mortality and wait upon the Lord for a renewing Spirit. This is a time for putting aside the sins and failures of the past in the light of who we are yet to become by the grace of God. These resources and services are part of a larger environment of repentance and growth in grace. We are to be tested by the Spirit so that our participation in the meaning of the Easter faith may be authentic and a true dying and rising with Christ to new life in God.

All this implies that careful planning for these services of worship is crucial. The local pastor cannot and should not do everything required. A significant portion of the congregation must be trained to assume various responsibilities throughout the whole of the time period covered here, but particularly in preparation for the Easter Triduum,[1] as will be made clear in the commentaries. Much of the planning and preparation can be done as part of the congregation's Lenten journey. This may provide a unique opportunity for persons to deepen their individual and corporate appreciation for, and involvement in, the Paschal Mystery. Liturgy becomes the "work of the people of God," as its root meaning suggests, and preparation for worship becomes the occasion for a more richly Christ-centered spirituality to develop.

Yet for all the intensity of Lent, we must seek a whole new pace for the season. Our church activities should not exhaust the congregation with mere "busyness." The point is not to sprint through a series of events, classes, services, and busy work only to collapse the day after Easter. Rather, the discipline of Lent should sustain and refresh us so that we may give full expression to church commitments on through the great Easter-Pentecost Season. The time from Ash Wednesday to Pentecost is also a natural time of the secular year in which many persons give themselves with renewed vigor to church programs. The Easter faith should overflow into our mission to do God's will in the world.

Easter Triduum: The Paschal Event

The aim of these three great days of observance is to dramatize and to proclaim the events of our Lord's passion and death, and to awaken in us a sense of God's ever-present saving power through the cross and resurrection. It is not an occasion for mere sentimental remembrance of past events. It is a *way of participating* in these saving events through a unified sequence of actions, Scripture, and common prayer. By faithful participation in the liturgy of Holy Week and Easter, we encounter Christ who, through his redemptive suffering and death and his triumphal rising, comes to deliver all humanity from bondage and death.

The narrative of Holy Week focuses on the Paschal Mystery. While the dynamic of Christian life in all seasons is that same mystery, it is manifest with explicit power in the celebrations of Passion/Palm Sunday and especially in the climactic last three days of the week (sunset of Holy Thursday to sunset Easter Day) known as the *Triduum*.[1] The early church, following a rigorous fast, celebrated the whole mystery on Easter Eve and into Easter Day in one unified liturgy. Everything was contained in the great Easter Vigil: the reading of the mighty acts of God, the telling of our Lord's passion, the lighting of the new fire and the paschal (or Easter) candle, the presentation of candidates for baptism, the full initiation rites with the renewal of baptismal vows for the whole church, and the glorious Easter communion, or Eucharist. Even though we have inherited a pattern of narrating and enacting the sweep of events over several days, our intent should be to dwell within the fundamental unity of Christ's one saving action in the self-giving of his life and his being raised from the dead.

The historical sequence of events was first systematically dramatized over the course of Holy Week in fourth-century Jerusalem. We are familiar with that sequence: the triumphal entry into the city; the final days of teaching and confrontation with authorities; the Last Supper in the context of the Passover; the subsequent arrest, trial, and crucifixion on Good Friday; the burial and rest in the tomb; and finally, the resurrection early on the first day of the week. Our worship through Holy Week follows this pattern. We begin with Passion/Palm Sunday. The name derives from a combination of two ideas that are in powerful tension with each other: a triumphal entry of the palm-bearing procession into Jerusalem shouting "Hosanna," and the sober realization that Jesus faces the gathering storm of human sin and death. It is a day of contrast and irony. Here we enter into a reenactment of something Scripture tells us vividly the followers of Jesus and others in Jerusalem did on this day. With the extended reading (or other expression) of the passion account from the Evangelists, we encounter anew the tension and reality of his "royal" procession. In no other week and on no other day of the year do we attend to the recounting of so much detailed history. Our worship on Passion/Palm Sunday is a reliving of the final chapters of Jesus' earthly ministry.

On the minor days from Monday through Thursday afternoon, we continue to read the accounts and to ponder them and to pray. On Thursday evening we relive with the disciples that fellowship meal on the very threshold of the Passover in which Jesus uttered the unforgettable words with the sharing of the bread and the cup—"This is my body," "This is my blood of the new covenant"—and commanded that we forever "Do this in remembrance of me." We experience anew that which was enacted on this extraordinary evening, including (if we choose) the act of mutual servanthood in the washing of feet. This may be followed by a service of Tenebrae (see p. 170) in which we recall and symbolize the growing darkness of the next hours' events: betrayal in the garden, arrest, and the condemnation of the trial.

Then, on Friday, we recall the crucifixion and death of Christ by again attending to the narration of events. Here the reality of his death is encountered, a death we remember also at the beginning of

Lent on the day of ashes. But now we experience the anguish of our own sin and evil intensified, and our own complicity in his betrayal. The altar table is stripped and made bare. We may also enter into the shadows of death by using the form of Tenebrae if it was not used Thursday evening. We keep watch and pray as we move through the time of burial and rest in the tomb. Fasting appropriately marks our watch. We await the unfolding of the great mystery which has been accomplished once and for all, yet remains an ever-renewing and amazing present reality throughout every age.

Thus, Holy Week—especially in its final days—proclaims and enacts the richness of meaning contained in the whole Paschal Mystery. In approaching these services of worship, we should think of each event not as an independent entity but rather as a continually unfolding unified drama of our salvation.

It is our prayer and hope that these resources will be a means of renewing our faith experience and that the church's worship may more fully and adequately proclaim "Jesus is Lord." We are not concerned merely with becoming more "formal" or "ceremonial" in our style of worship. The essential reality lying behind the recovery of the Paschal Mystery for our tradition is *theological*. In Christ we pass over from death to life, from the present age to the age which is yet to come in fullness. This is God's grace and doing alone. Just as the Hebrews passed from slavery in Egypt to life in God's promised land, and as Jesus Christ was raised from death to life, so the church proclaims and enacts its faith that, by God's saving grace, we pass from sin and death to life with God. The whole world is in the process of being redeemed. Every time we truly proclaim Christ and celebrate the Meal at his table, we "proclaim the Lord's death until he comes." The Paschal Mystery comprehends the entire range of life with God, including the eschatological hope of a new heaven and a new earth.

Black American Christians' experience has kept alive for the whole church the vivid power of the exodus themes of deliverance from death and liberation from slavery. Passover-Easter may be immeasurably deepened by celebrating that experience and using resources of proclamation and song from those traditions. There are also themes in native American and other ethnic traditions that may be drawn from to show the universality of the exodus experience. With respect to Good Friday, we inherit devotions based on the "seven last words" tradition from Peruvian sources, and from the Hispanic cultures of New Mexico and Colorado, the powerful Good Friday art of the *penitentes*.

Easter Day, and the Great Fifty Days of Easter

Holy Week and the Easter celebrations contain the entire gospel of salvation. The First Service of Easter, whether celebrated Easter Eve as the vigil or on Easter in the early morning, is both the source and the summit of the entire Christian Year. Here we are overwhelmed by God's victory and by the vastness of the divine mercy and love. We proclaim Christ crucified, dead, and buried, risen and exalted as the head of the church—the Savior of humanity and the Lord of all things. The whole faith of the church now comes into focus in the continuing life of union with Christ. That faith lives in expectant hope of the kingdom in its fullness. Whatever life we have is a reflection of the life of God manifest in Jesus Christ through the power of the Holy Spirit. Hence, cross-resurrection theology can never be separated from the exaltation of Christ and the sending forth of his truth and life in the Holy Spirit of God.

The burst of praise and resurrection joy of Easter permeates the entire period from Easter morning through Pentecost. This is known as the Great Fifty Days.[2] While Easter is the Sunday of all Sundays, gathering up and transfiguring the narrative of Holy Week, and indeed the whole history of God's mighty works, the resurrection courses through the days and weeks of the Easter Season as a never-ending day—a prolonged and sustained Lord's Day. The paschal candle, symbolizing the morning star that never sets, should be visible and lighted for every gathering for worship during these days of the Easter-Pentecost Season.

Our celebration of the paschal feast does not end with Easter Day, however. Easter Day initiates the time that transforms the passion of Holy Week; the world of the first creation, subject to sin and death, is becoming the new creation. Easter is the Eighth Day which ushers in the end time, promising the never-ending light of eternal life. Special events may take place this week, particularly in connection with those who have been initiated through baptism, whether as infants or adults, and with those confirmed. Family worship and devotions may emphasize the Easter appearances of Jesus with the apostles and others, as recorded in the scriptures. We rejoice as the disciples witness to the experience of the glorified Lord. The whole week and the whole of the fifty days should echo the song of victory. "For we know that Christ being raised from the dead will never die again; death no longer has dominion over him. . . . So you also must consider yourselves dead to sin and alive to God in Christ Jesus" (Rom. 6:9, 11). The Easter "Alleluias" should resound throughout this whole season which unfolds the reality of life in the Spirit. It comes to full consciousness when the whole church celebrates the feast of the new age of the Holy Spirit on Pentecost. On that day we make explicit again the fact that the gospel is proclaimed in every tongue, in every place, unto all the world.

The contrasts between Lent and Easter-Pentecost are dramatic. Lent is sober, reflective, and watchful. This quality is reflected in the ancient practice of omitting "Alleluias" and "Glorias." On the other hand, Easter is exuberant. This should be expressed visually and musically as well. Leaders of worship should be aware of such contrasts and enable the congregation to participate fully in them.

In planning worship for the Easter-Pentecost Season, we must bear in mind the intimate connection between resurrection, the exaltation of the Lord, and the sending of the Holy Spirit which characterizes the Great Fifty Days in the witness of Scripture and in praise. The biblical, historical, and theological bases of this Passover-Pentecost festival time are clear and compelling. While it is not possible to establish with absolute certainty its full observance during the apostolic days of the church, there is little doubt that some of the churches knew such a celebration in the late first or early second century. First Corinthians has been described as a paschal letter which testifies to the immediate anticipation of Pentecost (I Cor. 16:8; see also Acts 20:6, 16). Its resounding phrases may testify to the apostolic observance of the Easter Pascha: "Christ, our paschal lamb, has been sacrificed. Let us, therefore, celebrate the festival, not with the old leaven . . . of malice and evil, but with the unleavened bread of sincerity and truth" (I Cor. 5:7-8). Furthermore, from at least the fourth century, the church has regarded the reading of Acts as the continuing preaching of the apostles and the outpouring of the Easter gospel. Saint John Chrysostom called this the "demonstration of the resurrection."

The Passover-Pentecost time is, in essence, one great extended Lord's Day feast. It lifts up all the facets of the redeeming work of God in Christ. Pentecost is a reliving of all that the Easter Season has come to mean for the people of God. In the Old Testament, Israel celebrated the Feast of Weeks, a day of great thanksgiving for the wheat harvest. In later times this also came to be the day commemorating the giving of the Law on Mount Sinai. These meanings carry over but are transformed by the church's experience of the outpouring of the Holy Spirit and the giving of the Spirit by Jesus Christ to the disciples in their post-resurrection encounter (John 20). It is a day marking the universality of the new age in which "there is neither Jew nor Greek, . . . slave nor free, . . . male nor female; for you are all one in Christ Jesus" (Gal. 3:28). This shows the new unity of the Spirit of the Lord through whom all nations may be reconciled; yet it also celebrates the "birthday" of the church.

Ten days earlier we celebrate Ascension Day—the fortieth day after Easter, based upon the scriptural account of Jesus' forty days on earth following the resurrection, according to Acts 1. We should not, however, think of this as a completely separate historical commemoration. In fact, until at least the end of the fourth century, the ascension of Christ and the descent of the Spirit were celebrated on the same Lord's Day. For us as well, the exaltation of the risen Christ is intimately linked with his giving of the Holy Spirit. As John's Gospel brings out, Jesus must go to the Father so that the Counselor, the Spirit of Truth, may abide with those who believe and love.

If we use the expression "Season of Pentecost" at all, it is most fittingly applied to the Easter Season itself. The day of Pentecost is its culmination. Our worship during these days makes manifest what we confess in the Apostles' Creed: "He ascended into heaven, and sitteth at the right hand of God the Father Almighty." Jesus promises not to leave his followers comfortless; this promise is fulfilled. The Holy Spirit comes to teach the church all truth and to enliven our common remembrance of all that Jesus was and is for us and for the whole world. The Holy Spirit illuminates what is yet to come. "Amen. Come, Lord Jesus!" (Rev. 22:20)—this is the church's final cry.

For all these reasons, baptisms and renewals of baptism are most appropriate on Pentecost. Tertullian, whose writings reflect second-century practices, mentions that the church normally baptizes on Easter and Pentecost. However, he goes on to say that any Lord's Day is suitable. In larger congregations, the whole season of the Great Fifty Days is particularly opportune if there are large numbers of families with children or of adult initiates who have undergone instruction and Lenten preparation. Pentecost is the second climax of the Paschal Season; its proper and joyful celebration gives sustaining power to all the ordinary time of the season after Pentecost.

From ashes to fire, from repentance to rebirth, from sin and death to resurrection and eternal life: these are the themes we have been given to recover and celebrate again in our common worship. These are the heart of our existence before God. The services and resources that follow invite every local church to worship anew the living Lord, to enact the drama of salvation "in spirit and in truth," and to receive the abundance of God's grace.

NOTES FOR CHAPTER VI–A

1. The Easter Triduum (literally "three days") is the Latin name given to the span of time from the celebration of Holy Thursday sunset up to the sunset of Easter Day. If we adopt the biblical reckoning of days, beginning with sunset and ending at the next sunset, we find that three days include the events of the Last Supper, the arrest and trial, the crucifixion, the burial, and the resurrection "on the first day of the week"—that is, on Sunday following the Jewish Sabbath. The intention is theological and liturgical integrity rather than temporal accuracy.
2. The Great Fifty Days takes its name from the period of time, reckoned from the book of Acts, between the resurrection and the receiving of the Holy Spirit by the whole church at Jerusalem. Forty days is the symbolic number, inherited also from the Old Testament, of days which marked Jesus' post-resurrection appearances until his ascension. The Fifty Days also echoes the ancient Hebrew celebration of Pentecost as well.

B. Ash Wednesday

GATHERING   *In silence and meditation.*

> *If a brief exposition of the service is necessary, it may be done quietly during this time, allowing for a return to silence before the greeting. If a choir is to process, let it be done in silence just prior to the greeting.*

GREETING

> The grace of our Lord Jesus Christ be with you.
> **And also with you.**
>
> Bless the Lord, O my soul,
> and all that is within me, bless God's holy name.
>
> **Bless the Lord, O my soul,**
> **and forget not all God's benefits.**
>
> Who forgives all your sins
> and heals all your infirmities;
>
> **Who redeems your life from the grave,**
> **and crowns you with mercy and loving-kindness.**

OPENING PRAYER

Let us pray: *A brief silence.*
Most Holy God,
  your Son came to save sinners;
we come to this season of repentance,
  confessing our unworthiness,
  asking for new and honest hearts,
  and the healing power of your forgiveness.
Grant this through Christ our Lord. **Amen.**
         or
Almighty and everlasting God,
  you hate nothing you have made
  and forgive the sins of all who are penitent:
Create and make in us new and contrite hearts,
  that we, worthily lamenting our sins
  and acknowledging our wretchedness,
  may obtain of you, the God of all mercy,
  perfect remission and forgiveness;
through Jesus Christ our Lord,
  who lives and reigns with you and the Holy Spirit,
  one God, for ever and ever. **Amen.**

HYMN   "Lord, Who Throughout These Forty Days," tune: ST. FLAVIAN or other CM.

Lord, who throughout these forty days,
  For us didst fast and pray,
Teach us with thee to mourn our sins,
  And close by thee to stay.

As thou with Satan didst contend,
  And didst the vict'ry win,
O give us strength in thee to fight,
  In thee to conquer sin.

And through these days of penitence,
  And through thy passiontide,
Yea, evermore, in life and death,
  Jesus! with us abide.

Abide with us, that so, this life
  Of suffering overpast,
An Easter of unending joy
  We may attain at last! *Amen.*

FIRST LESSON   Joel 2:1-2, 12-17a   (All years)

PSALM 51:1-12

A hymn or anthem that paraphrases portions of this psalm, such as "O for a Heart to Praise My God" (tune: AMAZING GRACE) *or* "Create in Me a Clean Heart," *may be sung.*

SECOND LESSON   II Corinthians 5:20b–6:2 (3-10)   (All years)

RESPONSE

    Cry, and God will answer.

    Call, and the Lord will say: "I am here."

    If you do away with the yoke,
        the clenched fist, the wicked word;
    if you give your bread to the hungry,
        and relief to the oppressed;

    Call, and the Lord will say: "I am here."

    Your light will rise in the darkness
        and your shadows become like noon.
    The Lord will always guide you,
        giving you relief in desert places.

    Cry, and God will answer.
    Call, and the Lord will say: "I am here."

GOSPEL   Matthew 6:1-6, 16-21   (All years)

SERMON

INVITATION TO THE OBSERVANCE OF LENTEN DISCIPLINE

    The following or similar words may be spoken:
Dear brothers and sisters in Christ: Christians have always observed with great devotion the days of our Lord's passion and resurrection. It became the custom of the church to prepare for Easter by a season of penitence, fasting, and prayer. This season of forty days provided a time in which converts to the faith were prepared for baptism into the body of Christ. It is also the time when persons who had committed serious sins and had been separated from the community of faith were reconciled by penitence and forgiveness, and restored to the fellowship of the church. The whole congregation is thus reminded of the mercy and forgiveness proclaimed in the gospel of Jesus Christ and the need we all have to renew our baptismal faith.

    I invite you, in the name of the Lord, to observe a holy Lent, by self-examination, penitence, prayer, fasting, and almsgiving; and by reading and meditating on the Word of God. To make a right beginning, and as a mark of our mortality, let us now kneel (bow) before our Creator and Redeemer.

                A brief silence is kept.

THANKSGIVING OVER THE ASHES

    The Lord be with you.

    And also with you.

    Let us pray:
    Almighty God,
        you have created us out of the dust of the earth;

Grant that these ashes may be to us
   a sign of our mortality and penitence,
   so we may remember that only by your gracious gift
are we given everlasting life;
   through Jesus Christ our Savior. **Amen.**   BCP

IMPOSITION OF ASHES

Suitable hymns or psalms may be sung during the imposition, or it may be done in silence.

Remember that you are dust, and to dust you shall return.
                       and/or
Repent, and believe the gospel.

A PSALM OF CONFESSION   Psalm 51:1-17

Have mercy on me, O God,
according to your loving-kindness;
   in your great compassion blot out my offenses.
Wash me through and through from my wickedness
   and cleanse me from my sin.

For I know my transgressions,
   and my sin is ever before me.
Against you only have I sinned.
   and done what is evil in your sight.

And so you are justified when you speak
   and upright in your judgment.
Indeed, I have been wicked from my birth,
   a sinner from my mother's womb.
For behold, you look for truth deep within me,
   and will make me understand wisdom secretly.

Purge me from my sin, and I shall be pure;
   wash me, and I shall be brighter than snow.
Make me hear of joy and gladness.
   that the body you have broken may rejoice.

Hide your face from my sins
   and blot out all my iniquities.
Create in me a clean heart, O God,
   and renew a right spirit within me.

Cast me not away from your presence
   and take not your Holy Spirit from me.
Give me the joy of your saving help again
   and sustain me with your bountiful Spirit.
I shall teach your ways to the wicked.
   and sinners shall return to you.

Deliver me from death, O God,
   and my tongue shall sing of your righteousness,
O God of my salvation.

> Open my lips, O Lord,
>   and my mouth shall proclaim your praise.
> Had you desired it, I would have offered sacrifice,
>   but you take no delight in burnt offering.
> The sacrifice of God is a troubled spirit;
>   a broken and contrite heart, O God,
>   you will not despise.

ABSOLUTION, or RECONCILIATION AND COMMENDATION

The minister may say:

The almighty and merciful God, Source of our salvation in Christ, who desires not the death of a sinner but rather that we turn from wickedness and live; accept your repentance, forgive your sins, and restore you by the Holy Spirit to newness of life. **Amen.**

Or the following mutual pardon may be exchanged between pastor and people:

In the name of Jesus Christ, you are forgiven!

In the name of Jesus Christ, you are forgiven!

Rejoicing in the fellowship of all the saints,
  let us commend ourselves, one another,
  and our whole life to Christ our Lord.

To you, O Lord.

PRAYERS OF THE PEOPLE
Response:

> **Lord, have mercy,**
>   *or*
> **Have mercy on your people.**

THE PEACE

The peace of the Lord be with you all.

And also with you.
  All may exchange signs of peace and reconciliation.

OFFERING

BRIEF PRAYER OF THANKSGIVING

THE LORD'S PRAYER

HYMN
"Jesus, Thy Boundless Love to Me"
"Have Thine Own Way, Lord"

DISMISSAL WITH BLESSING

Go forth into the world in the strength of God's mercy
   to live and to serve in newness of life.
      May Jesus Christ, the bread of heaven, bless and keep you.

   Amen.

      May the Lamb of God who laid down his life for all,
         graciously smile upon you.

   Amen.

      May the Lord God order all your days and deeds in peace.

   Amen. Thanks be to God.

All may depart in quietness.

Commentary

Ash Wednesday emphasizes a dual encounter: we confront our own mortality and confess our sins before God within the community of faith. The form of the service and the texts presented here are designed to focus our lives upon the dual themes of sin and death in the light of God's redeeming love in Jesus Christ. While the use of ashes as a sign of mortality and penance may be new to some congregations, it has a significant history in Jewish and Christian worship. The imposition of ashes is a powerful nonverbal and experiential way of participating in the call to repentance and reconciliation. This day can become in some manner a Yom Kippur, or Day of Atonement, for the Christian community.

In some circumstances this service may be held early in the morning, before the school and workday begin. Noonday is an especially suitable time, since many persons can attend from home, school, or work, and begin to observe a fast with the deletion of the regular noon meal. An early evening hour, following a shared sacrificial meal of bread and water, is also appropriate. Pastoral consideration should be given to the local situation to determine the best time and place, in the event no custom has already been established. Where more than one service is necessary in a church, modifications of the length of service can easily be made.

The visual environment should be solemn and stark. Purple is the most traditional color throughout Lent, but on Ash Wednesday gray, with its suggestion of ashes, is especially appropriate. Dark earth colors or any somber hues are also appropriate. Rough, coarse textures such as burlap suggest the character of the day and season.

The tone and atmosphere are sober and meditative. On this occasion silence should be experienced along with the gravity of the scripture readings. If a cross is used in silent procession with the choir (or with the ministers), it may be held a moment before each section of the congregation before being placed in a floor holder near the center of the actions that follow. Focus should be upon the reading of Scripture, the prayers, and the simple ritual actions with the ashes.

Various means of participation in the symbolism and sign-acts with the ashes may be considered. Here is one well-tested example: After the opening hymn, but before the Scripture lessons, ushers may distribute small cards or pieces of paper, or these may be picked up upon entering the room. Each person, having been instructed at the beginning of the service, may then write down before the end of the sermon a particular sin or characteristic in his or her life that is hurtful or unjust to others. These cards will then be brought by each person in procession (or by the ushers) following the sermon and placed upon a grate to be burned with palm branches for the ashes. If this is done, preparations for the burning, such as a receptacle for the ashes, should be made well in advance of the service, and the grate should be set in a visible place before the congregation.

If the ashes are prepared in advance, care should be taken to use palms or other leaves that produce a black or very dark ash. Pulverizing may be necessary. Light-colored ashes reduce the power of the symbolic cross mark. (Under no circumstances should wood ashes from a fireplace be used.)

It is essential that the whole service be permeated by genuine prayer. The sermon need not be long—eight to ten minutes at most—since the readings from Scripture and the penitential actions are themselves proclamatory. Alternative modes of proclamation include (1) a choral setting of the main themes; (2) silent meditation upon a few well-chosen slides or other visuals portraying mortality and penance (wilderness, desert, images of sin and human injury, injustice, reconciliation, water, wind and dust, oasis); (3) dramatic reading of Luke 3:1-17 (three readers: a narrator, John the Baptist, and the remaining sections—prophecy from Isaiah and the various questions). This may serve as the Gospel reading and may be followed by silence or a brief choral meditation or a suitable hymn; (4) a period of silence for examination of conscience, directed with appropriate sentences or readings.

The central congregational action is the rite of imposition of ashes. Particular sensitivity and grace must be exercised in the manner in which this is done. After the prayer over the ashes, the minister(s) and assistant(s) take their places at a focal point in the room and indicate with a gesture for the first rows of the congregation to come forward. The minister(s) and assistant(s), if any, make a cross of ashes on each forehead with the thumb, saying, "Remember that you are dust, and to dust you shall return," and/or "Repent, and believe the gospel." These could be said alternately.

A sense of solemnity and freedom is desired, no matter how humble or elaborate the church building. Ushering people stiffly, row by row, should be avoided. In a small congregation, people may simply come forward to the altar rail, kneel or stand to receive, and return by a side aisle to their seats. A continuously moving, yet unrushed, line is best. Those waiting may remain seated or bowed and rise in turn; those returning may join in singing, if hymns are used. In large congregations, there may be two or more "stations" at which ministers and assistants are standing. Worshipers in each section will come forward and then return to their seats by the opposite end of the pew or row. If there is a choir, those persons may receive first and then return to lead in the singing of hymns or psalms (most suitably, Ps. 23, 32, and 130).

The confession of sin takes the form of communal recital of Psalm 51. Following the return of the last person from the imposition of ashes, all should stand or kneel. The psalm may be read responsively between the minister and the people or by a leader and choir alternating with the people, or between two sections of the congregation. The particular style or grouping of the verses may be designated in the printed text. In some cases it may be possible to sing or chant the psalm to a simple tune or psalm-tone setting.

The confession of sins is followed by a brief silence and then a general absolution or a reconciliation and commendation—depending upon which is more appropriate to local convictions. The intercessions that follow should always include petitions for the church universal and for the brokenness of the world, emphasizing both social and personal dimensions of repentance and of solidarity with human suffering. Whenever possible, prepared petitions should be included along with time for spontaneous ones. A simple form for congregational response to each petition, such as "Lord, have mercy" or "Have mercy on your people," may be used. The minister or assistant would begin, "Most merciful God, hear our prayers for others as we say, 'Lord, have mercy.' " Then may follow petitions, such as "For the victims of our sin, and all who bear the burden of our faults, let us pray to the Lord"; the congregation responding, "Lord have mercy." And so on.

It is also possible to use a visual litany, each image or slide being responded to in the manner indicated above. For example, the images in Matthew 25 may be used, along with questions such as "Lord, when did we see you . . .?" or "Is it nothing to you, all you who pass by?"

The gravity and pace of this service may not lend itself to the inclusion of the sacrament of the Lord's Supper. If the sacrament is not celebrated, the congregation and choir still may wish to sing one of several settings of the *Agnus Dei* ("Lamb of God") instead of a hymn. This may give a powerful unity to the service as it comes to a conclusion. If there is both the imposition of ashes and a celebration of Holy Communion, these should always be separated, with the people coming forward for each particular action.

When a final hymn or other sung response is used, it may be sung before the dismissal with blessing while the ministers remain facing the congregation. The choir and ministers may then recess in silence with the cross going before them. The people depart in silence.

C. The Sundays in Lent

On the Sundays in Lent, there is a healthy tension between two facts: it is Lent, and it is the Lord's Day. It is important that we keep an appropriate balance in our worship on these Sundays.

On the one hand, these Sundays must be the heart of our congregational observance of Lent. In most local churches there are many more persons present on these Sundays than there are at any weekday service, even Ash Wednesday or the weekdays in Holy Week. Many, if not most, of the regular worshipers will not participate in congregational worship except on Sunday.

On the other hand, even in Lent every Sunday is a little Easter—a celebration of the resurrection. We noted earlier that Lent actually has forty-six days because the six Sundays in Lent are not counted as part of the forty days of Lent. The traditional usage that speaks of "Sundays *in* Lent" reminds us that the Lord's Day is "in but not of" the penitential Lenten Season.

One way to achieve balance and wholeness in the observance of Lent is to encourage attendance at weekly Lenten renewal meetings in addition to Sunday services. Since Lent begins on Ash Wednesday, many congregations hold such meetings on the Wednesdays following. These meetings with their emphasis on spiritual formation—including study, prayer, reflection, and action—help at least a nucleus of the congregation supplement what is possible in Sunday worship as they prepare to renew their baptismal covenant. If persons are to be baptized or confirmed at Easter, it is, of course, essential that there be classes or sessions in addition to Sunday worship at which they or (in the case of young children) their parents can be thoroughly prepared.

But it is also important that the Sunday services in this season have a balance of Lent and Lord's Day which enables the congregation as a whole to prepare for the renewal that is the focus of Easter. It is not enough that these Sundays be like other Sundays, glorious as any Lord's Day; they must be focused on the spiritual deepening that is essential if we are to be ready to celebrate the Paschal Mystery. Neither is it enough to treat these Sundays as if Lent were simply one long Holy Week, concentrating on the suffering and death of Christ, as if we could ignore for even a single Lord's Day the fact of the risen, living Christ in our midst.

The environment of worship should suggest this balance. The visual suggestions made in connection with Ash Wednesday (p. 115) apply to Lent in general, but if the effect produced on Ash Wednesday was extremely somber it may be moderated thereafter.

The lectionary readings are crucial in focusing our worship rightly on these Lenten Sundays, and they will be reliable guides to the selection of prayers and hymns. Even if we note the Lenten Season by the traditional omission of hymns and responses with "alleluia," this does not mean that we should sing passion hymns all through Lent. Some hymns related to the lessons are also listed.

FIRST SUNDAY IN LENT

Year A: 1993, 1996, 1999

Genesis 2:15-17; 3:1-7; Psalm 32; Romans 5:12-19; Matthew 4:1-11
"Amazing Grace" or "When I Survey the Wondrous Cross" (Rom.)
"Lord, Who Throughout These Forty Days" (Matt.) (see p. 111)

"O Love, How Deep" *or* "What a Friend We Have in Jesus" (Matt.)

Year B: 1994, 1997, 2000

Genesis 9:8-17; Psalm 25:1-10; I Peter 3:18-22; Mark 1:9-15
"Great Is Thy Faithfulness" (Gen.)
"Thy Holy Wings, O Savior" (Gen.; I Pet.)
" 'Tis the Old Ship of Zion" (Gen.; I Pet.)
"What Wondrous Love Is This" (Ps.; I Pet.)
"When Jesus Came to Jordan" (Mark)
The hymns related to Matthew 4:1-11 above also relate to Mark 1:9-15.

Year C: 1995, 1998, 2001

Deuteronomy 26:1-11; Psalm 91:1-2, 9-16; Romans 10:8b-13; Luke 4:1-13
"Guide Me, O Thou Great Jehovah" (Deut.)
"Jesus, Lover of My Soul" *or* "On Eagle's Wings" (Ps.)
"At the Name of Jesus" (Rom.)
"I Love to Tell the Story" (Rom.)
The hymns related to Matthew 4:1-11 above also relate to Luke 4:1-13.

SECOND SUNDAY IN LENT

Year A: 1993, 1996, 1999

Genesis 12:1-4a; Psalm 121; Romans 4:1-5, 13-17; John 3:1-17 *or* Matthew 17:1-9
"If Thou But Suffer God to Guide Thee" (Gen.; Rom.)
"The God of Abraham Praise" ("Praise to the Living God") (Gen.; Rom.)
"Where He Leads Me, I Will Follow" (Gen.; Rom.)
"My Faith Looks Up to Thee" (Rom.)
"Spirit of Faith, Come Down" (Rom.)
"How Firm a Foundation" (Rom.; John)
"I Know Whom I Have Believed" (Rom.; John)
"Love Divine, All Loves Excelling" (John)
"This Is a Day of New Beginnings" (John)
"Wash, O God, Our Sons and Daughters" (John)

Year B: 1994, 1997, 2000

Genesis 17:1-7, 15-16; Psalm 22:23-31; Romans 4:13-25; Mark 8:31-38 *or* Mark 9:2-9
"Standing on the Promises" (Gen.; Rom.)
"Make Me a Captive, Lord" (Gen.; Rom.; Mark 8:31-38)
"Where He Leads Me, I Will Follow" (Gen.; Rom.; Mark 8:31-38)
"Are Ye Able" (Mark 8:31-38)
"Jesus, I My Cross Have Taken" (Mark 8:31-38)
"Take Up Thy Cross" (Mark 8:31-38)
For hymns related to Mark 9:1-9, see Transfiguration Sunday.

Year C: 1995, 1998, 2001

Genesis 15:1-12, 17-18; Psalm 27; Philippians 3:17–4:1; Luke 13:31-35 *or* Luke 9:28-36
"If Thou But Suffer God to Guide Thee" (Gen.)
"The God of Abraham Praise" ("Praise to the Living God") (Gen.)
"On Jordan's Stormy Banks I Stand" (Phil.)
"Soldiers of Christ, Arise" (Phil.)
"Where Cross the Crowded Ways of Life" (Luke 13:31-35)
For hymns related to Luke 9:28-36, see Transfiguration Sunday.

THIRD SUNDAY IN LENT

Year A: 1993, 1996, 1999

Exodus 17:1-7; Psalm 95; Romans 5:1-11; John 4:5-42
"Come, Thou Fount of Every Blessing" (Exod.)
"Rock of Ages, Cleft for Me" (Exod.; Rom.)
"Alas, and Did My Savior Bleed" (Rom.)
"And Can It Be that I Should Gain" (Rom.)
"How Great Thou Art" (esp. v. 3) (Rom.)
"What Wondrous Love Is This" (Rom.)
"When I Survey the Wondrous Cross" (Rom.)
"Fill My Cup, Lord" (John)
"Glorious Things of Thee Are Spoken" (esp. v. 3) (John)
"Hope of the World" (John)

Year B: 1994, 1997, 2000

Exodus 20:1-17; Psalm 19; I Corinthians 1:18-25; John 2:13-22
"The God of Abraham Praise" ("Praise to the Living God") (Exod.; Ps.)
"Trust and Obey" (Exod.; Ps.)
"Let's Sing unto the Lord" (Ps.)
"Ask Ye What Great Thing I Know" (I Cor.)
"The Old Rugged Cross" (I Cor.)
"O Young and Fearless Prophet" (John)

Year C: 1995, 1998, 2001

Isaiah 55:1-9; Psalm 63:1-8; I Corinthians 10:1-13; Luke 13:1-9
"Come, All of You" (Isa.)
"A Charge to Keep I Have" (I Cor.; Luke)
"My Soul, Be on Thy Guard" (I Cor.; Luke)
"Come, Every Soul by Sin Oppressed" (Luke)

FOURTH SUNDAY IN LENT

Year A: 1993, 1996, 1999

I Samuel 16:1-13; Psalm 23; Ephesians 5:8-14; John 9:1-41
"Hail to the Lord's Anointed" (I Sam.)
"He Leadeth Me" (I Sam.; Ps.)
"The King of Love My Shepherd Is" (Ps.)
"The Lord's My Shepherd, I'll Not Want" (Ps.)
"Awake, O Sleeper" (Eph.)
"Amazing Grace" (John)
"Christ Is the World's Light" (John)
"O for a Thousand Tongues to Sing" (esp. v. 6) (John)
"Open My Eyes That I May See" (John)

Year B: 1994, 1997, 2000

Numbers 21:4-9; Psalm 107:1-3, 17-22; Ephesians 2:1-10; John 3:14-21
"Amazing Grace" *or* "Freely, Freely" (Eph.; John)
"How Great Thou Art" (esp. v. 3) *or* "Let Us Plead for Faith Alone" (Eph.; John)
"Love Divine, All Loves Excelling" (John)
"This Is a Day of New Beginnings" (John)

Year C: 1995, 1998, 2001

Joshua 5:9-12; Psalm 32; II Corinthians 5:16-21; Luke 15:1-3, 11*b*-32
"Love Divine, All Loves Excelling" *or* "O Come and Dwell in Me" (II Cor.)
"Come Back Quickly to the Lord" (Luke)
"Come, Ye Sinners, Poor and Needy" (Luke)
"Rock of Ages, Cleft for Me" (Luke)
"Savior, Like a Shepherd Lead Us" (Luke)
"Softly and Tenderly Jesus Is Calling" (Luke)
"There's a Wideness in God's Mercy" (Luke)

FIFTH SUNDAY IN LENT

Year A: 1993, 1996, 1999

Ezekiel 37:1-14; Psalm 130; Romans 8:6-11; John 11:1-45
"Breathe on Me, Breath of God" *or* "O Spirit of the Living God" (Ezek.)
"Great Spirit, Now I Pray" (Rom.)
"Spirit of Faith, Come Down" (Rom.)
"Spirit of God, Descend Upon My Heart" (Rom.)
"O for a Thousand Tongues to Sing" (esp. v. 5) (Rom.; John)

Year B: 1994, 1997, 2000

Jeremiah 31:31-34; Psalm 51:1-12 *or* Psalm 119:9-16; Hebrews 5:5-10; John 12:20-33
"Give Me a Clean Heart" (Jer.; Ps.)
"Lord, I Want to Be a Christian" (Jer.; Ps.)
"O for a Heart to Praise My God" (Jer.; Ps.)
"Thy Holy Wings, O Savior" (Ps.)
"When I Survey the Wondrous Cross" (Heb.)
"What Wondrous Love Is This" (Heb.; John)
"O Jesus, I Have Promised" (John)
"We Would See Jesus" (John)

Year C: 1995, 1998, 2001

Isaiah 43:16-21; Psalm 126; Philippians 3:4*b*-14; John 12:1-8
"Come, All of You" (Isa.; Ps.)
"Walk On, People of God" (Isa.; Ps.; Phil.)
"Many Gifts, One Spirit" (Isa.; Phil.)
"When I Survey the Wondrous Cross" (Phil.)
"Woman in the Night" (esp. v. 4) (John)

The First Sunday in Lent is of special significance because it is for a great many people the first service of the Lenten Season. Many congregations do not hold Ash Wednesday services, and they need on this Sunday to hear, and respond to, the Ash Wednesday call to repentance and discipline. In congregations in which Ash Wednesday services have been held, the call needs to be repeated on this Sunday clearly enough to be heard by those who did not come on Ash Wednesday, yet subtly enough not to be redundant for those who did.

On this Sunday in all three years, the accounts of Jesus' victory over temptation after forty days in the wilderness point to these themes. In congregations in which persons will present themselves for baptism at Easter, these candidates may be elected or enrolled. This emphasizes the baptismal character of Lent and reminds the faithful that for them the season is one of reexamination that will culminate in the reaffirmation of their faith at Easter. Thus, candidates and those already baptized are joined in a common, though differentiated, Lenten discipline.

On the Second through the Fifth Sundays of Lent, the lessons continue the themes of penitence, baptism, and new life in Christ. Note the number of readings that mention water and thereby point, at least subtly, to baptism.

Note that on the Second Sunday of Lent a choice of Gospels is offered in the lectionary. In the Roman Catholic calendar, Transfiguration is celebrated August 6, which does not usually fall on a Sunday; and the Gospel accounts of the transfiguration are read on the Second Sunday of Lent. In other denominations in which Transfiguration is celebrated on the Last Sunday After Epiphany with a reading of one of the Gospel accounts, other Gospel readings are used on the Second Sunday of Lent.

The Sixth (and Last) Sunday of Lent, Passion/Palm Sunday, is of such importance that it will be the subject of the next section.

Whatever provision a congregation may make for confession and pardon in its year-round Sunday worship, it is especially important that this dimension of worship find ample expression on the Sundays of Lent. Since the proclamation of the Word in this season repeatedly calls us to confession and renewal, there is much to be said for placing the confession and pardon as part of the response to the Word. Confession and pardon are then appropriately followed by the exchange of the peace and, when celebrated, Holy Communion.

This brings us to the crucial place of Holy Communion in the observance of Lent. This is obvious in those churches that have Holy Communion every Sunday, but even churches in which Holy Communion is only an occasional service are almost sure to have it at least once during Lent. A great many congregations celebrate Holy Communion on Ash Wednesday or the First Sunday of Lent. Many others celebrate it on the first Sunday of each month, and either the first Sunday in March or the first Sunday in April, or both, will fall in Lent. Still other congregations are given the opportunity for weekly communion during Lent, even if that is not their practice the rest of the year.

When Holy Communion is celebrated on a Sunday of Lent, it is important to keep the balance between the Lord's Day and Lenten emphases. While it is good that we are recovering the experience of Holy Communion as a joyous celebration of all God's saving work in Christ, the common understanding of communion as solemn and penitential has an important element of truth in it which is appropriately acknowleged in Lent.

The following service shows one way in which Lenten Sunday worship can be ordered, with or without Holy Communion. The Great Thanksgiving given is especially suited to occasions early in Lent, such as Ash Wednesday, the First Sunday of Lent, or the first Sunday in March (if it falls within Lent). The Great Thanksgiving given in the section on Passion/Palm Sunday is also suited to other occasions later in Lent, such as the first Sunday in April (if it falls within Lent) or the early days in Holy Week. The section "Holy Thursday Evening" includes a Great Thanksgiving especially suited to that occasion.

GATHERING   *In silence and meditation.*

GREETING   *See greeting for Ash Wednesday.*

HYMN   *A solemn hymn of praise, without "alleluia."*

PRAYER FOR PURITY

> **Almighty God,**
> **to you all hearts are open, all desires known,**
> **and from you no secrets are hidden.**

**Cleanse the thoughts of our hearts
by the inspiration of your Holy Spirit,
that we may perfectly love you,
and worthily magnify your holy name,
through Christ our Lord.
Amen.**

FIRST LESSON

PSALM

SECOND LESSON

HYMN

GOSPEL

SERMON

RESPONSE TO THE WORD

PRAYERS OF THE PEOPLE OR PASTORAL PRAYER

INVITATION, CONFESSION, AND PARDON

At Holy Communion:
Christ our Lord invites to his table all who love him,
who earnestly repent of their sin
and seek to live in peace with one another.
Therefore, let us confess our sin before God and one another.

At Other Services:

Christ our Lord calls all who love him
earnestly to repent of their sin
and live in peace with one another.
Therefore, let us confess our sin before God and one another.

**Most merciful God,
we confess that we have sinned against you
in thought, word, and deed,
by what we have done, and by what we have left undone.
We have not loved you with our whole heart;
we have not loved our neighbors as ourselves.
We are truly sorry and we humbly repent.
For the sake of your Son Jesus Christ,
have mercy on us and forgive us;
that we may delight in your will,
and walk in your ways,
to the glory of your name.
Amen.** (BCP)

All pray in silence.

Minister to people:
Hear the good news:
"Christ died for us while we were yet sinners;
that proves God's love toward us."
In the name of Jesus Christ, you are forgiven!

People to minister:
In the name of Jesus Christ, you are forgiven!

Minister and people:
Glory to God. Amen.

THE PEACE

Let us offer one another signs of reconciliation and love.

All exchange signs and words of God's peace.

As a forgiven and reconciled people,
let us offer ourselves and our gifts to God.

OFFERING

If Holy Communion is not to be celebrated, the service concludes with a prayer of thanksgiving, the Lord's Prayer, a hymn, and the dismissal with blessing.

GREAT THANKSGIVING

The Lord be with you.

And also with you.

Lift up your hearts.

We lift them to the Lord.

Let us give thanks to the Lord our God.

It is right to give our thanks and praise.

It is right, and a good and joyful thing,
always and everywhere to give thanks to you,
Father Almighty, Creator of heaven and earth.

You brought all things into being and called them good.
From the dust of the earth you formed us into your image
and breathed into us the breath of life.
When we turned away, and our love failed,
your love remained steadfast.
When rain fell upon the earth forty days and forty nights
you bore up the ark on the waters,
saved Noah and his family,
and established an everlasting covenant
with every living creature upon the earth.

When you delivered us from slavery
and made us your covenant people,
you led Moses to your mountain
for forty days and forty nights
and gave us your teachings.
You led us through the wilderness
and fed us manna for forty years
and brought us to the promised land.

When we forsook your covenant,
you led your prophet Elijah to your mountain,
where, as he fasted forty days and forty nights,
he heard your still small voice.

And so, with your people on earth
and all the company of heaven,
we praise your name and join their unending hymn:

Holy, holy, holy Lord, God of power and might,
heaven and earth are full of your glory.
Hosanna in the highest.
Blessed is he who comes in the name of the Lord.
Hosanna in the highest.

Holy are you, and blessed is your Son Jesus Christ.
When you gave him to save us from our sin,
your Spirit led him into the wilderness,
where he fasted forty days and forty nights
in preparation for his ministry.

When he suffered and died on a cross for our sin,
you raised him to life,
presented him alive to the apostles during forty days,
and exalted him at your right hand.
By the baptism of his suffering, death, and resurrection
you gave birth to your church,
delivered us from slavery to sin and death,
and made with us a new covenant by water and the Spirit.

Now, when we your people
prepare for the yearly Paschal feast
of your Son's death and resurrection,
you lead us to repentance for our sin
and the cleansing of our hearts,
that during these forty days of Lent
we may be gifted and graced
to renew the covenant you made with us through Christ.

On the night in which he gave himself up for us
he took bread, gave thanks to you, broke the bread,
gave it to his disciples, and said:

"Take, eat; this is my body which is given for you.
Do this in remembrance of me."

When the supper was over he took the cup,
gave thanks to you, gave it to his disciples, and said;
"Drink from this, all of you;
this is my blood of the new covenant,
poured out for you and for many
for the forgiveness of sins.
Do this, as often as you drink it, in remembrance of me."
And so,
in remembrance of these your mighty acts in Jesus Christ,
we offer ourselves in praise and thanksgiving
as a holy and living sacrifice,
in union with Christ's offering for us,
as we proclaim the mystery of faith.

Christ has died, Christ is risen, Christ will come again.

Pour out your Holy Spirit on us, gathered here,
and on these gifts of bread and wine.
Make them be for us the body and blood of Christ,
that we may be for the world the body of Christ, '
redeemed by his blood.

By your Spirit make us one with Christ,
one with each other,
and one in ministry to all the world,
until Christ comes in final victory
and we feast at his heavenly banquet.

Through your Son Jesus Christ,
with the Holy Spirit in your holy church,
all honor and glory is yours, Almighty Father,
now and for ever.

Amen.

THE LORD'S PRAYER

BREAKING THE BREAD

COMMUNION

PRAYER AFTER COMMUNION

HYMN OR SONG

DISMISSAL WITH BLESSING

D. Passion/Palm Sunday

Preparing the Environment

The Lenten colors and other visuals may be continued into Holy Week, or there may be changes to
set Holy Week apart from the rest of Lent. In some churches the color for Holy Week, beginning with

Passion/Palm Sunday, is a deep hue of red, symbolizing the blood of Christ. All crosses and images may be veiled for Holy Week and no flowers used. Symbols of the passion—crown of thorns, whip, ladder, headboard, sponge, spears, nails, crowing cock, drops of blood, bag of coins—are especially appropriate during Holy Week.

Procession with the Palms

GATHERING

The congregation may gather at a designated place outside the church building or in the fellowship hall or other suitable place. Here palm branches, festive reeds, or green branches are distributed to all, and a brief introduction to the whole service may be given. At the processional hymn, the congregation, musicians, and leaders process into the place of worship.

GREETING   *May be sung by choir and congregation.*

Hosanna to the Son of David, the King of Israel.

Blessed is he who comes in the name of the Lord.
Hosanna in the highest!

OPENING PRAYER

The Lord be with you.

And also with you.

Let us pray: *A brief silence is kept.*
God our hope,
today we joyfully acclaim Jesus our Messiah and King.
Help us to honor him every day
   so we may enjoy his kingship in the new Jerusalem,
where he reigns with you and the Holy Spirit
for ever and ever. **Amen.**

   Or, if a thanksgiving over the palms is used.

The Lord be with you.

And also with you.

Let us give thanks to the Lord our God.

It is right to give our thanks and praise.

We praise and bless you, ever-living God,
   for the acts of love by which you redeem the world
   through Jesus Christ our Lord.
This day he entered the holy city of Jerusalem
   and was proclaimed king
by those who spread their garments and palm branches
   along his way.
Let these branches be for us signs of his victory;

and grant that we who bear them
may always acclaim Jesus Messiah
   by walking the way of his suffering and cross;
   that, dying and rising with him,
we may enter into your kingdom.
Through Jesus Christ, who lives and reigns
   with you and the Holy Spirit, now and forever. **Amen.**

PROCLAMATION OF THE ENTRANCE INTO JERUSALEM

Here is read the Gospel narrative appointed for the year and Psalm 118:1-2, 19-29 (all years), after which the response is said or sung by all, and the procession begins.

Matthew 21:1-11	(Year A: 1993, 1996, 1999)
Mark 11:1-11	(Year B: 1994, 1997, 2000)
Luke 19:28-40	(Year C: 1995, 1998, 2001)

Blessed is he who comes in the name of the Lord!

Hosanna in the highest!

PROCESSIONAL HYMN   "All Glory, Laud, and Honor"
                           "Filled with Excitement"
                           "Hosanna, Loud Hosanna"
                           "Rejoice, Ye Pure in Heart"
                           "Tell Me the Stories of Jesus"
                           "Lift Up Your Heads, Ye Mighty Gates"

Service of the Passion

PRAYER FOR ILLUMINATION   *Congregation remains standing.*

God our Redeemer,
   you sent your Son to be born of a woman
   and to die for us on a cross;
By your Holy Spirit, illumine our lives with your Word
   so, as the Scripture is read and proclaimed this day,
   we may be reconciled and won wholly to your will;
through Jesus Christ our Lord. **Amen.**

FIRST LESSON Isaiah 50:4-9*a*	(All years)
PSALM Psalm 31:9-16	(All years)
SECOND LESSON Philippians 2:5-11	(All years)

A PASSION HYMN

PROCLAMATION OF THE PASSION STORY

Matthew 26:14–27:66 *or* Matthew 27:11-54   (Year A: 1993, 1996, 1999)
Mark 14:1–15:47 *or* Mark 15:1-39 (40-47)   (Year B: 1994, 1997, 2000)
Luke 22:14–23:56 *or* Luke 23:1-49   (Year C: 1995, 1998, 2001)

[SERMON] *See commentary for various modes of proclamation with detailed suggestions.*

Responses and Offerings

CONCERNS AND PRAYERS OF THE PEOPLE

THE PEACE

OFFERING

When Holy Communion is not celebrated, the service concludes with a prayer of thanksgiving, the Lord's Prayer, hymn, and dismissal with blessing.

Thanksgiving and Communion

GREAT THANKSGIVING

The Lord be with you

And also with you.

Lift up your hearts.

We lift them to the Lord.

Let us give thanks to the Lord our God.

It is right to give our thanks and praise.

It is right, and a good and joyful thing,
always and everywhere to give thanks to you,
Father Almighty, Creator of heaven and earth.

In infinite love you made us for yourself;
and when we had fallen into sin
and become subject to evil and death,
your love remained steadfast.
You bid your faithful people cleanse their hearts
and prepare with joy for the Paschal feast;
that, fervent in prayer and works of mercy
and renewed by your Word and sacraments
we may come to the fullness of grace
which you have prepared for those who love you.

And so, with your people on earth
and all the company of heaven,
we praise your name and join their unending hymn:

**Holy, holy, holy Lord, God of power and might,
heaven and earth are full of your glory.
Hosanna in the highest.
Blessed is he who comes in the name of the Lord.
Hosanna in the highest.**

Holy are you, and blessed is your Son Jesus Christ,
whom you sent in the fullness of time to redeem the world.
He emptied himself, taking the form of a servant,
being born in our likeness.

He humbled himself and became obedient unto death,
even death on a cross.
He took upon himself our sin and death and offered himself,
a perfect sacrifice for the sin of the whole world.
By the baptism of his suffering, death, and resurrection
you gave birth to your church,
delivered us from slavery to sin and death,
and made with us a new covenant by water and the Spirit.

On the night in which he gave himself up for us
he took bread, gave thanks to you, broke the bread,
gave it to his disciples, and said:
"Take, eat; this is my body which is given for you.
Do this in remembrance of me."

When the supper was over he took the cup,
gave thanks to you, gave it to his disciples, and said:
"Drink from this, all of you;
this is my blood of the new covenant,
poured out for you and for many
for the forgiveness of sins.
Do this, as often as you drink it, in remembrance of me."

And so,
in remembrance of these your mighty acts in Jesus Christ,
we offer ourselves in praise and thanksgiving.
as a holy and living sacrifice,
in union with Christ's offering for us,
as we proclaim the mystery of faith.

Christ has died, Christ is risen, Christ will come again.

Pour out your Holy Spirit on us, gathered here,
and on these gifts of bread and wine.
Make them be for us the body and blood of Christ,
that we may be for the world the body of Christ,
redeemed by his blood.

By your Spirit make us one with Christ,
one with each other,

and one in ministry to all the world,
until Christ comes in final victory
and we feast at his heavenly banquet.

Through your Son Jesus Christ,
with the Holy Spirit in your holy church,
all honor and glory is yours, Almighty Father,
now and for ever.

Amen.

THE LORD'S PRAYER

BREAKING OF BREAD

COMMUNION

Choir and congregation may sing the following and/or suitable hymns during communion.

Lamb of God, you take away the sins of the world.
   Have mercy on us.
Lamb of God, you take away the sins of the world.
   Have mercy on us.
Lamb of God, you take away the sins of the world.
   Grant us peace.

or

Jesus, Lamb of God,
   have mercy on us.
Jesus, bearer of our sins,
   have mercy on us.
Jesus, redeemer of the world,
   give us your peace.

PRAYER AFTER COMMUNION

Lord,
we give you thanks for satisfying our hungry hearts
with this holy meal shared in the Spirit with your Son;
as his death brings us life and hope,
so may his resurrection lead us to salvation.
This we ask through Jesus Christ our Lord. **Amen.**

HYMN

DISMISSAL WITH BLESSING

May Jesus Christ, the bread of heaven broken for all,
   bless you and keep you.

Amen.

May the Lamb of God, who takes away the sins of the world,
   heal and restore you.

Amen.

May the Lord God order all your days and deeds in peace.

Amen.

Go in love to serve God and your neighbor in all things.

Amen. Thanks be to God.

Commentary

The church's worship on this day is inherently dramatic. It provides us with many possibilities for proclaiming the Word of God and entering fully into the events recalled this day. The proclamatory readings and the presentation of the narrative of our Lord's passion is the heart of the service of the Word. We experience more Scripture in public worship today than on almost any other occasion of the year.

This is one reason why Passion/Palm Sunday is not a particularly suitable day for celebrating baptism, confirmation, or the reception of new members. It is strongly advised that baptisms and confirmations (first renewal of baptismal vows) be celebrated during the Easter Vigil, the First Service of Easter, or on any of the Sundays during the season of the Great Fifty Days between Easter and Pentecost.

The structure of this service is simple, focusing in four principal sections: the procession with the palms, the celebration of the Word of God (passion), responses and offerings, and the sacrament of the Lord's Supper. Though many Protestant congregations have not celebrated communion on this day in the recent past, it is to be encouraged, since this is a natural completion of the whole narrative flow of the Word, of God, hence, the completion of our participation in the salvation wrought by Christ's passion, death, and resurrection. Congregations should be made aware that on this occasion, the service may be longer than on a usual Lord's Day.

Passion/Palm Sunday is a day of contrasts. In the first part we experience the joyous demonstration of loyalty to Jesus, who comes in the name of the Lord. The music for gathering may be festive. Yet the shouts of Hosanna are under a shadow cast by the crucifixion to come. The service should embody the sharp contrasts of the week ahead. Indeed, it should enable the congregation to recognize the contrasts within the whole Lenten journey that culminates in the mystery of Christ's dying and rising. We encounter anew the ambiguity of our own participation in the triumphal entry and the passion of our Lord. Thus the music, which may include use of brass or other instruments, must reflect this range of theme. If the organ is used, the gathering place may be within hearing through the open doors of the church building. A choir is very helpful in the opening section of the service. Where a procession starts from a considerable distance, a short response may be sung along the way by all.

Increasingly, congregations are exploring the following possibility: When weather and circumstances permit, the people gather outside or in a hall or assembly room other than the usual worship area. At an appointed time the celebrant or other designated person welcomes the people and gives a brief introduction to the whole service. The various musical responses may be learned at this time, the palms distributed, and necessary instructions given. In this case the introduction precedes the responsory greeting, which should be sung if possible. This in turn may become the refrain sung in response to the proclamation of the entrance into Jerusalem and, if needed, in procession to the entrance of the church building where the hymn is begun.

If it is not possible to have a procession from outside the place of worship, the congregation may gather in the worship area and conduct the procession carrying palms, with the choir and perhaps a representative group of children and families. This may be easily done with such a group (or the whole congregation) moving around the outside aisles and back to their appointed seats, while the ministers and the choir move into their places. In either case palms or green branches should be distributed to all and may be held and spontaneously waved during the entrance hymn.

In the second section of the service—the celebration of the Word of God—the focus is intensely on the proclamation of the Scriptures, principally the passion narrative appointed for the year. Particular care should be taken to help the people understand this aspect of worship and to explore various ways in which the dramatic qualities of the Word may be brought to light.

Many persons have asked why the new calendar and lectionary now shared by historic Christian traditions have combined Passion and Palm Sunday into one and have suggested such an extensive amount of Scripture. To understand why this has been done, one must first recognize that the passion story is a highly dramatic and unified whole and is absolutely central to each of the Gospels. It demands to be heard in its wholeness, rather than in small bits and pieces. To focus on this story one Sunday and then on the following Sunday to back up to the entry of Jesus into Jerusalem breaks the unity of the whole sweep of events from the triumphal entry through the passion and crucifixion to the resurrection. (From the beginning of their written form, each of the four Gospels contained the passion as a continuous narrative. These narratives are quite different in form from the rest of the materials in the Gospels that were handed down in various collections of oral traditions. The center point of the Gospel accounts is preserved in the church's proclamatory reading of these narratives in their fullness.)

There is also a pastoral reality to face. Most persons in church on Passion/Palm Sunday will not be there again until Easter Day. To go abruptly from the lesser joy of the entry into Jerusalem to the joy of Easter, without being addressed by the passion and the cross of our Lord, is to impoverish our experience of the gospel. There is no crown and triumph without the suffering and the cross.

How can such a long passage of Scripture be included without unduly lengthening the service and rendering it monotonous? It is essential to envision the telling of the story itself as a proclamation. There is no need to read the whole account and then to preach a full sermon as well. Here are four basic possibilities.

1. The Scripture can be read by the minister and other readers, with brief interpretive comments before, during, or following the reading. Of particular interest is *A Liturgical Interpretation of Our Lord's Passion in Narrative Form,* by John T. Townsend, included in the service of Tenebrae on page 170, for both study and use. The reading of the passion may be accompanied by silent mime or by dramatization of certain key scenes by a group of players. Here as elsewhere, careful preparation and a well-disciplined, understated presentation is crucial.

2. More effectively, the passion account may be read or sung by laypersons. Specific roles are designated: narrator, Jesus, Pilate, the apostles, other characters, and the crowd. As few as three persons are required if all the voices except the narrator and Jesus are spoken by one person. If members of the congregation are provided a text, or proper cues, they can take the role of the crowd. The choir may also take this role. In the following pages, texts from the three Synoptic Gospels are divided for easy dramatic presentation.

Positioning is important. The narrator may use the pulpit, and the remaining readers may be clustered in groups at reading stands. Audibility is absolutely crucial. The readers should be well rehearsed and, where necessary, should be amplified. Microphones and electronic hardware should not, however, clutter the worship space. The movement as well as the positioning of the readers should be carefully planned.

3. The passion narrative may also be sung by the choir. While one of the traditional settings, such as J. S. Bach's, would be far too long, there are many shorter choral settings available. Selections from the larger works may be woven together with dramatized readings as well. Advanced planning

and rehearsal are essential, as is wise choice in the level of difficulty of the music. It is better to offer something simple that is done well than something beyond the capacity of the choir.

4. Another possibility is a lessons-and-hymns pattern similar to the lessons and carols that many churches use at Christmastime for special services. Here are some suggestions for the three yearly cycles of readings:

Year A: Isaiah 50:4-9*a*
              Sung Psalter (Ps. 31:9-16) or anthem
              Philippians 2:5-11
              Hymn: "All Praise to Thee, for Thou, O King Divine"
                      or "At the Name of Jesus"
                      or "Creator of the Stars of Night"
              Matthew 26:14-29
              Hymn: "According to Thy Gracious Word"
                      or "O Master, Let Me Walk with Thee"
                      or "Are Ye Able"
              Matthew 26:30-56
              Hymn: "In the Hour of Trial"
                      or "'Tis Midnight, and on Olive's Brow"
                      or "Go to Dark Gethsemane"
              Matthew 26:57-75
              Hymn: "Sinners, Turn: Why Will You Die"
                      or "Ah, Holy Jesus"
                      or "O Sacred Head, Now Wounded"
              Matthew 27:1-23
              Hymn: "Sinners, Turn: Why Will You Die"
                      or "There Is a Green Hill Far Away"
                      or "Alas! and Did My Savior Bleed"
                      or "Cross of Jesus, Cross of Sorrow"
                      or "What Wondrous Love Is This"
              Matthew 27:24-50
              Hymn: "O Sacred Head, Now Wounded"
                      or "O Love Divine, What Hast Thou Done"
                      or "'Tis Finished! The Messiah Dies"
              Matthew 27:51-66
              Hymn: "Behold the Savior of Mankind"
                      or "Never Further Than Thy Cross"
                      or "When I Survey the Wondrous Cross"

Year B: Isaiah 50:4-9*a*
              Sung Psalter (Ps. 31:9-16) or anthem
              Philippians 2:5-11
              Hymn: "All Praise to Thee, for Thou, O King Divine"
                      or "At the Name of Jesus"
                      or "Take the Name of Jesus with You"
              Mark 14:1-25
              Hymn: "According to Thy Gracious Word"
                      or "Are Ye Able"
                      or "O Master, Let Me Walk with Thee"

Mark 14:26-50
Hymn: "In the Hour of Trial"
or " 'Tis Midnight, and on Olive's Brow"
or "Go to Dark Gethsemane"
Mark 14:53-72
Hymn: "Sinners, Turn: Why Will You Die"
or "Ah, Holy Jesus"
or "O Sacred Head, Now Wounded"
Mark 15:1-15
Hymn: "Sinners, Turn: Why Will You Die"
or "There Is a Green Hill Far Away"
or "Alas! and Did My Savior Bleed"
or "Cross of Jesus, Cross of Sorrow"
or "What Wondrous Love Is This"
Mark 15:16-39
Hymn: "O Sacred Head, Now Wounded"
or "O Love Divine, What Hast Thou Done"
or "'Tis Finished! The Messiah Dies"
Mark 15:40-47
Hymn: "Behold the Savior of Mankind"
or "Never Further Than Thy Cross"
or "When I Survey the Wondrous Cross"

Year C: Isaiah 50:4-9a
Sung Psalter (Ps. 31:9-16) or anthem
Philippians 2:5-11
Hymn: "All Praise to Thee, for Thou, O King Divine"
or "At the Name of Jesus"
or "Creator of the Stars of Night"
Luke 22:14-30 or 14-23
Hymn: "According to Thy Gracious Word"
or "Are Ye Able"
or "O Master, Let Me Walk with Thee"
Luke 22:31-62 or 39-48, 54-62
Hymn: "In the Hour of Trial"
or "'Tis Midnight, and on Olive's Brow"
or "Go to Dark Gethsemane"
Luke 22:63–23:25 or 23:1-5, 13-25
Hymn: "Ah, Holy Jesus"
or "O Sacred Head, Now Wounded"
Luke 23:26-43
Hymn: "There Is a Green Hill Far Away"
or "Alas! and Did My Savior Bleed"
or "Beneath the Cross of Jesus"
Luke 23:44-56
Hymn: "'Tis Midnight, and on Olive's Brow"
or "When I Survey the Wondrous Cross"
or "Were You There?"

There will be a few situations when it may be necessary to preach a full sermon and to shorten the reading of the passion narrative. In this case a selected section upon which the sermon is based may be read. If this is done, it is strongly urged that the other portions of the story be read sometime during the next days of Holy Week. This may be possible on Sunday evening where evening services are the custom. Passion/Palm Sunday evening presents a number of possibilities, especially along the patterns developed above in 2 and 4. Note also the suggestions for using the passion narrative during Monday, Tuesday, and Wednesday services, mentioned in the next section. Other translations may, of course, be used, and will be divided according to the pattern that follows for each of the three years.

The Passion Narratives for the Three Years

Year A:..1993, 1996, 1999
Full form:.. Matthew 26:14–27:66
[Short form:..Matthew 27:11-54]

The symbols in the margin represent the following: N–narrator, †–Christ, S–speakers other than Christ (these may be subdivided into male and female individual speakers, indicated by S₁, S₂, S₃, and Sps), C–the crowd.

N Then one of the twelve, who was called Judas Iscariot, went to the chief priests and said,

S₁ "What will you give me if I deliver him to you?"

N And they paid him thirty pieces of silver. And from that moment he sought an opportunity to betray him.
   Now on the first day of Unleavened Bread the disciples came to Jesus, saying,

Sps "Where will you have us prepare for you to eat the passover?"

N He said,

† "Go into the city to a certain one, and say to him, 'The Teacher says, My time is at hand; I will keep the passover at your house with my disciples.' "

N And the disciples did as Jesus had directed them, and they prepared the passover.
   When it was evening, he sat at table with the twelve disciples; and as they were eating, he said,

† "Truly, I say to you, one of you will betray me."

N And they were very sorrowful, and began to say to him one after another,

S₂₍₃₎ "Is it I, Lord?" *(May be repeated.)*

N He answered,

† "He who has dipped his hand in the dish with me, will betray me. The Son of man goes as it is written of him, but woe to that man by whom the Son of man is betrayed! It would have been better for that man if he had not been born."

N Judas, who betrayed him, said,

S₁ "Is it I, master?"

N He said to him,

†   "You have said so."

N   Now as they were eating, Jesus took bread, and blessed, and broke it, and gave it to the disciples and said,

†   "Take, eat; this is my body."

N   And he took the cup, and when he had given thanks he gave it to them, saying,

†   "Drink of it, all of you; for this is my blood of the covenant, which is poured out for many for the forgiveness of sins. I tell you I shall not drink again of this fruit of the vine until that day when I drink it new with you in my Father's kingdom."

N   And when they had sung a hymn, they went out to the Mount of Olives. Then Jesus said to them:

†   "You will all fall away because of me this night; for it is written, 'I will strike the shepherd, and the sheep of the flock will be scattered.' But after I am raised up, I will go before you to Galilee."

N   Peter declared to him,

S_2 "Though they all fall away because of you, I will never fall away."

N   Jesus said to him,

†   "Truly, I say to you, this very night, before the cock crows, you will deny me three times."

N   Peter said to him,

S_2 "Even if I must die with you, I will not deny you."

N   And so said all the disciples.
        Then Jesus went with them to a place called Gethsemane, and he said to his disciples,

†   "Sit here, while I go yonder and pray."

N   And taking with him Peter and the two sons of Zebedee, he began to be sorrowful and troubled. Then he said to them,

†   "My soul is very sorrowful, even to death; remain here, and watch with me."

N   And going a little farther he fell on his face and prayed,

†   "My Father, if it be possible, let this cup pass from me; nevertheless, not as I will, but as thou wilt."

N   And he came to the disciples and found them sleeping; and he said to Peter,

†   "So, could you not watch with me one hour? Watch and pray that you may not enter into temptation; the spirit indeed is willing, but the flesh is weak."

N   Again, for the second time, he went away and prayed,

†   "My Father, if this cannot pass unless I drink it, thy will be done."

N   And again he came and found them sleeping, for their eyes were heavy. So, leaving them again, he went away and prayed for the third time, saying the same words. Then he came to the disciples and said to them,

†   "Are you still sleeping and taking your rest? Behold, the hour is at hand, and the Son of man is betrayed into the hands of sinners. Rise, let us be going; see, my betrayer is at hand."

N   While he was still speaking, Judas came, one of the twelve, and with him a great crowd with swords and clubs, from the chief priests and the elders of the people. Now the betrayer had given them a sign, saying,

S₁   "The one I shall kiss is the man; seize him."

N   And he came up to Jesus at once and said,

S₁   "Hail, Master!"

N   And he kissed him. Jesus said to him,

†   "Friend, why are you here?"

N   Then they came up and laid hands on Jesus and seized him. And behold, one of those who were with Jesus stretched out his hand and drew his sword, and struck the slave of the high priest, and cut off his ear. Then Jesus said to him,

†   "Put your sword back into its place; for all who take the sword will perish by the sword. Do you think that I cannot appeal to my Father, and he will at once send me more than twelve legions of angels? But how then should the Scriptures be fulfilled, that it must be so?"

N   At that hour Jesus said to the crowds,

†   "Have you come out as against a robber, with swords and clubs to capture me? Day after day I sat in the temple teaching, and you did not seize me. But all this has taken place, that the Scriptures of the prophets might be fulfilled."

N   Then all the disciples forsook him and fled.

Then those who had seized Jesus led him to Caiaphas the high priest, where the scribes and the elders had gathered. But Peter followed him at a distance, as far as the courtyard of the high priest, and going inside he sat with the guards to see the end. Now the chief priests and the whole council sought false testimony against Jesus that they might put him to death, but they found none, though many false witnesses came forward. At last two came forward and said,

S₃   "This fellow said 'I am able to destroy the temple of God, and to build it in three days.' "

N   And the high priest stood up and said,

S₄   "Have you no answer to make? What is it that these men testify against you?"

N   But Jesus was silent. And the high priest said to him,

S₄   "I adjure you by the living God, tell us if you are the Christ, the Son of God."

N   Jesus said to him,

† "You have said so. But I tell you, hereafter you will see the Son of man seated at the right hand of Power, and coming on the clouds of heaven."

N Then the high priest tore his robes, and said,

S₄ "He has uttered blasphemy. Why do we still need witnesses? You have now heard his blasphemy. What is your judgment?"

N They answered,

C "He deserves death."

N Then they spat in his face, and struck him; and some slapped him, saying,

C "Prophesy to us, you Christ! Who is it that struck you?"

N Now Peter was sitting outside in the courtyard. And a maid came up to him, and said,

S₅ "You also were with the Galilean."

N But he denied it before them all, saying,

S₂ "I do not know what you mean."

N And when he went out to the porch, another maid saw him, and she said to the bystanders,

S₅ "This man was with Jesus of Nazareth."

N And again he denied it with an oath,

S₂ "I do not know the men."

N After a little while the bystanders came up and said to Peter,

C "Certainly you are also one of them, for your accent betrays you."

N Then he began to invoke a curse on himself and to swear,

S₂ "I do not know the man."

N And immediately the cock crowed. And Peter remembered the saying of Jesus, "Before the cock crows, you will deny me three times." And he went out and wept bitterly.

When morning came, all the chief priests and the elders of the people took counsel against Jesus to put him to death; and they bound him and led him away and delivered him to Pilate the governor.
When Judas, his betrayer, saw that he was condemned, he repented and brought back the thirty pieces of silver to the chief priests and the elders, saying,

S₁ "I have sinned in betraying innocent blood."

N They said,

Sps "What is that to us? See to it yourself."

N And throwing down the pieces of silver in the temple, he departed; and he went and hanged himself. But the chief priests, taking the pieces of silver, said,

Sps   "It is not lawful to put them into the treasury, since they are blood money."

N   So they took counsel, and bought with them the potter's field, to bury strangers in. Therefore that field has been called the Field of Blood to this day. Then was fulfilled what had been spoken by the prophet Jeremiah, saying, "And they took the thirty pieces of silver, the price of him on whom a price had been set by some of the sons of Israel, and they gave them for the potter's field, as the Lord directed me."

Short form begins.
Now Jesus stood before the governor; and the governor asked him,

S₆   "Are you the King of the Jews?"

N   Jesus said to him,

†   "You have said so."

N   But when he was accused by the chief priests and elders, he made no answer. Then Pilate said to him,

S₆   "Do you not hear how many things they testify against you?"

N   But he gave no answer, not even to a single charge; so that the governor wondered greatly.
   Now at the feast the governor was accustomed to release for the crowd any one prisoner whom they wanted. And they had then a notorious prisoner, called Barabbas. So when they had gathered, Pilate said to them,

S₆   "Whom do you want me to release for you, Barabbas or Jesus who is called Christ?"

N   For he knew that it was out of envy that they had delivered him up. Besides, while he was sitting on the judgment seat, his wife sent word to him,

S₇   "Have nothing to do with that righteous man, for I have suffered much over him today in a dream."

N   Now the chief priests and the elders persuaded the people to ask for Barabbas and destroy Jesus. The governor again said to them,

S₆   "Which of the two do you want me to release for you?"

N   And they said,

C   "Barabbas."

N   Pilate said to them,

S₆   "Then what shall I do with Jesus who is called Christ?"

N   They all said,

C   "Let him be crucified."

N   And he said,

S₆   "Why, what evil has he done?"

N   But they shouted all the more,

C   "Let him be crucified!"

N   So when Pilate saw that he was gaining nothing, but rather that a riot was beginning, he took water and washed his hands before the crowd, saying,

S₆   "I am innocent of this man's blood; see to it yourselves."

N   Then he released for them Barabbas, and having scourged Jesus, delivered him to be crucified.
    Then the soldiers of the governor took Jesus into the praetorium, and they gathered the whole battalion before him. And they stripped him and put a scarlet robe upon him, and plaiting a crown of thorns they put it on his head, and put a reed in his right hand. And kneeling before him they mocked him, saying,

C   "Hail, King of the Jews!"

N   And they spat upon him, and took the reed and struck him on the head. And when they had mocked him, they stripped him of the robe, and put his own clothes on him, and led him away to crucify him.
    As they went out, they came upon a man of Cyrene, Simon by name; this man they compelled to carry his cross. And when they came to a place called Golgotha (which means the place of a skull), they offered him wine to drink, mingled with gall; but when he tasted it, he would not drink it. And when they had crucified him, they divided his garments among them by casting lots; then they sat down and kept watch over him there. And over his head they put the charge against him, which read, "This is Jesus the King of the Jews." Then two robbers were crucified with him, one on the right and one on the left. And those who passed by derided him, wagging their heads and saying,

C   "You who would destroy the temple and build it in three days, save yourself! If you are the Son of God, come down from the cross."

N   So also the chief priests, with the scribes and elders, mocked him, saying,

Sps   "He saved others; he cannot save himself. He is the King of Israel; let him come down now from the cross, and we will believe in him. He trusts in God; let God deliver him now, if he desires him; for he said, 'I am the Son of God.' "

N   And the robbers who were crucified with him also reviled him in the same way.
    Now from the sixth hour there was darkness over all the land until the ninth hour. And about the ninth hour Jesus cried with a loud voice,

†   "Eli, Eli lama sabach-tha'ni?"

N   that is,

†   "My God, my God, why hast thou forsaken me?"

N   And some of the bystanders hearing it said,

Sps   "This man is calling Elijah."

N   And one of them at once ran and took a sponge, filled it with vinegar, and put it on a reed, and gave it to him to drink. But the others said,

Sps   "Wait, let us see whether Elijah will come to save him."

N   And Jesus cried again with a loud voice and yielded up his spirit.

A brief pause.

And behold, the curtain of the temple was torn in two, from top to bottom; and the earth shook, and the rocks were split; the tombs also were opened, and many bodies of the saints who had fallen asleep were raised, and coming out of the tombs after his resurrection they went into the holy city and appeared to many. When the centurion and those who were with him, keeping watch over Jesus, saw the earthquake and what took place, they were filled with awe, and said,

Sps   "Truly this was the Son of God!"

Short form ends.

N   There were also many women there, looking on from afar, who had followed Jesus from Galilee, ministering to him; among whom were Mary Magdalene, and Mary the mother of James and Joseph, and the mother of the sons of Zebedee.

When it was evening, there came a rich man from Arimathea, named Joseph, who also was a disciple of Jesus. He went to Pilate and asked for the body of Jesus. Then Pilate ordered it to be given to him. And Joseph took the body, and wrapped it in a clean linen shroud, and laid it in his own new tomb, which he had hewn in the rock; and he rolled a great stone to the door of the tomb, and departed. Mary Magdalene and the other Mary were there, sitting opposite the sepulchre.

Next day, that is, after the day of Preparation, the chief priests and the Pharisees gathered before Pilate and said,

Sps   "Sir, we remember how that imposter said, while he was still alive, 'After three days I will rise again.' Therefore order the sepulchre to be made secure until the third day, lest his disciples go and steal him away, and tell the people, 'He has risen from the dead,' and the last fraud will be worse than the first."

N   Pilate said to them,

S_6 "You have a guard of soldiers; go, make it as secure as you can."

N   So they went and made the sepulchre secure by sealing the stone and setting a guard.

Year B:...	1994, 1997, 2000
Full form:..	Mark 14:1–15:47
[Short form:..	Mark 15:1-39]

The symbols in the margin represent the following: N–narrator, †–Christ, S–speakers other than Christ (these may be subdivided into male and female individual speakers, indicated by S_1, S_2, S_3, and Sps), C–the crowd.

N   It was now two days before the Passover and the feast of Unleavened Bread. And the chief priests and the scribes were seeking how to arrest him by stealth, and kill him; for they said,

Sps   "Not during the feast, lest there be a tumult of the people."

N   And while he was at Bethany in the house of Simon the leper, as he sat at table, a woman came with an alabaster flask of ointment of pure nard, very costly, and she broke the flask and poured it over his head. But there were some who said to themselves indignantly,

Sps   "Why was the ointment thus wasted? For this ointment might have been sold for more than three hundred denarii, and given to the poor."

N   And they reproached her. But Jesus said,

†   "Let her alone; why do you trouble her? She has done a beautiful thing to me. For you always have the poor with you, and whenever you will, you can do good to them; but you will not always have me. She has done what she could; she has anointed my body beforehand for burying. And truly, I say to you, wherever the gospel is preached in the whole world, what she has done will be told in memory of her."

N   Then Judas Iscariot, who was one of the twelve, went to the chief priests in order to betray him to them. And when they heard it they were glad, and promised to give him money. And he sought an opportunity to betray him.

    And on the first day of Unleavened Bread, when they sacrificed the passover lamb, his disciples said to him,

Sps   "Where will you have us go and prepare for you to eat the passover?"

N   And he sent two of his disciples, and said to them,

†   "Go into the city, and a man carrying a jar of water will meet you; follow him, and wherever he enters, say to the householder, 'The Teacher says, Where is my guest room, where I am to eat the passover with my disciples?' And he will show you a large upper room furnished and ready; there prepare for us."

N   And the disciples set out and went to the city, and found it as he had told them; and they prepared the passover.

    And when it was evening he came with the twelve. And as they were at table eating, Jesus said,

†   "Truly, I say to you, one of you will betray me, one who is eating with me."

N   They began to be sorrowful, and to say to him one after another,

Sps   "Is it I?" *(May be repeated.)*

N   He said to them,

†   "It is one of the twelve, one who is dipping bread in the same dish with me. For the Son of man goes as it is written of him, but woe to that man by whom the Son of man is betrayed! It would have been better for that man if he had not been born."

N   And as they were eating, he took bread, and blessed, and broke it, and gave it to them, and said,

†   "Take; this is my body."

N   And he took a cup, and when he had given thanks he gave it to them, and they all drank of it. And he said to them,

†   "This is my blood of the covenant, which is poured out for many. Truly, I say to you, I shall not drink again of the fruit of the vine until that day when I drink it new in the kingdom of God."

N And when they had sung a hymn, they went out to the Mount of Olives. And Jesus said to them,

† "You will all fall away; for it is written, 'I will strike the shepherd, and the sheep will be scattered.' But after I am raised up, I will go before you to Galilee."

N Peter said to him,

S₁ "Even though they all fall away, I will not."

N And Jesus said to him,

† "Truly, I say to you, this very night, before the cock crows twice, you will deny me three times."

N But he said vehemently,

S₁ "If I must die with you, I will not deny you."

N And they all said the same.
   And they went to a place which was called Gethsemane; and he said to his disciples,

† "Sit here, while I pray."

N And he took with him Peter and James and John, and began to be greatly distressed and troubled. And he said to them,

† "My soul is very sorrowful, even to death; remain here, and watch."

N And going a little farther, he fell on the ground and prayed that, if it were possible, the hour might pass from him. And he said,

† "Abba, Father, all things are possible to thee; remove this cup from me; yet not what I will, but what thou wilt."

N And he came and found them sleeping, and he said to Peter,

† "Simon, are you asleep? Could you not watch one hour? Watch and pray that you may not enter into temptation; the spirit indeed is willing, but the flesh is weak."

N And again he went away and prayed, saying the same words. And again he came and found them sleeping, for their eyes were very heavy; and they did not know what to answer him. And he came the third time, and said to them,

† "Are you still sleeping and taking your rest? It is enough; the hour has come; the Son of man is betrayed into the hands of sinners. Rise, let us be going; see, my betrayer is at hand."

N And immediately, while he was still speaking, Judas came, one of the twelve, and with him a crowd with swords and clubs, from the chief priests and the scribes and the elders. Now the betrayer had given them a sign, saying,

S₂ "The one I shall kiss is the man; seize him and lead him away under guard."

N And when he came, he went up to him at once, and said,

S₂ "Master!"

N   And he kissed him. And they laid hands on him and seized him. But one of those who stood by drew his sword, and struck the slave of the high priest and cut off his ear. And Jesus said to them,

†   "Have you come out as against a robber, with swords and clubs to capture me? Day after day I was with you in the temple teaching, and you did not seize me. But let the scriptures be fulfilled."

N   And they all forsook him, and fled.

       And a young man followed him, with nothing but a linen cloth about his body; and they seized him, but he left the linen cloth and ran away naked.

       And they led Jesus to the high priest; and all the chief priests and the elders and the scribes were assembled. And Peter had followed him at a distance, right into the courtyard of the high priest; and he was sitting with the guards, and warming himself at the fire. Now the chief priests and the whole council sought testimony against Jesus to put him to death; but they found none. For many bore false witness against him, and their witness did not agree. And some stood up and bore false witness against him, saying,

Sps   "We heard him say, 'I will destroy this temple that is made with hands, and in three days I will build another, not made with hands.'"

N   Yet not even so did their testimony agree. And the high priest stood up in the midst, and asked Jesus,

S₃   "Have you no answer to make? What is it that these men testify against you?"

N   But he was silent and made no answer. Again the high priest asked him,

S₃   "Are you the Christ, the Son of the Blessed?"

N   And Jesus said,

†   "I am; and you will see the Son of man seated at the right hand of Power, and coming with the clouds of heaven."

N   And the high priest tore his garments, and said,

S₃   "Why do we still need witnesses! You have heard his blasphemy. What is your decision?"

N   And they all condemned him as deserving death. And some began to spit on him, and to cover his face, and to strike him, saying to him,

Sps   "Prophesy!"

N   And the guards received him with blows.

       And as Peter was below in the courtyard, one of the maids of the high priest came: and seeing Peter warming himself, she looked at him, and said,

S₄   "You also were with the Nazarene, Jesus."

N   But he denied it, saying,

S₁   "I neither know nor understand what you mean."

N   And he went out into the gateway. And the maid saw him, and began to say to the bystanders,

S₄ "This man is one of them."

N But again he denied it. And after a little while again the bystanders said to Peter,

Sps "Certainly you are one of them; for you are a Galilean."

N But he began to invoke a curse on himself and to swear,

S₁ "I do not know this man of whom you speak."

N And immediately the cock crowed a second time. And Peter remembered how Jesus had said to him, "Before the cock crows twice, you will deny me three times." And he broke down and wept.

Short form begins.

And as soon as it was morning the chief priests, with the elders and scribes, and the whole council held a consultation; and they bound Jesus and led him away and delivered him to Pilate. And Pilate asked him,

S₅ "Are you the King of the Jews?"

N And he answered him,

† "You have said so."

N And the chief priests accused him of many things. And Pilate again asked him,

S₅ "Have you no answer to make? See how many charges they bring against you."

N But Jesus made no further answer, so that Pilate wondered.
   Now at the feast he used to release for them one prisoner for whom they asked. And among the rebels in prison, who had committed murder in the insurrection, there was a man called Barabbas. And the crowd came up and began to ask Pilate to do as he was wont to do for them. And he answered them,

S₅ "Do you want me to release for you the King of the Jews?"

N For he perceived that it was out of envy that the chief priests had delivered him up. But the chief priests stirred up the crowd to have him release for them Barabbas instead. And Pilate again said to them,

S₅ "Then what shall I do with the man whom you call the King of the Jews?"

N And they cried out again,

C "Crucify him."

N So Pilate, wishing to satisfy the crowd, released for them Barabbas; and having scourged Jesus, he delivered him to be crucified.
   And the soldiers led him away inside the palace (that is, the praetorium); and they called together the whole battalion. And they clothed him in a purple cloak, and plaiting a crown of thorns they put it on him. And they began to salute him,

Sps "Hail, King of the Jews!"

N   And they struck his head with a reed, and spat upon him, and they knelt down in homage to him. And when they had mocked him, they stripped him of the purple cloak, and put his own clothes on him. And they led him out to crucify him.

And they compelled a passer-by, Simon of Cyrene, who was coming in from the country, the father of Alexander and Rufus, to carry his cross. And they brought him to the place called Golgotha (which means the place of a skull). And they offered him wine mingled with myrrh; but he did not take it. And they crucified him, and divided his garments among them, casting lots for them, to decide what each should take. And it was the third hour, when they crucified him. And the inscription of the charge against him read, "The King of the Jews." And with him they crucified two robbers, one on his right and one on his left. And those who passed by derided him, wagging their heads, and saying,

C   "Aha! You who would destroy the temple and build it in three days, save yourself, and come down from the cross!"

N   So also the chief priests mocked him to one another with the scribes, saying,

Sps   "He saved others; he cannot save himself. Let the Christ, the King of Israel, come down now from the cross, that we may see and believe."

N   Those who were crucified with him also reviled him.

And when the sixth hour had come, there was darkness over the whole land until the ninth hour. And at the ninth hour Jesus cried with a loud voice,

†   "Eloi, Eloi, lama sabach-tha'ni?"

N   which means,

†   "My God, my God, why hast thou forsaken me?

N   And some of the bystanders hearing it said,

Sps   "Behold, he is calling Elijah."

N   And one ran and, filling a sponge full of vinegar, put it on a reed and gave it to him to drink, saying,

S₆   "Wait, let us see whether Elijah will come to take him down."

N   And Jesus uttered a loud cry, and breathed his last. And the curtain of the temple was torn in two, from top to bottom. And when the centurion, who stood facing him, saw that he thus breathed his last, he said,

S₇   "Truly this man was the Son of God!"

Short form ends.

N   There were also women looking on from afar, among whom were Mary Magdalene, and Mary the mother of James the younger and of Joses, and Salome, who, when he was in Galilee, followed him, and ministered to him; and also many other women who came up with him to Jerusalem.

And when evening had come, since it was the day of Preparation, that is, the day before the sabbath, Joseph of Arimathea, a respected member of the council, who was also himself looking for the kingdom of God, took courage and went to Pilate, and asked for the body of Jesus. And Pilate wondered if he were already dead; and summoning the centurion, he asked him whether he was already dead. And when he learned from the centurion that he was dead, he granted the body to Joseph. And he bought a linen shroud, and taking him down, wrapped him in the linen shroud, and laid him in a tomb which had been hewn out of the rock; and he rolled a stone against the door of the tomb. Mary Magdalene and Mary the mother of Joses saw where he was laid.

> Year C:... 1995, 1998, 2001
> Full form:...Luke 22:14–23:56
> [Short form:... Luke 23:1-49]

The symbols in the margin represent the following: N–narrator, †–Christ, S–speakers other than Christ (these may be subdivided into male and female individual speakers, indicated by S₁, S₂, S₃, and Sps), C–the crowd.

N   And when the hour came, he sat at table, and the apostles with him. And he said to them,

†   "I have earnestly desired to eat this passover with you before I suffer; for I tell you I shall not eat it until it is fulfilled in the kingdom of God."

N   And he took a cup, and when he had given thanks he said,

†   "Take this, and divide it among yourselves; for I tell you that from now on I shall not drink of the fruit of the vine until the kingdom of God comes."

N   And he took bread, and when he had given thanks he broke it and gave it to them, saying,

†   "This is my body which is given for you. Do this in remembrance of me."

N   And likewise the cup after supper, saying,

†   "This cup which is poured out for you is the new covenant in my blood. But behold the hand of him who betrays me is with me on the table. For the Son of man goes as it has been determined; but woe to that man by whom he is betrayed!"

N   And they began to question one another, which of them it was that would do this.

     A dispute also arose among them, which of them was to be regarded as the greatest. And he said to them,

†   "The kings of the Gentiles exercise lordship over them; and those in authority over them are called benefactors. But not so with you; rather let the greatest among you become as the youngest, and the leader as one who serves. For which is the greater, one who sits at table, or one who serves? Is it not the one who sits at table? But I am among you as one who serves.

     "You are those who have continued with me in my trials; and I assign to you, as my Father assigned to me, a kingdom, that you may eat and drink at my table in my kingdom, and sit on thrones judging the twelve tribes of Israel.

     "Simon, Simon, behold, Satan demanded to have you, that he might sift you like wheat, but I have prayed for you that your faith may not fail; and when you have turned again, strengthen your brethren."

N   And he said to him,

S₁   "Lord, I am ready to go with you to prison and to death."

N   He said,

†   "I tell you, Peter, the cock will not crow this day, until you three times deny that you know me."

N   And he said to them,

† "When I sent you out with no purse or bag or sandals, did you lack anything?"

N They said,

Sps "Nothing."

N He said to them,

† "But now, let him who has a purse take it, and likewise a bag. And let him who has no sword sell his mantle and buy one. For I tell you that this scripture must be fulfilled in me, 'And he was reckoned with transgressors'; for what is written about me has its fulfilment."

N And they said,

Sps "Look, Lord, here are two swords."

N And he said to them,

† "It is enough."

N And he came out, and went, as was his custom, to the Mount of Olives; and the disciples followed him. And when he came to the place he said to them,

† "Pray that you may not enter into temptation."

N And he withdrew from them about a stone's throw, and knelt down and prayed,

† "Father, if thou art willing, remove this cup from me; nevertheless not my will, but thine, be done."

N And when he rose from prayer, he came to the disciples and found them sleeping for sorrow, and he said to them,

† "Why do you sleep? Rise and pray that you may not enter into temptation."

N While he was still speaking, there came a crowd, and the man called Judas, one of the twelve, was leading them. He drew near to Jesus to kiss him; but Jesus said to him,

† "Judas, would you betray the Son of man with a kiss?"

N And when those who were about him saw what would follow, they said,

Sps "Lord, shall we strike with the sword?"

N And one of them struck the slave of the high priest and cut off his right ear. But Jesus said,

† "No more of this!"

N And he touched his ear and healed him. Then Jesus said to the chief priests and officers of the temple and elders, who had come out against him,

† "Have you come out as against a robber, with swords and clubs? When I was with you day after day in the temple, you did not lay hands on me. But this is your hour, and the power of darkness."

N Then they seized him and led him away, bringing him into the high priest's house. Peter followed at a distance; and when they had kindled a fire in the middle of the courtyard and sat down together, Peter sat among them. Then a maid, seeing him as he sat in the light and gazing at him, said,

S₂   "This man also was with him."

N   But he denied it, saying,

S₁   "Woman, I do not know him."

N   And a little later some one else saw him and said,

S₃   "You also are one of them."

N   But Peter said,

S₁   "Man, I am not."

N   And after an interval of about an hour still another insisted, saying,

S₄   "Certainly this man also was with him; for he is a Galilean."

N   But Peter said,

S₁   "Man, I do not know what you are saying."

N   And immediately, while he was still speaking, the cock crowed. And the Lord turned and looked at Peter. And Peter remembered the word of the Lord, how he had said to him, "Before the cock crows today, you will deny me three times." And he went out and wept bitterly.
Now the men who were holding Jesus mocked him and beat him; they also blindfolded him and asked him,

Sps   "Prophesy! Who is it that struck you?"

N   And they spoke many other words against him, reviling him.
When day came, the assembly of the elders of the people gathered together, both chief priests and scribes; and they led him away to their council, and they said,

Sps   "If you are the Christ, tell us."

N   But he said to them,

†   "If I tell you, you will not believe; and if I ask you, you will not answer. But from now on the Son of man shall be seated at the right hand of the power of God."

N   And they all said,

Sps   "Are you the Son of God, then?"

N   And he said to them,

†   "You say that I am."

N   And they said,

Sps   "What further testimony do we need? We have heard it ourselves from his own lips."

Short form begins.

N   Then the whole company of them arose, and brought him before Pilate. And they began to accuse him, saying,

Sps   "We found this man perverting our nation, and forbidding us to give tribute to Caesar, and saying that he himself is Christ a king."

N   And Pilate asked him,

S₅   "Are you the King of the Jews?"

N   And he answered him,

†   "You have said so."

N   And Pilate said to the chief priests and the multitudes,

S₅   "I find no crime in this man."

N   But they were urgent, saying,

Sps   "He stirs up the people, teaching throughout all Judea, from Galilee even to this place."

N   When Pilate heard this, he asked whether the man was a Galilean. And when he learned that he belonged to Herod's jurisdiction, he sent him over to Herod, who was himself in Jerusalem at that time. When Herod saw Jesus, he was very glad, for he had long desired to see him, because he had heard about him, and he was hoping to see some sign done by him. So he questioned him at some length; but he made no answer. The chief priests and the scribes stood by, vehemently accusing him. And Herod with his soldiers treated him with contempt and mocked him, then, arraying him in gorgeous apparel, he sent him back to Pilate. And Herod and Pilate became friends with each other that very day, for before this they had been at enmity with each other.

    Pilate then called together the chief priests and the rulers and the people, and said to them.

S₅   "You brought me this man as one who was perverting the people; and after examining him before you, behold, I did not find this man guilty of any of your charges against him; neither did Herod, for he sent him back to us. Behold, nothing deserving death has been done by him; I will therefore chastise him and release him."

N   But they all cried out together,

C   "Away with this man, and release to us Barabbas"—

N   a man who had been thrown into prison for an insurrection started in the city, and for murder. Pilate addressed them once more, desiring to release Jesus; but they shouted out,

C   "Crucify, crucify him!"

N   A third time he said to them,

S₅   "Why, what evil has he done? I have found in him no crime deserving death; I will therefore chastise him and release him."

N   But they were urgent, demanding with loud cries that he should be crucified. And their voices prevailed. So Pilate gave sentence that their demand should be granted. He released the man who had been thrown into prison for insurrection and murder, whom they asked for; but Jesus he delivered up to their will.

    And as they led him away, they seized one Simon of Cyrene, who was coming in from the country, and laid on him the cross, to carry it behind Jesus. And there followed him a great multitude of the people, and of women who bewailed and lamented him. But Jesus turning to them said,

†   "Daughters of Jerusalem, do not weep for me, but weep for yourselves and for your children. For behold, the days are coming when they will say, 'Blessed are the barren, and the wombs that never bore, and the breasts that never gave suck!' Then they will begin to say to the mountains, 'Fall on us'; and to the hills, 'Cover us.' For if they do this when the wood is green, what will happen when it is dry?''

N   Two others also, who were criminals, were led away to be put to death with him. And when they came to the place which is called The Skull, there they crucified him, and the criminals, one on the right and one on the left. And Jesus said,

†   "Father, forgive them; for they know not what they do."

N   And they cast lots to divide his garments. And the people stood by, watching; but the rulers scoffed at him, saying,

Sps   "He saved others; let him save himself, if he is the Christ of God, his Chosen One!"

N   The soldiers also mocked him, coming up and offering him vinegar, and saying,

Sps   "If you are the King of the Jews, save yourself!"

N   There was also an inscription over him, "This is the King of the Jews."
    One of the criminals who were hanged railed at him, saying,

S_6 "Are you not the Christ? Save yourself and us!"

N   But the other rebuked him, saying,

S_7 "Do you not fear God, since you are under the same sentence of condemnation? And we indeed justly; for we are receiving the due reward of our deeds; but this man has done nothing wrong."

N   And he said,

S_7 "Jesus, remember me when you come into your kingdom."

N   And he said to him,

†   "Truly, I say to you, today you will be with me in Paradise."

N   It was now about the sixth hour, and there was darkness over the whole land until the ninth hour, while the sun's light failed; and the curtain of the temple was torn in two. Then Jesus, crying with a loud voice, said,

†   "Father, into thy hands I commit my spirit!"

N   And having said this he breathed his last. Now when the centurion saw what had taken place, he praised God, and said,

S_8 "Certainly this man was innocent!"

N   And all the multitudes who assembled to see the sight, when they saw what had taken place, returned home beating their breasts. And all his acquaintances and the women who had followed him from Galilee stood at a distance and saw these things.

Short form ends.

N   Now there was a man named Joseph from the Jewish town of Arimathea. He was a member of the council, a good and righteous man, who had not consented to their purpose and deed, and he was looking for the kingdom of God. This man went to Pilate and asked for the body of Jesus. Then he took it down and wrapped it in a linen shroud, and laid him in a rock-hewn tomb, where no one had ever yet been laid. It was the day of Preparation, and the sabbath was beginning. The women who had come with him from Galilee followed, and saw the tomb, and how his body was laid; then they returned, and prepared spices and ointments.

On the sabbath they rested according to the commandment.

E. Monday, Tuesday, and Wednesday in Holy Week

Monday

GATHERING   *Suitable music may be offered.*

GREETING

> Grace and peace from God our Father
> and the Lord Jesus Christ.
>
> **Amen.**
>
> Come, let us worship the Lord,
> who was obedient even unto death on a cross.
>
> **We come in spirit and in truth.**

HYMN

OPENING PRAYER

> The Lord be with you.
>
> **And also with you.**
>
> Let us pray: *A brief silence.*
>
> **God of strength and mercy,**
>   **by the suffering and death of your Son,**
>   **free us from slavery to sin and death**
>   **and protect us in all our weakness;**
> **through Jesus Christ our Lord. Amen.**

FIRST LESSON   Isaiah 42:1-9   (All years)

PSALM 36:5-10   (BCP)

Response: **How priceless is your love, O God!**

> Your love, O Lord, reaches to the heavens,
>   and your faithfulness to the clouds.

Your righteousness is like the strong mountains,
your justice like the great deep;
   you save both man and beast, O Lord.

Response
Your people take refuge under the shadow of your wings.

They feast upon the abundance of your house;
   you give them drink from the river of your delights.

For with you is the well of life,
   and in your light we see light.

Continue your loving-kindness to those who know you,
   and your favor to those who are true of heart.

Response

SECOND LESSON   Hebrews 9:11-15   (All years)

RESPONSORY

Now is the acceptable time.

Now is the time of salvation.

Let us prove ourselves in patience.
in the power of the Lord.

Now is the acceptable time,

Now is the time of salvation.

Let us live as God's servants,
watching in the word of truth,
in the power of redeeming love.

Now is the season of hope,
Now is the acceptable time,
Now is the day of salvation near.

THE GOSPEL   John 12:1-11   (All years)

MEDITATION   *Silent, or other; see commentary.*

INTERCESSIONS

In peace, let us pray to the Lord:

Response: **Lord, have mercy,** *or* **Hear us in your mercy.**

For the unity, peace and welfare of the church
   and for all our sisters and brothers in Christ,
   let us pray to the Lord.

Response

For all ministers of the gospel who speak the truth in love,
   let us pray to the Lord.

Response

For all prophets of justice, and those who bring mercy,
   and for all who serve and defend human life,
   let us pray to the Lord.

Response

For the destruction of demonic powers,
   the elimination of slavery, human exploitation, and war,
   let us pray to the Lord.

Spontaneous petitions may be added.

Help, save, pity, and defend us, O God, by your grace.

A brief silence is kept.

Rejoicing in the fellowship of all the saints,
   let us commend ourselves, one another
   and the whole world to Christ our Lord.
To you, O Lord.   (BCP)

[COLLECT   *The following may be used:*

   Almighty God,
      whose dear Son went not up to joy
      before he suffered pain,
      and entered not into glory before he was crucified:
   Mercifully grant that we,
      walking in the way of the cross,
      may find it the way of life and peace;
   through Jesus Christ your Son our Lord,
      who lives and reigns with you and the Holy Spirit,
      one God, for ever. **Amen.**]   (BCP)

THE LORD'S PRAYER

HYMN

DISMISSAL WITH BLESSING

   Go forth in peace to walk the way of life.

   We go in the name of the Lord.

   Now may the God of peace who brought again from the dead
   Our Lord Jesus, the great shepherd of the sheep,
   by the blood of the eternal covenant,
   equip you with everything good that you may do his will,

working in you that which is pleasing in his sight;
through Jesus Christ, to whom be glory for ever and ever.

Amen. Thanks be to God.

The hymn may be used following the dismissal with blessing, the congregation departing quietly so that some may remain for meditation.

Tuesday

GATHERING   *Suitable music may be offered.*

GREETING

Grace and peace from the Lord Jesus Christ be with you all.

And also with you.

Come, let us worship the Lord,
who was obedient even unto death on a cross.

We come in spirit and in truth.

HYMN

OPENING PRAYER

Let us pray: *A brief silence.*

God of strength and mercy,
   By the passion of your blessed Son
   you made an instrument of shameful death
   to be for us the means of life:
Grant us so to glory in the cross of Christ,
   that we may gladly suffer shame and loss
   for the sake of Jesus Christ our Savior;
through whom in the Holy Spirit we pray. Amen.

FIRST LESSON   Isaiah 49:1-7   (All years)

PSALM   71:1-12

Response: **I will sing of your salvation.**

In you, O Lord, have I taken refuge;
   let me never be ashamed.
In your righteousness, deliver me and set me free;
   incline your ear to me and save me.

Response

Be my strong rock, a castle to keep me safe;
   you are my crag and my stronghold.

Deliver me, my God, from the hand of the wicked,
from the clutches of the evildoer and the oppressor.

Response

For you are my hope, O Lord God,
my confidence since I was young.
I have been sustained by you ever since I was born;
from my mother's womb you have been my strength;
my praise shall be always of you.

Response

I have become a portent to many;
but you are my refuge and my strength.
Let my mouth be full of your praise
and your glory all the day long.
Do not cast me off in my old age;
forsake me not when my strength fails.
For my enemies are talking against me,
and those who lie in wait for my life take counsel together.

Response

They say, "God has forsaken him;
go after him and seize him;
because there is one who will save."
O God, be not far from me;
come quickly to help me, O my God.

Response

SECOND LESSON   I Corinthians 1:18-31   (All years)

RESPONSORY

Let us glory in the cross of Jesus Christ.
Through him we have salvation,
life and resurrection.

Cross of Christ, tree of hope.

For us he became obedient even to death on a cross;
because of this God exalted him above every name.

Cross of Christ, tree of hope,
Wisdom of God.

When I am lifted up from the earth,
I will draw all unto myself.

Cross of Christ, tree of hope, wisdom of God.
We worship and praise you, O Christ;
by your cross the world is redeemed.   *(adapted from St. John's Abbey prayer)*

THE GOSPEL   John 12:20-36   (All years)

MEDITATION   *Silent, or other; see commentary.*

INTERCESSIONS

[COLLECT]

THE LORD'S PRAYER

HYMN

DISMISSAL WITH BLESSING

Go forth to walk the way of the cross;
May God bless and keep you in his mercy.

We go in the name of the Lord.

Now to him who by the power at work within us
is able to do far more abundantly than all we ask or think
to him be glory in the church
and in Christ Jesus to all generations,
for ever and ever.

Amen. Thanks be to God.

*The hymn may be sung following the dismissal with blessing, the congregation departing quietly so that
some may remain for meditation.*

Wednesday

GATHERING   *Suitable music may be offered.*

GREETING

Grace and peace from God our Father
and the Lord Jesus Christ.

Amen.

Come, let us worship the Lord,
who was obedient even unto death on a cross.

We come in spirit and in truth.

HYMN

OPENING PRAYER

The Lord be with you.

And also with you.

Let us pray: *A brief silence.*
Most merciful God,
    whose blessed Son our Savior was betrayed, whipped,

and his face spat upon:
Grant us grace to take joyfully
   the sufferings of the present time,
   confident of the glory that shall yet be revealed;
Through Jesus Christ our Lord,
   who lives and reigns with you and the Holy Spirit,
   one God, for ever and ever. **Amen.**

FIRST LESSON   Isaiah 50:4-9*a*   (All years)

PSALM 70

Response: **O Lord, make haste to help me.**

Be pleased, O God, to deliver me;
   O Lord, make haste to help me.
Let those who seek my life be ashamed
and altogether dismayed;
   let those who take pleasure in my misfortune
   draw back and be disgraced.
Let those who say to me "Aha!" and gloat over me turn back,
   because they are ashamed.
Let all who seek you rejoice and be glad in you;
   let those who love your salvation say for ever,
   "Great is the Lord!"
But as for me, I am poor and needy;
   come to me speedily, O God.
You are my helper and my deliverer;
   O Lord, do not tarry.

               Response

SECOND LESSON   Hebrews 12:1-3   (All years)

HYMN

THE GOSPEL   John 13:21-30   (All years)

MEDITATION   *Silent, or other; see commentary.*

INTERCESSIONS

[COLLECT]

THE LORD'S PRAYER

HYMN

DISMISSAL WITH BLESSING

Go forth in peace to walk the way of his suffering.

We go in the name of the Lord.

May the God of peace enable us to do his will
in every kind of goodness,
working in us what pleases him
in the Holy Spirit;
through Jesus Christ our Lord.

Amen. Thanks be to God.

Commentary

On Passion/Palm Sunday the whole congregation has gathered to recall and to celebrate the dramatic beginning of these days of the passion and death of our Lord. Thus begins the period of time traditionally known as Holy Week. These are among the most intense days in the church's year of grace, culminating in the Easter Triduum (Thursday sunset to Sunday sunset). We here approach the yearly renewal of our incorporation into the central mystery of Christian life and faith.

Monday through Thursday afternoon comprise the minor days in Holy Week, but nonetheless they are occasions for dwelling together upon Scripture, particularly the portrayal of the final events, and for pondering their meaning for us in the context of prayer and meditation. Note that a service has not been provided for Thursday; but if one is needed, the same pattern as for the first three days may be followed. While many churches cannot expect most of the congregation to gather each of these days, increasingly we find the need for services that may be held in church buildings or in homes. In many communities, there is a well-established tradition of noonday worship, often of an ecumenical nature; many others hold brief early evening services for which these resources are appropriate.

The order and texts of these services are designed for communal gatherings in a church building; but with some adaptation they are suitable for family use as well. The psalms, prayers, and various responsories are integrated with the readings from Scripture and are extensions of the Holy Week themes. The meditative style and tone of these services should be preserved in the hymn selection and in other musical elements, such as choral settings. This is especially important in a congregational setting. Careful choice in the light of the themes and images found in the Word of God is required.

In some cases the psalms may be sung by the choir, and the congregation may respond; or the congregation may sing or recite the whole psalm in sections. Pastors and church musicians should discuss the use of existing choral literature that may be adaptable to congregational participation. Of course, in some circumstances, having no music may be effective and in keeping with the austerity of the time and the setting.

Several persons may be involved in leading these services: readers, leaders of prayer, musicians, acolytes, book-bearers, and the presiding ministers. On ecumenical occasions, several denominations can thus take part. Lay involvement is to be encouraged whenever possible. Adequate preparation of the participants is essential. Since these are primarily meditative services, a solemnity and reserve coupled with pastoral grace are desirable. A spirit of communal prayer should be present.

There are a variety of ways in which Scripture may be incorporated. If for some reason the full passion narrative was not proclaimed on Sunday, selections from the synoptic account for the particular year may be read or enacted in addition to, or in the place of, the Johannine readings that are indicated. Nonbiblical readings may also be used as a commentary and as response to the Scripture, if a slightly longer service is possible.

In many instances music, both instrumental and vocal, may play a significant part. It should always be kept in mind that these services prepare us for the paschal celebrations of the Easter Triduum. We follow Jesus along the way of his passion and cross, yet always in the yearning toward Easter. To the expression of our Lord's suffering, we join the prayers of intercession for the broken world that his prayer and his life embrace. The prayers need not be printed, except in the case of the opening prayers when they are prayed in unison. Pastoral sensitivity with respect to free prayer should be exercised; the need may vary from place to place, and even from one day to the next, depending upon events in the community and upon the people gathered. In no case should the prayers neglect the more universal themes and petitions expressed in the texts given. Those intercessions may be used as models.

Worshipers are increasingly receptive to nonverbal witness to the Holy Week events. With such extensive use of readings from the Bible during these days, nonverbal dimensions are not to be overlooked. In some cases, visual arts can create prayerful and meditative environments as well as strong commentary on Scripture. Images of the passion are vivid and varied: the jar of costly perfume, thirty pieces of silver, spears and swords and clubs, the crowing rooster, cross and nails, a crown of thorns, wheat and grapes, a lamb for sacrifice, and others. Projected images or banners, preferably without words, may provide a focus for silent meditation. Liturgical dance or simple mime may enact the events or themes from Scripture. These may be woven together into a unity with silences and prayer, together with appropriate hymnody, choral pieces, or instrumental music. The key to this is thoughtful preparation and a deep simplicity arising out of meditation on the principal texts to be used.

One further dimension of our worship during these final days of Lent deserves special mention, fasting and almsgiving. While the pattern of fasting and almsgiving for Lent cannot be legislated or imposed apart from pastoral realities in local churches, these final days present an especially appropriate time for such practices, so largely missing in contemporary Protestant circles. For example, a partial fast could accompany the midday or evening services Monday through Wednesday. The family setting could include a "sacrificial meal" in which money normally spent for the supper would be contributed by the household or assembled group for a special project such as world hunger or a local need.

Good Friday is, of course, the traditional day of fasting for Christians. In the first three centuries, the paschal celebrations were always preceded by a two-day fast, and in some cases a modified fast took place over six days. This was mentioned in Athanasius' Festal Letter in A.D. 329. The practices of fasting and almsgiving were taught by Jesus and were widespread in the apostolic church. In contrast to the Lenten restraint that recalls our sinfulness, the Easter feast makes evident the abundance of God's goodness which we are empowered to share with others.

In any event, we need to recover the connection between fasting, almsgiving, and prayer. This can be especially meaningful during the prayer vigils on Friday and Saturday of Holy Week. The great Easter celebration, whether the Vigil or the First Service of Easter, then breaks the fast after the baptismal initiation of those who, with the whole church, have prepared themselves throughout the Lenten Season.

F. Holy Thursday Evening

On this night we remember and celebrate the final supper Jesus shared with his disciples in the context of Passover. This event, which reveals the holiness of all subsequent meals eaten in his name, institutes the mystery of his abiding redemptive presence in the church's celebrations of the Lord's Supper, or Holy Communion, or Eucharist. This evening also marks the beginning of the most solemn and joyful celebration of the entire Christian Year. We enter what Augustine referred to as "the triduum during which the Lord died, was buried, and rose again."

Historically, Holy Thursday has included a series of distinctive elements, which have been quite complex and elaborate in certain periods, especially in the Middle Ages. Yet there is a profound simplicity about the essentials, since they arise out of Scripture and the early church's worship, which unfolded the meaning of Christ's redemptive action. From the history of this pattern of elements, we have included six: (1) introductory rites emphasizing penitence, (2) the liturgy of the Word of God, (3) footwashing, (4) Holy Communion (with optional agape, or love feast), (5) the stripping of the church, and (6) Tenebrae, or service of the shadows.

This day is sometimes called "Maundy Thursday," a term derived through the Old French *mandé* from the Latin *mandatum novum*, "a new commandment" associated with John 13:34 and perhaps also with the footwashing reported earlier in the same chapter.

The Lenten or Holy Week visual environment continues through this service until the stripping of the church, but white may be used as an alternative to purple, red, or other Lenten colors.

Worship may be simple or elaborate, depending upon the resources and situation of the local community involved. Options will be noted in the rubrics and in the commentary. The order of service with its texts and actions is designed to focus on the central theological and experiential realities arising from the scriptural events we commemorate and relive this night. In the commentary, numerous suggestions are made concerning the inherent drama and flexibility of the whole liturgy.

GATHERING

Suitable instrumental or choral music may be offered, or the people may assemble in silence.

GREETING

Return to the Lord, God of all mercies,
for a feast of love has been prepared for his own.

I will bless the Lord at all times.
His praise shall be continually in my mouth.

O taste and see the goodness of the Lord.

Happy are they who take refuge in God.

O magnify the Lord with me,

And let us exalt God's name together.

HYMN

A wide variety of hymns about the Lord's Supper and passion hymns are suitable for this occasion. If footwashing is included or mentioned, the hymn "Jesu, Jesu" is especially appropriate.

PRAYERS OF CONFESSION AND PARDON

My brothers and sisters, Christ shows us his love by becoming a humble servant. Let us draw near to God and confess our sin in the truth of his Spirit.

A brief silence for individual reflection.

A. Merciful God, we have not loved you with all our heart and mind and strength and soul. Lord have mercy.

Lord have mercy.

We have not loved our neighbors as you have taught us.
Christ have mercy.

Christ have mercy.

We have not fully received the saving grace of your word and life.
Lord, have mercy.

Lord, have mercy.

May the Lord have mercy upon you,
forgive and heal you by his steadfast love
made known to us by the passion, death, and
resurrection of Jesus Christ our Lord.

Amen. Thanks be to God.

Or, following the silent prayers.

B. **Most merciful God,**
   We your church confess
      that often our spirit has not been that of Christ.
   Where we have failed to love one another as he loves us,
   Where we have pledged loyalty to him with our lips
      and then betrayed, deserted, or denied him.
   Forgive us, we pray, and by your Spirit
      make us faithful in every time of trial;
   Through Jesus Christ our Lord. Amen.

Who is in a position to condemn? Only Christ.
But Christ suffered and died for us,
was raised from the dead and ascended on high for us,
and continues to intercede for us.
Believe the good news:
In the name of Jesus Christ, you are forgiven!

In the name of Jesus Christ, you are forgiven!
Thanks be to God. Amen.

ACT OF PRAISE

FIRST LESSON

    Exodus 12:1-4 (5-10), 11-14   (All years)

PSALM   Psalm 116:1-2, 12-19   (All years)

Response:
I will lift up the cup of salvation
and call upon the name of the Lord.

I love the Lord, because he has heard
  my voice and my supplications.
Because he inclined his ear to me,
  therefore I will call on him as long as I live.
What shall I render to the Lord
  for all his bounty to me?
I will lift up the cup of salvation
  and call upon the name of the Lord.
I will fulfill my vows to the Lord
  in the presence of all his people.
Precious in the sight of the Lord
  is the death of his servants.

Response

O Lord, I am your servant;
  I am your servant and the child of your handmaid;
  you have freed me from my bonds.
I will offer you the sacrifice of thanksgiving
  and call upon the name of the Lord.
I will fulfill my vows to the Lord
  in the presence of all his people,
In the courts of the Lord's house,
  in the midst of you, O Jerusalem.
  Hallelujah!

Response

SECOND LESSON

I Corinthians 11:23-26   (All years)

HYMN OR RESPONSORY

Glory to you, Word of God, Lord Jesus Christ.

Glory to you, Word of God, Lord Jesus Christ.

A new commandment I give to you:
Love one another as I have loved you.

Glory to you, Word of God, Lord Jesus Christ.

THE GOSPEL

John 13:1-17, 31*b*-35   (All years)

SERMON

RESPONSES TO THE WORD

[FOOTWASHING]   *See commentary.*

PRAYERS OF THE PEOPLE

THE PEACE

The following responsory may be used:

The Lord Jesus after he had supped with his disciples and washed their feet, said to them, "I have given you an example, that you should do as I have done."

**"Peace I leave with you; my peace I give to you;
peace which the world cannot give, I give to you."**

"Love one another, as I have loved you."
The peace of our Lord Jesus Christ be with you all.

And also with you.

Reconciled by his love, let us offer one another
signs of peace and reconciliation.

OFFERING

A hymn or anthem may be sung, during which the table is prepared.

GREAT THANKSGIVING

The Lord be with you.

And also with you.

Lift up your hearts.

We lift them to the Lord.

Let us give thanks to the Lord our God.

It is right to give our thanks and praise.

It is right, and a good and joyful thing,
always and everywhere to give thanks to you,
Father Almighty, Creator of heaven and earth.

From the earth you bring forth bread
and create the fruit of the vine.
You formed us in your image,
delivered us from captivity,
and made covenant to be our sovereign God.
You fed us manna in the wilderness,
and gave grapes to evidence the promised land.

And so, with your people on earth
and all the company of heaven,
we praise your name and join their unending hymn:

**Holy, holy, holy Lord, God of power and might,
heaven and earth are full of your glory.
Hosanna in the highest.
Blessed is he who comes in the name of the Lord.
Hosanna in the highest.**

Holy are you, and blessed is your Son Jesus Christ.
When we had turned aside from your way
and abused your gifts,
you gave us in him your crowning gift.
Emptying himself, that our joy might be full,
he fed the hungry, healed the afflicted,
ate with the scorned and forgotten,
washed his disciples' feet,
and gave a holy meal as the pledge of his abiding presence.

By the baptism of his suffering, death, and resurrection
you gave birth to your church,
delivered us from slavery to sin and death,
and made with us a new covenant, by water and the Spirit.

On the night in which he gave himself up for us
he took bread, gave thanks to you, broke the bread,
gave it to his disciples, and said:
"Take, eat; this is my body which is given for you.
Do this in remembrance of me."

When the supper was over he took the cup,
gave thanks to you, gave it to his disciples, and said:
"Drink from this, all of you;
this is my blood of the new covenant,
poured out for you and for many
for the forgiveness of sins.
Do this, as often as you drink it, in remembrance of me."

And so,
in remembrance of these your mighty acts in Jesus Christ,
we offer ourselves in praise and thanksgiving
as a holy and living sacrifice,
in union with Christ's offering for us,
as we proclaim the mystery of faith.

Christ has died, Christ is risen, Christ will come again.

Pour out your Holy Spirit on us, gathered here,
and on these gifts of bread and wine.
Make them be for us the body and blood of Christ,
that we may be for the world the body of Christ,
redeemed by his blood.

By your Spirit make us one with Christ,
one with each other,
and one in ministry to all the world,
until Christ comes in final victory
and we feast at his heavenly banquet.

Through your Son Jesus Christ,
with the Holy Spirit in your holy church,

all honor and glory is yours, Almighty Father,
now and for ever.

Amen.

THE LORD'S PRAYER

BREAKING THE BREAD

COMMUNION   *Hymns may be sung during the communion.*

PRAYER AFTER COMMUNION

We thank you, holy God,
for giving us this meal, shared in the Spirit,
which sustains us with the food and drink of your life.
Grace our lives that we may at the last come to share
in the heavenly banquet of your kingdom,
through Jesus Christ our Lord.
Amen.

[THE STRIPPING OF THE CHURCH]

See commentary.

HYMN   *Where the Tenebrae (see Section G) or the footwashing is to follow, this hymn should be chosen to introduce that service. When it does not follow, the service concludes with the following dismissal with blessing.*

DISMISSAL WITH BLESSING

Go forth in peace to walk the way of his cross and resurrection.

We are sent in the name of the Lord.

May Jesus Christ, who was put to death for our sins, bless you and keep you.

Amen.

May Jesus Christ, who was raised to life for our salvation, let light shine upon you.

Amen.

May Jesus Christ be your life and peace, now and for ever.

Amen. Thanks be to God.

Commentary

Since Holy Thursday evening is, both by the solemnity of its meaning and structure and by custom, one of the most significant worship experiences of the year, careful planning is crucial. Decisions regarding the various elements in the whole liturgy and the degree of simplicity or elaboration should be made well in advance, preferably at the beginning of Lent. In this way preparations for the whole Easter Triduum can become part of the Lenten discipline of the congregation, and particularly of the worship planning committee, the musicians, and others who may contribute.

A balance between flexibility and a well-ordered set of texts and actions is found in the preceding pages. Careful study and pastorally sensitive imagination may envision various adaptations for local circumstances. If all six of the basic elements are incorporated—introductory penitential rite, the Word of God, footwashing, Holy Communion (or agape), the stripping of the church, and Tenebrae—the length of the service will last from one and a half to two hours. It could follow a community meal or, in some circumstances, be incorporated into such a meal. On the occasion of the first night of the three high holy days of the Christian Year, such a gathering of the whole community is a powerful witness. Depending upon the space available and the room environment as well as the customs of the people, these services may be either quite intimate and casual or highly structured liturgically. The whole service, for example, may take place in a fellowship hall. In any case, the whole service should be understood as evangelical in the most profound sense: a proclamation, encounter, and participation in the mystery of our redemption through the saving action of God in Christ.

While the first part of the service is penitential in nature, there may be extensions of forgiveness and reconciliation that echo and become visible throughout. For example, during the responses to the Word, acts of reconciliation are quite appropriate. If there are persons who have been intentionally separated from the church for a period of time, either from grave sin or out of personal alienation or animosity, and who wish to publicly renew their commitment to the church, this is a most opportune moment. In earlier church practice, public penitents were received by the bishop on Holy Thursday evening. Such an act may take the form of a brief personal witness and an act of reconciliation with the laying on of hands. The minister may say: "In the name of Jesus Christ you are forgiven and reconciled to his body, the church. As you have witnessed to your faith and new intention, by the mercy of Christ we receive you as restored members in this family of faith. God bless you this night and grant you peace. Amen."

Other responses to the Word might include silent meditation, with or without visual images of the passion. This would be particularly suitable if the Tenebrae is not included (either as part of the liturgy of the Word of God, or as the concluding element in the whole service). A choral presentation may also be appropriate, especially if it involves congregational participation.

Also fitting, and a very powerful symbolic response to the Word, is the *rite of footwashing*. This dramatizes vividly the humility and servanthood of Jesus, both on the night of his betrayal and in his continuing presence in our midst. When entered into prayerfully and openly, without embarrassment, it is a clear witness to our own role in his actions. It is a response to his "new commandment"—that we love one another as he has loved us.

In a large congregation it is advisable to select certain representatives from the people. At the designated time, they will be invited to come forward to a place where chairs, a basin and pitcher of water, and towels have already been placed. These articles may also be brought forward by deacons or ushers. Depending upon the context, the minister may wash only one foot of each person, though the mutual footwashing among minister(s) and laypersons would be more symbolic of servanthood. These actions should be clearly visible, yet not overly dramatic. Love and care for one another must be expressed in these ritual gestures. It is best not to include persons for whom this seems unduly embarrassing.

During the footwashing, the choir may sing appropriate pieces or the congregation may sing hymns or songs. The actions may be done as well in silence.

Where the congregation is small, it may be possible for everyone to participate. Among the Church of the Brethren, even in larger congregations, this has always been done by the whole congregation. The movement of persons should not be forced or regimented, but natural, with an air of hospitality and care. It can be suggested that where possible the worshipers come in sandals, and it can be made clear that persons are welcome simply to observe rather than participate. Basins may be scattered among the congregation, and a small group may form around each basin; or persons may come forward to the basins as they feel led to participate. Sponge and towel are provided at each basin. Persons who have had their feet washed wash their neighbor's in turn.

A strikingly beautiful hymn text which may be sung by choir and congregation is *Ubi Caritas* ("Where charity and love are found, there is God"). This may be used at the offertory if it is not used here.

Refrain:	Where charity and love are found, there is God.
Verse 1:	The love of Christ has gathered us together into one. Let us rejoice and be glad in him. Let us fear and love the living God, and love each other from the depths of our hearts.
Refrain repeated	
Verse 2:	Therefore when we are together, let us take heed not to be divided in mind. Let there be an end to bitterness and quarrels, an end to strife, and in our midst be Christ our God.
Refrain repeated	
Verse 3:	And, in company with the blessed, may we see your face in glory, Christ our God, with pure and unbounded joy for ever and for ever.
Refrain repeated	

Another text which may be set to a simple melodic line is
Faith, hope, and love,
let these endure among you;
and the greatest of these is love.

Or other versions of I Corinthians 13 may be employed. Another well-known hymn that picks up the theme of John 13:35 is "They'll Know We Are Christians by Our Love."

The prayers of the people may be a traditional form for intercession, such as was included in the services for Monday through Wednesday in Holy Week. Several forms are provided in the *Book of Common Prayer*. If free prayer is invited, it is best to give a simple form such as "For N.; that she/he may be . . . , let us pray to the Lord," with the congregation responding "Lord, have mercy," or "Hear us in your mercy."

The offering is taken as usual. During this time the table is prepared for the celebration of the Lord's Supper, or the agape (love feast) if for some reason the sacrament cannot be celebrated. If the elements are already in place, the cloth coverings may be removed. It is appropriate to use a chalice and several additional drinking vessels if the congregation is large. A whole loaf of specially prepared unsliced bread should be used whenever possible. The containers of wine and the bread may be brought forward by laypersons in procession to the table with the offerings, or brought from a credence table nearby, and placed on the altar table. The sung doxology is not necessary during the bringing of the gifts and offerings. The hymn, *Ubi Caritas* (given above), is particularly suitable for this evening's offertory.

After the ushers and gift-bearers return, the congregation remains standing for the Great

Thanksgiving. Note the particular resonance of the prayer on this evening. The service is made even more powerful when, following the communion, the practice known as the stripping of the church occurs.

A highly vivid and dramatic way of showing forth the desolation and abandonment of the long night in Gethsemane is through stripping the altar table and removing all textile hangings and candles. This practice dates from the seventh century and began for the utilitarian purpose of cleaning and washing the church in preparation for Easter. But the stark, bare church reflected so clearly the fitting tone of the occasion that the stripping became an evocative ceremony in its own right. The ceremony is probably best done in complete silence. Altar-table cloths and frontals (if any), pulpit and lectern hangings, banners, and candlesticks or other altar-table furnishings are simply picked up by designated persons and quietly carried out of the sanctuary. In a matter of minutes, the visual aspect of the room is completely changed, and the church remains bare until Easter Eve, when the process is reversed.

If no one is present who is authorized to administer Holy Communion, an agape may be celebrated instead. At the conclusions of the prayers of the people and the sharing of the peace, the congregation may process to a fellowship hall or to another room where a meal has been prepared. The people may wish to sing a familiar hymn on their way, or a psalm could be chanted or sung by the choir, or between choir and people in responsive style. The entire service may take place in the fellowship hall. If this is the case, the food is brought out following the prayers of the people. The following is a brief model order.

READING   John 15:4–5*a*, 8-9

HYMN or SONG

BLESSING OF THE BREAD

> *At each table a loaf of bread is placed. Each person takes a piece and holds it while the blessing is prayed.*

> Blessed are you, O Lord our God, King of the universe,
> you bring forth bread from the earth to sustain us.
> Blessed is your name for all the life and food we share this night,
> through Jesus Christ our Lord. **Amen.**

THE MEAL

> *During the meal readings may be given, such as Isaiah 25:6-9; I John 4:7-21; Colossians 3:12-17.*

BLESSING OF THE CUP

> *At each table a pitcher of fresh fruit juice is saved and poured out to each person at the end of the meal, at which time all stand for the blessing prayer.*

> Blessed are you, O Lord our God, King of the universe,
>   you create the fruit of the vine.
> Blessed is your name for refreshing our lives
>   from the cup of life and salvation,
> through Jesus Christ our Lord. **Amen.**

HYMNS or SONGS OF PRAISE

> *Especially suitable are Psalms 103; 107:1-9, 33-34; Psalm 136 (omitting verses 17-22) which may be sung or recited.*

If the footwashing has not occurred earlier, it may follow the love feast; or if Tenebrae is to be celebrated, the congregation may move back to the usual place of worship. If the whole service takes place in the fellowship hall, hymns may be sung during the clearing of the tables. There should be absolute quiet and no distracting dishes remaining for the Tenebrae.

Note again that a fellowship meal, structured in a similar manner, may *precede* the liturgy of the Word and Sacrament as well.

G. Tenebrae

This may be incorporated into the Holy Thursday communion service. It is, however, most appropriately used on the evening of Good Friday, marking the beginning of a prayer vigil through Saturday.

[GATHERING]

[GREETING

> And this is the judgment, that the light has come into the world,
> and we loved darkness rather than light.
>
> **God is light, in whom there is no darkness at all.**
>
> For God sent the Son into the world, not to condemn the
> world, but that the world might be saved through him.
>
> **Every one who does evil hates the light,**
> **and does not come to the light.**
> **But all who do what is true come to the light.**
>
> Come, let us worship in spirit and in truth.]

HYMN   *A passion hymn.*

OPENING PRAYER

> The Lord be with you.
>
> **And also with you.**
>
> Let us pray: *A brief silence.*
> Most gracious God,
>   Look with mercy upon your family gathered here
>   for whom our Lord Jesus Christ was betrayed,
>   given into sinful hands, and suffered death upon the cross.
> Strengthen our faith and forgive our betrayals
>   as we enter the way of his passion;
> through him who lives and reigns with you and the Holy Spirit,
>   for ever and ever. **Amen.**

THE PASSION OF OUR LORD

> *Twelve candles, along with a central Christ candle, remain lighted through the first five sections of the*
> *reading; then they are extinguished one by one at the conclusion of each of the next twelve sections. At the*

last, the Christ candle is either extinguished, or it may be removed or hidden, and then returned for the final reading from Isaiah.

1

It was two days before the Passover and the Feast of Unleavened Bread. The religious leaders who collaborated with the Roman occupation were conspiring against Jesus. They had gathered in the palace of Caiaphas the high priest. This man had received the high priesthood at the hand of Valerius Gratus, the former Roman governor, and now retained the office under Pontius Pilate. They all were planning to arrest and destroy Jesus quietly so as to avoid a popular revolt among the Jews.

2

At this time Jesus was lodging at Bethany in the house of Simon the leper. While he was there, a woman approached and anointed him from an alabaster jar of pure nard. When his disciples saw the act, they were outraged. "Why this waste?" they demanded. "Such costly ointment might have been sold for a large sum and given to the poor." Jesus responded, "Why do you bother the woman? The poor are always with you. Indeed, I tell you that, wherever the gospel is preached throughout the world, what she has done will be told in her memory."

3

Then one of the twelve named Judas, son of Simon the Iscariot, went to the chief priests and asked, "What will you give me if I deliver Jesus to you for the governor?" When they heard the offer, they were glad and promised Judas thirty pieces of silver. From that hour he sought an opportunity to betray Jesus.

4

At the beginning of the feast, when the passover lamb was sacrificed, the disciples of Jesus approached him and asked, "Where do you wish us to prepare the Paschal meal?" Jesus took two of his disciples and instructed them, "Go into the city, and you will see there a man carrying a water jar. He will show you a suitable place." The two did as Jesus commanded. They entered the city where they found the man with the water jar, who brought them to a large upper room.

5

When evening had come, Jesus arrived with the twelve. While they were eating, he said, "I tell you truly that one of you is going to betray me." The disciples were stunned with grief and began to protest one after the other, "Surely not I!" Jesus replied, "The betrayer is one of you dipping his hand in the dish with me. The Son of man is fulfilling Scripture, but woe to that man through whom the Son of man is betrayed." Then Judas slipped out into the night.

One of the readers extinguishes the first candle.

6

As they were eating, Jesus took bread. After reciting the blessing, he broke it and gave it to his disciples as he said, "Take, eat; this is my body." Then taking the cup with the traditional blessing, he gave it to his disciples as he said, "This is my blood of the covenant which is being shed for many. I tell you in truth that I shall not drink again from the fruit of the vine until that day when I drink it fresh in the kingdom of God." Then, having sung a hymn, they left the city for the Mount of Olives.

7

As they walked, Jesus said to his disciples, "You will all desert me this very night. So it is written in the prophet Zechariah, 'Strike the shepherd, and the sheep will be scattered.' " Then Peter protested, "Though all desert, I will remain by you." Jesus replied, "I tell you truly that in this very night, before the cock crows twice you shall deny me three times." Still Peter maintained, "Even though I must die with you, I will never deny you": and so declared all the disciples.

The extinguishing of the second candle.

8

Jesus halted at an olive grove called Gethsemane. Then going apart with Peter, James, and John, he left them on watch and continued a little farther alone. There he fell on his face in anguished prayer. Soon he returned to the three on watch and found them sleeping. Rousing them, he asked Peter, "Could you not watch with me for just one hour? Watch and pray that you are not put to the test; for the spirit is willing but the flesh is weak." Again Jesus went apart in troubled prayer; and again he returned to find the disciples sleeping, for their eyes were heavy. A third time Jesus withdrew to pray, and a third time he found the disciples sleeping. Then Jesus said, "Sleep on and finish your rest. Now is the time for the Son of man to be delivered into the hands of sinners. Here comes my betrayer."

The extinguishing of the third candle.

9

Jesus had not finished speaking before Judas, one of his own disciples, arrived with a group of Roman soldiers and other armed men from the Temple. Now the betrayer had arranged with the authorities for a sign and had said, "The man whom I kiss is the one you want." In accord with this arrangement Judas went directly to Jesus and cried out, "Greetings, Master." Then he gave him the kiss. Jesus responded, "Judas, would you betray the Son of man with a kiss?"

Immediately the soldiers laid hands on Jesus and held him fast. Then one of the disciples with Jesus drew his sword and cut off an ear from the slave of the high priest; but Jesus said to him, "Sheathe your sword. All who take up the sword will perish by the sword. Do you not know that I can call upon my Father and that he will respond at once with more than twelve legions of angels?" Then turning to the mob, Jesus continued, "Have you come for me as against a rebel bandit with swords and clubs? Why did you not seize me in the Temple, where I sat teaching by day? Were you so afraid of the Jewish people that you must come for me by stealth? Nevertheless, your actions are fulfilling the words of the prophets." Then all of his disciples forsook him and fled.

The extinguishing of the fourth candle.

10

Those who had seized Jesus brought him to Caiaphas, whom the Romans had made a high priest. Peter followed at a distance as far as the courtyard. There he sat with the attendants and warmed himself by the fire. The high priest had gathered his whole council, and they began to arrange the case against Jesus which they would present to Pontius Pilate the governor. The charge was that Jesus claimed to be King of the Jews; and they brought in many false witnesses, but to no avail. Finally two came forward and testified, "We heard this man say, 'I will tear down this temple made with hands and within three days build another not made with hands.' " The testimony was evidence that Jesus claimed an authority over temple affairs which traditionally belonged only to the rulers of Israel, and in those days Israel was ruled from Rome. Yet even these witnesses were unable to agree on their testimony.

Finally Caiaphas stood up and examined Jesus directly. "Have you no answer to these charges?" demanded the high priest. Jesus remained silent and answered nothing. Then the high priest put the question of kingship in terms of the royal titles "Anointed" and "Son of God." "Are you the Anointed One, the Son of the Blessed?" he probed. Jesus answered, "I am, and you shall see the Son of man seated on the right hand of power and coming in the clouds of heaven." The high priest turned and said, "What need have we of witnesses? He has condemned himself." They all concurred that Jesus was indeed worthy of death.

Then those holding Jesus began to spit on him. They covered his face and were striking him as they taunted him and said, "O Anointed One, prophesy who it is who is striking you."

The extinguishing of the fifth candle.

11

Now Peter was warming himself in the courtyard when a small slave girl entered. She confronted Peter and said, "You also were with this Jesus the Nazarene." Peter quickly gave a denial. "I do not know what you are talking about," he replied and went outside into the gateway. Meanwhile, the cock crowed. The slave girl followed Peter out and said to the bystanders, "This man is one of them." Again Peter denied knowing Jesus. After a little while the bystanders said directly to Peter, "Surely you are one of them, for you speak with a Galilean accent." Then Peter began to swear with an oath, "I do not know this person of whom you are speaking"; but the cock interrupted him as it crowed for the second time. Immediately Peter remembered how Jesus had said to him, "Before the cock crows twice, you will deny me three times." He went out and wept bitterly.

The extinguishing of the sixth candle.

12

When morning arrived, all of the chief priests, along with the other Roman collaborators, bound Jesus and delivered him over to Pontius Pilate, the imperial Roman governor. When Judas saw what was happening, he knew that Jesus was doomed, and he repented. He returned the thirty pieces of silver to the chief priests and confessed, "I have sinned in betraying innocent blood." "What is that to us?" they responded. "That is your affair." Judas threw down the thirty pieces of silver in the Temple. Then he went out and hanged himself. Picking up the silver pieces, the chief priests said, "It is unlawful to put this silver into the treasury; for it is blood money." Whereupon they used the money to buy the Potter's Field for the burial of strangers. Therefore, that field is known to this day as the Field of Blood.

The extinguishing of the seventh candle.

13

Jesus stood before the Roman governor as the accusers made their charge, "We found this man perverting our nation," they said. "He was forbidding us to pay taxes to the Emperor and proclaiming himself Anointed King." The governor asked, "Are you the King of the Jews?" Jesus answered, "You say so." The chief priests were accusing him of many things. Therefore, Pilate again spoke to Jesus. "Have you no answer to give?" he asked. "Look at how many accusations they are making!" Jesus astonished Pilate by remaining silent.

The extinguishing of the eighth candle.

14

At that festival the governor used to release a prisoner, and some were urging Pilate to do so at this time. Now there was a notable rebel in prison with those who had committed murder during the insurrection. His name was Jesus Barabbas. Therefore, the chief priests arranged a demonstration to demand Barabbas. Pilate asked them, "Whom do you want me to release for you, Jesus Barabbas, or Jesus the Anointed One?" The demonstrators shouted, "Barabbas!" Pilate responded, "What shall I do then with Jesus the Anointed One?" The crowd shouted, "Crucify him!" Pilate continued, "Are you certain of his guilt?" The crowd took up the chant, "Crucify him! Crucify him!" Again Pilate spoke, "Shall I crucify your king?" "We have no king but Caesar," cried the demonstrators. Then Pilate agreed to release Jesus Barabbas, but Jesus the Anointed One he handed over to his soldiers for scourging and crucifixion.

The extinguishing of the ninth candle.

15

The soldiers led Jesus away within the governor's palace. There they assembled the whole battalion. They clothed Jesus in royal purple. They set a crown of thorns upon his head and shoved a reed between his fingers for a scepter. They began to mock him by kneeling before him and proclaiming, "Hail King of the Jews." They also spat upon him and smote him on the head with a stick. Then, after mocking him, they took away the purple, returned his own clothes, and brought him out to crucify him.

The extinguishing of the tenth candle.

16

On the road they met an African of Cyrene named Simon coming in from the countryside. Him they compelled to carry the cross. They brought Jesus to a place called Golgotha (which means "skull"). There they crucified him. . . . They offered him wine mingled with myrrh, but he refused it. His garments they divided among themselves, casting lots for them. Over his head they inscribed the charge against him, The King of the Jews. Also there were two insurrectionists crucified with him, one to his right and one to his left. Those who passed by were shaking their heads in derision and saying, "So you would destroy the Temple and rebuild it in three days! Save yourself. Come down from the cross." Likewise the priestly collaborators mocked him as they said to one another, "He saved others; himself he cannot save. Let the Anointed One, the King of Israel, come down from the cross that we may see and believe." Even the two crucified with him reviled him.

The extinguishing of the eleventh candle.

17

Now from midday there was darkness over the whole land until three in the afternoon. At that hour Jesus cried out in a loud voice, "Eli, Eli, lema shevaqtani!" words that mean, "My God, my God, why have you forsaken me?" Some of the bystanders said, "Look, he is calling for Elijah." One of them put a sponge full of vinegar on a stick and laid it to his lips. Others said, "Wait! let us see whether Elijah will come to take him down." Then Jesus having uttered a loud cry, breathed his last breath.

The extinguishing of the twelfth candle and the Christ candle. A loud noise is made by use of a cymbal or other means of harsh sound; the last section is read in darkness, after which the Christ candle may be returned or relighted.

18

Suddenly the curtain of the Temple was torn in two from the top to the bottom. The earth shook, and the rocks were split. Even the tombs of the dead were opened. Now, when the centurion on watch and the others who were with him saw all that was taking place, they were filled with awe and said, "This man truly was God's royal Son!"

Silence. Then return of light.

[SONG OF THE SUFFERING SERVANT]

Isaiah 53:4-9 [or 4-6]
This may be spoken by the congregation, or sung by the choir, or done responsively.

Surely he has borne our griefs
   and carried our sorrows;
yet we esteemed him stricken,
   smitten by God, and afflicted.
But he was wounded for our transgressions,
   he was bruised for our iniquities;
upon him was the chastisement that made us whole,
   and with his stripes we are healed.
All we like sheep have gone astray;
   we have turned every one to his own way;
and the Lord has laid on him
   the iniquity of us all.

He was oppressed, and he was afflicted,
   yet he opened not his mouth;
like a lamb that is led to the slaughter,
   and like a sheep that before its shearers is dumb,
   so he opened not his mouth.
By oppression and judgment he was taken away;
   and as for his generation, who considered
that he was cut off out of the land of the living,
   stricken for the transgression of my people?
And they made his grave with the wicked
   and with a rich man in his death,
although he had done no violence,
   and there was no deceit in his mouth.
Or a passion hymn may be sung.

DISMISSAL

May Jesus Christ, who for our sake became obedient unto death, even death on a cross, keep you and strengthen you this night and for ever. **Amen.**

All depart in quietness, except those beginning the prayer vigil.

Alternate A

With this form, seven or fourteen candles are used, and the Christ candle. Then, following each section, one or two are extinguished until the eighth reading, at which time the loud noise is made and the Christ candle is hidden or removed. At suitable times, hymns that express the scene just portrayed, or express a response to it, may be sung.

(Year A)	(Year B)	(Year C)
1. Matthew 26:30-46	Mark 14:26-42	Luke 22:39-46
	First candle(s) extinguished.	
2. Matthew 26:47-56	Mark 14:43-50	Luke 22:47-53
	Second candle(s) extinguished.	
3. Matthew 26:57-75	Mark 14:51-72	Luke 22:54-62
	Third candle(s) extinguished.	
4. Matthew 27:1-5	Mark 15:1-5	Luke 22:63-71
	Fourth candle(s) extinguished.	
5. Matthew 27:6-23	Mark 15:6-15	Luke 23:1-12
	Fifth candle(s) extinguished.	
6. Matthew 27:24-31	Mark 15:16-20	Luke 23:13-25
	Sixth candle(s) extinguished.	
7. Matthew 27:32-44	Mark 15:21-32	Luke 23:26-38
	Seventh candle(s) extinguished.	
8. Matthew 27:45-50	Mark 15:33-37	Luke 23:39-46
	Christ candle removed or hidden, and harsh sound.	
9. Matthew 27:51-54	Mark 15:38-39	Luke 23:47-56a
	Christ candle returned after a brief silence.	

SONG OF THE SUFFERING SERVANT

Isaiah 53:4-9 [or 4-6]

[HYMN]

DISMISSAL WITH BLESSING

Go in peace. May Jesus Christ, who for our sake became obedient unto death, even death on a cross, keep you and strengthen you this night and for ever. **Amen.**

All depart in quietness, except those beginning the prayer vigil.

Alternate B

In communities where the passion narrative is read on Passion/Palm Sunday and Good Friday, it is wise to use this form of the Tenebrae, which centers in the reading of appropriate psalms. It may be done on Thursday, Friday, and Saturday in Holy Week. During the first set of psalms, seven candles are extinguished at suitable intervals; during the second set of three psalms, seven more candles are extinguished. All other candles and lights are extinguished during the Benedictus (Luke 1:68-79) except for one candle which is hidden, usually behind the altar table. The people remain seated during the recital of these psalms and the reading from Lamentations, and the Gloria Patri is, of course, not used.

In the darkened church, people may kneel for the Lord's Prayer (which follows the short responsory), for the final Psalm 51 (which may be recited responsively by the choir), and for the final prayer. The hidden candle is brought out again just before the final prayer. The congregation is dismissed and departs in silence.

Thursday	*Friday*	*Saturday*
GATHERING	GATHERING	GATHERING
GREETING	GREETING	GREETING
PSALMS 69, 70, 71	PSALMS 72, 73, 74	PSALMS 2, 22, 27
READING Lam. 1:1-14	READING Lam. 2:10-19	READING Lam. 3:1-21
PSALMS 75, 76, 77	PSALMS 38, 40, 54	PSALMS 59, 88, 94
GOSPEL John 13	GOSPEL John 16	GOSPEL John 17
BENEDICTUS	BENEDICTUS	BENEDICTUS

Blessed be the Lord, the God of Israel;
he has come to his people and set them free.
He has raised up for us a mighty Savior,
born of the house of his servant David.
Through his holy prophets he promised of old
  that he would save us from our enemies,
  from the hands of all who hate us.
He promised to show mercy to our fathers
and to remember his holy covenant.
This was the oath he swore to our father Abraham:
to set us free from the hands of our enemies,
free to worship him without fear,
holy and righteous in his sight
  all the days of our life.

You, my child, shall be called the prophet of the Most High,
for you will go before the Lord to prepare his way
to give his people knowledge of salvation
by the forgiveness of their sins.
In the tender compassion of our God
the dawn from on high shall break upon us,
to shine on those who dwell in darkness
  and the shadow of death,
and to guide our feet into the way of peace.
      A brief silence.
Christ, for our sake, became obedient unto death;

Even unto the death of the cross.

THE LORD'S PRAYER

A brief silence; the Christ candle is returned.

[PSALM 51:1-17   *See pp. 113-14 for text.*]

CLOSING PRAYER

> Lord Jesus, one of us betrayed you,
>   another denied you,
>   and all of us have forsaken you.
> Yet you remained faithful to death,
>   even death upon a cross.
> Strengthen us so we do not turn aside
>   but follow you through sunlight and shadow alike.
> For the final victory belongs to you, Lord Jesus.
> **Amen.**

DISMISSAL

> Go in peace.
> May Jesus Christ, who for our sake became obedient
> unto death, even death on a cross,
> keep you and strengthen you this night and for ever.
> **Amen.**

All depart in quietness.

Commentary

The service of Tenebrae, or "shadows," grew out of a combination night prayer and early morning prayer, with an additional focus on the commemoration of the passion. The latter was usually read by several deacons and later, in the Middle Ages, was read by monastic choirs. The most significant feature of this service is the gradual extinguishing of the lights and candles in the room and on the altar. The bare altar table and the unvested furnishings emphasize the starkness of the events recalled. The candles represent the apostles and all followers of Christ, and the larger candle represents Christ. The dramatic high point occurs with the complete darkness and the loud noise, or *strepitus*, at the death of Jesus.

This service may be used in one of three ways: (1) as preparation for a Holy Thursday rite of repentance and forgiveness; (2) as a concluding service following Holy Communion on Holy Thursday; (3) or as the evening service on Good Friday, particularly as the beginning of a prayer vigil lasting through Saturday, or in a retreat. Alternate B may be used on all three evenings.

Three basic alternates for the meditation on the passion are included. The first is a specially composed liturgical interpretation by John T. Townsend[1]; the second uses the text of the Gospel appointed for the year. The third is based on psalms of distress, passages from Lamentations, and John's Gospel. In the first two alternatives, the passion narrative is divided into sections, and candles are extinguished at certain specific times. Hymns or psalms may also be sung in response to these sections. An atmosphere of quiet and sober reflection should permeate the readings and the prayers. Several readers may be used, alternating the sections. The readers also extinguish the candles.

Care sould be taken to rehearse the readings for pace, audibility, and coherent meaning. The larger candle is either hidden at the death passage or removed from the room. Such actions must not be hurried. When the candle is removed, after suitable time for silence in total darkness, it is returned; and the lights of the room are at least partially turned up for the final reading and dismissal.

Alternate B provides several possibilities for reciting the psalms. Visuals may be appropriate between the psalms for meditation. The Benedictus (Luke 1:68-79) may be recited or sung by the choir, it may be recited responsively by the congregation. Because this will be done in diminishing light, provision must be made for seeing the texts. The brief response which follows should be known by the congregation beforehand. The penitential Psalm 51 is optional, and the closing prayer is prayed by the minister or lay leader. Care should be taken to allow space for silence between the readings.

NOTE FOR CHAPTER VI–G

1. A booklet containing the full text with introduction and extensive documentation for further study may be obtained from the National Conference of Christians and Jews, 43 West 75th Street, New York, NY 10019 or from any of their regional offices in metropolitan areas.

H. Good Friday
with Provision for a Prayer Vigil Through Holy Saturday

GATHERING

No colors, flowers, images, or decorative materials should be used on Good Friday except, perhaps, representations of the way of the cross. The Lord's table, pulpit, and lectern should be bare of cloth, candles, or anything else not actually used in the service. The cross remains, but it and any permanently fixed images should be veiled if possible. The veil may be made from mesh or cheesecloth dyed a deep hue of red, black, purple, or gray. It covers the cross or images completely and may be gathered at the bottom. Because of the transparent nature of the veil, the cross remains visible though shrouded. The veil, by partly concealing the cross, also calls attention to it.

Appropriate choral or instrumental music may be offered while the people gather, though silence is preferable. The ministers and readers enter in silence. A brief introduction may be given if necessary. After another silence, the minister invites the people to stand, then says:

GREETING

Blessed be the name of the Lord our God.

Who redeems us from sin and death.

For us and for the salvation of all,
Christ became obedient unto death,
even death on a cross.

Blessed be the name of the Lord.

HYMN

OPENING PRAYER

Let us pray: *A brief pause.*
Holy and ever-living God,
   by the suffering and death of Jesus
   you save us from Adam's fall.
Grant in your mercy that we may be drawn
   to Christ lifted high on the cross,
   and by his redeeming love be raised
   to everlasting life with him,
who lives and reigns with you in the Holy Spirit,
   for ever and ever. **Amen.**

FIRST LESSON Isaiah 52:13–53:12 (All years)

PSALM Psalm 22:1-18 (BCP)
My God, my God, why have you forsaken me?
    and are so far from my cry
    and from the words of my distress?
O my God, I cry in the daytime, but you do not answer;
    by night as well, but I find no rest.

Yet you are the Holy One,
    enthroned upon the praises of Israel.
Our ancestors put their trust in you;
    they trusted in you and were not put to shame.

But as for me, I am a worm, and no man,
    scorned by all and despised by the people.
All who see me laugh me to scorn;
    they curl their lips and wag their heads, saying,
"He trusted in the Lord; let him deliver him;
    let him rescue him, if he delights in him."
Yet you are the one who took me out of the womb,
    and kept me safe upon my mother's breast.
I have been entrusted to you ever since I was born;
    you were my God when I was still in my mother's womb.
Be not far from me, for trouble is near,
    and there is none to help.

Many young bulls encircle me;
    strong bulls of Bashan surround me.
They open wide their jaws at me,
    like a ravening and a roaring lion.

I am poured out like water;
    all my bones are out of joint;
    my heart within my breast is melting wax.
My mouth is dried out like a potsherd;
    my tongue sticks to the roof of my mouth;
    and you have laid me in the dust of the grave.

Packs of dogs close me in,
    and gangs of evildoers circle around me;
    they pierce my hands and my feet;
I can count all my bones.
    They stare and gloat over me;
they divide my garments among them;
    they cast lots for my clothing.

SECOND LESSON Hebrews 4:14-16; 5:7-9 (All years)

HYMN or RESPONSORY

Christ became obedient unto death,
even death on a cross.

Have mercy on us, Lord Jesus.

Therefore, God raised him on high
and gave him a name above all other names.

Praise to you, Lord Jesus Christ.

THE PASSION OF OUR LORD ACCORDING TO JOHN

Full form: John 18:1–19:42 [Short form: John 19:17-30]
This is most suitably proclaimed as a dramatic reading. Specific roles may be assigned. The principal designations are N–narrator; †–Christ; S–speakers other than Christ (these may be divided into separate male and female voices, indicated by S₁, S₂, S₃, and Sps); C–crowd (or congregation).

N   Jesus . . . went forth with his disciples across the Kidron Valley, where there was a garden, which he and his disciples entered. Now Judas, who betrayed him, also knew the place; for Jesus often met there with his disciples. So Judas, procuring a band of soldiers and some officers from the chief priests and the Pharisees, went there with lanterns and torches and weapons. Then Jesus, knowing all that was to befall him, came forward and said to them,

†   "Whom do you seek?"

N   They answered him,

Sps "Jesus of Nazareth."

N   Jesus said to them,

†   "I am he."

N   Judas, who betrayed him, was standing with them. When he said to them, "I am he," they drew back and fell to the ground. Again he asked them,

†   "Whom do you seek?"

N   And they said,

Sps "Jesus of Nazareth."

N   Jesus answered,

†   "I told you that I am he; so, if you seek me, let these men go."

N   This was to fulfill the word which he had spoken, "Of those whom thou gavest me I lost not one." Then Simon Peter, having a sword, drew it and struck the high priest's slave and cut off his right ear. The slave's name was Malchus. Jesus said to Peter,

†   "Put your sword into its sheath; shall I not drink the cup which the Father has given me?"

N   So the band of soldiers and their captain and the officers of the Jews seized Jesus and bound him. First they led him to Annas; for he was the father-in-law of Caiaphas, who was high priest that year. It was Caiaphas who had given counsel to the Jews that it was expedient that one man should die for the people.

Simon Peter followed Jesus, and so did another disciple. As this disciple was known to the high priest, he entered the court of the high priest along with Jesus, while Peter stood outside at the door. So the other disciple, who was known to the high priest, went out and spoke to the maid who kept the door, and brought Peter in. The maid who kept the door said to Peter,

S₁   "Are not you also one of this man's disciples?"

N   He said,

S₂   "I am not."

N   Now the servants and officers had made a charcoal fire, because it was cold, and they were standing and warming themselves; Peter also was with them, standing and warming himself.

The high priest then questioned Jesus about his disciples and his teaching. Jesus answered him,

†   "I have spoken openly to the world; I have always taught in synagogues and in the temple, where all Jews come together; I have said nothing secretly. Why do you ask me? Ask those who have heard me, what I said to them; they know what I said."

N   When he had said this, one of the officers standing by struck Jesus with his hand, saying,

S₃   "Is that how you answer the high priest?"

N   Jesus answered him,

†   "If I have spoken wrongly, bear witness to the wrong; but if I have spoken rightly, why do you strike me?"

N   Annas then sent him bound to Caiaphas the high priest.

Now Simon Peter was standing and warming himself. They said to him,

Sps   "Are not you also one of his disciples?"

N   He denied it and said,

S₂   "I am not."

N   One of the servants of the high priest, a kinsman of the man whose ear Peter had cut off, asked,

S₄   "Did I not see you in the garden with him?"

N   Peter again denied it; and at once the cock crowed.

Then they led Jesus from the house of Caiaphas to the praetorium. It was early. They themselves did not enter the praetorium, so that they might not be defiled, but might eat the passover. So Pilate went out to them and said,

S₅   "What accusation do you bring against this man?"

N   They answered him,

Sps   "If this man were not an evildoer, we would not have handed him over."

N   Pilate said to them,

S₅   "Take him yourselves and judge him by your own law."

N   The Jews said to him,

Sps "It is not lawful for us to put any man to death."

N   This was to fulfil the word which Jesus had spoken to show by what death he was to die. Pilate entered the praetorium again and called Jesus, and said to him,

S₅   "Are you the King of the Jews?"

N   Jesus answered,

†   "Do you say this of your own accord, or did others say it to you about me?"

N   Pilate answered,

S₅   "Am I a Jew? Your own nation and the chief priests have handed you over to me; what have you done?"

N   Jesus answered,

†   "My kingship is not of this world; if my kingship were of this world, my servants would fight, that I might not be handed over to the Jews; but my kingship is not from the world."

N   Pilate said to him,

S₅   "So you are a king?"

N   Jesus answered,

†   "You say that I am a king. For this I was born, and for this I have come into the world, to bear witness to the truth. Every one who is of the truth hears my voice."

N   Pilate said to him,

S₅   "What is truth?"

N   After he had said this, he went out to the Jews again, and told them,

S₅   "I find no crime in him. But you have a custom that I should release one man for you at the Passover; will you have me release for you the King of the Jews?"

N   They cried out again,

Sps "Not this man, but Barabbas!"

N   Now Barabbas was a robber.
     Then Pilate took Jesus and scourged him. And the soldiers plaited a crown of thorns, and put it on his head, and arrayed him in a purple robe; they came up to him saying,

Sps "Hail, King of the Jews!"

N   and struck him with their hands. Pilate went out again, and said to them,

S₅   "See, I am bringing him out to you, that you may know that I find no crime in him."

N   So Jesus came out, wearing the crown of thorns and the purple robe. Pilate said to them,

S₅ "Behold the man!"

N   When the chief priests and the officers saw him, they cried out,

C   "Crucify him, crucify him!"

N   Pilate said to them,

S₅ "Take him yourselves and crucify him, for I find no crime in him."

N   The Jews answered him,

C   "We have a law, and by that law he ought to die, because he has made himself the Son of God."

N   When Pilate heard these words, he was the more afraid; he entered the praetorium again and said to Jesus,

S₅ "Where are you from?"

N   But Jesus gave no answer. Pilate therefore said to him,

S₅ "You will not speak to me? Do you not know that I have power to release you, and power to crucify you?"

N   Jesus answered him,

†   "You would have no power over me unless it had been given you from above; therefore he who delivered me to you has the greater sin."

N   Upon this Pilate sought to release him, but the Jews cried out,

Sps "If you release this man, you are not Caesar's friend; every one who makes himself a king sets himself against Caesar."

N   When Pilate heard these words, he brought Jesus out and sat down on the judgment seat at a place called The Pavement, and in Hebrew, Gabbatha. Now it was the day of Preparation for the Passover; it was about the sixth hour. He said to the Jews,

S₅ "Behold your king!"

N   They cried out,

C   "Away with him, away with him, crucify him!"

N   Pilate said to them,

S₅ "Shall I crucify your King?"

N   The chief priests answered,

Sps "We have no king but Caesar."

N   Then he handed him over to them to be crucified.

Short form begins.

So they took Jesus, and he went out, bearing his own cross, to the place called the place of a skull, which is called in Hebrew Golgotha. There they crucified him, and with him two others, one on either side, and Jesus between them. Pilate also wrote a title and put it on the cross; it read, "Jesus of Nazareth, the King of the Jews." Many of the Jews read this title, for the place where Jesus was crucified was near the city; and it was written in Hebrew, in Latin, and in Greek. The chief priests of the Jews then said to Pilate,

Sps   "Do not write, 'The King of the Jews,' but, "This man said, 'I am King of the Jews.' ' "

N   Pilate answered,

S₅   "What I have written I have written."

N   When the soldiers had crucified Jesus they took his garments and made four parts, one for each soldier. But his tunic was without seam, woven from top to bottom; so they said to one another,

Sps   "Let us not tear it, but cast lots for it to see whose it shall be."

N   This was to fulfil the scripture, "They parted my garments among them, and for my clothing they cast lots."

     So the soldiers did this. But standing by the cross of Jesus were his mother, and his mother's sister, Mary the wife of Clopas, and Mary Magdalene. When Jesus saw his mother, and the disciple whom he loved standing near, he said to his mother,

†   "Woman, behold, your son!"

N   Then he said to the disciple,

†   "Behold, your mother!"

N   And from that hour the disciple took her to his own home.

     After this Jesus, knowing that all was now finished, said (to fulfil the scripture),

†   "I thirst."

N   A bowl full of vinegar stood there; so they put a sponge full of the vinegar on hyssop and held it to his mouth. When Jesus had received the vinegar, he said,

†   "It is finished";

N   and he bowed his head and gave up his spirit.

Short form ends.

Since it was the day of Preparation, in order to prevent the bodies from remaining on the cross on the sabbath (for that sabbath was a high day), the Jews asked Pilate that their legs might be broken, and that they might be taken away. So the soldiers came and broke the legs of the first, and of the other who had been crucified with him; but when they came to Jesus and saw that he was already dead, they did not break his legs. But one of the soldiers pierced his side with a spear, and at once there came out blood and water. He who saw it has borne witness—his testimony is true, and he knows that he tells the truth—that you also may believe. For these things took place that the scripture might be fulfilled. "Not a bone of him shall be broken." And again another scripture says, "They shall look on him whom they have pierced."

After this Joseph of Arimathea, who was a disciple of Jesus, but secretly, for fear of the Jews, asked Pilate that he might take away the body of Jesus, and Pilate gave him leave. So he ame and took away his body. Nicodemus also, who had at first come to him by night, came bringing a mixture of myrrh and aloes, about a hundred pounds' weight. They took the body of Jesus, and bound it in linen cloths with the spices, as is the burial custom of the Jews. Now in the place where he was crucified there was a garden, and in the garden a new tomb where no one had ever been laid. So because of the Jewish day of Preparation, as the tomb was close at hand, they laid Jesus there.

[SERMON]

HYMN

PRAYERS OF THE PEOPLE

The minister or other appointed person may say:

My brothers and sisters: God sent Christ into the world, not to condemn the world, but that the world through him might be saved; that all who believe in him might be delivered from the power of sin and death, and become heirs with him of everlasting life.

Therefore, let us pray with the whole church for people everywhere in their needs, and for the whole world.

The service concludes with one of the following alternates.

Alternative A: A Brief Closing

HYMN or ANTHEM

THE LORD'S PRAYER

[CONCLUDING PRAYER

Lord Jesus Christ, Son of God,
   set your passion, cross, and death between your judgment and our souls,
now and in the hour of our death.
Give mercy and grace to the living;
   pardon and rest to the dead and the dying;
   to your church, peace and unity;
   and to us sinners, everlasting life;
for you live and reign with the Father and the Holy Spirit,
   one God, now and for ever. **Amen.**]   (BCP)

All depart in silence.

Alternative B: Meditations on the Cross

Following the prayers, a wooden cross may be brought silently into the church and positioned in a visible, accessible place. If there is a procession, the following verse and response may be said or sung two or three times by the ministers, the choir, and the people—pausing at the place in the church where it is sung—depending upon the space involved.

This is the wood of the cross, on which hung
   the Savior of the world.
Come let us worship and bow down.

After the cross has been positioned, a hymn or anthem of the cross may be said or sung.

HYMN or ANTHEM

and/or

We glory in your cross, O Lord,

and praise and glorify your resurrection victory;
for by virtue of your cross
joy has come to the whole world.

May God be merciful to us and bless us,
shed the light of his countenance on us, and come to us.

We glory in your cross, O Lord,
and praise and glorify your resurrection,
for by virtue of your cross
joy has come to the whole world.

or

We adore you, O Christ, and we bless you,
By your holy cross you have redeemed the world.

If we have died with him, we shall also live with him;
if we endure, we shall also reign with him.

We adore you, O Christ, and we bless you,
By your holy cross you have redeemed the world.

or

O Savior of the world,
who by your cross and precious blood did redeem us:
Help, save, pity, and defend us, we pray, O Lord.

SILENT MEDITATION or
DEVOTIONS AT THE CROSS

In some circumstances, the ministers and the congregation may wish to come forward in an informal procession to the cross, with each person making a sign of reverence such as touching the cross, kneeling briefly, or bowing. The people should move freely and return to their seats. No one should be coerced or regimented.

During this time any or all of the following Reproaches—questions and responses of Christ's lament against his faithless church—may be sung or spoken, with the congregation responding.

1. Is it nothing to you, all you who pass by?
   Look and see if there is any sorrow like my sorrow
   which was brought upon me,
   which the Lord inflicted on the day of his fierce anger.

   Holy God,
   Holy and Mighty.
   Holy and Immortal One,
   Have mercy upon us.

2. O my people, O my church,
   What have I done to you,

or in what have I offended you?
Testify against me.
I led you forth from the land of Egypt
and delivered you by the waters of baptism,
but you have prepared a cross for your Savior.

Holy God,
Holy and Mighty.
Holy and Immortal One,
Have mercy upon us.

3. I led you through the desert forty years,
   and fed you with manna:
   I brought you through tribulation and penitence,
   and gave you my body, the bread of heaven,
   but you have prepared a cross for your Savior.

   Holy God . . .

4. What more could I have done for you
   that I have not done?
   I planted you, my chosen and fairest vineyard,
   I made you the branches of my vine;
   but when I was thirsty, you gave me vinegar to drink
   and pierced with a spear the side of your Savior.

   Holy God . . .

5. I went before you in a pillar of cloud,
   and you have led me to the judgment hall of Pilate.
   I scourged your enemies and brought you to a land of freedom,
   but you have scourged, mocked, and beaten me.
   I gave you the water of salvation from the rock,
   but you have given me gall and left me to thirst.

   Holy God . . .

6. I gave you a royal scepter,
   and bestowed the keys to the kingdom,
   but you have given me a crown of thorns.
   I raised you on high with great power,
   but you have hanged me on the cross.

   Holy God . . .

7. My peace I gave, which the world cannot give,
   and washed your feet as a sign of my love,
   but you draw the sword to strike in my name
   and seek high places in my kingdom.
   I offered you my body and blood,
   but you scatter and deny and abandon me.

   Holy God . . .

8. I sent the Spirit of truth to guide you,
   and you close your hearts to the Counselor.
   I pray that all may be one in the Father and me,
   but you continue to quarrel and divide.
   I call you to go and bring forth fruit,
   but you cast lots for my clothing.

   Holy God . . .

9. I grafted you into the tree of my chosen Israel,
   and you turned on them with persecution and mass murder.
   I made you joint heirs with them of my covenants,
   but you made them scapegoats for your own guilt.

   Holy God . . .

10. I came to you as the least of your brothers and sisters;
    I was hungry and you gave me no food,
    I was thirsty and you gave me no drink,
    I was a stranger and you did not welcome me,
    naked and you did not clothe me,
    sick and in prison and you did not visit me.

    Holy God . . .

A brief silence follows.

THE LORD'S PRAYER

[CONCLUDING PRAYER]

All depart in silence.

Commentary

Many local churches have an already established tradition of a two- or three-hour service on Good Friday afternoon, usually beginning at noon. It is often ecumenical in nature. In many places the service is based upon the Word of God and upon musical offerings, focusing on the seven last words of Christ, a composite of several Gospel accounts, with hymns and music by a number of composers.

The service presented here is designed to focus even more intensely on the proclamatory reading and experience of the context and meaning of the crucifixion for us today. In particular, it uses the passion according to Saint John, since the three Synoptic Gospels are used on Passion/Palm Sunday. This service has three principal sections: the proclamation of the Word of God, the intercessory prayers for the afflictions of the world, and the meditations at the cross. The latter section may be omitted, or other suitable devotions may be substituted, such as the stations of the cross or silent prayer with directed reflection or hymns and free prayer. The service can easily incorporate parts of various musical settings of the Saint John passion, of which the most well-known is that of J. S. Bach.

As with other services for Holy Week and Easter Triduum, this may be quite simple in style and relatively brief; or it may be more elaborate and fully developed, depending upon the resources and the local circumstances. The more elaborate devotional form could last up to two hours.

A sizable wooden cross (for example, six feet by four feet) may be positioned before the service in the narthex or foyer of the building or just outside the main entrance. Then, following the prayers of the people, it may be brought in procession as indicated. Several persons may take part in the procession, including laypersons. In this manner the congregation passes by the wooden cross upon entering, and then again experiences the cross as a focus for meditation and devotional acts as the concluding section of the service.

Many congregations have found that nonverbal expressions of devotion to Christ and the cross are powerful though somewhat unfamiliar. It is crucial that the sign-acts with the cross be introduced in prayerful reflection and discussion with the work area on worship or the worship committee well before the Good Friday service. If possible, the congregation may be instructed as well. More harm than good may result without careful teaching and pastoral direction here. On the other hand, Alternative B should be considered by each congregation since it provides a strong expression of encounter and witness to the redeeming love of Christ.

With respect to the Service of the Word, the reading of the passion may be shortened, if necessary, to John 19:17-30 (indicated in the text). In some cases, chancel drama may be used and integrated into the whole of the service. Hymns may be interspersed at appropriate intervals within the reading, as was suggested for Passion/Palm Sunday and the service of Tenebrae.

A special word must be said concerning the Reproaches. Traditionally these were used to dramatize the accusations that God brings against his people in the light of the passion and death of Christ. They ask questions that reveal our own rebellion and complicity in the sufferings of Christ and in the evil and sufferings in the world. Images from scripture are used concerning Israel and God's hand in that holy history, but the accusations are clearly aimed at the faithlessness of all who would call upon God, particularly at all Christians in the church who presume to be grafted into the tree of Israel (Rom. 11:17-24). The accusations are like an inversion of the holy history we recite and recall in the Great Thanksgivings at the Lord's table.

We must all be aware, however, of the history of anti-Jewish sentiment which has often seen the crucifixion to be the work of the Jews. This is abhorrent, especially in the light of modern consequences of anti-Semitism and its continuing presence within the Christian community. For those situations where the Reproaches may give the impression of anti-Jewish convictions, they should not be used. But these texts have been carefully recast, based upon the excellent work done by the Inter-Lutheran Commission on Worship and upon serious reflection. In fact, by the inclusion of verse 9, the Reproaches become a specific act of repentance by Christians for anti-Semitism, appropriate to the day that has been the occasion in our history for overt expressions of anti-Semitism.

If all ten verses are too many for a given service, only those verses that are most appropriate may be used. Verses 1, 2, 6, 7, and 8 are one possible shortened form. It is also possible to create a contemporary version from images born of our own rebellion and abuse of God's good gifts—though care should be taken not to make this ecological alone; the *theological* point of the accusations and responses is central. This may be done visually using slides or other projections of events, persons, and situations that show us our complicity in rejecting Christ. The images from verse 10 are particularly suggestive and are based upon Matthew 25.

When Tenebrae is not celebrated on Holy Thursday, it is quite appropriate for Good Friday evening. Increasing numbers of churches are holding continuous prayer vigils from Friday evening through the afternoon on Holy Saturday. One possibility is to use the Tenebrae service described earlier as the beginning of such a prayer vigil. Persons and families sign up for certain designated hours (in thirty- or sixty-minute periods). The church building would be open during these hours up to the beginning of the Easter Vigil on Saturday evening. A set of resources might be provided, based upon the images and the passion narrative, to those who keep vigil. This could take the form of a brief printed set of meditations and prayers or a tape of directed meditation or a tableau of images or icons. The persons would bring their own Bibles.

Holy Saturday

On Holy Saturday, the church continues in prayer, waiting with the women at the Lord's tomb. The meditation continues to focus on the themes of redemptive suffering and death. The altar table remains bare. If a brief liturgy of the Word is part of the devotions of those on the prayer vigil—say at noon—it could be patterned after Alternative B of Tenebrae. Or the following may be used.

PRAYER

Merciful and ever-living God,
Creator of heaven and earth:
   As the crucified body of your Son was laid in the tomb
   and rested on this holy day,
   Grant that we may await with him the dawning
   of the third day as he promised,
   and rise with him in newness of life;
through Jesus Christ our Lord. **Amen.**

READINGS

Job 14:1-14
Psalm 130 or Psalm 31:1-5 as responsorial psalms
I Peter 4:1-8
Matthew 27:57-66 or John 19:38-42

RESPONSORY

In the midst of life we are in death;
from whom can we seek help?
From you alone, O Lord,
who by our sins are justly angered.

Holy God, Holy and Mighty,
Holy and merciful Savior,
Deliver us from the bitterness of eternal death.

Good Friday and Holy Saturday are traditional days of fasting. The whole church may be invited to fast along with those on prayer vigil or on retreat during this period.

These two days are also a significant time for a retreat. Historically, these hours were the last period of intensive preparation for those persons who were to be baptized at the first Easter service—in ancient times, always the great Easter Vigil. We wish to encourage this possibility. Such a retreat may be for any group within the church. Elements of the Good Friday services, both the afternoon sections and the Tenebrae, may be used to structure common prayer. There should be periods of common prayer and reflection on scripture, with times for personal solitude throughout the day. In the case of those preparing for baptism, some of the great patristic (early church) writings, catechetical lectures, and Easter homilies may be read and shared. Writings of Saint Ambrose, Saint John Chrysostom, Saint Cyril of Jerusalem, and Theodore of Mopsuestia are rich in instruction and spiritual insight for this period. These may be found in Edward Yarnold's *The Awe-Inspiring Rites of Initiation: Baptismal Homilies of the Fourth Century* (London: St. Paul's Publications, 1971).

I. Easter Vigil, or the First Service of Easter

Introduction

(The following introductory remarks may be duplicated and distributed to the congregation as part of their preparation for Holy Week. In churches celebrating the vigil for the first time, a preparatory meeting or study group may be formed during Lent.)

During the Easter Triduum, from sunset Thursday to sunset Sunday, we celebrate the saving events of our Lord's passion, death, and resurrection. In the development of Christian worship, each event came to be remembered on a separate day. In the earliest centuries, however, the whole of the Paschal Mystery was celebrated in an extraordinary single liturgy which began on Saturday night and continued until the dawn of what we now call Easter Day. This was known as the great Paschal (Easter) Vigil. It was the most holy and joyful night of the entire Christian Year, for it proclaimed and celebrated the whole of salvation history and Christ's saving work.

On this holy and joyous paschal night, the fullness of the sacraments of Christian initiation are joined to the Word of God, as we participate in the passing from death to life, and to rebirth into the kingdom of God. Justin Martyr, writing in the second century, tells us that persons preparing for baptism fasted as discipline. By the fourth century the period of preparation and instruction lasted forty days (the origin of our modern Lent). In his *Homilies,* Saint Basil declares: "What time is more appropriate for Baptism than this day of the Pasch? It is the memorial day of the resurrection. Baptism implants in us the seed of resurrection. Let us then receive the grace of resurrection on the day of the resurrection."[1] The whole community's participation in this most dramatic occasion of worship reveals the original unity of the rites of Christian initiation. This liturgy is for all members of the household of faith and presents the grace of renewal which is at the heart of being raised to new life in Christ.

The Easter Vigil has both historic and symbolic roots in the Jewish Passover. This is why so many images are from the Old Testament and why so many analogies are experienced in Christ. In this service we experience the passage from slavery to freedom, from sin to salvation, from death to life. The vigil of the Christian Passover marks the beginning of the Sunday of all Sundays, the Lord's Day above all others.

In recent times, there has been widespread interest in the recovery of this ancient First Service of Easter. Many Protestants are familiar with Easter sunrise services and the main Easter morning service bathed in a sea of lilies and special music. Relatively few have celebrated this most glorious and fitting occasion for the Lord's Supper, and fewer still have experienced the intensity of the whole drama of salvation that the Easter Vigil proclaims and presents.

The order of service which follows is patterned after the ancient vigil service. It may be celebrated beginning Saturday night and culminating early Sunday morning after midnight, or as a predawn Sunday morning service. In the former case, we call it the Easter Vigil; in the latter, the First Service of Easter. When it is held in the early morning hours, it may be followed by a festive Easter breakfast. In either case, the whole liturgy has four principal parts:

1. The Service of Light
2. The Service of the Word
3. The Service of the Water
4. The Service of the Bread and Cup

Two primary characteristics of this celebration are to be noted: first, the dominant symbols of light, water, and the heavenly banquet; and second, the powerful sweep of the Scriptures, the whole history of God's creating and redeeming work focused in Jesus Christ. Thus, we may say that this is at one and the same time the most evangelical, biblical, sacramental, and liturgical occasion of worship in the whole of Christian life.

As with other services in this book, the basic pattern may be carried out quite simply or in a richly elaborated manner. The pattern and the texts with actions are designed for flexible adaptation without sacrificing the theological depth and meaning of this most glorious gathering in the Christian Year. The following pattern and texts resemble closely the traditional vigil, which is now being recovered by almost all Christian traditions, and yet allow for contemporary accents as well. It may be modified according to pastoral realities and local circumstances, but the integrity of the four principal elements and the primary characteristics should be preserved—especially the sacraments of baptism (or baptismal renewal) and the Lord's Supper, or Eucharist. If the whole liturgy is celebrated, the people should be made aware of the length of the service and should prepare accordingly.

1. The Service of Light

The vigil begins in darkness. Wherever possible, the lighting of the new fire should take place outside the building in a suitable place, or in another room or fellowship hall which can accommodate the whole gathering. This allows a congregational procession into the room of worship.

The fire is kindled while some of the people may still be gathering. Silence is kept for a time until all are assembled. Then the presiding minister, or someone appointed, addresses the people with these or similar words:

GREETING AND INTRODUCTION

Grace and peace to you from Jesus Christ our Lord.

My brothers and sisters in Christ: On this most holy night (morning) in which Jesus Christ passed over from death to life, we gather as the church to pray and to watch for the dawning of his triumph and resurrection. We join with the whole company of God's people in heaven and on earth in recalling and celebrating his victory over death, and our deliverance from the bondage of sin and darkness to everlasting light. *A brief pause.*

Hear the Word of God: "In the beginning was the Word, and the Word was with God, and the Word was God. . . . In him was life, and the life was the light of all people. The light shines in the darkness, and the darkness has not overcome it" (John 1:1, 4-5).

OPENING PRAYER

Let us pray: *A brief pause.*
Eternal Lord of life,

Through your Son you have bestwed the light of life upon all the world. Sanctify this new fire and grant that our hearts and minds also be kindled with holy desire to shine forth with the brightness of Christ's rising, and to feat at the heavenly banquet; through jesus Christ our Lord. **Amen.**

LIGHTING OF THE PASCHAL CANDLE

The paschal candle is lighted from the fire, and these words are spoken:

> The light of Christ rises in glory,
> overcoming the darkness of sin and death.

The candle is lifted that all may see it, and immediately a procession forms, with choir or singers leading the candle-bearers and the ministers, followed by the people, into the worship area.

PROCESSION INTO THE CHURCH

Depending upon the distance, the procession pauses three times at various places—the third being when all are in position in the worship area—to sing:

Or a hymn may be sung as the procession enters the church, particularly "Christ, Whose Glory Fills the Skies." If candles have been given to members of the congregation, they may be lighted from others which

have been lighted from the paschal candle. As the room fills, other lights and stationary candles may be lighted.

EASTER PROCLAMATION

When the paschal candle is placed on a stand visible to the people, the Exsultet *is sung or recited. Various forms of this ancient and glorious hymn are given in the commentary.*

Rejoice, heavenly powers! Sing, choirs of angels!
Exult, all creation around God's throne!
Jesus Christ, our King is risen!
Sound the trumpet of salvation!

Rejoice, O earth, in shining splendor,
   radiant in the brightness of our King!
Christ has conquered! Glory fills you!
Darkness vanishes for ever!

Rejoice, O Holy Church! Exult in glory!
The risen Savior shines upon you!
Let this place resound with joy,
   echoing the mighty song of all God's people!

[My dearest friends, standing with me in this holy light,
   join me in asking God for mercy,
   that he may give his unworthy minister
   grace to sing his Easter praises.
The Lord be with you.

And also with you.]

Lift up your hearts.

We lift them up to the Lord.

Let us give thanks to the Lord our God.

It is right to give our thanks and praise.

It is truly right that with full hearts and
   minds, and voices we should praise you,
   invisible, almighty, and eternal God,
   and your only Son, our Lord Jesus Christ.
For Christ has ransomed us with his blood,
   and paid for us the debt of Adam's sin
   to deliver your faithful people.

This is our Passover feast,
   when Christ, the true Lamb, is slain,
   whose blood consecrates the homes of all believers.
This is the night when first you saved our forebears:
   you freed the people of Israel from their slavery
   and led them dry-shod through the sea.

This is the night when the pillar of fire
    destroyed the darkness of sin!
This is the night when Christians everywhere,
    washed clean of sin and freed from all defilement,
    are restored to grace and grow together in holiness.
This is the night when Jesus Christ broke the chains of
    death and rose triumphant from the grave.

Father, how wonderful your care for us!
How boundless your merciful love!
To ransom a slave you gave away your Son.

[O happy fault, O necessary sin of Adam,
    which gained for us so great a Redeemer!
Most blessed of all nights, chosen by God
    to see Christ rising from the dead!
Of this night scripture says:
    "The night will be as clear as day:
    it will become my light, my joy."

The power of this holy night
    dispels all evil, washes guilt away.
    restores lost innocence, brings mourners joy;
    it casts out hatred, brings us peace,
    and humbles earthly pride.]
Night truly blessed, when heaven is wedded to earth,
    and we are reconciled with God!
Therefore, Heavenly Father, in the joy of this night,
    receive our evening sacrifice of praise,
    your church's solemn offering.
Accept this Easter candle,
    a flame divided but undimmed,
    a pillar of fire that glows to your honor.
Let it mingle with the lights of heaven
    and continue bravely burning to dispel the darkness of the night!

May the Morning Star which never sets
    find this flame still burning:
Christ, that Morning Star, who
    came back from the dead,
    and shed his peaceful light on all creation,
    your Son who lives and reigns for ever and ever. **Amen.**

[HYMN]

2. The Service of the Word

The celebrant may say:
    Dear sisters and brothers in Christ, we now begin our solemn vigil. Let us attend to the Word of God, recalling God's saving deeds in history; and, in the fulness of time, how God's own Son was sent to be our Redeemer. May the Holy Spirit illumine our hearts and minds in the hearing of this Word.

OLD TESTAMENT READINGS

The number of readings may vary according to the length of the service, but there should always be at least three from the Old Testament, including Exodus 14. Each reading is followed by brief silence or a responsorial psalm, then a prayer. See the commentary for other variations.

The creation

Genesis 1:1–2:2
Psalm 33 *or* "Morning Has Broken"
Let us pray:
Almighty God, who wonderfully created, yet more wonderfully restored, the dignity of human nature, grant that we may share the divine life of him who humbled himself to share our humanity, through Jesus Christ our Lord. **Amen.**   BCP

The covenant between God and the earth

Genesis 7:1-5; 11-18; 8:6-18; 9:8-13
Psalm 46 *or* "A Mighty Fortress Is Our God"
Let us pray:
Almighty God of heaven and earth, who set in the clouds a rainbow, to be a sign of your covenant with every living creature: Grant that we may be faithful stewards of the dominion you have entrusted to us on earth, according to your grace given to us through Jesus Christ our Lord. **Amen.**

Abraham's obedience

Genesis 22:1-18
Psalm 16
Let us pray:
Gracious God of all believers, through Abraham's obedience you made known your faithful love to countless numbers; by the grace of Christ's sacrifice fulfill in your church and in all creation the joy of your promise and new covenant. **Amen.**

Israel's deliverance at the Red Sea

Exodus 14:10–15:1
(song) Exodus 15:1-6, 11-13, 17-18
 or "Come, Ye Faithful, Raise the Strain"
 or "Oh, Mary, Don't You Weep, Don't You Mourn"
Let us pray:
God our Savior, as once you delivered by the power of your mighty arm your chosen Israel through the waters of the sea, so now deliver your church and all the peoples of the earth from bondage and oppression to rejoice and serve you in freedom, through Jesus Christ our Lord. **Amen.**

Love calls us back

Isaiah 54:5-14
Psalm 30 *or* "Great Is Thy Faithfulness"
Let us pray:
Holy One of Israel, our Redeemer, your love is unending and your covenant is not shaken, even when our sin carries us away from you; take pity again, establish us in righteousness, and through our baptism lead us to safety in Jesus Christ our Lord. **Amen.**

Salvation offered freely to all

> Isaiah 55:1-11
> (song) Isaiah 12:2-6
> *or* "God Is My Strong Salvation"
> *or* "Fill My Cup"
> Let us pray:
> Creator of all things, you freely offer water to the thirsty and food to the hungry; refresh us by the water of baptism and feed us with the bread and wine of your table, that your Word may bear fruit in our lives, and bring all to your glorious kingdom; through Jesus Christ our Lord. **Amen.**

God's incomparable wisdom

> Baruch 3:9-15; 3:32–4:4
> Psalm 19 *or* "The Spacious Firmament on High"
> Let us pray:
> Almighty God, whose wisdom is proclaimed by all creation: Grant us grace faithfully to turn to you, that in your wisdom we find life abundant and eternal; through Jesus Christ our Lord. **Amen.**

A new heart and a new spirit

> Ezekiel 36:24-28
> Psalm 42 *or* "Spirit of God, Descend upon My Heart"
> Let us pray:
> God of holiness and light, in the mystery of dying and rising with Christ you have established a new covenant of reconciliation; cleanse our hearts and give a new spirit to all your people, that your saving grace may be professed and made known to the whole world; through Jesus Christ our Lord. **Amen.**

New life for God's people

> Ezekiel 37:1-14
> Psalm 143 *or* "O Spirit of the Living God" *or* "Breathe on Me, Breath of God"
> Let us pray:
> Eternal God, you raised from the dead our Lord Jesus and by your Holy Spirit brought to life your church; breathe upon us again with your Spirit and give new life to your people, through the same Jesus Christ our Lord. **Amen.**

The gathering of God's people

> Zephaniah 3:14-20
> Psalm 98 *or* "Joy to the World"
> Let us pray:
> Ever-living God of power and light, look with mercy on your whole church; bring to completion your lasting salvation, that the whole world may see the fallen lifted up, the old made new, and all things brought to perfection in him through whom all things were made, our Lord Jesus Christ. **Amen.**

[ACT OF PRAISE, such as "Glory to God in the Highest"]

EPISTLE   Romans 6:3-11

PSALM 114   *Introduced with sung or spoken "alleluia."*

GOSPEL	Matthew 28:1-10	(Year A: 1993, 1996, 1999)
	Mark 16:1-8	(Year B: 1994, 1997, 2000)
	Luke 24:1-12	(Year C: 1995, 1998, 2001)

SERMON

A short sermon may be given after any of the Old Testament lessons as well, depending upon the length of the service. In any case, the sermon after the Gospel lesson should not be long, since the readings are the proclamation in this service.

3. The Service of the Water

BAPTISM AND REAFFIRMATION OF THE BAPTISMAL COVENANT

See Annotated Bibliography for listing of denominational liturgies of baptism and reaffirmation of the baptismal covenant.

4. The Service of the Bread and Cup (Easter Communion)

OFFERING (TAKING OF THE BREAD AND CUP)

While the offering is being received, an Easter hymn or anthem may be sung. During this time, the table is prepared. The gifts of bread and wine are brought forward from the congregation with the other gifts or from a nearby table. When the table is ready, the minister says:

Beloved in Christ! People shall be gathered from north and south, from east and west, to feast at the heavenly banquet of the Lord. Christ our Paschal Lamb has been sacrificed. Let us therefore celebrate the feast. Alleluia!

GREAT THANKSGIVING

The Lord be with you.

And also with you.

Lift up your hearts.

We lift them to the Lord.

Let us give thanks to the Lord our God.

It is right to give our thanks and praise.

It is right, and a good and joyful thing,
always and everywhere to give thanks to you,
Father Almighty, Creator of heaven and earth.
You formed us in your image
and breathed into us the breath of life.
When we turned away, and our love failed,
your love remained steadfast.

You delivered us from captivity,
made covenant to be our sovereign God,

brought us to a land flowing with milk and honey,
and set before us the way of life.

And so, with your people on earth
and all the company of heaven,
we praise your name and join their unending hymn:

**Holy, holy, holy Lord, God of power and might,
heaven and earth are full of your glory.
Hosanna in the highest.
Blessed is he who comes in the name of the Lord.
Hosanna in the highest.**

Holy are you, and blessed is your Son Jesus Christ.
Your Spirit anointed him
to preach good news to the poor,
to proclaim release to the captives
and recovering of sight to the blind,
to set at liberty those who are oppressed,
and to announce that the time had come
when you would save your people.
He healed the sick, fed the hungry, and ate with sinners.

By the baptism of his suffering, death, and resurrection
you gave birth to your church,
delivered us from slavery to sin and death,
and made with us a new covenant by water and the Spirit.

By your great mercy we have been born anew to a living hope
through the resurrection of your Son from the dead,
and to an inheritance
which is imperishable, undefiled, and unfading.

Once we were no people, but now we are your people,
declaring your wonderful deeds in Christ,
who called us out of darkness into his marvelous light.
When the Lord Jesus ascended,
he promised to be with us always,
in the power of your Word and Holy Spirit.

On the night in which he gave himself up for us
he took bread, gave thanks to you, broke the bread,
gave it to his disciples, and said:
"Take, eat; this is my body which is given for you.
Do this in remembrance of me."

When the supper was over he took the cup,
gave thanks to you, gave it to his disciples, and said:
"Drink from this, all of you;
this is my blood of the new covenant,
poured out for you and for many
for the forgiveness of sins.
Do this, as often as you drink it, in remembrance of me."

On the day you raised him from the dead
he was recognized by his disciples
in the breaking of the bread,
and in the power of your Holy Spirit
your church has continued
in the breaking of bread and the sharing of the cup.
And so,
in remembrance of these your mighty acts in Jesus Christ,
we offer ourselves in praise and thanksgiving
as a holy and living sacrifice,
in union with Christ's offering for us,
as we proclaim the mystery of faith.

Christ has died, Christ is risen, Christ will come again.

Pour out your Holy Spirit on us, gathered here,
and on these gifts of bread and wine.
Make them be for us the body and blood of Christ,
that we may be for the world the body of Christ,
redeemed by his blood.

By your Spirit make us one with Christ,
one with each other,
and one in ministry to all the world,
until Christ comes in final victory
and we feast at his heavenly banquet.

Through your Son Jesus Christ,
with the Holy Spirit in your holy church,
all honor and glory is yours, Almighty Father,
now and for ever.

Amen.

THE LORD'S PRAYER

BREAKING OF BREAD

COMMUNION

During the communion, joyous Easter hymns or anthems may be sung.

PRAYER AFTER COMMUNION

You have given yourself to us, Lord.

Now we give ourselves for others.

You have raised us with Christ, and made us a new people.

As people of the resurrection, we will serve you with joy.

Your glory has filled our hearts.

Help us to glorify you in all things. Amen.

HYMN   *An Easter hymn or doxological stanza.*

DISMISSAL WITH BLESSING

Go in peace to love and serve the Lord.

We are sent in the power of Christ's resurrection. Alleluia!

The blessing of Almighty God,
Father, Son, and Holy Spirit,
be with you always. Amen.

Amen. Alleluia, alleluia!

Commentary

Because this service is the richest and most glorious occasion for worship in the entire year, great care must be taken in preparation for it. The key decision is whether to hold the great Easter Vigil at night or to hold an early Sunday morning service. It may be celebrated at a suitable time between midevening on Saturday and the Second Service of Easter. It should be celebrated only once. The mid- and late-morning services on Sunday are called "the Resurrection of the Lord," or the Second Service of Easter. In several respects, the Saturday night time, beginning around 10:30 P.M. and ending just after midnight, is the most dramatic time. It may, of course, be held any time after nightfall. If, however, a night service is unrealistic for the majority of the congregation who wish to attend, then the early morning hour is fitting, provided that it begins in darkness. Either may be followed by a joyful paschal breakfast.

A third option for celebrating the First Service of Easter may be considered in some circumstances. The Service of Light and the Service of the Word may be held through the reading of the Easter Gospel and the sermon. Then a hymn is sung, and the congregation may have breakfast together. At a suitable time, the liturgy resumes with the baptism and renewal, followed by the Easter communion. This has an advantage of permitting a slightly later starting time, though still near dawn; and it permits those who prepare the breakfast to attend the second half of the service. This option, of course, lessens the unity and full dramatic sweep of the whole liturgy. If either the second or third option is followed, ample preparation time must be allowed for the Second Service of Easter.

Recall again the fourfold structure of the Easter Vigil: (1) the Service of Light, (2) the Service of the Word, (3) the Service of the Water, or baptism and renewal, and (4) the Service of the Bread and Cup, or Easter communion. In the Service of Light, we carry forth an ancient Jewish practice which the primitive church inherited and gave a new significance. The *Lucernarium* (service of the lights) was done at nightfall at the beginning of vigils before the Lord's Day. Rooted in Jewish home ritual—the lighting of the lamps on Sabbath eve—it was discontinued in time, but maintained with special meaning in the Easter Vigil.

The kindling of the new fire can be done quite simply. It is best done outside in an ample container of metal, standing at least three feet high on strong supports. Dry wood arranged in a small "tent" shape on a covering of gravel or crushed stone in the base of the container works well. If done inside, a portable grate may be used, and a safe flammable substance, is useful in some instances. The container for the fire should express the dignity and simplicity of the action. Care should be taken to see that the fire is completely extinguished after the paschal candle and other candles are lighted and the procession begins. A smothering lid may be designed to place over the burning materials by an assistant after the celebrants leave the position of the fire.

During the procession, the celebrant or assistant, or a soloist or the choir, sings the "Light of Christ," and the congregation responds singing, "Thanks Be to God." Where a procession does not form outside, the choir and minister may process from the place of assembly or from the entranceway, pausing the three times indicated for the sung versicle and response.

If there is a congregational procession and the people are given individual candles, it is best to wait until the congregation has taken its place in the pews or seats before the candles are lighted. Designated persons or ushers will then light tapers from the paschal candle and initiate the light at the end of each row. The congregation then holds the lighted candles throughout the *Exsultet*, at the conclusion of which they are extinguished.

The *Exsultet* is one of the great sung poetic treasures of the church. This ancient paschal hymn is sung only once each year. The text given is suitable for traditional chanting by a song leader or soloist. There are three other possibilities as well, including variation in translations available. (1) The opening verses are treated as a responsory with the congregation. (2) The response is sung by the congregation at various points in response to the choir or soloist. (3) A brief version with opening responsory is used. The traditional chant may be found in the Roman Sacramentary or in the *Holy Week Offices,* edited by Massey H. Shepherd, Jr. (Greenwich, Conn.: Seabury Press, 1958). For a different translation of the *Exsultet,* see the *Book of Common Prayer* used in Option 1. Here are the three options.

OPTION 1

Rejoice now, heavenly hosts and choirs of angels,
and let your trumpets shout Salvation
for the victory of our mighty King.

**Rejoice and sing now, all the round earth,
bright with a glorious splendor.
for the darkness has been vanquished by our eternal King.**

Rejoice and be glad now, Holy Church,
and let your holy courts, in radiant light,
resound with the praises of your people.

[All who stand near this marvelous and holy flame,
pray with me to God the Almighty
for the grace to sing the worthy praise of this great light;
through Jesus Christ his Son our Lord,
who lives and reigns with him,
in the unity of the Holy Spirit,
one God, for ever and ever. **Amen.**

The Lord be with you.

And also with you.

Let us give thanks to the Lord our God.

It is right to give our thanks and praise.]

It is truly right and good, always and everywhere,
with our whole heart and mind and voice, to praise you,
the invisible, almighty, and eternal God, and your only
begotten Son, Jesus Christ our Lord;

for he is the true Paschal Lamb, who at the feast of the
Passover paid for us the debt of Adam's sin,
and by his blood delivered your faithful people.

This is the night, when you brought our forebears,
the children of Israel, out of bondage in Egypt,
and led them through the Red Sea on dry land.
This is the night, when all who believe in Christ
are delivered from the gloom of sin,
and are restored to grace and holiness of life.
This is the night, when Christ broke the bonds of death and hell,
    and rose victorious from the grave.

[How wonderful and beyond our knowing, O God, is your
mercy and loving-kindness to us,
that to redeem a slave, you gave a Son.
How holy is this night, when wickedness is put to flight,
and sin is washed away.
It restores innocence to the fallen and joy to those who mourn.
It casts out pride and hatred, and brings peace and concord.
How blessed is this night, when earth and heaven are joined
and we are reconciled to God.]

Holy Father, accept our evening sacrifice,
the offering of this candle in your honor.
May it shine continually to drive away all darkness.
May Christ, the Morning Star who knows no setting,
find it ever burning—he who gives his light to all creation,
and who lives and reigns for ever and ever. **Amen.**   BCP

OPTION 2   *Response*

(First sung by the choir, then all repeat; then all sing it each of the five times as a responsory. The congregation needs only the printed music for the response.)

Re-joice, heav-en-ly pow-ers! Sing, choirs of an - gels!

Je - sus Christ, our King is ri - sen!

I. Choir:
    Rejoice heavenly powers! Sing choirs of angels!
    Exult, all creation around God's throne!

Jesus Christ, our King is risen!
Sound the trumpet of salvation!
Rejoice, O earth, in shining splendor,
radiant in the brightness of your King!
Christ has conquered! Glory fills you!
Darkness vanishes for ever!

Response: *All sing.*
Rejoice, heavenly powers! Sing, choirs of angels!
Jesus Christ, our King is risen!

II. Choir:
For Christ has ransomed us with his blood,
and paid for us the price of Adam's sin to our eternal Father!
This is our Passover feast, when Christ, the true Lamb, is slain,
whose blood consecrates the homes of all believers.
This is the night when first you saved our forebears:
you freed the people of Israel from their slavery
and led them dry-shod through the sea.
This is the night
when the pillar of fire destroyed the darkness of sin!
This is the night when Christians everywhere,
washed clean of sin and freed from all defilement,
are restored to grace and grow together in holiness.
This is the night when Jesus Christ broke the chains of death
and rose triumphant from the grave.

Response: *All sing.*

III. Choir:
What good would life have been to us,
had Christ not come as our Redeemer?
Father, how wonderful your care for us!
How boundless your merciful love!
To ransom a slave you gave away your Son.
O happy fault, O necessary sin of Adam,
which gained for us so great a Redeemer!
Most blessed of all nights,
chosen by God to see Christ rising from the dead!
Of this night Scripture says:
"The night will be clear as day: it will become my light, my joy."

Response: *All sing.*

IV. Choir:
The power of this holy day dispels all evil,
washes guilt away,
restores lost innocence and brings mourners joy.
Night truly blessed when heaven is wedded to earth
    and we are reconciled with God!

Therefore, Heavenly Father, in the joy of this night
  receive our evening [morning] sacrifice of praise,
your church's solemn offering.

Response: *All sing.*

V. Choir:
  Accept this Easter candle.
  May it always dispel the darkness of this night!
  May the Morning Star which never sets
    find this flame still burning:
  Christ, that Morning Star, who came back from the dead,
  and shed his peaceful light on all humankind,
  your Son who lives and reigns for ever and ever. Amen.

Response: *All sing.*

(Note: The translation used above may employ the musical setting found in the Roman Catholic
Liturgy of Holy Week, published by the Liturgical Press, Collegeville, Minn. 56321. In some cases,
church musicians may wish to compose new settings suitable for choir and congregation.)

OPTION 3

  Rejoice, heavenly choirs of angels.

  Rejoice, all creation around God's throne.

  Jesus Christ, our King, is risen!

  Sound the trumpet of salvation.

  Rejoice, O earth, in shining splendor,

  Radiant in the brightness of your King.

  Christ has conquered! Glory fills you!

  Darkness vanishes for ever.

  This is our Passover feast when Christ,
    the true Lamb, is slain,
    whose blood consecrates the homes of all believers.

  This is the night when you, Lord our God,
    first saved our ancestors in the faith;
  you delivered the people of Israel from their slavery
    and led them dry-shod through the sea.

  This is the night when Christ broke the chains of death
    and rose triumphant from the grave.
  This is the night truly blessed,
  when heaven is wedded to earth,
  and all creation is reconciled with God.

Therefore, Father, in the joy of this night,
receive our sacrifice of praise and thanksgiving.
Let us sing with joy,
joining the mighty chorus of all God's people!

HYMN   *An Easter hymn, or:*

Rejoice, heavenly choirs of angels.

Rejoice, all creation around God's throne.

Christ has conquered! Glory fills you!

Darkness vanishes for ever.

Followed by this hymn, to the tune TALLIS' CANON:

All praise to thee, my God, this night,
For all the blessings of the light!
Keep me, O keep me, King of kings,
Beneath thine own almighty wings!

O Christ, who art the Light and Day,
Thou drivest death and night away!
We know thee as the Light of light,
Illuminating mortal sight.

Teach us to live, that we may dread
The grave as little as our bed;
Teach us to die, that so we may
Rise glorious at the Judgment Day.

Praise God, from whom all blessings flow;
Praise him, all creatures here below;
Praise him above, ye heavenly host;
Praise Father, Son, and Holy Ghost.

In some situations the order of the first two parts of the liturgy may be reversed; following the vigil readings with the service of light. This is particularly suitable when the new fire cannot take place outside the worship area, or when the prayer vigil of Friday and Saturday continues until the beginning of the Easter Vigil itself.

In this case, the congregation assembles in the semi-darkness, joining those in the last of the "watch," with only a few small stationary lights or candles near the reading stand. After a brief introduction, the ministers enter in silence and take their places. In a small church, this may be done after the minister and choir are already in place. The readings from holy history continue up through the Epistle lesson from Romans 6. At this time, the ministers move to the place where the new fire is to be kindled. The fire is lighted and the paschal candle lighted from it; and a procession forms, moving toward the front of the worship area again, singing "Christ Our Light," with the congregational response. At each pause, other candles are lighted and, in turn, the congregation's individual candles, row by row. At the third response, when all are in position at the front, all the lights come on as the paschal candle is placed in its holder, and the *Exsultet* is sung or recited. The celebrant then proclaims the Easter Gospel, in reading and in sermon. The baptisms and renewals then take place, followed by the Easter communion, according to the pattern given above.

This arrangement allows a more austere vigil, though it does not allow the presence of the lighted paschal candle, symbolizing the light of Christ, in the midst of the reading of holy history from Genesis through the prophets. This is a choice between a continuing vigil—with a more dramatic and close connection between the symbolism of light and the water of baptism—and the more traditional ancient symbolism of the initial service of light and the new fire.

In the case of a continuing Friday-Saturday prayer vigil, the cross may be unveiled and the Easter paraments, banners, flowers, and other visuals placed during the final hour before the whole congregation assembles. Or it may occur as the people process into the worship area. As people gather, they participate in the extended vigil and, in some situations, witness the transformation of the church before moving into the readings.

The Service of the Word focuses on the history of salvation and is fundamental to our participation in the Easter-Passover Mystery. There are twelve lessons appointed, including the Epistle and Gospel. Throughout history the number has varied from as many as seventeen in some Eastern liturgies to as few as five. Ideally, all or most of the Old Testament lessons should be read. In any case, at least three of them should be read, including Genesis 1 and the Exodus 14 passage. The readings from the New Testament are, of course, essential.

The basic structure of this part of the liturgy consists of a lesson, a psalm (or biblical canticle), followed by a brief collect form of prayer. This may be varied in a number of ways. For example, hymn verses may be substituted for some of the psalms; or there may be readings followed by a brief silence, or by psalms, with one common prayer at the beginning of the whole series. Psalm 136 may be used as a common response throughout, with the congregation reciting, "For God's steadfast love endures for ever." One or two of the verses may be used in response to each lesson, followed by the congregational response.

Once the basic dynamic and point of the reading of salvation history is understood, a great deal of creativity may be exercised in how the Service of the Word is done. There is ample historical precedent, for example, in having various groups of readings done at different places or stations—both inside and outside the building. One can imagine beginning with the Genesis-Exodus readings, then a short drama or media response, then a procession to another place for readings from the prophets, followed by a drama or nonbiblical reading and, finally, a movement back to the worship area for Romans 6 and the Easter Gospel. If the circumstances of time and place permit such an elaboration (for example, in a college or university chapel), a special committee to work solely on the Service of the Word should be formed well in advance.

Of course much simpler variations may also be done effectively with careful planning. For example, the Genesis-Exodus readings lend themselves well to a media presentation. A plain white reflective cloth may be brought in by two persons and held in place during slides interpreting the creation, then quietly removed by the same persons. This avoids setting up screens. The projectors may be unobtrusively placed in the pews or aisles and removed immediately after use.

After the Old Testament lesson, the "Glory to God in the Highest" may be sung, and church bells rung out, according to local custom. Or this act of praise may follow after the Romans 6 reading, in which case Psalm 114 is quite fitting, especially when sung. A short sermon may follow any of the readings, or there may be a sermon following the reading of the Easter Gospel. In any case, these proclamations should be brief and powerfully to the point. Some may consider reading one of the beautiful patristic Easter sermons such as those of John Chrysostom, Basil of Caesarea, or Gregory the Great. These are found in *The Awe-Inspiring Rites of Initiation.*[2]

Following the Easter Gospel and sermon, a brief silence may be kept. This provides a moment for assimilation and a pause before moving to the deep mystery of Christian initiation and the renewal of the congregation's baptismal promises. If this is an early Sunday morning service, an Easter breakfast may come at this point and a hymn may be sung in procession to the fellowship hall.

The Service of the Water proclaims in sign-actions the central fact of our rebirth and identity in Christ. Before any specific plans are made, the minister(s) and worship planning committee should be familiar with the new rites of baptism, confirmation, and reaffirmation in their denomination. If there are to be no baptisms or confirmations, there can at least be the congregational reaffirmation of the baptismal covenant.

In some churches a form of the litany of saints may be used in connection with the baptismal rite. Here are some possibilities, depending upon time and space, and the theological convictions of the congregation and ministers.

1. Following the brief introduction, "In this we enter the communion of saints . . . ," there may occur a *naming of the saints,* a proclaiming of a select list beginning with Mary and the apostles, and including names through the centuries. For example: Mary and Martha, Benedict, Francis, Theresa, Martin Luther, John Wesley, Mary McLeod Bethune, Martin Luther King, Jr., and ending with "all holy men and women. In their company we pray to the Lord"; and the congregation responds, "Lord, have mercy," or, "Lord, save your people."

2. In the same pattern, naming persons of the particular local church, the congregation may then be led in specific bidding prayers.

3. A more elaborate form involves the list of saints by groups: martyrs, preachers and pastors, theologians, missionaries and evangelists, reformers and prophets of social justice, and "those faithful in obscurity." Each group would include saints from both ancient and modern periods. For example: (martyrs) Peter, Stephen, Paul, Perpetua, Polycarp, Thomas More, Michael Servetus, Joan of Arc, Dietrich Bonhoeffer, Martin Luther King, Jr.; (preachers and pastors) Apostle Paul, Saint Francis, Lancelot Andrewes, John Wesley, Jonathan Edwards, Harry Emerson Fosdick; (prophets and workers for social justice) Harriet Tubman, Dag Hammarskjold, John Woolman, Walter Rauschenbusch, Clara Barton, Rachel Carson; (artists, musicians, and writers) J. S. Bach, John Donne, Pearl S. Buck, John Milton, Michelangelo, Mahalia Jackson, John Bunyan, Rembrandt, Palestrina, Dante, Charles Wesley.

As each group is called, persons could stand to be identified with them, or process to a place near the baptismal font, if the space is ample. After all have gathered under a banner or other sign of each group, the prayers of the people are offered.

4. An alternate litany may be done, beginning with the responses, preferably sung:

Lord, have mercy	**Lord, have mercy.**
Christ, have mercy	**Christ, have mercy.**
Lord, have mercy	**Lord, have mercy.**

Then the saints' names may be sung, followed again by responses:

Lord, be merciful	**Lord, save your people.**
From all evil	**Lord, save your people.**
From every sin	**Lord, save your people.**
From everlasting death	**Lord . . .**
By your incarnation	**Lord . . .**
By your death and rising to new life	**Lord . . .**
By the gift of your Holy Spirit	**Lord . . . Amen.**

Note that if the litany of the saints is used, prayers for the church may be better placed after the baptismal blessing. At that point, the peace may be given and signs of reconciliation and love are exchanged. This has the added advantage, if there are adult baptisms, of permitting candidates to participate in the prayers of the people and the Easter communion immediately after baptism, as was the custom in the early church. If the font is not in the front of the worship area and there has been a procession to it, the hymn of preparation may be sung in procession back to the seats, during which time the table is prepared and the elements brought forward.

On this occasion the finest bread should be prepared. It is particularly significant if one of the families who has prepared it assists in bringing the gifts forward. In some churches, where an Easter breakfast will follow the service, it is a glorious custom to invite each household to bring breads of various sorts, some of which will be used for the Holy Communion. The remaining breads will be used at the breakfast. People of various folk and ethnic backgrounds bring their special breads, and other suitable foods, to be placed in containers at the church entrance. These, along with such items as fruits of various kinds, olives, honey, cheese, and eggs, may be then taken to the place where the breakfast is to be held.

Throughout the service, particular care should be given to the musical settings of the texts, the hymn selection and the instrumental music to be used. Brass fanfares and instrumental variations on the hymn tunes can be most effective. The choir need not prepare special anthems for the Easter Vigil but rather should concentrate on leading the congregational song. The Second Service of Easter is a better time for anthems or larger choral pieces, such as traditional selections from Handel's *Messiah* or contemporary forms. However, during the communion, appropriate Easter chorales and anthems may be sung by the choir if desired. Brass and choral work may resound at the conclusion of the service as well, continuing the great themes of the paschal feast.

NOTES FOR CHAPTER VI-I

1. Saint Basil of Caesarea, *Baptismal Homilies,* in Edward Yarnold's *The Awe-Inspiring Rites of Initiation: Baptismal Homilies of the Fourth Century* (London: St. Paul's Publications, 1971).
2. Ibid.

J. Easter Day, or the Second Service of Easter

GATHERING

Festive music may be offered during the gathering of the people. Music may include brass and may begin ten to fifteen minutes before the normal time, particularly when there is one main Sunday service following the Easter Vigil or First Service of Easter. In some situations the bringing in and placing of flowers may be done as an informal procession as various families and members arrive.

GREETING

Christ is risen!

The Lord is risen indeed!

Glory and honor, dominion and power,
be to God for ever and ever.

Christ is risen! Alleluia!

HYMN OF PRAISE

If the hymn is to be an entrance hymn with procession, it precedes the greeting.
Appropriate hymns for this service include:
"Christ the Lord Is Risen Today"
"Jesus Christ Is Risen Today"
"The Day of Resurrection"
"Sing with All the Sons of Glory"
"Come, Ye Faithful, Raise the Strain"
"Welcome, Happy Morning"

OPENING PRAYER

> O God, who for our redemption
> gave your only begotten Son
> to the death of the cross,
> and by his glorious resurrection
> delivered us from the power of our enemy:
> grant us so to die daily to sin
> that we may evermore live with him
> in the joy of his resurrection;
> through Jesus Christ your Son our Lord,
> who lives and reigns with you and the Holy Spirit,
> one God, now and for ever. **Amen.**
>
> *or*
>
> God our Father,
> by raising Christ your Son,
> you conquered the power of death
> and opened to us the way of eternal life.
> Let our celebration today
> raise us up and renew our lives
> by the Spirit that is within us.
> Grant this through our Lord Jesus Christ,
> your Son, who lives and reigns
> with you and the Holy Spirit,
> one God, for ever and ever. **Amen.**

FIRST LESSON

> Acts 10:34-43 *or* Jeremiah 31:1-6 (Year A: 1993, 1996, 1999)
> Acts 10:34-43 *or* Isaiah 25:6-9 (Year B: 1994, 1997, 2000)
> Acts 10:34-43 *or* Isaiah 65:17-25 (Year C: 1995, 1998, 2001)

PSALM 118:1-2, 14-24 (All years)

> *Response:* **This is the day the Lord has made;**
> **let us rejoice and be glad in it.**
>
> Give thanks to the Lord, for he is good;
> his mercy endures for ever.
> Let Israel now proclaim,
> "His mercy endures for ever."
>
> *Response*
>
> The Lord is my strength and my song,
> and he has become my salvation.
> There is a sound of exultation and victory
> in the tents of the righteous;
> "The right hand of the Lord has triumphed!
> The right hand of the Lord is exalted!
> The right hand of the Lord has triumphed!"

Response

I shall not die, but live,
and declare the word of the Lord.
The Lord has punished me sorely,
but he did not hand me over to death.

Response

Open for me the gates of righteousness;
I will enter them;
I will offer thanks to the Lord.
"This is the gate of the Lord;
he who is righteous may enter."
I will give thanks to you,
for you answered me
and have become my salvation.

Response

The Stone which the builders rejected
has become the chief Cornerstone.
This is the Lord's doing,
and it is marvelous in our eyes.
On this day the Lord has acted;
we will rejoice and be glad in it.

Response

SECOND LESSON

Colossians 3:1-4 *or* Acts 10:34-43	(Year A: 1993, 1996, 1999)
I Corinthians 15:1-11 *or* Acts 10:34-43	(Year B: 1994, 1997, 2000)
I Corinthians 15:19-26 *or* Acts 10:34-43	(Year C: 1995, 1998, 2001)

HYMN

GOSPEL

John 20:1-18 *or* Matthew 28:1-10	(Year A: 1993, 1996, 1999)
John 20:1-18 *or* Mark 16:1-8	(Year B: 1994, 1997, 2000)
John 20:1-18 *or* Luke 24:1-12	(Year C: 1995, 1998, 2001)

SERMON

RESPONSES TO THE WORD

REAFFIRMATION OF THE BAPTISMAL COVENANT

See Annotated Bibliography for listing of denominational liturgies of baptism and reaffirmation of the baptismal covenant.

PRAYERS OF THE PEOPLE OR PASTORAL PRAYER

THE PEACE

By dying, Christ destroyed our death;
in rising, he restores our life;
in giving us his Spirit, he grants us peace.
The peace of the Lord be with you.

And also with you.

Signs and words of peace and reconciliation are exchanged among all, using words such as "He is risen" or "The peace of Christ be with you."

OFFERING

When Holy Communion is not celebrated, the service concludes after the presentation of the offering with the following prayers, a hymn, and dismissal with blessing:

PRAYER OF THANKSGIVING

Blessed are you, O Lord our God,
Creator and Redeemer of the whole world;
 from you we receive the gift of life,
 and by your grace we have gifts to offer you.
Accept our offerings and our lives in praise and thanksgiving,
 through Jesus Christ our Lord,
 who brings us again from death to life,
 and holds forth the promise of your everlasting kingdom. **Amen.**

As Jesus has taught us, we are bold to pray:

THE LORD'S PRAYER

HYMN

DISMISSAL WITH BLESSING

Go forth in joy to love and serve God in all that you do.

We are sent in the name of the risen Christ.

Let us bless the Lord.

Thanks be to God. Alleluia!

May the God of peace, who raised to life the great Shepherd of the sheep,
make us ready to do his will in every good thing,
through Jesus Christ, to whom be glory for ever and ever.

Amen. Alleluia!

* * *

If Holy Communion is celebrated, the table is prepared at the offering, during which a hymn or anthem is sung.

GREAT THANKSGIVING

The text for the Easter Vigil is used; see pages 198–200.

BREAKING THE BREAD

COMMUNION

PRAYER AFTER COMMUNION

Lord, we bless and praise you for nourishing us
with this Easter feast of redemption.
Fill us with your Spirit,
and make us living signs of your love;
through Jesus Christ our Lord. **Amen.**

HYMN

DISMISSAL WITH BLESSING

Go forth in joy to love and serve God in all that you do.

We are sent in the name of the risen Christ.

Let us bless our Lord.

Thanks be to God. Alleluia!

May the God of peace, who raised to life the great Shepherd of the sheep,
make us ready to do his will in every good thing,
through Jesus Christ, to whom be glory for ever and ever.

Amen. Alleluia!

Commentary

Easter morning is an occasion of great joy and renewal. Even in churches that have not followed the full Christian Year, this is a day of many rituals and local customs. In particular, people expect to hear the Easter Gospel and special music, to sing the Easter hymns, and to see the beautiful flowers and vestments. This service is designed to give these expectations a substantial framework and pattern and also to heighten the Word of God and the theological meaning of paschal renewal—of dying and rising with Jesus our Lord.

The visual environment should powerfully enhance the joy of the occasion. An abundance of lilies and other bright flowers is traditional at this service, and this is appropriate as long as they do not detract from such basic visual symbols as the cross, Lord's table, pulpit, and baptismal font. White and gold are traditional Easter colors, but other colors that are regarded as festive by the people may also be used. Textiles should be the finest available, with elegant textures. Bolts of brightly colored cloth may be slit halfway lengthwise and hung across the worship area, or bright colors can be used in various ways to transform the building. The contrast to Lenten array should be striking; somberness of hue and roughly textured material should be put away for another day. Appropriate symbols for this season include the open tomb, shining Chi Rho, resurrection banner, glorified cross, phoenix, butterflies, peacocks, and pomegranate.

The paschal candle is a particularly important visual symbol. It is a large white candle, at least two inches in diameter and at least two feet tall, placed in a candlestand at least three feet high. Like the morning star that never sets, it signifies Christ shining eternally. It is first lighted at the Easter Vigil, or the First Service of Easter if there is no vigil, and remains lighted at the front of the church for all services through the Great Fifty Days. After Pentecost it is placed near the baptismal font for the remainder of the year, where it is lighted for all baptisms and at church funerals where it is placed at the coffin and memorial services to signify the resurrection. Paschal candles and candlestands are widely available in religious goods stores and mail-order supply houses.

If the Easter Vigil or the First Service of Easter is followed by a breakfast, thought should be given as to how the lilies and other flowers may be placed in the worship area, since not all of them could be positioned and still leave space for the various actions surrounding baptism and eucharist. Here is one suggestion: A group of persons may be responsible for arranging and placing the flowers and other visuals. As persons arrive they may present flowers (including lilies) brought from their homes. This may be done quite festively, yet without show. Banners, paraments, and other visuals may also be placed at this time. A genuine atmosphere of offering and sharing may be experienced. If this is done while special music is offered, it should be done quietly. The gifts of flowers will then be taken to the sick and shut-in following the service. Not only will this save the church the expense of filling the worship area, but it will link the beauty of Easter worship with acts of love and ministry. Care should be taken not to overload the room. Varieties of flowers with several lilies can be more striking than huge banks of nothing but lilies.

Concerning the readings from scripture, note that if the first lesson is from the Old Testament, then the reading from Acts 10 may be used in place of the appointed second lesson. Careful consideration for preaching must be given to the interaction of the lessons. Differing themes and accents can be brought out for the congregation with different combinations of lessons. Note also the alternative possibilities in the Gospel lessons as well.

The responses to the Word present many possibilities. A hymn of joyful response may be sung, or an anthem which lifts up a theme of the Easter Gospel and the sermon may be offered. This is an excellent occasion for hymn-anthems which involve both choir and congregation in dialogue. The affirmation of faith or one of the historic creeds is particularly appropriate this Sunday of all Sundays. It is especially fitting that the congregation be invited to reaffirm the baptismal covenant, the heart of Christian life and the Easter faith.

We must frankly recognize that this raises serious pastoral questions concerning the number of persons attending Easter services who are infrequent worshipers, or whose faith is nominal at best. Care should be taken to let the congregation know by a note in the bulletin or by a simple remark that this rite is for those desiring to renew their baptismal promises. This does not coerce; yet it has a powerful symbolic meaning for increasing numbers of Christians. It is an evangelical witness in the deepest sense. This reaffirmation of the baptismal covenant shows vividly the essentials of Easter faith: being incorporated into the death and resurrection of Jesus Christ and his body, the church.

If the sacrament of the Lord's Supper is celebrated, it should be in the spirit of Easter joy. During the communing of the people, it is especially recommended that people receive standing, and preferably in a continuing movement, rather than in a lengthy series of table dismissals. Here is an occasion for the great Easter choral music to be sung. Where this is not possible, the congregation should sing Easter hymns or carols throughout the communion rite.

K. The First Week of Easter

The first week of Easter deserves particular attention, beginning with the vesper service of Easter evening, sometimes known as the "Great Paschal Vespers." Though the service is unfamiliar to many Protestant churches, its great beauty and solemnity provide a deeply prayerful way of acknowledging and receiving the joy of Easter. The following service of song and lessons is based on the ancient Roman Office for Easter Day and the week following. It may be used on any of the days of Easter week, including the following Sunday evening, with different but suitable lessons and other verses for the Alleluias.

Because this service celebrates the presence of the risen Christ and our awareness of baptism into the Paschal Mystery, we may give a place of special honor to those who were baptized at the Easter Vigil.

GATHERING

The paschal candle is the only light burning as the congregation assembles in silence. The presiding minister and any assistants enter in silence, taking their places near the paschal candle.

The Service of Light

ACCLAMATION

Light and peace in Jesus Christ our Lord!

Thanks be to God!

Stay with us, Lord, it is near evening.

And the day is almost over. Alleluia, Alleluia!

HYMN

The Phos Hilaron *or appropriate Easter hymn during which the assistant lights a taper from the paschal candle to light other candles, and the lights of the room, if needed, are turned on.*

THANKSGIVING*

Let us give thanks to God the Father, always and for everything!

In the name of our Lord Jesus Christ.

The Service of the Word

The three places (or stations) mentioned may be within the sanctuary, the first and third being the same, or they may be in spaces related to the sanctuary. The gathering space for the second station is at the baptismal font.

FIRST STATION   *All are seated.*

Response:
Alleluia! Alleluia! Alleluia!
The Lord reigns with majesty enrobed;
the Lord has robed himself with might,
and has girded himself with power.

Response
The world you made firm, not to be moved;
your throne has stood firm from all ages.
From all eternity, O Lord, you are.

*The text and music for the Thanksgiving may be taken from *Praise God in Song: Ecumenical Daily Prayer,* by J. A. Melloh and W. G. Storey (Chicago: G.I.A. Publications, 1979), pp. 236-37.

Response

The waters have lifted up, O Lord,
the waters have lifted up their voice,
the waters have thundered their praise.

FIRST LESSON   Daniel 12:1-3 *or* Acts 5:29-32   (All years)

PSALM   150   (All years)

PRAYER   *All standing.*

God our Father, through the mystery of the cross your Son destroyed death and brought us the forgiveness of sins. Let our voices join in the thundering praise of all creation as we celebrate his resurrection. May this festival raise us up and renew our lives in your Holy Spirit. In the name of Jesus, the Lord.   **Amen.**

PROCESSION TO THE FONT

An Easter or baptismal hymn such as "Come, Ye Faithful, Raise the Strain," "Christ Jesus Lay in Death's Strong Bands," *or* "The Strife Is O'er" *may be sung as the people gather at the font, led by the minister(s), the newly baptized and their family, sponsors, and friends, with the book carried by the reader of the second lesson.*

SECOND STATION   *All remain standing.*

Response:
Alleluia! Alleluia! Alleluia!

When Israel came forth from Egypt,
Jacob's children from an alien land,
Judah became the Lord's sanctuary,
Israel became his possession.

Response

The sea fled at the sight:
the Jordan turned back on its course,
the mountains leapt like rams
and the hills like yearling sheep.

Response

Why was it, sea, that you fled,
that you turned back, Jordan, on your course?
Mountains, that you leapt like rams,
hills like yearling sheep?

Response

Tremble, O earth, at the coming of the Lord,
in the presence of the God of Jacob,
who turns the rock into a pool
and stone into a spring of water.

Response

216

SECOND LESSON   Romans 6:8-11   (All years)

SILENCE

PRAYER   *All standing.*

O God, our Rescuer and our Redeemer, you led your people out of slavery and darkness into your own freedom and light. You make a covenant with us in the waters of baptism and call us to continue our pilgrimage, following the Lord Jesus on his way of the cross to new and eternal life. Help us persevere on this journey, trusting in your continual guidance and endless love, through Jesus Christ our Lord.   **Amen.**

PROCESSION TO STATION THREE

Sing the remaining verses of the first hymn or another Easter hymn or anthem. As persons pass by the font, they may touch the water and make signs of devotion in recommitment to their baptismal covenant.

THIRD STATION

Response:
Alleluia! Alleluia! Alleluia!

Christ our Passover has been sacrificed;
let us feast with the unleavened bread of sincerity and truth.

Response
The Stone which the builders rejected
has become the Cornerstone.
This is the work of the Lord, a marvel in our eyes.

Response
This is the day the Lord has made.
Let us rejoice and be glad!

Response
Come, sing out your joy to the Lord;
hail the Rock who saves us.
Let us come before him giving thanks;
with songs let us hail the Lord.

Response
GOSPEL   Luke 24:13-49   (All years)

SERMON and/or SILENCE

THE CANTICLE OF MARY   (Luke 1:46-55)

Response *(before and after the canticle):*

**Jesus stood in the midst of his disciples.
and said: "Peace to you: Alleluia!"**

INTERCESSIONS

The following or some other litany is prayed:
   Response:
   Lord, hear our prayer, *or* **Lord, have mercy.**
   In the peace of the risen Christ, let us pray to the Lord;

   That our risen Savior may grant us victory over all our enemies, seen and unseen,
   let us pray to the Lord;

   That he may crush beneath our feet the prince of darkness and his power,
   let us pray to the Lord;

   That he may raise us up and set us with himself in heaven,
   let us pray to the Lord;

   That he may fill us with the joy of his holy and life-giving resurrection,
   let us pray to the Lord;

   That he may provide for those who lack food, work, and shelter through us,
   let us pray to the Lord;

   That by his love, wars and famine may cease through all the earth,
   let us pray to the Lord;

   That isolated and persecuted churches find fresh strength in the Paschal Mystery,
   let us pray to the Lord;

   That all those who have gone before us in the faith of Christ
   may find refreshment, light, and peace,
   let us pray to the Lord;

   Again and again in peace, let us pray to the Lord.

COLLECT

   Gracious and loving God, on this Easter evening,
   the Lord Jesus appeared to his disciples who had begun to lose hope
   and opened their eyes to what the Scriptures had foretold.
   May the risen Christ breathe on our minds and open our hearts
   that we may know him in the breaking of bread,
   and follow him in his risen life;
   joining with all our brothers and sisters in the prayer he gave us:

THE LORD'S PRAYER

BLESSING AND DISMISSAL

   Assistant: Bow to the Lord and ask his blessing.

               May God the Father, who raised Christ Jesus from the dead,
               continually show us his loving-kindness.

   All: **Amen.**

   Presider: May God the Son, Victor over sin and death,
               grant us a share in the joy of his resurrection.

   All: **Amen.**

Presider: May God the Spirit, giver of light and peace, renew our hearts in God's love.

All: **Amen.**

Presider: May Almighty God continue to bless us, the Father, the Son, and the Holy Spirit.

All: **Amen. Alleluia!**

Assistant: Let us go forth in peace. Alleluia, Alleluia!

All: **Thanks be to God. Alleluia, Alleluia!**

   All may greet one another with the peace.

It is an ancient custom that after this service, at least on Easter Day itself, this evening prayer be followed by a simple agape, at which the minister is host(ess), and at which Easter eggs, breads, and fruits may be served. The agape may conclude informally or with a suitable song.

L. The Second Through the Sixth Sundays of Easter

The Great Fifty Days should be the greatest, most festive season of the Christian Year; and if this is to happen, the joy and festivity of Easter Day should continue in the Sundays following. These Sundays are not only the Lord's Day, they are in the season that is to the rest of the Christian Year what the Lord's Day is to the week.

A study of the Scriptures in the lectionary will reveal what a rich variety of meanings this season has. Most obviously, we remember the accounts of Jesus' appearances during the forty days between his resurrection and his ascension and then the ten days of waiting for the coming of the Holy Spirit at Pentecost. But there is far more to the season. As the readings make clear, it is also the Pentecost Season, the time when passages are read concerning the Holy Spirit and the life of the earliest church as it was empowered by the Spirit. We are reminded of the presence of the risen, living Christ in our midst, and we are also reminded that it is only through the work of the Holy Spirit that we can know the risen Christ. It is also the season of God's new creation, especially for those of us who live in the North Temperate Zone of the earth where this season is also spring.

The environment of worship should reflect the spirit and significance of this season. The visual suggestions given for Easter should be carried through the season. The lighting of the paschal candle will continue to be a reminder that this is the greatest season of the year. To be sure, the Easter flowers will be missing from the sanctuary the next Sunday, but with imagination something can be added.

Take the matter of seasonal colors, for instance. The color most commonly and traditionally used in this season is white—except on Pentecost, when the color becomes flame red to symbolize the fire of the Holy Spirit. Since plain white becomes more effective if used with another color, and since gold is also a color that suggests festivity and joy, we commonly use gold with white in our Easter visuals. Also, gold is commonly used with red at Pentecost. Since this whole season is Pentecost as well as Easter, and since on the Second Sunday of Easter every year the Gospel tells how Jesus breathed the Holy Spirit on the disciples on the evening of the first Easter Day, we could on that Sunday add touches of red to the white and gold visuals. These touches of red could continue through the season until on Pentecost the red suddenly expands to become the dominant color.

Several program suggestions may also help us recover the Great Fifty Days. We clergy, choirs, and faithful church people should not plan such a heavy program of Lenten and Holy Week services and activities that we feel like dropping from exhaustion after Easter. We should set a pace in Lent that can be continued through the Great Fifty Days. If new members are received at Easter, it is essential in the following several weeks that they be assimilated into the life of the congregation, including some small group if the congregation is other than very small itself. If it is not feasible for a congregation to hold baptisms and confirmations and receive new members at an Easter Vigil or on Easter Day, then rather than having these rites on Passion/Palm Sunday or during Holy Week, it is much better that they be at some other time in the Great Fifty Days. Pentecost is a good time; but if that is too long to wait, perhaps the Second Sunday of Easter, with its Holy Spirit message, would be suitable. If there are numbers of persons to be baptized, confirmed, or received on that day, then the Sunday after Easter will surely not be "Low Sunday."

It is important that music during these Sundays should be joyous and festive. Hymns and anthems of praise should predominate. To the hymn suggestions given below, it should be added that one can hardly go wrong on these Sundays with a good, beloved hymn of praise and joy in Christ.

Holy Communion on any of these Sundays can be a joyous eucharist (thanksgiving) and a resurrection meal with the living Christ. Churches that celebrate Holy Communion monthly will do so on one or another of these Sundays, and congregations moving toward weekly communion might offer the opportunity of weekly communion in this season even if they are not prepared to do so the rest of the year. The Great Thanksgiving text for the Easter Vigil is suitable for these Sundays as well.

An Opening Prayer for Use in the Easter Season

Lord of Life, by submitting to death you conquered the grave.
By being lifted on a cross you draw all peoples to you.
By being raised from the dead
you restored to humanity all that we had lost through sin.
Throughout these fifty days of Easter
we proclaim the marvelous mystery of your death and resurrection.
For all praise is yours, now and throughout eternity. **Amen.**

SECOND SUNDAY OF EASTER

Year A: 1993, 1996, 1999

Acts 2:14*a*, 22-32; Psalm 16; I Peter 1:3-9; John 20:19-31
"The Day of Resurrection" (Acts)
"How Firm a Foundation" (I Pet.)
"O Sons and Daughters, Let Us Sing" (I Pet.; John)
"Breathe on Me, Breath of God" (John)
"Let It Breathe on Me" (John)
"O Breath of Life" (John)
"Spirit of Faith, Come Down" (John)

Year B: 1994, 1997, 2000

Acts 4:32-35; Psalm 133; I John 1:1–2:2; John 20:19-31
"All Praise to Our Redeeming Lord" (Acts)
"Jesus, United by Thy Grace" (Acts)
"Trust and Obey" (I John)
See Year A for hymns related to John 20:19-31.

Year C: 1995, 1998, 2001

Acts 5:27-32; Psalm 118:14-29 *or* Psalm 150; Revelation 1:4-8; John 20:19-31
"This Is the Day" *or* "This Is the Day the Lord Hath Made" (Psalm 118:14-29)
"Crown Him with Many Crowns" (Rev.)
"Lo, He Comes with Clouds Descending" (Rev.)
See Year A for hymns related to John 20:19-31.

THIRD SUNDAY OF EASTER

Year A: 1993, 1996, 1999

Acts 2:14*a*, 36-41; Psalm 116:1-4, 12-19; I Peter 1:17-23; Luke 24:13-35
"The Church's One Foundation" (Acts)
"Abide with Me" (Luke)
"O Thou Who This Mysterious Bread" (Luke)
"On the Day of Resurrection" (Luke)
"Thine Be the Glory" (Luke)

Year B: 1994, 1997, 2000

Acts 3:12-19; Psalm 4; I John 3:1-7; Luke 24:36*b*-48
"Lead Me, Lord" (Ps.)
"Children of the Heavenly Father" (I John)
"Take Time to Be Holy" (I John)
"Blessed Assurance, Jesus Is Mine" (I John; Luke)
"Go, Make of All Disciples" (Luke)
"See How Great a Flame Aspires" (Luke)
"Thine Be the Glory" (Luke)

Year C: 1995, 1998, 2001

Acts 9:1-6 (7-20); Psalm 30; Revelation 5:11-14; John 21:1-19
"And Can It Be That I Should Gain" (Acts)
"Amazing Grace" (Acts)
"Crown Him with Many Crowns" (Rev.)
"See the Morning Sun Ascending" (esp. v. 4) (Rev.)
"This Is the Feast of Victory" (Rev.)
"Lord God, Your Love Has Called Us Here" (John)
"Lord, You Have Come to the Lakeshore" (John)

FOURTH SUNDAY OF EASTER

Year A: 1993, 1996, 1999

Acts 2:42-47; Psalm 23; I Peter 2:19-25; John 10:1-10
"Jesus, United by Thy Grace" (Acts)
"Let Us Break Bread Together" (Acts)
"The Lord's My Shepherd, I'll Not Want" (Ps.)
"He Leadeth Me: O Blessed Thought" (Ps.; I Pet.; John)
"O Thou in Whose Presence" (Ps.; I Pet.; John)
"Savior, Like a Shepherd Lead Us" (Ps.; I Pet.; John)
"The King of Love My Shepherd Is" (Ps.; I Pet.; John)
"You Satisfy the Hungry Heart" (Ps.; I Pet.; John)

Year B: 1994, 1997, 2000

Acts 4:5-12; Psalm 23; I John 3:16-24; John 10:11-18
"All Hail the Power of Jesus' Name" (Acts)
"At the Name of Jesus" (Acts)
"Christ Is Made the Sure Foundation" (Acts)
"O for a Heart to Praise My God" (I John)
See Year A for hymns related to Psalm 23 and John 10.

Year C: 1995, 1998, 2001

Acts 9:36-43; Psalm 23; Revelation 7:9-17; John 10:22-30
"Crown Him with Many Crowns" (Rev.)
"Fix Me, Jesus" (Rev.)
"See the Morning Sun Ascending" (esp. v. 4) (Rev.)
"Ye Servants of God" (Rev.)
See Year A for hymns related to Psalm 23 and John 10.

FIFTH SUNDAY OF EASTER

Year A: 1993, 1996, 1999

Acts 7:55-60; Psalm 31:1-5, 15-16; I Peter 2:2-10; John 14:1-14
"I'll Praise My Maker While I've Breath" (Acts)
"Christ Is Made the Sure Foundation" (I Pet.)
"The Church's One Foundation" (I Pet.)
"Come, My Way, My Truth, My Life" (John)
"O Jesus, I Have Promised" (John)

Year B: 1994, 1997, 2000

Acts 8:26-40; Psalm 22:25-31; I John 4:7-12; John 15:1-8
"Christ for the World We Sing" (Acts)
"We've a Story to Tell to the Nations" (Acts)
"I Need Thee Every Hour" (I John; John)
"Love Divine, All Loves Excelling" (I John; John)
"Where Charity and Love Prevail" (I John)
"When We Are Living" (John)

Year C: 1995, 1998, 2001

Acts 11:1-18; Psalm 148; Revelation 21:1-6; John 13:31-35
"Spirit of the Living God" (Acts)
"Mountains Are All Aglow" (Ps.)
"Glorious Things of Thee Are Spoken" (Rev.)
"I Want to Be Ready" (Rev.)
"O Holy City, Seen of John" (Rev.)
"On Jordan's Stormy Banks I Stand" (Rev.)
"Soon and Very Soon" (Rev.)
"This Is a Day of New Beginnings" (Rev.)
"Blest Be the Tie That Binds" (John)
"Jesus, United by Thy Grace" (John)
"They'll Know We Are Christians by Our Love" (John)

SIXTH SUNDAY OF EASTER

Year A: 1993, 1996, 1999

Acts 17:22-31; Psalm 66:8-20; I Peter 3:13-22; John 14:15-21
"I Sing the Almighty Power of God" (Acts)
"O Zion, Haste" (Acts)
"Open My Eyes, That I May See" (Acts)
"Let All the World in Every Corner Sing" (Acts; Ps.)
"Thy Holy Wings, O Savior" (I Pet.)
"Come Down, O Love Divine" (John)
"Love Divine, All Loves Excelling" (John)

Year B: 1994, 1997, 2000

Acts 10:44-48; Psalm 98; I John 5:1-6; John 15:9-17
"O Spirit of the Living God" (Acts)
"Spirit of Faith, Come Down" (Acts)
"Trust and Obey" (I John)
"Victory in Jesus" (I John)
"Help Us Accept Each Other" (John)
"Jesus Our Friend and Brother" (John)
"What a Friend We Have in Jesus" (John)

Year C: 1995, 1998, 2001

Acts 16:9-15; Psalm 67; Revelation 21:10; 21:22–22:5; John 14:23-29 *or* John 5:1-9
"There's a Wideness in God's Mercy" (Acts)
"Christ Is the World's Light" (Rev.)
"For the Healing of the Nations" (Rev.)
"Shall We Gather at the River" (Rev.)
"Blessed Jesus, at Thy Word" (John 14:23-29)

M. Ascension Day and the Sunday Following

The church has traditionally marked the biblical reality of the ascension of the Lord who now sits at the right hand of the Father with a special feast. This day marks the rightful assumption of glory and power by the Crucified One. While we mark the fortieth day of the Easter Season, or the sixth Thursday, this is not merely a historical commemoration of the forty days of Jesus' post-resurrection appearances to his disciples (Acts 1:3); rather it is a highlighting of an integral part of the Easter event according to the earliest traditions.

In many churches it is not feasible to hold a special service on Thursday, in which case the ascension may be celebrated the following Sunday, the Seventh Sunday of Easter. If this is done, the lessons for Ascension Day should be used, with the reading from Acts perhaps extended to verse 14 or even including verses 15-17 and 21-26.

In any event, the liturgy should make abundantly clear the connection between the resurrection and the ascension: Christ died and rose that we might have eternal life; and he ascended that we might be given a share in his divinity, his continuing presence and, hence, life with God. A careful study of all the lessons of this season leading up to the ascension texts is essential to any planning. This biblical understanding will help avoid a shallow interpretation of the ascension.

GATHERING

GREETING

Risen with Christ, let us seek the realities of the Spirit.

Our life is hidden with Christ in God.

He who descended
is also ascended far above the heavens,
that he might fill all things.

**When Christ, our Life, appears,
we shall appear with him in glory! Alleluia!**

HYMN OF PRAISE   *Suitable hymns for this day include:*

"All Hail the Power of Jesus' Name"
"All Praise to Thee, for Thou, O King Divine"
"Christ Is the World's Light"
"Crown Him with Many Crowns"
"Hail, Thou Once Despised Jesus"
"Jesus Shall Reign"
"Rejoice, the Lord Is King"
"The Head That Once Was Crowned"

OPENING PRAYER

The risen Christ is with you.

And also with you.

Let us pray:
Almighty God,
whose blessed Son our Savior
ascended far above all heavens
that he might fill all things:
mercifully grant us faith
to recognize his abiding presence
with his people on earth,
even to the end of the ages;
through Jesus Christ our Lord,
who lives and reigns with you and the Holy Spirit,
one God, in glory for ever.

Amen.

or

Ever-loving God,
your only Son was taken up into heaven
that he might prepare a place for us
and bestow the Spirit of Truth.
Make us joyful in his ascension
so that we might worship him in his glory;
through Jesus Christ our Lord.

Illumine our hearts and minds
by the power of the Holy Spirit,
that the Scriptures may be the living Word to us this day;
through Jesus Christ our Lord.

Amen.

FIRST LESSON

Ascension Day:	Acts 1:1-11	(All years)
Seventh Sunday:	Acts 1:6-14	(Year A: 1993, 1996, 1999)
	Acts 1:15-17, 21-26	(Year B: 1994, 1997, 2000)
	Acts 16:16-34	(Year C: 1995, 1998, 2001)

PSALM

Ascension Day:	Psalm 47 *or* Psalm 110	(All years)
Seventh Sunday:	Psalm 68:1-10, 32-35	(Year A: 1993, 1996, 1999)
	Psalm 1	(Year B: 1994, 1997, 2000)
	Psalm 97	(Year C: 1995, 1998, 2001)

SECOND LESSON

Ascension Day:	Ephesians 1:15-23	(All years)
Seventh Sunday:	I Peter 4:12-14, 5:6-11	(Year A: 1993, 1996, 1999)
	I John 5:9-13	(Year B: 1994, 1997, 2000)
	Revelation 22:12-14, 16-17, 20-21	(Year C: 1995, 1998, 2001)

HYMN

GOSPEL

Ascension Day:	Luke 24:44-53	(All years)
Seventh Sunday:	John 17:1-11	(Year A: 1993, 1996, 1999)
	John 17:6-19	(Year B: 1994, 1997, 2000)
	John 17:20-26	(Year C: 1995, 1998, 2001)

SERMON

RESPONSE TO THE WORD

PRAYERS OF THE PEOPLE OR PASTORAL PRAYER

To each petition responding: **King of Glory, hear our prayer.**

THE PEACE

OFFERING

If Holy Communion is celebrated, the Great Thanksgiving for the Easter Vigil and the dismissal with blessing given below may be used.

If Holy Communion is not celebrated, the service may conclude with the following prayers, a hymn, and the dismissal with blessing.

PRAYER OF THANKSGIVING

Blessed are you,
God and Father of our Lord Jesus Christ!
By your mercy we have been born anew to a living hope.

As once you brought your people through the Red Sea waters,
so from the waters of death you raise us to life with Christ.
Once we were no people, but now we are your people.
Help us to grow as people of your new covenant
toward the fullness of the life our Savior bestows.
Accept these gifts and our lives,
that we may live always
in the Spirit you share with Jesus Christ,
in whom and through whom we pray.

Amen.

THE LORD'S PRAYER

HYMN

DISMISSAL WITH BLESSING

Go in the peace of Christ to serve God and your neighbor.

We are sent in the name of the risen and glorified Lord.

May the blessing of Almighty God, the Father, Son, and Holy Spirit,
  be upon you now and for ever.

Amen. Alleluia!

Commentary

The theme of the gathering could center on the meaning of "Christ filling all things." The ascension theme could be carried out in a number of ways. Presentations centering on key scriptural images, both as dramatizations and as media events, might be given. (1) Christ is seated at the right hand of the Father in victory; (2) "All authority in heaven and on earth has been given to me"; (3) "Lo, I am with you always, even to the end of the age"; (4) "It is to your advantage that I go away"—"I will send the Counselor, the Spirit of Truth, to you"; (5) "You shall receive power when the Holy Spirit has come upon you, and you shall by my witnesses . . . to the end of the earth"; (6) "Why do you stand, gazing into heaven?"

This evening presents a good time to reflect together on the meaning for the concrete life of the church today of Christ's promise to be with us in witness and mission. Thus, a presentation or discussion of specific forms of the church's witness and mission in the community might also form the focus of the gathering. If this service is celebrated on Thursday evening, it may be held in connection with a congregational supper. Worship could precede the meal. This might allow for a movement following communion in an informal procession to a fellowship room from the worship area.

The same themes mentioned above form the basis of the prayers of the people (intercessions) and, most certainly, the sermon. These images also suggest the possibility of a simple media presentation in the context of the service, as part of the response to the Word, or in combination with the verbal proclamation. In general, the atmosphere of our worship on this occasion should be a joyful solemnity. There is at the heart of this feast a profound mystery which cannot be expressed by mere hilarity and balloons, though the release of helium-filled balloons containing messages of the witness and mission of the gospel may be a suitable sign-act and a way of involving children, for example.

The visual experience of the sanctuary and the fellowship hall should be of strong vertical lines and simple, bold colors: white, gold, purple, and red. The quality of Ascension Day and its meaning are beautifully expressed in the following prayer from the *Verona Sacramentary*.

> Rightly do we exult and rejoice on today's feast. The ascension into heaven of Jesus Christ, Mediator between God and man, is not an abandonment of us to our lowly state, for he exists now in the glory that he always had with you and in the nature he took from us and made his own. He deigned to become a man, in order that he might make us sharers in his divinity.[1]

"Christ enthroned in glory" opens up several strong visual possibilities, including the use of Pantocrator iconography—i.e., representations of Christ as Ruler of all.

When the ascension is celebrated on the following Sunday, these same themes should be considered. It is crucial that the entire Great Fifty Days be kept in mind, so that Ascension becomes not an isolated event but rather a specific witness to the meaning of the Great Fifty Days as the season of the Spirit. As the narrative of the Apostles' Creed expresses it, "the third day he rose from the dead; he ascended into heaven, and sits at the right hand of God"; he sends the Holy Spirit and will "come to judge the quick and the dead." The hymns suitable for this occasion are among the most powerful in Christian tradition.

N. Pentecost

GATHERING

Weather permitting, the people may gather outside or in a bright, airy space before the service begins. There may be special music and special displays of arts, handcrafts, flowers, and anything representing the gifts God has given to the congregation. Following the service, this may be a place for gathering and eating. At the appointed time, the paschal candle may be brought forward, the people gathered attentively into the opening litany, and everyone may then process into the worship area, singing the opening hymn.

GREETING AND LITANY OF PRAISE

Our help is in the name of the Lord,
who created heaven and earth.

**Sing to God, O kingdoms of the earth;
sing praises to the Lord.
Alleluia!**

He rides in the heavens, and sends forth his mighty voice.

Alleluia!

How wonderful is God in his holy places,
the God of Israel,
giving strength and power to his people!

Alleluia!

All who are led by the Spirit of God are children of God.
Lord, send forth your Spirit,
and renew the face of the earth.

[1]Cited in *The Liturgical Year*, by Adrian Nocent, O.S.B., translated by M. J. O'Connell (Collegeville, Minn.: Liturgical Press, 1977), Vol. III, pp. 235-36. The whole four-volume set is an excellent resource for serious study of the Christian Year. Though based on the Roman Catholic version of the three-year lectionary, it provides valuable theological and homiletical insights for anyone using the new ecumenical lectionary upon which *Word and Table*, *Seasons of the Gospel*, and *From Ashes to Fire* are based.

Alleluia!

or

Response:
Listen! you nations of the world:
listen to the Word of the Lord.
Proclaim it from coast to coast,
declare it to distant islands.

The Lord who scattered Israel
will gather his people again;
and he will keep watch over them
as a shepherd watches his flock.

Response

With shouts of joy they will come,
their faces radiantly happy,
for the Lord is so generous to them;
he showers his people with gifts.

Response

Young women will dance for joy,
and men young and old will make merry.
Like a garden refreshed by the rain,
they will never be in want again.
Break into shouts of great joy:
Jacob is free again!
Teach nations to sing the song:
"The Lord has saved his people!"

Response

After this the minister says:
I was glad when they said to me:
"Let us go into the house of the Lord."

HYMN OF PRAISE   *Suitable hymns for this day include:*

"See How Great a Flame Aspires"
"O Spirit of the Living God"
"Spirit of Faith, Come Down"
"Come, Holy Ghost, Our Hearts Inspire"
"Come, Holy Ghost, Our Souls Inspire"
"Come Down, O Love Divine"
"Spirit of Life, in This New Dawn"
"Spirit of God, Descend upon My Heart"
"Breathe on Me, Breath of God"

OPENING PRAYER

Almighty God,
on this day you opened the way of eternal life
to every race and nation
by the promised gift of your Holy Spirit.
Shed abroad this gift throughout the world
by the preaching of the gospel,
that it may reach to the ends of the earth;
through Jesus Christ our Lord,
who lives and reigns with you,
in the unity of the Holy Spirit,
for ever and ever.

Amen.

or

Spirit of the living God,
visit us again on the day of Pentecost.

Come, Holy Spirit.

With rushing wind that sweeps away all barriers,

Come, Holy Spirit.

With tongues of fire that set our hearts aflame,

Come, Holy Spirit.

With speech that unites the Babel of our tongues,

Come, Holy Spirit.

With love that overleaps the boundaries of race and nations,

Come, Holy Spirit.

With power from above to make our weakness strong,

Come, Holy Spirit.

In the name of Jesus Christ our Lord.

Amen.

FIRST LESSON

Acts 2:1-21 *or* (All years)
Numbers 11:24-30 (Year A: 1993, 1996, 1999)
Ezekiel 37:1-14 (Year B: 1994, 1997, 2000)
Genesis 11:1-9 (Year C: 1995, 1998, 2001)

PSALM 104:24-34   (All years)

Response:

**Send forth your Spirit,
and renew the face of the earth.**

O Lord, how manifold are your works!
In wisdom you have made them all;
the earth is full of your creatures.
Yonder is the great and wide sea
with its living things too many to number,
creatures both small and great.
There move the ships,
and there is that Leviathan,
which you have made for the sport of it.

Response

All creatures look to you
to give them their food in due season.
You give it to them; they gather it;
you open your hand,
and they are filled with good things.
You hide your face, and they are terrified;
you take away their breath,
and they die and return to their dust.
You send forth your Spirit,
and they are created;
and so you renew the face of the earth.

Response

May the glory of the Lord endure for ever;
may the Lord rejoice in all his works.
He looks at the earth and it trembles;
he touches the mountains and they smoke.

Response

I will sing to the Lord as long as I live;
I will sing praises to my God as long as I have being.
May my meditation be pleasing to him,
for I rejoice in the Lord.

Response

SECOND LESSON

If Acts 2:1-21 was not used as the first lesson it should be used as the second lesson; otherwise, the lessons are as follows:

I Corinthians 12:3*b*-13	(Year A: 1993, 1996, 1999)
Romans 8:22-27	(Year B: 1994, 1997, 2000)
Romans 8:14-17	(Year C: 1995, 1998, 2001)

HYMN OR RESPONSORY

The alternate litany of praise from the opening of the service may be used.

GOSPEL

John 20:19-23 *or* John 7:37-39	(Year A: 1993, 1996, 1999)
John 15:26-27; 16:4*b*-15	(Year B: 1994, 1997, 2000)
John 14:8-17 (25-27)	(Year C: 1995, 1998, 2001)

SERMON

RESPONSE TO THE WORD

[BAPTISM, CONFIRMATION, AND RENEWAL OF THE BAPTISMAL COVENANT]

See Annotated Bibliography for listing of denominational liturgies of baptism, confirmation, and renewal of the baptismal covenant.

PRAYERS OF THE PEOPLE

THE PEACE

Jesus said: "My peace I give to you, not as the world gives."
The peace of the Lord be with you.

And also with you.

Let us exchange signs of reconciliation and peace.

OFFERING

If Holy Communion is not celebrated, the service concludes with the following prayers, the final hymn, and the dismissal with blessing.

PRAYER OF THANKSGIVING

God of wind, word, and fire,
we bless your name this day for sending
the light and strength of your Holy Spirit.
We give you thanks for all the gifts, great and small,
which have been poured out upon your children.
Accept us with our gifts to be living praise and witness
to your love throughout all the earth;
through Jesus Christ who lives with you
in the unity of the Holy Spirit,
one God, for ever.

Amen.

THE LORD'S PRAYER

DISMISSAL WITH BLESSING

> Go forth in the power of the Holy Spirit!
> Proclaim the gospel throughout the earth!
> Serve the Lord with gladness,
> with deeds of justice and mercy!

> **We are sent in the name and power of the Lord!**

> May the God who raised Jesus from the dead bless you.

> **Amen.**

> May the God to whom our Lord ascended
> make his face shine upon you and be gracious to you.

> **Amen.**

> May the Spirit
> who is the unity of love between Father and Son,
> grant you peace forevermore.

> **Amen. Thanks be to God.**

**   ****   ****

If Holy Communion is celebrated, the table is prepared during the offering. The bread and wine may be brought forward with the offerings.

GREAT THANKSGIVING

> The Lord be with you.

> **And also with you.**

> Lift up your hearts.

> **We lift them to the Lord.**

> Let us give thanks to the Lord our God.

> **It is right to give our thanks and praise.**

> It is right, and a good and joyful thing,
> always and everywhere to give thanks to you,
> Father Almighty, Creator of heaven and earth.

In the beginning
your Spirit moved over the face of the waters.
You formed us in your image
and breathed into us the breath of life.
When we turned away, and our love failed,
your love remained steadfast.
Your Spirit came upon prophets and teachers,
anointing them to speak your Word.

And so, with your people on earth
and all the company of heaven,
we praise your name and join their unending hymn:

Holy, holy, holy Lord, God of power and might,
heaven and earth are full of your glory.
Hosanna in the highest.
Blessed is he who comes in the name of the Lord.
Hosanna in the highest.

Holy are you, and blessed is your Son Jesus Christ.
At his baptism in the Jordan your Spirit descended upon him
and declared him your beloved Son.
With your Spirit upon him
he turned away the temptation of sin.
Your Spirit anointed him
to preach good news to the poor,
to proclaim release to the captives
and recovering of sight to the blind,
to set at liberty those who are oppressed,
and to announce that the time had come
when you would save your people.
He healed the sick, fed the hungry, and ate with sinners.

By the baptism of his suffering, death, and resurrection
you gave birth to your church,
delivered us from slavery to sin and death,
and made with us a new covenant by water and the Spirit.
When the Lord Jesus ascended,
he promised to be with us always,
baptizing us with the Holy Spirit and with fire,
as on the Day of Pentecost.

On the night in which he gave himself up for us
he took bread, gave thanks to you, broke the bread,
gave it to his disciples, and said:
"Take, eat; this is my body which is given for you.
Do this in remembrance of me."

When the supper was over he took the cup,
gave thanks to you, gave it to his disciples, and said:
"Drink from this, all of you;
this is my blood of the new covenant,

poured out for you and for many
for the forgiveness of sins.
Do this, as often as you drink it, in remembrance of me."

On the day you raised him from the dead
he was recognized by his disciples
in the breaking of the bread,
and in the power of your Holy Spirit
your church has continued
in the breaking of bread and the sharing of the cup.

And so,
in remembrance of these your mighty acts in Jesus Christ,
we offer ourselves in praise and thanksgiving
as a holy and living sacrifice,
in union with Christ's offering for us,
as we proclaim the mystery of faith.

Christ has died, Christ is risen, Christ will come again.

Pour out your Holy Spirit on us, gathered here,
and on these gifts of bread and wine.
Make them be for us the body and blood of Christ,
that we may be for the world the body of Christ,
redeemed by his blood.

By your Spirit make us one with Christ,
one with each other,
and one in ministry to all the world,
until Christ comes in final victory
and we feast at his heavenly banquet.

Through your Son Jesus Christ,
with the Holy Spirit in your holy church,
all honor and glory is yours, Almighty Father,
now and for ever.

Amen.

THE LORD'S PRAYER

BREAKING THE BREAD

COMMUNION

PRAYER AFTER COMMUNION

HYMN

DISMISSAL WITH BLESSING

Go forth into the world,
rejoicing in the power of the Holy Spirit!

Thanks be to God. Alleluia!

The blessing of Almighty God,
Father, Son, and Holy Spirit,
be with you this day and for ever.

Amen! Alleluia!

Commentary

This is the great climax of the Easter-Pentecost Season. On this day we remember and celebrate the fullness of God's promises in Jesus Christ. Before us this day is the whole sweep of Christ's death and resurrection, his ascension, and the sending of the Holy Spirit with all God's gifts and commissioning power for our ministries. This great occasion should be marked with special gatherings and a festive common meal. It is especially fitting to celebrate the Lord's Supper with great joy.

The visual environment should reflect the great joy and festivity of the day. Flame red is the dominant color, supplemented by other bright colors such as gold. The finest textures are appropriate. Appropriate Pentecost symbols include a descending dove, tongues of flame, symbols of the church (ship, rainbow), and a downward arrow.

The music should be glorious and may include Easter as well as Pentecost texts. If there is to be a gathering outside the church building, instrumental music is appropriate. We may draw, for example, upon the French medieval and Moravian traditions in having brass fanfare and/or chorales, perhaps from a church tower or other high place. If a procession is formed behind the paschal candle, the choir and congregation may wish to sing a canticle of praise or a suitable Pentecost hymn.

There may be a festival or display of the "varieties of gifts" given to the church: images of its various ministries and missions, its common life, the arts, and its hopes and expectations. This should be an occasion of freedom, sharing, and hospitality among all. This in itself is a sign and a witness to the Spirit which has been poured out into our hearts.

The congregation may return to the same fellowship room or outdoor space for a fellowship meal following the service. Festivities and arts displays may last on into the afternoon.

This day presents several opportunities for responses to the Word. There may be musical responses or a period of witness and testimony to the faith—particularly to the service ministries of the local and global church in which the Holy Spirit is at work. A creed may be said by the entire congregation, or there may be a period of free prayer.

This day is also a most suitable time for baptisms, confirmations, and renewal of the baptismal covenant. If a baptismal renewal has not been celebrated on Easter Day, it is strongly urged that it be used as the main response to the Word. This should be given ample time to unfold with power and not be rushed or merely sandwiched in. This may require shortening the sermon slightly. Again, the proclamatory power of the sacrament speaks for itself, if done well and prayerfully. Careful preparations must be made and particular attention given to the instructions leading to baptism, confirmation, or renewal of the baptismal covenant. Those being prepared should have a clear appreciation for the rite which takes place in the context of the Pentecost Gospel and the whole congregational service.

Another possibility for the service, or perhaps for presentation at a common meal, is a drama based upon the disciples' experience on Pentecost. In particular, people may experience the contrast between Babel (texts read simultaneously in several languages) and the unity of utterance in the preaching of the gospel. The scripture lessons suggest various possible media presentations as well: the valley of dry bones, the wind and fire, water and the Spirit—all these may be presented along with nonbiblical or contemporary readings as interpretations. Babel and Pentecost provide rich and inexhaustible themes.

FROM SUNDAY TO SUNDAY: THE SEASON AFTER PENTECOST

A. Trinity Sunday

*T*he first and last Sundays in the season After Pentecost are days with special themes—Trinity and Christ the King, respectively. Although the basic color for this half of the year is green, it is customary to use white on these Sundays. These are transitional Sundays between the high seasons and what is often called "ordinary time," and while they are not in the first rank of great days in the Christian Year, they are nevertheless significant celebrations.

On Trinity Sunday we celebrate the mystery of God's being as Holy Trinity. Often the emphasis of this day has been placed on the Trinity as an abstract concept, idea, or doctrine—an intellectual emphasis that tends to produce sermons and liturgies which attempt to interpret or explain this doctrine to those who find it confusing or incredible. Whatever the pastoral justification for this approach may be in certain situations, it seems generally more in keeping with the character of worship and of the Christian Year to treat Trinity Sunday as a day in which we praise and adore the infinitely complex and unfathomable mystery of God's being to which we point when we speak of the Holy Trinity. Because our celebration of the Easter cycle is based upon the mighty acts of the triune God, and because we are entering upon the Sunday-to-Sunday half of the year when the emphasis is wholeheartedly upon each Sunday as the Lord's Day, whose celebration is also based upon the mighty acts of the triune God, it is appropriate that we pause on this transitional Sunday to give ourselves over to the adoration and praise of the *being*—as distinct from the *acts*—of the triune God.

The visual environment should be conducive to adoration and praise and suggestive of the mystery of the Holy Trinity. White can be supplemented by such other colors as gold. Symbols of the Trinity can be used: equilateral triangle, trefoil, fleur-de-lis, three intertwined circles, triquetra, and shamrock (see Glossary of Christian Symbols).

Music that eloquently expresses adoration and praise to the inexhaustible mystery of God's being is crucial to worship on this day.

Use of a creed is particularly appropriate on Trinity Sunday. The Nicene Creed is a more fully expressive witness to the church's faith in the Trinity than are modern affirmations or even the Apostles' Creed. The Athanasian Creed is in some ways an even more comprehensive witness to the church's faith, although its anathemas against unbelievers have caused much offense and led many churches to reject its use. An abbreviated form of the Athanasian Creed, including the positive affirmations but not the anathemas, is printed below.

Holy Communion is supremely expressive of our celebration of the mystery of the Holy Trinity. In addition to those congregations that celebrate Holy Communion every Sunday, congregations that celebrate Holy Communion on the first Sunday of every month will do so on Trinity Sunday when it falls on the first Sunday in June. The Great Thanksgiving printed below, while it is suitable for use at any time of the year, is by its thoroughly trinitarian character well suited for Trinity Sunday.

GATHERING   *Instrumental music should express adoration.*

GREETING

In the name of the Father, and of the Son, and of the Holy Spirit.

Amen.

HYMN OF PRAISE   *Suitable hymns for this day include*

"Holy, Holy, Holy!"
"Come, Thou Almighty King"
"Ancient of Days"
"Holy God, We Praise Thy Name"
"Praise God, from Whom All Blessings Flow" ("The Doxology")
"Come, Father, Son, and Holy Ghost"
"We Believe in One True God"
"Thou, Whose Almighty Word"

OPENING PRAYER

Father, you sent your Word to bring us truth
and your Spirit to make us holy.
Through them we come to know
the mystery of your life.
Help us to worship you, one God in three persons,
by proclaiming and living our faith in you.
Grant this through our Lord Jesus Christ, your Son,
who lives and reigns with you and the Holy Spirit,
one God, for ever and ever. **Amen.**

FIRST LESSON

Genesis 1:1–2:4*a*	(Year A: 1996, 1999, 2002)
Isaiah 6:1-8	(Year B: 1997, 2000, 2003)
Proverbs 8:1-4, 22-31	(Year C: 1998, 2001, 2004)

PSALM

Psalm 82	(Year A: 1996, 1999, 2002)
Psalm 29	(Year B: 1997, 2000, 2003)
Psalm 8	(Year C: 1998, 2001, 2004)

SECOND LESSON

II Corinthians 13:11-13	(Year A: 1996, 1999, 2002)
Romans 8:12-17	(Year B: 1997, 2000, 2003)
Romans 5:1-5	(Year C: 1998, 2001, 2004)

HYMN

GOSPEL

Matthew 28:16-20   (Year A: 1996, 1999, 2002)
John 3:1-17   (Year B: 1997, 2000, 2003)
John 16:12-15   (Year C: 1998, 2001, 2004)

SERMON

RESPONSE TO THE WORD

The Nicene Creed or this abbreviated version of the Athanasian Creed:

Whoever wants to be saved
must, above all, hold the catholic faith:
Now this is the catholic faith,
that we worship one God in three persons
and three persons in one God
without confusing the persons
nor dividing the divine being.
For the Father is one person,
the Son is another,
and the Holy Spirit is still another;
but there is one God, the Father, the Son, and the Holy Spirit,
all equal in glory and eternal in majesty.
It is necessary that one also believe faithfully
that our Lord Jesus Christ became human.
For this is the true faith, that we believe and confess,
that our Lord Jesus Christ, the Son of God,
is both God and human:
God, begotten before all worlds from the being of the Father,
and human, born in the world from the being of his mother,
perfect God and perfect human,
with a rational soul and a human body.
For just as soul and body are one in a human being,
so God and human are one in Christ,
who suffered for our salvation, descended to the dead,
rose from the dead on the third day, ascended into heaven,
sits at the right hand of God, the Father Almighty
and will come to judge the living and the dead.
At whose coming, all shall rise with their bodies
to give account of their own deeds.
Those who have done what is good will enter eternal life.
This is the catholic faith.

PRAYERS OF THE PEOPLE OR PASTORAL PRAYER

THE PEACE

OFFERING

If Holy Communion is not celebrated, the service concludes with a prayer of thanksgiving, the Lord's Prayer, and a clearly trinitarian dismissal with blessing such as that given below.

If Holy Communion is celebrated, the table is prepared during the offering and the service continues as follows:

GREAT THANKSGIVING

The Lord be with you.

And also with you.

Lift up your hearts.

We lift them to the Lord.

Let us give thanks to the Lord our God.

It is right to give our thanks and praise.

It is right, and a good and joyful thing,
always and everywhere to give thanks to you,
Father Almighty, Creator of heaven and earth.

You formed us in your image
and breathed into us the breath of life.
When we turned away, and our love failed,
your love remained steadfast.
You delivered us from captivity,
made covenant to be our sovereign God,
and spoke to us through your prophets.

And so with your people on earth
and all the company of heaven,
we praise your name and join their unending hymn:

**Holy, holy, holy Lord, God of power and might,
heaven and earth are full of your glory.
Hosanna in the highest.
Blessed is he who comes in the name of the Lord.
Hosanna in the highest.**

Holy are you, and blessed is your Son Jesus Christ.
Your Spirit anointed him
to preach good news to the poor,

to proclaim release to the captives
and recovering of sight to the blind,
to set at liberty those who are oppressed,
and to announce that the time had come
when you would save your people.
He healed the sick, fed the hungry, and ate with sinners.

By the baptism of his suffering, death, and resurrection
you gave birth to your church,
delivered us from slavery to sin and death,
and made with us a new covenant by water and the Spirit.
When the Lord Jesus ascended,
he promised to be with us always
in the power of your Word and Holy Spirit.

On the night in which he gave himself up for us
he took bread, gave thanks to you, broke the bread,
gave it to his disciples, and said:
"Take, eat; this is my body which is given for you.
Do this in remembrance of me."

When the supper was over he took the cup,
gave thanks to you, gave it to his disciples, and said:
"Drink from this, all of you;
this is my blood of the new covenant,
poured out for you and for many
for the forgiveness of sins.
Do this, as often as you drink it, in remembrance of me."

And so,
in remembrance of these your mighty acts in Jesus Christ,
we offer ourselves in praise and thanksgiving
as a holy and living sacrifice,
in union with Christ's offering for us,
as we proclaim the mystery of faith.

Christ has died, Christ is risen, Christ will come again.

Pour out your Holy Spirit on us, gathered here,
and on these gifts of bread and wine.
Make them be for us the body and blood of Christ,
that we may be for the world the body of Christ,
redeemed by this blood.

By your Spirit make us one with Christ,
one with each other,
and one in ministry to all the world,
until Christ comes in final victory
and we feast at his heavenly banquet.

Through your Son Jesus Christ,
with the Holy Spirit in your holy church,

all honor and glory is yours, Almighty Father,
now and for ever.

Amen.

THE LORD'S PRAYER

BREAKING THE BREAD

COMMUNION

PRAYER AFTER COMMUNION

HYMN

DISMISSAL WITH BLESSING

Go in peace.
The blessing of God Almighty,
the Father, the Son, and the Holy Spirit,
be among you, and remain with you always.

Amen.

B. The Sundays After Pentecost

We have seen in part one of this book that the half of the year following Pentecost is different in character from the seasons of Advent, Christmas, Epiphany and Lent, Holy Week, Easter. Whether it is called "ordinary time," or "Season After Pentecost," or "Kingdomtide," each Sunday stands on its own as the Lord's Day and should be considered in the light of the Scriptures to be read that day.

Because there has been much confusion about this half of the year, some clarification needs to be made. The Season *After* Pentecost is just that; it is *not* the Pentecost Season. As we have seen, the term *Pentecost* both in the most ancient usage and in contemporary usage is reserved for the Great Fifty Days. Both the traditional and the new lectionaries make it clear that the Great Fifty Days are the time to celebrate not only the risen Christ but also the Holy Spirit. It is only through the work of the Holy Spirit that we know the risen Christ. The Christian calendar does not deal with the persons of the Trinity in sequence, as if we centered on the Father in the fall, the Son from Advent through Easter, and the Holy Spirit at Pentecost and thereafter. The persons of the Trinity cannot thus be separated and separately dealt with.

For those who choose to call this season "Kingdomtide," it is possible to note that the Gospel readings go in course through the teaching portions of Matthew (Year A), Mark (Year B), and Luke (Year C), in which Jesus' teaching about the kingdom of God is clearly central. This theme is sounded with particular strength on the last few Sundays after Pentecost and leads to the last Sunday, which is called "Christ the King." The emphasis on Christian social concerns that has been central to Kingdomtide observance since 1937 is amply provided for in the lectionary, not only by the Gospels but by the Old Testament and Epistle lessons as well.

It is also important to note, however, that Christ the King is not the climax of our centering on Christ the King but, rather, a transitional Sunday leading to Advent, which is in a more ancient and fuller sense a "kingdomtide." Indeed, the whole Christmas cycle and ultimately the Easter cycle are also "kingdomtides." Dieter Hessel's book *Social Themes of the Christian Year*, listed in the Annotated Bibliography, is one resource that shows the year-round relevance of the calendar to social concerns.

An examination of the lectionary readings will show that not only the Gospels but also the first and second lessons go in a semicontinuous cycle through books of the Bible. The second lessons go through Epistles, and the first lessons go through major portions of the Old Testament. Because continuous reading through books of the Bible *(lectio continua)* is an ancient tradition of proven effectiveness, it is fitting that this be the pattern for half of the year. This means that the three readings on any one Sunday should not be expected to relate to one another and that the preacher should preach on *one* of them. These readings provide a way for a pastor to preach directly and in depth from the Old Testament and from the Epistles as well as from the Gospels. In fact, the preacher has in these readings the basis for a *nine*-year cycle of preaching.

The preacher who wishes more information about the Sunday-by-Sunday reasoning behind these cycles of readings should read *Common Lectionary,* listed in the Annotated Bibliography, which is the book developed by the Consultation on Common Texts to present and interpret the common lectionary.

It is also important to note that, while Sundays are called "the _____ Sunday After Pentecost," the lectionary readings are determined not by how many Sundays it is since Pentecost but by the days within which a Sunday falls on the calendar. For instance, a given set of lessons will be appointed for "the Sunday between July 3 and 9 inclusive," regardless of the date of Pentecost.

Some confusion remains for pastors who are part of ecumenical lectionary study groups not all of whose members use the *Common Lectionary* or who use resources based on earlier versions of the three-year lectionary. This half of the year is when most of the confusion will take place, for two reasons: (1) the Old Testament lessons after Pentecost have been greatly changed and strengthened in the *Common Lectionary* as compared with earlier versions of the three-year lectionary, and (2) some older versions of the three-year lectionary set the readings by how many weeks it was after Pentecost and could therefore be one or more weeks out of phase with the *Common Lectionary.* As use of the *Common Lectionary* continues to increase, this confusion should continue to diminish.

This half of the year offers great freedom in creating the visual environment. The basic color is green, but this does *not* mean that a church must use green every Sunday for half the year. White is customary not only on Trinity Sunday and Christ the King but also on All Saints. For those who observe saints' days, red is used on the days of saints who were martyrs and white on the days of other saints. Those who do not observe martyrs' days do not need to feel deprived of the opportunity to use red during this season. Red, symbolizing the fire of the Holy Spirit and also the blood of Christ, can be used during evangelistic services, for ordinations and consecrations, for anniversaries and homecomings, and for civil observances such as Thanksgiving. Combinations of colors and colors other than the basic green, red, purple, and white are appropriate in this half of the year and are frequently seen today.

Both color and symbols can change from Sunday to Sunday to fit the Scripture readings, especially the reading on which the sermon is based. Some Christian symbols are listed in a special section in this book as a ready reference guide, and it is permissible to create new symbols whose meaning will either be obvious or can be interpreted to the people.

Great freedom is also possible in the choice of hymns and other music. It is often possible to relate the music to a scripture reading on a particular Sunday, and a few such possibilities are given here. On the other hand, general hymns and anthems of praise or hymns and songs that witness to the very heart of the Christian gospel can be appropriate even when there is no special relationship to the scriptures for a particular day. It is also a good time of year to learn new hymns, perhaps taking a whole month to learn a new hymn designated as "the hymn of the month."

When Holy Communion is celebrated on any of these Sundays, the Great Thanksgiving for Trinity is appropriate. So is the Great Thanksgiving for Christ the King, especially during the last several weeks, or if the time is considered to be Kingdomtide.

This half of the year, being less structured by tradition, can be the time when churches are challenged to be creative. Green symbolizes growth, and this time can be one of spiritual growth for any church.

If the Sunday between May 24 and 28 inclusive follows Trinity Sunday, use readings for the Eighth Sunday After Epiphany on that day.

SUNDAY BETWEEN MAY 29 AND JUNE 4 INCLUSIVE (if after Trinity Sunday)

> *Year A: 1993, 1996, 1999*
> Genesis 6:9-22, 7:24, 8:14-19; Psalm 46 *or* Deuteronomy 11:18-21, 26-28; Psalm 31:1-5, 19-24
> Romans 1:16-17; 3:22b-28 (29-31); Matthew 7:21-29
> "If Thou But Suffer God to Guide Thee" *or* "My Hope Is Built on Nothing Less" (Matt.)

> *Year B: 1994, 1997, 2000*
> I Samuel 3:1-10 (11-20); Psalm 139:1-6, 13-18 *or* Deuteronomy 5:12-15; Psalm 81:1-10
> II Corinthians 4:5-12; Mark 2:23–3:6
> "Lord, Speak to Me" (I Sam.); "This Little Light of Mine" (II Cor.)
> Any hymn on the Lord's Day (Deut.; Mark) or on healing (Mark)

> *Year C: 1995, 1998, 2001*
> I Kings 18:20-21 (22-29) 30-39; Psalm 96 *or* I Kings 8:22-23, 41-43; Psalm 96:1-9
> Galatians 1:1-12; Luke 7:1-10
> "Rejoice, the Lord Is King" (I Kings; Psalm); any hymn on healing (Luke)

SUNDAY BETWEEN JUNE 5 AND 11 INCLUSIVE (if after Trinity Sunday)

> *Year A: 1993, 1996, 1999*
> Genesis 12:1-9; Psalm 33:1-12 *or* Hosea 5:15–6:6; Psalm 50:7-15
> Romans 4:13-25; Matthew 9:9-13, 18-26
> "Where He Leads Me, I Will Follow" (Gen.; Rom.; Matt.)
> "Jesus Calls Us O'er the Tumult" (Gen.; Hosea; Rom.; Matt.)
> "The Voice of God Is Calling" (Matt.)
> "There Is a Balm in Gilead" *or* any hymn on healing (Matt.)

> *Year B: 1994, 1997, 2000*
> I Samuel 8:4-11 (12-15) 16-20 (11:14-15); Psalm 138 *or* Genesis 3:8-15; Psalm 130
> II Corinthians 4:13–5:1; Mark 3:20-35
> "Stand By Me" (II Cor.; Mark); any hymn on healing (Mark)

> *Year C: 1995, 1998, 2001*
> I Kings 17:8-16 (17-24); Psalm 146 *or* I Kings 17:17-24; Psalm 30
> Galatians 1:11-24; Luke 7:11-17
> "Amazing Grace" *or* "And Can It Be That I Should Gain" (Gal.)
> "Come, Ye Disconsolate" (Luke)

SUNDAY BETWEEN JUNE 12 AND 18 INCLUSIVE (if after Trinity Sunday)

> *Year A: 1993, 1996, 1999*
> Genesis 18:1-15 (21:1-7); Psalm 116:1-2, 12-19 *or* Exodus 19:2-8a; Psalm 100
> Romans 5:1-8; Matthew 9:35–10:8 (9-23)
> "How Great Thou Art" (esp. v. 3) (Rom.)
> "Freely, Freely" *or* any hymn on mission or evangelism (Rom.; Matt.)

Year B: 1994, 1997, 2000
 I Samuel 15:34–16:13; Psalm 20 *or* Ezekiel 17:22-24; Psalm 92:1-4, 12-15
 II Corinthians 5:6-10 (11-13), 14-17; Mark 4:26-34
 "O Come and Dwell in Me" (II Cor.); "Come, Ye Thankful People Come" (Mark)
 "The Kingdom of God Is Like a Grain of Mustard Seed" (Mark)

Year C: 1995, 1998, 2001
 I Kings 21:1-10 (11-14) 15-21*a*; Psalm 5:1-8 *or* II Samuel 11:26–12:10, 13-15; Psalm 32
 Galatians 2:15-21; Luke 7:36–8:3
 "Thou Hidden Love of God" (Gal.); "Forgive Our Sins as We Forgive" (Luke)
 "Freely, Freely," *or* "Just As I Am" *or* "Grace Greater Than Our Sin" (Luke)

SUNDAY BETWEEN JUNE 19 AND 25 INCLUSIVE (if after Trinity Sunday)

Year A: 1993, 1996, 1999
 Genesis 21:8-21; Psalm 86:1-10, 16-17 *or* Jeremiah 20:7-13; Psalm 69:7-10 (11-15) 16-18
 Romans 6:1*b*-11; Matthew 10:24-39
 "We Know That Christ Is Raised" (Rom.)
 "Stand Up, Stand Up for Jesus" *or* "How Firm a Foundation" (Matt.)

Year B: 1994, 1997, 2000
 I Samuel 17: (1*a*, 4-11, 19-23) 32-49; Psalm 9:9-20
  or I Samuel 17:57–18:5, 10-16; Psalm 133 *or* Job 38:1-11; Psalm 107:1-3, 23-32
 II Corinthians 6:1-13; Mark 4:35-41
 "Jesus, Savior, Pilot Me" *or* "Lonely the Boat" *or* "Stand By Me" (Mark)

Year C: 1995, 1998, 2001
 I Kings 19:1-4 (5-7) 8-15*a*; Psalms 42 and 43 *or* Isaiah 65:1-9; Psalm 22:19-28
 Galatians 3:23-29; Luke 8:26-39
 "Dear Lord and Father of Mankind" (esp. stanza 5) (I Kings) *or* "One Bread, One Body" (Gal.)
 "Christ, from Whom All Blessings Flow" *or* "In Christ There Is No East or West" (Gal.)
 "Silence, Frenzied, Unclean Spirit"; "Just As I Am" (esp. v. 3); any hymn on healing (Luke)

SUNDAY BETWEEN JUNE 26 AND JULY 2 INCLUSIVE

Year A: 1993, 1996, 1999
 Genesis 22:1-14; Psalm 13 *or* Jeremiah 28:5-9; Psalm 89:1-4, 15-18
 Romans 6:12-23; Matthew 10:40-42
 "Where Cross the Crowded Ways of Life" (esp. stanza 4) (Matt.)

Year B: 1994, 1997, 2000
 II Samuel 1:1, 17-27; Psalm 130
  or Wisdom of Solomon 1:13-15; 2:23-24; Lamentations 3:23-33 *or* Psalm 30
 II Corinthians 8:7-15; Mark 5:21-43
 "Great Is Thy Faithfulness" (Lam.) *or* "Ivory Palaces" (II Cor.)
 "Heal Us, Emmanuel" (esp. stanza 4) *or* any hymn on healing (Mark)

Year C: 1995, 1998, 2001
 II Kings 2:1-2, 6-14; Psalm 77:1-2, 11-20 *or* I Kings 19:15-16, 19-21; Psalm 16
 Galatians 5:1, 13-25; Luke 9:51-62
 "Spirit of God, Descend upon My Heart" *or* any hymn on the Holy Spirit (II Kings; Gal.)
 "Swing Low, Sweet Chariot" (II Kings) *or* "O Jesus, I Have Promised" (Luke)

SUNDAY BETWEEN JULY 3 AND 9 INCLUSIVE

Year A: 1993, 1996, 1999
  Genesis 24:34-38, 42-49, 58-67; Psalm 45:10-17 *or* Song of Solomon 2:8-13
    or Zechariah 9:9-12; Psalm 145:8-14
  Romans 7:15-25*a*; Matthew 11:16-19, 25-30
  "Dear Jesus, in Whose Life I See" (Rom.)
  "Come, All of You" *or* "What a Friend We Have in Jesus" (Matt.)

Year B: 1994, 1997, 2000
  II Samuel 5:1-5, 9-10; Psalm 48 *or* Ezekiel 2:1-5; Psalm 123
  II Corinthians 12:2-10; Mark 6:1-13
  "Be Thou My Vision" *or* "Spirit of God, Descend Upon My Heart" (II Cor.; Mark)

Year C: 1995, 1998, 2001
  II Kings 5:1-14; Psalm 30 *or* Isaiah 66:10-14; Psalm 66:1-9
  Galatians 6:(1-6) 7-16; Luke 10:1-11, 16-20
  Any hymn of healing (II Kings); "Ask Ye What Great Thing I Know"
    or "In the Cross of Christ I Glory" *or* "When I Survey the Wondrous Cross" (Gal.)

SUNDAY BETWEEN JULY 10 AND 16 INCLUSIVE

Year A: 1993, 1996, 1999
  Genesis 25:19-34; Psalm 119:105-112 *or* Isaiah 55:10-13; Psalm 65 (1-8) 9-13
  Romans 8:1-11; Matthew 13:1-9, 18-23
  Any hymn on the Holy Spirit (Rom.)

Year B: 1994, 1997, 2000
  II Samuel 6:1-5, 12*b*-19; Psalm 24 *or* Amos 7:7-15; Psalm 85:8-13
  Ephesians 1:3-14; Mark 6:14-29
  "Lord of the Dance" (II Sam.); "Lift Up Your Heads, Ye Mighty Gates" (Ps.)
  "Amazing Grace" *or* "How Great Thou Art" (Eph.)

Year C: 1995, 1998, 2001
  Amos 7:7-17; Psalm 82 *or* Deuteronomy 30:9-14; Psalm 25:1-10
  Colossians 1:1-14; Luke 10:25-37
  "In Christ There Is No East or West" *or* "Where Cross the Crowded Ways of Life" (Luke)

SUNDAY BETWEEN JULY 17 AND 23 INCLUSIVE

Year A: 1993, 1996, 1999
  Genesis 28:10-19*a*; Psalm 139:1-2, 23-24
    or Wisdom of Solomon 12:13, 16-19 *or* Isaiah 44:6-8; Psalm 86:11-17; Romans 8:12-25;
    Matthew 13:24-30, 36-43
  "We Are Climbing Jacob's Ladder" (Gen.); "Every Time I Feel the Spirit" (Rom.)
  "Hope of the World" *or* "My Hope Is Built" *or* any hymn on the Holy Spirit or on hope (Rom.)

Year B: 1994, 1997, 2000
  II Samuel 7:1-14*a*; Psalm 89:20-37 *or* Jeremiah 23:1-6; Psalm 23
  Ephesians 2:11-22; Mark 6:30-34, 53-56
  "The Church's One Foundation" *or* "Christ Is Made the Sure Foundation" (Eph.)
  "O Thou in Whose Presence" *or* "Savior, Like a Shepherd Lead Us" *or* "The Lord's My
    Shepherd, I'll Not Want" *or* "The King of Love My Shepherd Is" (Jer.; Ps.; Mark)

Year C: 1995, 1998, 2001
   Amos 8:1-12; Psalm 52 *or* Genesis 18:1-10*a*; Psalm 15
   Colossians 1:15-28; Luke 10:38-42
   "Dear Lord and Father of Mankind" *or* "Take Time to Be Holy" (Col.; Luke)

SUNDAY BETWEEN JULY 24 AND 30 INCLUSIVE

Year A: 1993, 1996, 1999
   Genesis 29:15-28; Psalm 105:1-11, 45*b or* Psalm 128 *or* I Kings 3:5-12; Psalm 119:129-136
   Romans 8:26-39; Matthew 13:31-33, 44-52
   "A Mighty Fortress Is Our God" (Rom.); "Jesus, Priceless Treasure" (Matt.)
   "Love Divine, All Loves Excelling" *or* "The Kingdom of God" (Matt.)

Year B: 1994, 1997, 2000
   II Samuel 11:1-15; Psalm 14 *or* II Kings 4:42-44; Psalm 145:10-18
   Ephesians 3:14-21; John 6:1-21
   "God of Grace and God of Glory" (Eph.); "Jesus, Savior, Pilot Me" (John)
   "Stand By Me" (John); "The King of Love My Shepherd Is" (II Kings; John)

Year C: 1995, 1998, 2001
   Hosea 1:2-10; Psalm 85 *or* Genesis 18:20-32; Psalm 138
   Colossians 2:6-15 (16-19); Luke 11:1-13
   "Rock of Ages, Cleft for Me" *or* "The Old Rugged Cross" (Col.)
   "Children of the Heavenly Father" *or* "Great Is Thy Faithfulness" (Luke)

SUNDAY BETWEEN JULY 31 AND AUGUST 6 INCLUSIVE

Year A: 1993, 1996, 1999
   Genesis 32:22-31; Psalm 17:1-7, 15 *or* Isaiah 55:1-5; Psalm 145:8-9, 14-21
   Romans 9:1-5; Matthew 14:13-21
   "Come, O Thou Traveler Unknown" (Gen.); "Come, All of You" (Isa.; Matt.)
   "Children of the Heavenly Father" *or* "Great Is Thy Faithfulness" (Matt.)

Year B: 1994, 1997, 2000
   II Samuel 11:26–12:13*a*; Psalm 51:1-12 *or* Exodus 16:2-4, 9-15; Psalm 78:23-29
   Ephesians 4:1-16; John 6:24-35
   "All Praise to Our Redeeming Lord" *or* "The Church's One Foundation" (Eph.)
   "Grace Greater than Our Sin" (II Sam.; Ps. 51); "Break Thou the Bread of Life" (John)

Year C: 1995, 1998, 2001
   Hosea 11:1-11; Psalm 107:1-9, 43 *or* Ecclesiastes 1:2, 12-14; 2:18-23; Psalm 49:1-12
   Colossians 3:1-11; Luke 12:13-21
   "Have Thine Own Way, Lord" *or* "Love Divine, All Loves Excelling" (Col.)
   "Jesus Calls Us" *or* "Take My Life, and Let It Be Consecrated" (Luke)

SUNDAY BETWEEN AUGUST 7 AND 13 INCLUSIVE

Year A: 1993, 1996, 1999
   Genesis 37:1-4, 12-28; Psalm 105:1-6, 16-22, 45*b or* I Kings 19:9-18; Psalm 85:8-13
   Romans 10:5-15; Matthew 14:22-33
   "How Shall They Hear the Word of God" *or* "In Christ There Is No East or West" (Rom.)
   "Jesus, Savior, Pilot Me" *or* "Stand By Me" (Gen.; I Kings; Matt.)

Year B: 1994, 1997, 2000

    II Samuel 18:5-9, 15, 31-33; Psalm 130 or I Kings 19:4-8; Psalm 34:1-8

    Ephesians 4:25–5:2; John 6:35, 41-51

    "All Praise to Our Redeeming Lord" *or* "Help Us Accept Each Other" (Eph.)

    "Become to Us the Living Bread" *or* "Bread of the World" *or* "Fill My Cup, Lord" (John)

Year C: 1995, 1998, 2001

    Isaiah 1:1, 10-20; Psalm 50:1-8, 22-23 *or* Genesis 15:1-6; Psalm 33:12-22

    Hebrews 11:1-3, 8-16; Luke 12:32-40

    "Marching to Zion" *or* "He Leadeth Me" (Gen.; Heb.); "A Charge to Keep I Have" (Luke)

SUNDAY BETWEEN AUGUST 14 AND 20 INCLUSIVE

Year A: 1993, 1996, 1999

    Genesis 45:1-15; Psalm 133 *or* Isaiah 56:1, 6-8; Psalm 67

    Romans 11:1-2a, 29-32; Matthew 15: (10-20) 21-28

    "The God of Abraham Praise" (Rom.); "There's a Wideness in God's Mercy" (Rom.; Matt.)

    "God of Many Names" *or* "In Christ There Is No East or West" (Rom.; Matt.)

Year B: 1994, 1997, 2000

    I Kings 2:10-12; 3:3-14; Psalm 111 *or* Proverbs 9:1-6; Psalm 34:9-14

    Ephesians 5:15-20; John 6:51-58

    "O Spirit of the Living God" (I Kings; Prov.); "When in Our Music God Is Glorified" (Eph.)

    "Deck Thyself, My Soul, with Gladness" *or* "Let All Mortal Flesh Keep Silence" (John)

Year C: 1995, 1998, 2001

    Isaiah 5:1-7; Psalm 80:1-2, 8-19 *or* Jeremiah 23:23-29; Psalm 82

    Hebrews 11:29–12:2; Luke 12:49-56

    "Come, Let Us Join" *or* "Faith of Our Fathers" *or* "For All the Saints" (Heb.)

    "O Young and Fearless Prophet" *or* "See How Great a Flame Aspires" (Isa.; Jer.; Luke)

SUNDAY BETWEEN AUGUST 21 AND 27 INCLUSIVE

Year A: 1993, 1996, 1999

    Exodus 1:8–2:10; Psalm 124 *or* Isaiah 51:1-6; Psalm 138

    Romans 12:1-8; Matthew 16:13-20

    "One Bread, One Body" *or* "Take My Life, and Let It Be Consecrated" (Rom.)

    "Onward, Christian Soldiers" *or* "The Church's One Foundation" (Matt.)

Year B: 1994, 1997, 2000

    I Kings 8:(1, 6, 10-11), 22-30, 41-43; Psalm 84 *or* Joshua 24:1-2a, 14-18; Psalm 34:15-22

    Ephesians 6:10-20; John 6:56-69

    "Soldiers of Christ, Arise" *or* "Stand Up, Stand Up for Jesus" (Eph.)

    "Christ Is Made the Sure Foundation" (I Kings); "Wonderful Words of Life" (John)

Year C: 1995, 1998, 2001

    Jeremiah 1:4-10; Psalm 71:1-6 *or* Isaiah 58:9b-14; Psalm 103:1-8

    Hebrews 12:18-29; Luke 13:10-17

    "Immortal, Invisible, God Only Wise" *or* "O Spirit of the Living God" (Heb.)

    "Heal Us, Emmanuel" *or* any hymn on healing (Luke)

SUNDAY BETWEEN AUGUST 28 AND SEPTEMBER 3 INCLUSIVE

Year A: 1993, 1996, 1999
Exodus 3:1-15; Psalm 105:1-6, 23-26, 45c *or* Jeremiah 15:15-21; Psalm 26:1-8
Romans 12:9-21; Matthew 16:21-28
"Go Down, Moses" *or* "Let My People Seek Their Freedom" (Exod.)
"The God of Abraham Praise" ("Praise to the Living God") (Exod.)
"Jesus, Lord, We Look to Thee" *or* "Jesus, United by Thy Grace" (Rom.)
"Must Jesus Bear the Cross Alone" *or* "Take Up Thy Cross" (Matt.)

Year B: 1994, 1997, 2000
Song of Solomon 2:8-13; Psalm 45:1-2, 6-9 *or* Deuteronomy 4:1-2, 6-9; Psalm 15
James 1:17-27; Mark 7:1-8, 14-15, 21-23
"Just a Closer Walk with Thee"; "Lord, I Want to Be a Christian"; "O for a Heart to Praise"

Year C: 1995, 1998, 2001
Jeremiah 2:4-13; Psalm 81:1, 10-16 *or* Sirach 10:12-18 *or* Proverbs 25:6-7; Psalm 112
Hebrews 13:1-8, 15-16; Luke 14:1, 7-14
"How Firm a Foundation" *or* "Saranam, Saranam" (Heb.)
"Jesu, Jesu" *or* "Lord, Whose Love Through Humble Service" (Heb.; Luke)

SUNDAY BETWEEN SEPTEMBER 4 AND 10 INCLUSIVE

Year A: 1993, 1996, 1999
Exodus 12:1-14; Psalm 149 *or* Ezekiel 33:7-11; Psalm 119:33-40
Romans 13:8-14; Matthew 18:15-20
"Awake, O Sleeper" *or* "Soldiers of Christ, Arise" (Rom.)
"All Praise to Our Redeeming Lord" *or* "Where Charity and Love Prevail" (Matt.)

Year B: 1994, 1997, 2000
Proverbs 22:1-2, 8-9, 22-23; Psalm 125 *or* Isaiah 35:4-7a; Psalm 146
James 2:1-10 (11-13), 14-17; Mark 7:24-37
"When the Church of Jesus" *or* "When the Poor Ones" (Proverbs; James)
"Open My Eyes, That I May See" *or* any hymn of healing (Mark)

Year C: 1995, 1998, 2001
Jeremiah 18:1-11; Psalm 139:1-6, 13-18 *or* Deuteronomy 30:15-20; Psalm 1
Philemon 1:21; Luke 14:25-33
"Have Thine Own Way, Lord" (Jer.) *or* "Take My Life, and Let It Be Consecrated" (Luke)

SUNDAY BETWEEN SEPTEMBER 11 AND 17 INCLUSIVE

Year A: 1993, 1996, 1999
Exodus 14:19-31; Psalm 114 *or* Genesis 50:15-21; Psalm 103: (1-7) 8-13
Romans 14:1-12; Matthew 18:21-35
"Lord, Speak to Me" *or* "When We Are Living" (Rom.)
"Forgive Our Sins as We Forgive"; "Help Us Accept Each Other" (Gen.; Rom.; Matt.)

Year B: 1994, 1997, 2000
Proverbs 1:20-33; Psalm 19 *or* Wisdom of Solomon 7:26–8:1 *or* Isaiah 50:4-9a; Psalm 116:1-9
James 3:1-12; Mark 8:27-38
"O Spirit of the Living God" (Prov.); "Take Up Thy Cross" *or* "Where He Leads Me" (Mark)

Year C: 1995, 1998, 2001
   Jeremiah 4:11-12, 22-28; Psalm 14 *or* Exodus 32:7-14; Psalm 51:1-10
   I Timothy 1:12-17; Luke 15:1-10
   "Amazing Grace" *or* "Depth of Mercy" *or* "Immortal, Invisible" (I Tim.)
   "O Zion, Haste" *or* "Rescue the Perishing" (Luke)

SUNDAY BETWEEN SEPTEMBER 18 AND 24 INCLUSIVE

Year A: 1993, 1996, 1999
   Exodus 16:2-15; Psalm 105:1-6, 37-45 *or* Jonah 3:10–4:11; Psalm 145:1-8
   Philippians 1:21-30; Matthew 20:1-16
   "Guide Me, O Thou Great Jehovah" (Exod.); "When We Are Living" (Phil.)
   "All Praise to Our Redeeming Lord" (Matt.)

Year B: 1994, 1997, 2000
   Proverbs 31:10-31; Psalm 1
      or Wisdom of Solomon 1:16–2:1, 12-22 *or* Jeremiah 11:18-20; Psalm 54
   James 3:13–4:3, 7-8*a*; Mark 9:30-37
   "Blest Be the Tie" (James); "Tell Me the Stories of Jesus" *or* "Jesus Loves Me" (Mark)

Year C: 1995, 1998, 2001
   Jeremiah 8:18–9:1; Psalm 79:1-9 *or* Amos 8:4-7; Psalm 113
   I Timothy 2:1-7; Luke 16:1-13
   "There Is a Balm in Gilead" (Jer.); "I Surrender All" *or* "Jesus Calls Us" (Luke)

SUNDAY BETWEEN SEPTEMBER 25 AND OCTOBER 1 INCLUSIVE

Year A: 1993, 1996, 1999
   Exodus 17:1-7; Psalm 78:1-4, 12-16 *or* Ezekiel 18:1-4, 25-32; Psalm 25:1-9
   Philippians 2:1-13; Matthew 21:23-32
   "All Praise to Thee, for Thou, O King Divine" *or* "At the Name of Jesus" (Phil.)
   "A Charge to Keep I Have" *or* "Forth in Thy Name" (Matt.)

Year B: 1994, 1997, 2000
   Esther 7:1-6, 9-10; 9:20-22; Psalm 124 *or* Numbers 11:4-6, 10-16, 24-29; Psalm 19:7-14
   James 5:13-20; Mark 9:38-50
   Any hymn on healing (James); "Where Cross the Crowded Ways of Life" (esp. v. 4) (Mark)

Year C: 1995, 1998, 2001
   Jeremiah 32:1-3*a*, 6-15; Psalm 91:1-6, 14-16 *or* Amos 8:4-7; Psalm 113
   I Timothy 6:6-19; Luke 16:19-31
   "O Young and Fearless Prophet" *or* "Where Cross the Crowded Ways"
      or "The Voice of God Is Calling" (all readings)

SUNDAY BETWEEN OCTOBER 2 AND 8 INCLUSIVE

Year A: 1993, 1996, 1999
   Exodus 20:1-4, 7-9, 12-20; Psalm 19 *or* Isaiah 5:1-7; Psalm 80:7-15
   Philippians 3:4*b*-14; Matthew 21:33-46
   "Trust and Obey" (Exod.); "All Praise to Our Redeeming Lord" (esp. v. 2) (Phil.)
   "God Hath Spoken by the Prophets" *or* "Rescue the Perishing" (Matt.)

Year B: 1994, 1997, 2000

   Job 1:1; 2:1-10; Psalm 26 *or* Genesis 2:18-24; Psalm 8

   Hebrews 1:1-4; 2:5-12; Mark 10:2-16

   "The Head That Once Was Crowned" (Heb.); "Tell Me the Stories of Jesus" (Mark)

   "As Man and Woman We Were Made" *or* "O Perfect Love" *or* "When Love Is Found" (Gen.; Mark)

Year C: 1995, 1998, 2001

   Lamentations 1:1-6; Lamentations 3:19-26 *or* Psalm 137

    or Habakkuk 1:1-4; 2:1-4; Psalm 37:1-9

   II Timothy 1:1-14; Luke 17:5-10

   "Great Is Thy Faithfulness" (Lam.); "I Know Whom I Have Believed" (II Tim.)

   "Give Me the Faith" *or* "Let Us Plead for Faith Alone" (Luke)

SUNDAY BETWEEN OCTOBER 9 AND 15 INCLUSIVE

Year A: 1993, 1996, 1999

   Exodus 32:1-14; Psalm 106:1-6, 19-23 *or* Isaiah 25:1-9; Psalm 23

   Philippians 4:1-9; Matthew 22:1-14

   "Rejoice, Ye Pure in Heart" (Phil.); "The King of Love My Shepherd Is" (Ps. 23; Matt.)

   "Come, Sinners, to the Gospel Feast" *or* "Where Cross the Crowded Ways of Life" (Matt.)

Year B: 1994, 1997, 2000

   Job 23:1-9, 16-17; Psalm 22:1-15 *or* Amos 5:6-7, 10-15; Psalm 90:12-17

   Hebrews 4:12-16; Mark 10:17-31

   "Leave It There" *or* "Precious Lord" *or* "What a Friend We Have in Jesus" (Job)

   "Jesus Calls Us" *or* "Take My Life, and Let It Be Consecrated" (Mark)

Year C: 1995, 1998, 2001

   Jeremiah 29:1, 4-7; Psalm 66:1-12 *or* II Kings 5:1-3, 7-15c; Psalm 111

   II Timothy 2:8-15; Luke 17:11-19

   "Faith of Our Fathers" (II Tim.); any hymn on healing (II Kings; Luke)

   "For the Beauty of the Earth" *or* "Now Thank We All Our God" (Luke)

SUNDAY BETWEEN OCTOBER 16 AND 22 INCLUSIVE

Year A: 1993, 1996, 1999

   Exodus 33:12-23; Psalm 99 *or* Isaiah 45:1-7; Psalm 96:1-9 (10-13)

   I Thessalonians 1:1-10; Matthew 22:15-22

   "Rock of Ages" (Exod.); "Jesus Calls Us" *or* "O Jesus, I Have Promised" (I Thess.; Matt.)

Year B: 1994, 1997, 2000

   Job 38:1-7 (34-41); Psalm 104:1-9, 24, 35c *or* Isaiah 53:4-12; Psalm 91:9-16

   Hebrews 5:1-10; Mark 10:35-45

   "God Moves in a Mysterious Way"; "Immortal, Invisible"; "O Worship the King" (Job; Ps. 104)

   "Hallelujah! What a Savior" (Isa.); "Are Ye Able"; "The Church of Christ in Every Age" (Mark)

Year C: 1995, 1998, 2001

   Jeremiah 31:27-34; Psalm 119:97-104 *or* Genesis 32:22-31; Psalm 121

   II Timothy 3:14–4:5; Luke 18:1-8

   "Break Thou the Bread of Life" *or* "Thy Word Is a Lamp"

    or "Wonderful Words of Life" (Jer.; Ps. 119; II Tim.)

   "Come, O Thou Traveler Unknown" (Gen.); "Precious Lord" (Luke)

SUNDAY BETWEEN OCTOBER 23 AND 29 INCLUSIVE

Year A: 1993, 1996, 1999
Deuteronomy 34:1-12; Psalm 90:1-6, 13-17 *or* Leviticus 19:1-2, 15-18; Psalm 1
I Thessalonians 2:1-8; Matthew 22:34-46
"Love Divine, All Loves Excelling" *or* "O Love That Wilt Not Let Me Go" (Lev.; Matt.)

Year B: 1994, 1997, 2000
Job 42:1-6, 10-17; Psalm 34:1-8, (19-22) *or* Jeremiah 31:7-9; Psalm 126
Hebrews 7:23-28; Mark 10:46-52
"Blow Ye the Trumpet, Blow" (Heb.); "Pass Me Not, O Gentle Savior" (Mark)

Year C: 1995, 1998, 2001
Joel 2:23-32; Psalm 65 *or* Sirach 35:12-17 *or* Jeremiah 14:7-10, 19-22; Psalm 84:1-7
II Timothy 4:6-8, 16-18; Luke 18:9-14
"Spirit Song" (Joel); "It's Me, It's Me, O Lord" *or* "Just as I Am" *or* "Rock of Ages" (Luke)

SUNDAY BETWEEN OCTOBER 30 AND NOVEMBER 5 INCLUSIVE

Year A: 1993, 1996, 1999
Joshua 3:7-17; Psalm 107:1-7, 33-37 *or* Micah 3:5-12; Psalm 43
I Thessalonians 2:9-13; Matthew 23:1-12
"Jesu, Jesu" *or* "O Master, Let Me Walk with Thee" (Matt.)

Year B: 1994, 1997, 2000
Ruth 1:1-18; Psalm 146 *or* Deuteronomy 6:1-9; Psalm 119:1-8
Hebrews 9:11-14; Mark 12:28-34
"Love Divine, All Loves Excelling" *or* "Where Charity and Love Prevail"
   or "O Love That Wilt Not Let Me Go" (Ruth; Deut.; Mark)

Year C: 1995, 1998, 2001
Habakkuk 1:1-4; 2:1-4; Psalm 119:137-144 *or* Isaiah 1:10-18; Psalm 32:1-7
II Thessalonians 1:1-4, 11-12; Luke 19:1-10
"I Know Whom I Have Believed" (II Thess.); "I Surrender All" *or* "Where He Leads Me" (Luke)

SUNDAY BETWEEN NOVEMBER 6 AND 12 INCLUSIVE

Year A: 1993, 1996, 1999
Joshua 24:1-3*a*, 14-25; Psalm 78:1-7
   or Wisdom of Solomon 6:12-16 *or* Amos 5:18-24; Wisdom of Solomon 6:17-20 *or* Psalm 70
I Thessalonians 4:13-18; Matthew 25:1-13
"How Great Thou Art" *or* "Rejoice, the Lord Is King" (I Thess.)
"God of Love and God of Power" *or* "Wake, Awake, for Night Is Flying" (Matt.)
" 'Sleepers, Wake!' A Voice Astounds Us" (Matt.)

Year B: 1994, 1997, 2000
Ruth 3:1-5; 4:13-17; Psalm 127 *or* I Kings 17:8-16; Psalm 146
Hebrews 9:24-28; Mark 12:38-44
"How Great Thou Art" (Heb.); "Take My Life, and Let It Be Consecrated" (Mark)

Year C: 1995, 1998, 2001
Haggai 1:15*b*–2:9; Psalm 145:1-5, 17-21 *or* Psalm 98 *or* Job 19:23-27*a*; Psalm 17:1-9

II Thessalonians 2:1-5, 13-17; Luke 20:27-38
"Hymn of Promise" *or* "Sing with All the Saints in Glory" *or* "When We Are Living" (Luke)

SUNDAY BETWEEN NOVEMBER 13 AND 19 INCLUSIVE

Year A: 1993, 1996, 1999
Judges 4:1-7; Psalm 123 *or* Zephaniah 1:7, 12-18; Psalm 90:1-8, (9-11), 12
I Thessalonians 5:1-11; Matthew 25:14-30
"A Charge to Keep I Have" *or* "Awake, O Sleeper" (I Thess.)
"Canta, Debora, Canta" (Judges); "Take My Life and Let It Be Consecrated" (Matt.)

Year B: 1994, 1997, 2000
I Samuel 1:4-20; I Samuel 2:1-10 *or* Daniel 12:1-3; Psalm 16
Hebrews 10:11-14 (15-18) 19-25; Mark 13:1-8
"How Great Thou Art" *or* "I Am Thine, O Lord" (Heb.)
"A Charge to Keep I Have" *or* "My Lord, What a Morning" (Mark)

Year C: 1995, 1998, 2001
Isaiah 65:17-25; Isaiah 12 *or* Malachi 4:1-2*a*; Psalm 98
II Thessalonians 3:6-13; Luke 21:5-19
"Marching to Zion" (Isa.); "Forth in Thy Name" (II Thess.)
"Must Jesus Bear the Cross Alone" *or* "Standing on the Promises" (Luke)

C. Christ the King

This is both the Last Sunday After Pentecost and the last Sunday in the Christian Year. It is not so much a climax in itself, however, as it is a transitional Sunday leading directly to Advent, the Christmas cycle, and the new Christian Year. People are already thinking about Christmas, and the observance of Christ the King can help them prepare by stressing the continuity between the celebration of the kingship, or sovereignty, of Christ and the expectation of Christ's coming again in sovereign glory which opens the Advent Season. We have more than a baby Jesus at Christmas; we have a sovereign Christ. "Joy to the world! the Lord is come: Let earth receive her King."

This day occurs between November 20 and 26 inclusive. Since Thanksgiving occurs the Thursday between November 22 and 28 inclusive, Christ the King, more often than not, coincides with the Sunday before Thanksgiving. If a congregation participates in union services, or holds services of its own, on Thanksgiving Eve or Thanksgiving Day, then it is redundant to celebrate the previous Sunday as Thanksgiving Sunday. It is also possible for a service to combine elements of the two celebrations. Thanksgiving resources will be found later in this book.

In preparing for the celebration of Christ the King it is important to study the Scripture readings. In a given year there will be the prefiguration of Christ's rule in the Old Testament, a particular unfolding of the meaning of the messianic age in the Epistle and a portrayal of the paradox: Servant/King.

White is the customary color for this day. Gold is also appropriate; even a little purple may be introduced, as the color of royalty and in anticipation of the coming transition into Advent. Symbols of royalty may be used—crown, orb, scepter—especially when these contain, or are combined with, a cross. Images of Christ as Pantocrator (ruler of all) are appropriate.

GATHERING

Festival music based upon the hymn tunes is particularly appropriate as the people gather. Symbols and banners of royalty may be brought in procession if the space and style permit.

GREETING

"I am the Alpha and the Omega," says the Lord God,
"who is, and who was, and who is to come, the Almighty."

Blessing and honor and glory and might be unto the Lamb!

Worthy is Christ who has ransomed us by his blood
from every tribe and tongue and nation,
and made his people a kingdom, and priests to our God.

**Holy, holy, holy, is the Lord God Almighty,
who was and is and is to come!**

HYMN OF PRAISE   *Appropriate hymns include:*

"O Worship the King"
"Jesus Shall Reign"
"Crown Him with Many Crowns"
"Hail, Thou Once Despised Jesus"
"The Head That Once Was Crowned"
"Hail to the Lord's Anointed"
"Rejoice, the Lord Is King"
"At the Name of Jesus"
If there is an entrance hymn with procession, it precedes the greeting.

OPENING PRAYER

All-powerful God,
your only Son came to earth
in the form of a slave
and is now enthroned at your right hand,
where he rules in glory.
As he reigns as King in our hearts,
may we rejoice in his peace,
glory in his justice,
and live in his love.
For with you and the Holy Spirit
he rules now and for ever.

Amen.

FIRST LESSON

Ezekiel 34:11-16, 20-24	(Year A: 1993, 1996, 1999)
II Samuel 23:1-7 *or* Daniel 7:9-10, 13-14	(Year B: 1994, 1997, 2000)
Jeremiah 23:1-6	(Year C: 1995, 1998, 2001)

PSALM

Psalm 100 *or* 95:1-7*a*	(Year A: 1993, 1996, 1999)
Psalm 132:1-12 (13-18) *or* Psalm 93	(Year B: 1994, 1997, 2000)
Luke 1:68-79 *or* Psalm 46	(Year C: 1995, 1998, 2001)

SECOND LESSON

Ephesians 1:15-23	(Year A: 1993, 1996, 1999)
Revelation 1:4*b*-8	(Year B: 1994, 1997, 2000)
Colossians 1:11-20	(Year C: 1995, 1998, 2001)

ALLELUIA (HYMN OR ANTHEM)

"Soon and Very Soon" or "Majesty, Worship His Majesty" might be suitable.

GOSPEL

Matthew 25:31-46	(Year A: 1993, 1996, 1999)
John 18:33-37	(Year B: 1994, 1997, 2000)
Luke 23:33-43	(Year C: 1995, 1998, 2001)

SERMON

[CREED] *(especially if Holy Communion is not celebrated)*

PRAYERS OF THE PEOPLE OR PASTORAL PRAYER

To each petition the people may respond: **By the mercies of Christ, hear us.** *Another possible response is* **Jesus, remember me when you come into your kingdom,** *available in a beautiful musical setting in* Music from Taize, *by Jacques Berthier (Chicago, G.I.A. Publications, 1981), p. 9.*

OFFERING

One of the above hymns may be sung, or at the presentation of the offerings one or two stanzas of a Christ-centered hymn such as "Rejoice, the Lord Is King"; "Lead On, O King Eternal" (stanza 4); or "Lord, Whose Love Through Humble Service" (stanza 1) may be sung.

If Holy Communion is not celebrated, the service concludes with a prayer of thanksgiving, the Lord's Prayer, and a dismissal with blessing.

If Holy Communion is celebrated, the table is prepared during the offering and the service continues as follows:

GREAT THANKSGIVING

The Lord be with you.

And also with you.

Lift up your hearts.

We lift them to the Lord.

Let us give thanks to the Lord our God.

It is right to give our thanks and praise.

It is right, and a good and joyful thing,
always and everywhere to give thanks to you,
Father Almighty, Creator of heaven and earth.

You formed us in your image
and breathed into us the breath of life.
When we turned away, and our love failed,
your love remained steadfast.
You delivered us from captivity,
made covenant to be our sovereign God,
and spoke to us through your prophets,
who looked for that day
when justice shall roll down like waters
and righteousness like an ever-flowing stream,
when nation shall not lift up sword against nation,
neither shall they learn war any more.

And so, with your people on earth
and all the company of heaven,
we praise your name and join their unending hymn:

Holy, holy, holy Lord, God of power and might,
heaven and earth are full of your glory.
Hosanna in the highest.
Blessed is he who comes in the name of the Lord.
Hosanna in the highest.

Holy are you, and blessed is your Son Jesus Christ,
who came in your name as our King.
Your Spirit anointed him
to preach good news to the poor,
to proclaim release to the captives
and recovering of sight to the blind,
to set at liberty those who are oppressed,
and to announce that the time had come
when you would save your people.
He healed the sick, fed the hungry, and ate with sinners.

By the baptism of his suffering, death, and resurrection
you gave birth to your church,
delivered us from slavery to sin and death,
and made with us a new covenant by water and the Spirit.
At his ascension you exalted him
to sit and reign with you at your right hand.

On the night in which he gave himself up for us
he took bread, gave thanks to you, broke the bread,

gave it to his disciples, and said:
"Take, eat; this is my body which is given for you.
Do this in remembrance of me."

When the supper was over he took the cup,
gave thanks to you, gave it to his disciples, and said:
"Drink from this, all of you;
this is my blood of the new covenant,
poured out for you and for many
for the forgiveness of sins.
Do this, as often as you drink it, in remembrance of me."

And so,
in remembrance of these your mighty acts in Jesus Christ,
we offer ourselves in praise and thanksgiving
as a holy and living sacrifice,
in union with Christ's offering for us,
as we proclaim the mystery of faith.

Christ has died, Christ is risen, Christ will come again.

Pour out your Holy Spirit on us, gathered here,
and on these gifts of bread and wine.
Make them be for us the body and blood of Christ,
that we may be for the world the body of Christ,
redeemed by his blood.

By your Spirit make us one with Christ,
one with each other,
and one in ministry to all the world,
until Christ comes in final victory
and we feast at his heavenly banquet.

Through your Son Jesus Christ,
with the Holy Spirit in your holy church,
all honor and glory is yours, Almighty Father,
now and for ever.

Amen.

THE LORD'S PRAYER

BREAKING THE BREAD

COMMUNION

PRAYER AFTER COMMUNION

You have given yourself to us, Lord.

Now we give ourselves for others.

Your love has made us a new people.

As a people of love we will serve you with joy.

Your glory has filled our hearts.

Help us to glorify you in all things.

HYMN   *Appropriate hymns include:*

"Jesus Shall Reign"
"Rejoice, the Lord Is King"
"O Jesus Christ, to You May Hymns"
"When the Church of Jesus"
"Soon and Very Soon, We Are Going to See the King"

DISMISSAL WITH BLESSING

May God who is, who was, and who is to come,
bless you and keep you.

Amen.

May Jesus Christ,
the faithful witness and ruler of all nations,
make his face to shine upon you.

Amen.

May the Holy Spirit, who guides us into all truth,
grant you peace.

Amen.

Go in the strong name of Jesus Christ.

Thanks be to God!

SPECIAL DAYS

A. Lesser Christological Days

*I*t was mentioned earlier in this book that in addition to the days and seasons that we have dealt with so far, there are a variety of observances that fall on fixed dates and, for that reason, usually fall on a weekday. The common calendar refers to them as "special days."

Several commemorations of events in the life of Christ make up the first set of these special days. They relate to Christmas and Easter and are part of the temporal cycle even if their dates do not fall within the Christmas and Easter cycles. We may refer to them as "lesser christological days" to distinguish them from the major commemorations of events in the life of Christ which we have already discussed.

Holy Name of Jesus is observed on January 1 to mark Jesus' circumcision and naming on his eighth day (Luke 2:21) and is included in the common calendar as part of the Christmas Season. For that reason it was discussed earlier (see p. 78), although its lesser importance in the calendar might have led us to discuss it here.

The following three days, which can be considered Christmas feasts outside the Christmas cycle, are in the Roman Catholic, Episcopal, and Lutheran calendars and are sometimes observed by other Protestants as well.

The Presentation [of our Lord Jesus Christ in the Temple] is observed on February 2 (the fortieth day counting from Christmas) to commemorate the visit of the holy family to the Temple on the fortieth day of Jesus' life, the purification of his mother according to Jewish ritual, and the role of Simeon and Anna in these events. The scriptures appointed in the *Common Lectionary* are Malachi 3:1-4, Psalm 84 or 24:7-10, Hebrews 2:14-18, and Luke 2:22-40. The color is white, and symbols include images of Anna and Simeon (white hair) and two turtledoves. The following opening prayer may be used:

> God of compassion,
> on this day your Holy Spirit revealed
> the salvation you had prepared for all peoples
> to the devout Simeon and Anna,
> who had waited until late in life.
> Grant that we, too, may adore your Son, Jesus Christ,
> a light to the Gentiles and the glory of Israel,
> so we may proclaim him to all your world.
> Through Jesus the Christ we pray. **Amen.**

The Annunciation [of our Lord Jesus Christ to the Blessed Virgin Mary] is observed on March 25, nine months before Christmas, marking the announcement of the angel to Mary that she will bear a son. The scriptures appointed in the *Common Lectionary* are Isaiah 7:10-14, Psalm 45 or 40:6-10, Hebrews 10:4-10, and Luke 1:26-38. The color is white, and the symbols include an angel (Gabriel) and the Virgin Mary. Frequently they are represented bowing to each other. The following opening prayer may be used:

> Gracious God,
> you entrusted our salvation to a woman,
> the Virgin Mary, who consented to be your handmaid.
> Grant that we, too, may welcome your will for us,
> that our lives may show forth your glory;
> through Jesus Christ our Lord. **Amen.**

The Visitation [of the Blessed Virgin Mary] to her cousin Elizabeth, when both were pregnant, is observed on May 31 because that is after the Annunciation and just before the birth of John the Baptist, identified as June 24 (Luke 1:26). The scriptures appointed in the *Common Lectionary* are I Samuel 2:1-10, Psalm 113, Romans 12:9-16b, and Luke 1:39-57. The color is white, and the symbol is two women—both pregnant, if shown in silhouette. The following opening prayer may be used:

> Almighty God,
> in choosing the Virgin Mary to be the mother of your Son,
> you made known your gracious care for the poor and lowly.
> Grant us, too, the grace to receive your Word in humility
> that we may be made one with your Son, Jesus Christ our Lord,
> who lives and reigns with you and the Holy Spirit,
> one God, now and for ever. **Amen.**

Holy Cross Day on September 14 is another lesser christological day in the common calendar. It is related in theme to Holy Week but is, of course, outside the Easter cycle. It is in the Roman Catholic, Episcopal, and Lutheran calendars. The scriptures appointed in the *Common Lectionary* are Numbers 21:4b-9; Psalm 98:1-5 or 78:1-2, 34-38; I Corinthians 1:18-24; John 3:13-17. The color is white, and the basic symbol is the cross itself and perhaps also a cross with a serpent on it. The following opening prayer may be used:

> Almighty God,
> your Son Jesus Christ was lifted high upon the cross
> so that he might draw the whole world to himself.
> Grant that we, who glory in his death for our salvation,
> may also glory in his call
> to take up our cross and follow him;
> through your Son, Jesus Christ our Lord,
> who lives and reigns with you and the Holy Spirit,
> one God, now and for ever. **Amen.**

The Transfiguration [of our Lord Jesus Christ] is, as was noted earlier, observed on August 6 in the Roman Catholic calendar rather than on the Last Sunday After Epiphany. It is also on August 6 in the Episcopal calendar, but in that lectionary the transfiguration scriptures are also read on the Last Sunday After Epiphany.

B. All Saints and the Sanctoral Cycle

All Saints falls on November 1 but may be celebrated on the first Sunday in November. In contemporary understanding, it commemorates all Christian people of every time and place. "The saints" in New Testament usage refers to Christians collectively, and it is with this biblical understanding that celebration of this day has been rapidly spreading among Protestants in recent years. Although it can be considered part of the sanctoral cycle and is listed under "special days" in the common calendar, it is now in the calendars of a number of Protestant denominations and is observed by many who do not commemorate any individual designated as a saint.

An Order of Worship for All Saints

GATHERING

GREETING

> Grace to you and peace from God
> who is, and was, and is to come.

> **Amen.**

> And from Jesus Christ the faithful witness,
> the firstborn of the dead,
> the ruler of kings on earth.

> **Amen.**

> The grace of the Lord Jesus be with all the saints.

> **Amen.**

HYMN OF PRAISE   *Appropriate hymns include:*

> "Rejoice, the Lord Is King"
> "All Praise to Our Redeeming Lord"
> "For All the Saints"
> "Come, Let Us Join Our Friends Above"
> "We Bear the Strain of Earthly Care"
> "Through All the Changing Scenes of Life"
> *If there is an entrance hymn with procession, it precedes the greeting.*

OPENING PRAYER

> God of all holiness,
> you gave your saints different gifts on earth
> but one holy city in heaven.
> Give us grace to follow their good example,
> that we may know the joy you have prepared
> for all who love you;
> through your Son Jesus Christ our Lord.

> **Amen.**

> *or*

> Almighty God,
> you have knit together your elect
> in one communion and fellowship
> in the mystical body of your Son Christ our Lord.
> Give us grace so to follow your blessed saints
> in all virtuous and godly living,

that we may come to those ineffable joys
which you have prepared
for those who truly love you;
through Jesus Christ our Lord,
who with you and the Holy Spirit lives and reigns,
one God, in glory everlasting.   BCP

Amen.

FIRST LESSON

Revelation 7:9-17   (Year A: 1993, 1996, 1999)
Wisdom of Solomon 3:1-9 *or* Isaiah 25:6-9 (Year B: 1994, 1997, 2000)
Daniel 7:1-3, 15-18   (Year C: 1995, 1998, 2001)

PSALM

Psalm 34:1-10, 22   (Year A: 1993, 1996, 1999)
Psalm 24   (Year B: 1994, 1997, 2000)
Psalm 149   (Year C: 1995, 1998, 2001)

SECOND LESSON

I John 3:1-3   (Year A: 1993, 1996, 1999)
Revelation 21:1-6*a*   (Year B: 1994, 1997, 2000)
Ephesians 1:11-23   (Year C: 1995, 1998, 2001)

ALLELUIA (HYMN OR ANTHEM)   *Appropriate hymns include:*

"Rejoice in God's Saints"
"Forward Through the Ages"
"Faith of Our Fathers"

GOSPEL

Matthew 5:1-12   (Year A: 1993, 1996, 1999)
John 11:32-44   (Year B: 1994, 1997, 2000)
Luke 6:20-31   (Year C: 1995, 1998, 2001)

SERMON

[NAMING OF THE HONORED DEAD]

The names of members of the congregation who have died within the past year may be solemnly read, the people standing. A minute of silence follows.

PRAYERS OF THE PEOPLE OR PASTORAL PRAYER

This may begin with a brief silence or with the following:

The Lord be with you.

And also with you.

Let us pray:

Holy God, we pray for your human family everywhere;

That we may be one.

Grant that all who are baptized into Christ may faithfully serve you;

That your name may be glorified on earth as in heaven.

We pray for all bishops, pastors, and deacons;

That there may be justice and peace on the earth.

Give us grace to do your will in all that we undertake;

That our works may find favor in your sight.

Have compassion on those who suffer from any grief or trouble;

That they may be delivered from their distress.

Give to the departed eternal rest;

Let light perpetual shine upon them.

We praise you for your saints who have entered into joy;

May we also come to share in your heavenly kingdom.

Let us pray for our own needs and those of others.

Silence

The people may add their petitions, following which the presiding minister may add a suitable collect or other brief concluding prayer.

or

PRAYERS FOR THE SAINTS AND FAITHFUL DEPARTED

This is especially appropriate if the names of all persons in the congregation who have died during the year are either read or commemorated in some other way.

O God of both the living and the dead,
  we praise your holy name for all your servants who have finished their course in faith,
especially . . . *(here the names may be given).*
We pray that, encouraged by their example and strengthened by their fellowship,
we may be partakers with them of the inheritance of the saints in light;
Through the merits of your Son Jesus Christ our Lord.
Amen.

or

PRAYER OF PRAISE FOR ALL THE SAINTS

If Holy Communion is to be celebrated using the Great Thanksgiving, this prayer should not be included.

Blessed are you,
God of creation and all beginnings,
God of Abraham and Sarah,
God of Miriam and Moses,
God of Joshua and Deborah,
God of Ruth and David,
God of the priests and the prophets,
God of Mary and Joseph,
God of apostles and martyrs,
God of our mothers and fathers,
God of our children to all generations.

You made us in your image;
and though we all have sinned
and fallen short of your glory,
you loved the world so much
you gave your only Son Jesus Christ to be our Savior.
Through his suffering and death,
his resurrection and ascension,
you gave birth to your church,
delivered us from slavery to sin and death,
made with us a new covenant,
and baptized us with the Holy Spirit and with fire.
Therefore, in remembrance of all your mighty acts in Jesus Christ,
we offer our lives in your service
as a living and holy surrender of ourselves.

Send the power of your Holy Spirit on us
that we may know the presence of the living Christ,
be one body in him,
and grow into his likeness.
Renew our communion with all your saints,
especially those whom we name before you
. . . [in our hearts].
May we run with perseverance the race that is set before us,
being surrounded by so great a cloud of witnesses
and looking to Jesus, the pioneer and perfecter of our faith,
and to his coming in final victory.
Through him, with him, in him,
in the unity of the Holy Spirit,
all honor and glory is yours,
Almighty God, now and for ever.
Amen.

[THE PEACE]

OFFERING

If Holy Communion is not celebrated, the service concludes with a prayer of thanksgiving, the Lord's Prayer, and a dismissal with blessing.

If Holy Communion is celebrated, the table is prepared during the offering and the service continues as follows:

GREAT THANKSGIVING

The Lord be with you.

And also with you.

Lift up your hearts.

We lift them to the Lord.

Let us give thanks to the Lord our God.

It is right to give our thanks and praise.

It is right, and a good and joyful thing,
always and everywhere to give thanks to you,
Father Almighty, Creator of heaven and earth.

Blessed are you,
God of creation and all beginnings,
God of Abraham and Sarah,
God of Miriam and Moses,
God of Joshua and Deborah,
God of Ruth and David,
God of the priests and the prophets,
God of Mary and Joseph,
God of apostles and martyrs,
God of our mothers and fathers,
God of our children to all generations.

And so, with your people on earth
and all of the company of heaven,
we praise your name and join their unending hymn:

**Holy, holy, holy Lord, God of power and might,
heaven and earth are full of your glory.
Hosanna in the highest.
Blessed is he who comes in the name of the Lord.
Hosanna in the highest.**

Holy are you, and blessed is your Son Jesus Christ.
By the baptism of his suffering, death, and resurrection
you gave birth to your church,
delivered us from slavery to sin and death,
and made with us a new covenant by water and the Spirit.

On the night in which he gave himself up for us
he took bread, gave thanks to you, broke the bread,
gave it to his disciples, and said:
"Take, eat; this is my body which is given for you.
Do this in remembrance of me."

When the supper was over he took the cup,
gave thanks to you, gave it to his disciples, and said:
"Drink from this, all of you;
this is my blood of the new covenant,
poured out for you and for many
for the forgiveness of sins.
Do this, as often as you drink it, in remembrance of me."

And so,
in remembrance of these your mighty acts in Jesus Christ,
we offer ourselves in praise and thanksgiving
as a holy and living sacrifice,
in union with Christ's offering for us,
as we proclaim the mystery of faith.

Christ has died, Christ is risen, Christ will come again.

Pour out your Holy Spirit on us, gathered here,
and on these gifts of bread and wine.
Make them be for us the body and blood of Christ,
that we may be for the world the body of Christ,
redeemed by his blood.

Renew our communion with all your saints,
especially those whom we name before you
. . . [in our hearts].
Since we are surrounded by so great a cloud of witnesses,
strengthen us to run with perseverance
the race that is set before us,
looking to Jesus, the pioneer and perfecter of our faith.
By your Spirit make us one with Christ,
one with each other,
and one in ministry to all the world,
until Christ comes in final victory
and we feast at his heavenly banquet.

Through your Son Jesus Christ,
with the Holy Spirit in your holy church,
all honor and glory is yours, Almighty Father,
now and for ever.

Amen.

THE LORD'S PRAYER

BREAKING THE BREAD

COMMUNION   *Appropriate communion hymns include:*

"Come, Let Us Join Our Friends Above"
"How Happy Every Child of Grace"
"On Jordan's Stormy Banks I Stand"

PRAYER AFTER COMMUNION

You have given yourself to us, Lord.

Now we give ourselves to others.

Your love has made us a new people.

As a people of love we will serve you with joy.

Your glory has filled our hearts.

Help us to glorify you in all things. Amen.

HYMN   *Appropriate closing hymns include:*

"For All the Saints"
"How Firm a Foundation"
"Blest Be the Tie That Binds"

DISMISSAL WITH BLESSING

Go in peace to serve God and your neighbor
in all that you do.

We are sent in Christ's name.

The grace of the Lord Jesus Christ
and the love of God
and the communion of the Holy Spirit
be with you all.

Amen.

or

Now unto him that is able to keep you from falling,
and to present you faultless
before the presence of his glory with exceeding joy:
to the only wise God our Savior,
be glory and majesty,
dominion and power,
both now and for ever.

Amen.

Commentary

In planning for the celebration of All Saints, whether on November 1 or on the first Sunday of November, we must ask several basic questions. What are the biblical and theological themes and images that are being proclaimed and expressed? What experience of faith does this particular congregation have with "the communion of saints"—the solidarity of the living and the dead in Jesus

Christ? Who are the examples of faith—people who have "walked with God" throughout the ages, and in this particular church—people who are sources of encouragement and holiness to us? What are the particular gifts and resources as well as limitations of this local church, and what are the possibilities and restrictions in the particular worship area and related spaces in which this service will take place? What style of music and congregational participation will both reach people and enable them to participate deeply in the meaning of the service?

This service is a deep remembrance in which we encounter anew the most profound dimensions of what it is to be the church. There is a clear eschatological vision and tone to this celebration, since it reminds us of those for whom the battle is over, the victory won, and also of our continuing pilgrimage toward God and the heavenly banquet. This is why Holy Communion ought to be celebrated on this day and with a particular joy and solemnity. Time and again John Wesley referred to All Saints in his journals as a day of triumphant joy. As he remarked in 1756, "Nov. 1 was a day of triumphant joy, as All Saints' Day generally is. How superstitious are they who scruple giving God solemn thanks for the lives and deaths of his saints!" To render thanks to God for the lives and deaths of the saints is to recognize the common bond between the church on earth and the church triumphant in God's love. It is this vision that is so marvelously expressed in the Great Thanksgiving prayer at the table.

It may be possible in some circumstances to begin the service with a procession of the congregation, or a representative group, along with the choir(s) and principal ministers. This could be done to the accompaniment of various instruments, depending upon what is available and appropriate. Care should be taken to choose music that does not trivialize the theme, yet which the people sing vigorously. In some churches, a strong version of "When the Saints Go Marching In" may be done with great integrity and allow spontaneous joy in the procession, with banners bearing the names of saints. Brass and organ may be used to good effect. A charming hymn for use between lessons is "I Sing a Song of the Saints of God." This could easily be done by a children's choir.

Such understandings of the themes of All Saints can be reflected in the visual environment. White is the basic color, supplemented by such other colors as are deemed appropriate. Among the many possible symbols are myriads of paper dolls (each marked by a cross), a cloud of witnesses, silhouettes representing all races and both sexes, an assemblage of vertical arrows of different colors, different types of the numeral or word *one*, or symbols of the church used on Pentecost. Particular groups within the congregation may wish to make a calendar of saints or particular symbols of favorite saints to be posted at the church door or in the worship area.

The tone of the whole service may reflect the solemnity of remembering specific local persons who have died as well—making this, in effect, a Christian Memorial Day. This needs to be approached with sensitivity and may be best handled by the common practice of solemnly naming those in the congregation who have died within the past year, with these names also being printed in the bulletin. It is customary to use full names without titles of any kind. Sometimes specific persons may be named in the prayers of the people following the sermon. When using the Beatitudes as the Gospel reading, the preacher may find it appropriate to connect them with specific lives. In some circumstances it is possible to have a time of witnessing to the lives of the saints directly from the congregation following the sermon. It may be helpful to have one or two laypersons who have prepared testimonies to provide a model to others who may then be led to speak. This might also be correlated with particular traditional or "classical" saints whose lives have influenced persons we have known and who have encouraged us.

If a hymn such as "Blest Be the Tie That Binds" is used in closing, the congregation may join hands. In that case the second form of the dismissal with blessing may be used, followed by the exchange of the peace (instead of having it earlier in the service). Again, the final hymn may be a strong recessional with cross, Bible, and banners. In this case the presiding minister would remain in front to give the dismissal with blessing.

The Sanctoral Cycle

Very early the church began to commemorate its deceased leaders. This was particularly true of martyrs, whose day of death was considered their "birthday" into Christ's eternal realm. New Testament figures and other widely known leaders were remembered universally; but parishes and dioceses had local lists of saints to be commemorated, and eventually the sanctoral calendar became crowded. Some of the "saints" were of spurious evidence historically, as were many of the deeds attributed to others. Superstition and folly became attached to the celebration of many of the days of the saints.

It was to such excesses that the Protestant Reformers reacted negatively and, to one degree or another, threw out the sanctoral cycle on the theory that it obscured the place that should be accorded to Christ. Indeed, the most extreme Reformers abolished everything in the calendar except for the Lord's Day itself.

Properly understood, however, the saints are manifestations of the continuing work of Jesus Christ in human life. Holy men and women are not testimonies to works-righteousness but to the transforming grace of God. Futhermore, human beings have an inherent need for heroes or "role models." The very people who threw out the sanctoral cycle soon unofficially canonized Luther, Zwingli, Calvin, and others and came to commemorate significant days in their lives and ministries. The secular world has its own sanctoral cycle of civic and political figures, as well as stars of sports and entertainment. Hence, increasingly there is a return to an appreciation for the sanctoral cycle on the part of Protestants, at the same time that Roman Catholics are recognizing the legitimacy of Reformation objections by removing from their calendar persons for whose existence there is no historical evidence and by making the sanctoral cycle lean and clearly subsidiary to other calendar concerns.

In their recent service books, Lutherans and Episcopalians have published rather ample calendars of the saints, extending from Saint Stephen through Thomas Aquinas (Episcopal) to Dietrich Bonhoeffer and Martin Luther King, Jr. (Lutheran). Presbyterians and United Methodists have issued no such lists, but their stance is evidenced by the increasing number of their churches named after New Testament saints, at least—to say nothing of Calvin and Knox on the one hand, and Wesley, Asbury, Albright, and Otterbein on the other.

At a minimum, then, there are congregations in such denominations that may be introduced to some or all of the following calendar of New Testament saints. Asterisks and notes indicate where this listing, taken from the calendars of the Episcopal and Lutheran churches, differs from the Roman calendar.

	Holy Family	Apostles	Others
February 24		Matthias*	
March 19	Joseph		
April 25			Mark
May 1		Philip and James the Less**	
June 11		Barnabas	
June 24	John the Baptist		
June 29		Peter and Paul	
July 22			Magdalene
July 25		James	
August 15	Mary		
August 24		Bartholomew	
September 21		Matthew	

October 18		Luke
October 23	James, brother of Jesus***	
October 28	Simon and Jude	
November 1		All Saints
November 30	Andrew	
December 21	Thomas****	
December 26		Stephen
December 27	John the Evangelist	
December 28		Holy Innocents

Alternative Roman Catholic dates:
* Matthias—May 13
** Philip and James the Less—May 3
*** James, brother of the Lord—not so designated
**** Thomas—July 3

Most of these will not be given major celebrations but may be noted briefly and included in prayers of thanksgiving on the Sundays nearest their day. In many cases, mention of their faith and work may be included in the sermon without committing either exegetical or homiletic violence. Certainly, churches that are named after one of these saints may well mark the annual feast of that saint with greater attention. The observance of All Saints with a special service is a commendable and increasingly common practice which gives substance to the brief mention of the others throughout the year.

Once a congregation has become accustomed to the sanctoral cycle through the commemoration of major New Testament saints, the list can be expanded. Figures such as the Wesleys, Calvin, Knox, or Martin Luther King, Jr., are obvious examples, and examination of the Lutheran and Episcopal calendars will reveal persons who are of interest to particular congregations or in special circumstances.

C. Thanksgiving

In addition to the Christian temporal and sanctoral cycles, there are days in the civil calendars that are marked by services in many Christian churches. Thanksgiving Day and New Year's are the two days in the civil calendar that are widely enough celebrated with church services in North America to have been included in the common calendar. New Year's is included in the common calendar as part of the Christmas Season, but Thanksgiving is included with the special days.

In the United States, Thanksgiving is celebrated on the fourth Thursday in November, which can occur between November 22 and 28 inclusive. It has a decidedly religious cast to it, but its religious character is broad enough to include not only Christians but Jews and others as well. Some have called it the chief annual celebration of American civil religion. It is the chief occasion in the year when significant numbers of communities hold interreligious worship services that include both Jewish and Christian congregations. The widespread custom of family Thanksgiving dinner, which may bring together a family reunion and be for many persons their biggest meal of the year, is often marked by a table blessing or other expression of thanks to God for the blessings of the year. While the secular ritual of football has made considerable inroads on more traditional observances, no realistic calendar of the American Christian Year can ignore Thanksgiving services, even if they are often moved back to Thanksgiving Eve or the Sunday before Thanksgiving (Thanksgiving Sunday).

Because most Thanksgiving (or Thanksgiving Eve, or Thanksgiving Sunday) services are held by a single congregation or a group of Christian congregations, the majority of such services are Christian worship services. Many of them, especially when held by a single congregation, include Holy Communion.

An Order of Worship for Thanksgiving

GATHERING

Suitable choral or instrumental music may be offered as the people gather. Congregational singing of hymns of thanksgiving may provide an alternative in some circumstances. If this is an ecumenical gathering, hymns or songs from the various traditions represented may be sung.

GREETING

Let the nations be glad and sing for joy,
for you judge the peoples with equity
and guide all the nations upon the earth.

**Let all the peoples praise you, O God;
let all the peoples praise you.**

The earth has brought forth its increase;
may God, our own God, bless us.

**Let all the peoples praise you, O God;
let all the peoples praise you.**

HYMN

"Now Thank We All Our God" and "Praise to the Lord, the Almighty" are especially appropriate as an entrance hymn or processional. Other appropriate hymns for this day include:

"All People That on Earth Do Dwell"
"Come, Ye Thankful People, Come"
"For All the Blessings of the Year"
"For the Beauty of the Earth"
"From All That Dwell Below the Skies"
"God, Whose Farm Is All Creation"
"How Great Thou Art"
"Let Us with a Gladsome Mind"
"Many and Great, O God"
"O God, Thou Giver of All Good"
"O Lord of Heaven and Earth and Sea"
"Thanks to God Whose Word Was Spoken"
"To Bless the Earth, God Sendeth"
"We Plow the Fields"
"We, Thy People, Praise Thee"
"When All Thy Mercies, O My God"

The greeting will follow the hymn if there is a processional. Appropriate signs of harvest, cross, and Bible may be carried in procession.

OPENING PRAYER

Lord our God,
love began with you
and has filled our cup to overflowing.
In the abundance of your countless gifts,
give us your grace
to fill others' lives with love,
that we may more nearly be worthy
of all you have given us.
We ask this in the name of Jesus the Lord.

Amen.

or

Almighty and gracious Father, we give you thanks
for the fruits of the earth in their season,
and for the labors of those who harvest them.
Make us, we pray, faithful stewards of your great bounty,
in the provision for our necessities,
and the relief of all who are in need,
to the glory of your name;
through Jesus Christ our Lord,
who lives and reigns with you and the Holy Spirit,
one God, now and for ever.

Amen.

Or, if a prayer of confession is desired, the minister may address the people:

Dear friends in Christ, aware of God's providence and grace,
let us bow in silence before God
to confess our sins and receive forgiveness.

A brief silence.

**Most merciful God,
we confess that we have sinned against you
in thought, word, and deed.
We have not loved you with our whole heart;
we have not loved our neighbors as ourselves.
We pray you: in your mercy
forgive what we have been,
amend what we are,
direct what we shall be;
that we may delight in your will,
and walk in your ways,
giving thanks in all circumstances
through Jesus Christ our Lord. Amen.**

Minister to people:
Friends, hear the good news:
In the name of Jesus Christ, you are forgiven!

People to minister:
In the name of Jesus Christ, you are forgiven!

People and minister:
Glory to God. Amen.

[ACT OF PRAISE]

Here may be sung the Gloria in Excelsis, *the* Jubilate Deo, *or the* Te Deum. *A choral setting of these or similar canticles may be sung by the choir.*

FIRST LESSON

Deuteronomy 8:7-18	(Year A: 1993, 1996, 1999)
Joel 2:21-27	(Year B: 1994, 1997, 2000)
Deuteronomy 26:1-11	(Year C: 1995, 1998, 2001)

PSALM

Psalm 65	(Year A: 1993, 1996, 1999)
Psalm 126	(Year B: 1994, 1997, 2000)
Psalm 100	(Year C: 1995, 1998, 2001)

SECOND LESSON

II Corinthians 9:6-15	(Year A: 1993, 1996, 1999)
I Timothy 2:1-7	(Year B: 1994, 1997, 2000)
Philippians 4:4-9	(Year C: 1995, 1998, 2001)

ALLELUIA (HYMN OR ANTHEM)

GOSPEL

Luke 17:11-19	(Year A: 1993, 1996, 1999)
Matthew 6:25-33	(Year B: 1994, 1997, 2000)
John 6:25-35	(Year C: 1995, 1998, 2001)

SERMON

PRAYERS OF THE PEOPLE OR PASTORAL PRAYER

If a special offering of food gifts is to be brought by the people in procession or by representatives, these prayers or the litany of thanksgiving may follow the Offering. If the people make their own petitions, the common response to each may be: **Most gracious God, hear our prayer.** *Or, the following litany of thanksgiving may be prayed:*

Let us give thanks to God our Creator
for all gifts so freely bestowed upon us:

A brief silence.

For the beauty and wonder of creation,
in earth and sky and sea,

We thank you, Lord.

For all that is gracious in the lives of men and women,
revealing the image of Christ,

We thank you, Lord.

For our daily food and drink,
our homes and families, and our friends,

We thank you, Lord.

For minds to think, and hearts to love, and hands to serve,

We thank you, Lord.

For health and strength to work,
and leisure to rest and play,

We thank you, Lord.

For the brave and courageous
who are patient in suffering and faithful in adversity,

We thank you, Lord.

For all valiant seekers after truth, liberty, justice, and peace,

We thank you, Lord.

For the communion of saints, in all times and places,

We thank you, Lord.

Above all,
let us give thanks for the great promises and mercies
given to us and to all the world
in Jesus Christ, our Lord.

**To Christ be praise and glory,
with the Father and the Holy Spirit,
now and for ever. Amen.**

[THE PEACE]

All may exchange signs of reconciliation and peace, silently, or with the traditional "The peace of the Lord be with you."

OFFERING

When the offerings are presented, the following may be sung:

"Praise God from Whom All Blessings Flow"
"We Give Thee But Thine Own" (stanza 1)

Or the following hymn by Charles Wesley:

Father, Son, and Holy Ghost,
One in Three, and Three in One,
As by the celestial host,
Let thy will on earth be done;
Praise by all to thee be given,
Gracious Lord of earth and heaven!

Take my soul and body's powers,
Take my memory, mind, and will,
All my goods, and all my hours,
All I know, and all I feel,
All I think, and speak, and do:
Take my heart—but make it new.

If Holy Communion is not celebrated, the service concludes with a hymn and dismissal with blessing.

If Holy Communion is celebrated, the table is prepared during the offering and the service continues as follows:

GREAT THANKSGIVING

The Lord be with you.

And also with you.

Lift up your hearts.

We lift them to the Lord.

Let us give thanks to the Lord our God.

It is right to give him thanks and praise.

It is right, and a good and joyful thing,
always and everywhere to give thanks to you,
Father Almighty, Creator of heaven and earth.
By your appointment the seasons come and go.
You bring forth bread from the earth
and create the fruit of the vine.
You have made us in your image
and given us dominion over the world.
Earth has yielded its treasure,
and from your hand we have received blessing on blessing.

And so, with your people on earth
and all the company of heaven,
we praise your name and join their unending hymn:

**Holy, holy, holy Lord, God of power and might,
heaven and earth are full of your glory.
Hosanna in the highest.
Blessed is he who comes in the name of the Lord.
Hosanna in the highest.**

Holy are you, and blessed is your Son Jesus Christ.
Though he was rich, yet for our sake he became poor.
When hungry and tempted,
he refused to make bread for himself
that he might be the bread of life for others.
When the multitudes were hungry, he fed them.
He broke bread with the outcast
but drove the greedy out of the Temple.

By the baptism of his suffering, death, and resurrection
you gave birth to your church,
delivered us from slavery to sin and death,
and made with us a new covenant by water and the Spirit.

On the night in which he gave himself up for us
he took bread, gave thanks to you, broke the bread,
gave it to his disciples, and said:
"Take, eat; this is my body which is given for you.
Do this in remembrance of me."

When the supper was over he took the cup,
gave thanks to you, gave it to his disciples, and said:
"Drink from this, all of you;
this is my blood of the new covenant,
poured out for you and for many
for the forgiveness of sins.
Do this, as often as you drink it, in remembrance of me."

And so,
in remembrance of these your mighty acts in Jesus Christ,
we offer ourselves in praise and thanksgiving
as a holy and living sacrifice,
in union with Christ's offering for us,
as we proclaim the mystery of faith.

Christ has died, Christ is risen, Christ will come again.

Pour out your Holy Spirit on us, gathered here,
and on these gifts of bread and wine.
Make them be for us the body and blood of Christ,
that we may be for the world the body of Christ,
redeemed by his blood.

By your Spirit make us one with Christ,
one with each other,
and one in ministry to all the world,
until Christ comes in final victory
and we feast at his heavenly banquet.

Through your Son Jesus Christ,
with the Holy Spirit in your holy church,
all honor and glory is yours, Almighty Father,
now and for ever.

Amen.

THE LORD'S PRAYER

BREAKING THE BREAD

COMMUNION

PRAYER AFTER COMMUNION

> You have given yourself to us, Lord.
>
> **Now we give ourselves to others.**
>
> Your love has made us a new people.
>
> **As a people of love we will serve you with joy.**
>
> Your glory has filled our hearts.
>
> **Help us to glorify you in all things. Amen.**

> *or*

> Eternal God, Heavenly Father,
> you have graciously accepted us
> as living members of your Son our Savior Jesus Christ,
> and you have fed us with spiritual food
> in the sacrament of his body and blood.
> Send us now into the world in peace,
> and grant us strength and courage
> to love and serve you
> with gladness and singleness of heart;
> through Christ our Lord.

> **Amen.**   BCP

HYMN   *Appropriate closing hymns include:*

> "Now Thank We All Our God"
> "Lord, Whose Love Through Humble Service"
> "O God, Thou Giver of All Good"

DISMISSAL WITH BLESSING

> Go in peace to love and serve the Lord.
>
> **Thanks be to God.**
>
> The grace of the Lord Jesus Christ
> and the love of God
> and the communion of the Holy Spirit
> be with you all, now and for ever.
>
> **Amen.**

Commentary

Thanksgiving presents us with a number of possibilities. If it is celebrated on Thursday, it may be a gathering of several churches for an ecumenical service. Such an occasion provides an excellent opportunity for shared ministry among choirs and worship leaders from the various traditions, and especially for congregational singing of hymns and songs from the respective churches. This would be an appropriate occasion to use both choral and congregational music from ethnic minority traditions. An order of worship alternative to the one given here could be prepared in which readings were interspersed with hymns and anthems in the manner of the service of lessons and carols and several of the Holy Week/Easter orders. If there were several choirs involved, the sermon could be shortened appropriately, and the accent would fall on praise and thanksgiving.

Sensitivity is required whenever congregations with differing traditions worship together. It is important that every congregation be represented in the planning from the beginning. If the service is to be interreligious in character—for instance, involving one or more Jewish congregations—special sensitivity is required. Obviously an interreligious service would be radically different from what was suggested above, yet the experience of local persons in planning such a service could be an important learning experience for everyone. Even an ecumenical Christian service would not necessarily find all of what was suggested above to be acceptable. There may be one or more of the participating congregations not free to share in Holy Communion, or not at home with the use of certain liturgical forms. On the other hand, where congregations are ready to share in an ecumenical communion service and use unfamiliar liturgical forms, this can be a time of spiritual growth for everyone concerned. The ecumenical service that meets the needs of one community may not be at all suited to the needs of another community.

There are many possibilities regarding the visual environment. Red and white are both appropriate colors for the day, and one could see appropriate symbolic meaning in the use of green, gold, and earth colors in general. Harvest displays—grains, fruits, vegetables—are often set up. If gifts of food are being collected for the needy or offerings received for an appropriate cause, the way in which they are collected and gathered in front of the people can be a powerful symbolic statement. Intercessory prayers may be offered for the specific persons or agencies for whom the offering is being received. Special banners can be made and used at this service each year.

If it is possible to celebrate Holy Communion, this can be an expression of a profound dimension of the sacrament. The word *eucharist* means "thanksgiving"; and what could be more appropriate for a Christian congregation at Thanksgiving than to celebrate the great thanksgiving that is the eucharist—setting our gratitude for God's countless acts of bounty in the context of our gratitude for God's greatest gift to us in Jesus Christ.

PART THREE

APPENDICES

GLOSSARY OF CHRISTIAN SYMBOLS

A symbol is an object or other visible (perceptual) sign pointing to a reality greater in meaning and power than the sign itself. Christian symbols which occur in worship gather and combine ranges of meaning that no literal statement or representation can fully communicate. Thus, over time, the worshiping community deepens its faith experience with the symbols since they open up several levels of meaning. Sometimes they hold certain meanings in tension. For example, water may signify both life and death, cleansing and chaos. Yet the symbol of water as it is encountered in the Easter Vigil, for instance, conveys all of these at once. As the praying and celebrating community grows in the Word of God and experiences its own life in ministry, the signs become symbolic by opening up maturing levels of insight into the gospel.

In the history of Christian worship, many different types of symbols occur. Some—the cross, bread and wine, water—are primary. They are found widely in scripture and are linked directly to specific ways in which God has acted toward the world. Others, such as an emblem of a triangle or a circle, may refer to a particular doctrine or to an attribute of God—the Trinity and eternity, respectively. Still others are figures or images associated with divine realities such as the dove and the Holy Spirit, the ark and the history of God's promises, the pelican and Christ's redeeming nurture. These latter two categories belong to Christian symbolism that is derived from the primary type. Finally, there are actions or gestures that are symbolic of the divine-human interaction in worship itself, such as the kiss of peace or the laying on of hands.

All of these are depicted and used in various ways in liturgical art—in stained glass windows, stoles, altar frontals, furnishings, architecture, and the like. The following list of symbols is not exhaustive, but it is intended to be a guide to the major types of symbolism that occur frequently in the art and ritual related to Word and sacrament over the course of the Christian Year.

Agape (Love feast): A simple, ritual meal in the context of which hymns are sung, Scripture is read, and testimonies and stories of faith are shared. John Wesley instituted this after the Moravian pattern. All such meals derive from Jewish and early church meals such as are referred to by Paul, and they symbolize the unity of fellowship in the love of Christ which the saints at rest will share. Signs of the agape are the loving cup and bread.

Alpha and Omega: The first and last letters of the Greek alphabet. They are used to refer to Christ's person and work in the book of Revelation, and they are often depicted as a monogram or emblem of his comprehensive revelation. His eternal reign is expressed in the phrase: "I am the Alpha and the Omega, the first and the last, the beginning and the end" (Rev. 22:13).

Alpha  *Omega*

Altar: The focal point of sacramental encounter with God, the place of offering and receiving God's self-giving. The altar gathers meaning from ancient Hebrew holy places (for example, Shechem or Penuel) which acknowledge and honor Yahweh and, more specifically, are places of sacrifice and prayer. For Protestants, the altar is symbolic of kneeling before God in self-surrender and the table upon which the Lord's Supper is celebrated.

Anchor: Often used as an emblem or image of hope, the anchor is related to the ship as a type of the church. The anchor image derives from Hebrews 6:18-19.

Anchor

Anointing (with Oil): Anointing with oil recalls the Old Testament anointing of prophets, priests, and kings, signifying God's power to empower and confirm particular virtues and roles in the community as well as the authority given to fulfill these respective roles. Anointing with oil is also a profound symbol of healing and, hence, of God's goodness toward all.

Ark: One of the earliest Christian symbols for Christ and the church and, more generally, for salvation, derived directly from the story of God's covenant promises with Noah. More recently it has become a common ecumenical symbol of the whole church. (See also **Ship**.)

Ark

Ashes: A primary symbol of penitence and mourning found in several instances throughout Scripture and brought to particular focus in Christian rites of Ash Wednesday and in the burial rites. Thus the words: "You are dust, and to dust you shall return" (Gen. 3:19). "Repent, and believe in the gospel" (Mark 1:15). Ashes are also used as a symbol of mortality.

Banners: Signs of victory and triumph, originally used in the context of battle to lead the way or to identify particular groups. Specifically in the ancient hymn "Forth the Royal Banners Go" Christ's redemptive work is heralded by their appearance. More recently banners have become specially designed for processions or for wall hangings, often bearing specific seasonal symbols and texts.

Banners

Baptismal Font: The place of water for the sacrament of baptism. Originally large and suitable for immersion, the font has classically been at the entrance of the church or in the chancel area on an axis with altar and pulpit. Fonts are focal points for remembrance of covenant for initiation, cleansings, incorporation, and the many levels of association with the primary symbol of water and water imagery in Scripture.

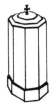
Baptismal Font

Bible (Liturgical books): The primary book is the Bible which, when opened on the lectern or pulpit, signifies the opening of God's living Word for the people. When carried in procession at the beginning of worship, or in preparation for the reading of the gospel, for example, it shows the movement of God's Word toward us and creates the symbol of the Word in the midst of the people. There are other liturgical books, such as a Psalter or a lectionary, which may become visible signs of the Word of God and the responsive word of the church's worship.

Bread: This inexhaustible primary symbol functions as a natural representation of food and also in the Scriptures as God's Word—the "bread of life." This in turn connects bread with Jesus Christ who speaks in John's Gospel of himself as the "Bread of Life." As employed in the Eucharist or Lord's Supper, bread becomes the transforming, living sign of Christ's presence. Throughout the Christian Year we encounter many references to bread in the Scriptures—manna in the desert, the cakes made by Sarah for the three visitors, the feeding of the multitudes, and the bread of the Last Supper, to name a few. The loaves and fishes thus are a powerful symbol of nurture, and the relationship between bread broken, bread scattered, and bread made one refers to the reality of the church as Christ's body.

Bread

Butterfly: A symbol of the resurrection, or of transformation of life, frequently used on a Chrismon Tree but also on Easter banners during the Great Fifty Days.

Butterfly

Candles: Candles or lamps are places of light and illumination; hence, they refer to the archetypal symbol of light. The paschal candle is the chief symbolic candle in the Christian tradition, standing for the risen Christ beginning each year at the Easter Vigil and remaining during the Sundays of the Great Fifty Days, used also at funerals and occasions of great solemnity referring to death and resurrection. Candlelight services, especially at Christmas Eve, are times of group symbolization of the divine illumination. (See also **Light.**)

Chalice (Cup): A symbol of Christ's self-giving in the Eucharist. The chalice has come to signify the whole of his suffering for us and the redeeming benefits of his passion as well. In various periods the chalice became heavily adorned with designs and jewels, expressing the honor and preciousness of the blood of Christ. Occasionally, a monogram with a pointed cross in the cup is used to indicate this particular symbol as a cup of the passion, while the cup and a radiant host just above it symbolize the whole of the eucharistic presence and self-giving sacrifice of Christ.

Chalice

Chi Rho: A chief form of sacred monogram signifying Jesus Christ by using the first two letters of the Greek word *Christos*. It has appeared in many forms since the fourth century, including without the "P" as ✗ or, ✳ as well as elaborated combinations with the Alpha and Omega ✸ sometimes surrounded by a wreath of leaves signifying victory.

Chi Rho

Chrismon Tree: This tree, used by many congregations instead of a secular Christmas tree and placed in the sanctuary, is decorated with various monograms and emblems standing for Christ and the story of salvation. Several of these "chrismons," or Christ monograms, are mentioned in this list—for example, the Chi Rho, butterfly, the Alpha and Omega, and the letters IHS.

Cross: Perhaps the fundamental symbol in Christianity representing the whole meaning of Christ's saving death and resurrection, life and ministry, incarnation and coming in glory. There are many forms of the cross, including the crucifix with the suffering figure of Christ and a cross with a triumphant Christ upon it, reigning and exalted. Some of the most common resurrection, or empty, crosses are the *Latin*, with lower arm longer than the others; the *Greek*, with four arms of equal length; the *Celtic*, with a circle symbolizing eternity; the *Budded Cross*, with a trefoil on each end of four arms signifying life and the Trinity; the *Saint Andrew's Cross* shaped like an X; the *Jerusalem Cross*, representing the spread of the gospel to the four corners of the earth; the *Maltese Cross*, whose spreading arms and eight points show human regeneration and the eight Beatitudes; the *Tau Cross*, named for its shape resembling the Greek letter *tau*; and the *Cross with Crown*, either of thorns or of a kingly crown.

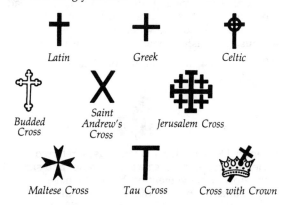

Latin *Greek* *Celtic*

Budded Cross *Saint Andrew's Cross* *Jerusalem Cross*

Maltese Cross *Tau Cross* *Cross with Crown*

Cross, Sign of: In some traditions, especially in Orthodoxy, Roman Catholicism, and Anglicanism, the gesture of crossing oneself—head, heart and both shoulders, or with small crosses on the forehead, lips, and breast—is an act of devotion in response to the trinitarian name.

Dove, Descending: Symbolizes the Holy Spirit, originating in the account of Jesus' baptism in Matthew 3:16. It sometimes refers to the peace of God.

Descending Dove

Eggs: While this tends to be a secular symbol outside the church, in some Christian traditions elaborately decorated eggs symbolize new life. They are painted with icons and used in ritual acts following their distribution at the church.

Fire: Especially at the Easter Vigil, the new fire kindled symbolizes the dawning of the resurrection and the light that shines with the splendor of day in the darkness.

Fish: The figure of the fish was first drawn by early Christians in the time of persecution as a mark of identity and it appears in early Christian iconography. The first letters of the Greek words "Jesus

Christ, God's Son, Savior" also make up the word *fish* or *ichthus* in Greek.

Fish

Footwashing: Symbolic of Jesus' own act of ministry to the disciples, used in some traditions on Holy Thursday and other occasions. A sign of the love and care the Christian community has from Jesus.

Fraction: The breaking of the eucharistic bread, occurring just after the eucharistic prayer, of Christ's body for the whole world.

Ichthus: (See **Fish**.) Sometimes written IXTHUS.

IHS: The first three letters of "Jesus" in Greek (IHSOUS).

IHS

Incense: Deriving from several uses referred to in Hebrew scripture, the sweet fragrance and sight of the upward movement of the smoke have come to symbolize the prayers of the saints (cf. Ps. 141) and are a primary sign of honor and sanctification, both of the people and of the altar, book, and sanctuary.

Keys, Crossed: A sign of the "keys of the kingdom" given to Peter (Matt. 16:18-19), hence of the authority of the church. Keys are also used as a basic image in the O Antiphons to refer to the "Key of David" and, therefore, are an image of messianic hope in the prophetic literature.

Crossed Keys

Kiss of Peace: A sign of fellowship, greeting (as in Rom. 16:16 and I Pet. 5:14), and reconciliation, used in various liturgies. More recently it has been restored to a place between the prayers of the people and the offertory in reformed eucharistic rites.

Lamb: Often depicted standing with a banner of victory flying from a cross held by the front leg of the lamb, this emblem signifies the victorious nature of the sacrifice of Jesus Christ; but it is also a figure of the Lamb of God "slain from the foundation of the world" (Rev. 13:8 KJV). It is a symbol of the eternal redemptive work of Christ.

Lamb

Laying on of Hands: A gesture used in various services, such as in baptism, confirmation, ordination, and investiture, to signify the conferring of the Holy Spirit. It is also used in healing services where it symbolizes both the conferral of the Spirit and the role God gives human touch in empowering and healing.

Lectern: A reading stand upon which the Bible is placed. It symbolizes a reading of the Word and singing of psalms and canticles.

Light: The archetypal symbol of light is found throughout Scripture and finds many expressions in Christian worship—the lights of evening, the vigil lights, processional lights, and the like. Not only a natural symbol for life and the visible goodness of creation, light in the Bible is associated with the divine activity and with the very nature of God in Christ ("God from God, Light from Light"). Christ is referred to as the light of the world. God's acts are epiphanies of the light of the divine nature, from the burning bush and the pillar of fire by night to the vision of the new Jerusalem where God will be the only light required.

Lily: A flower of the resurrection, but also a symbol of the care of God, as in the Sermon on the Mount: "Consider the lilies of the field" (Matt. 6:28). Also frequently used as a symbol of the Annunciation in which the angel extends a lily to the virgin—an allusion to a christological interpretation of the frequent image of the lilies in the Song of Solomon (especially 2:1).

Lily

Menorah: The seven-branched candleholder from Jewish tradition, often said to represent the sevenfold gifts of the Holy Spirit.

Menorah

Monograms: Emblems of Christ or of some aspect of his person and work, usually based on Greek letters such as IHS. Monograms may also be shapes of specific symbols used on a Chrismon Tree.

Oil: A primary symbol of anointing, used in various aspects of initiation, healing, and renewal.

Paraments: Linens and cloth hangings used to adorn altars, pulpits, and lecterns, bearing the symbolic colors of the Christian Year and often adorned with specific emblems appropriate to the seasons—the cross, the crown, the Epiphany star, or the trefoil.

Passion, Symbols of:

Crown of thorns—mockery, humiliation, and suffering.

Crown of thorns

Crowing cock—the warning and rebuke of Peter and, generally, of Peter's denial of Jesus.

Crowing cock

Palm leaves or branches—entry into Jerusalem; honor and victory.

Palm leaves

Scourge and pillar—symbolizing Jesus' physical suffering and humiliation.

Scourge and pillar

Ladder crossed with reed and sponge—symbolizing the crucifixion, and the cruelty of the vinegar given him (Matt. 27:48).

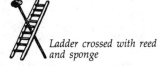
Ladder crossed with reed and sponge

Money bag and/or silver coins—smbolizing the treachery of Judas (Matt. 26:15).

Money bag

Pelican: A redemptive figure of Christ derived from the popular belief that the pelican gives of its own blood to feed its young, usually depicted in wood carvings or drawings with a brood of young.

Pelican

Pulpit: The place of preaching, generally symbolizing the proclaimed and living Word, as well as the authority of those called to preach.

Salt: A sign of incorruptibility (Mark 9:50), integrity, and wisdom (Col. 4:6), used as a chief image by Jesus in the Sermon on the Mount (Matt. 5:13). The liturgical use of salt is related to the baptism of infants and in rites with catechumens, persons preparing for baptism.

Shell: A symbol of baptism, sometimes used in the rite to administer the water.

Shell

Shepherd: One of the earliest iconographic depictions of Jesus, often shown with a lamb about his shoulders, deriving from the scriptural identity of Jesus as the Good Shepherd.

Shepherd

Ship: A symbol of the church. (See also **Ark.**)

Ship

Stars: The five-sided star with rays symbolizes Epiphany and the star followed by the Wise Men. Six-sided star (or shield) of David, a common Jewish symbol also used by Christians.

Epiphany Star   *Star of David*

Stole: A symbol of authority worn over the left shoulder by deacons and around the shoulders of bishops and presbyters (elders). It can be adorned with specific symbols such as cross, chalice, and host or with seasonal symbols.

Towel and Basin: Symbols of Christ's servanthood, especially shown in his act of washing the disciples' feet on Holy Thursday. Images are interwoven into the Holy Thursday ritual.

Towel and Basin

Tree: The Jesse Tree, derived from Isaiah 11:1, decorated with biblical images and figures. The general symbol of life and death, found in Genesis—the fruit of the tree in the midst of the garden signifying human choice for good and evil. Symbolic connections are made in many traditions between the tree of life and the tree of Calvary—the cross made of wood, especially in the Good Friday liturgy. (See also **Chrismon Tree.**)

Jesse Tree

Trinity, Symbols of:

Fleur-de-lis:

Shamrock:

Three intertwined circles:

Trefoil:

Triquetra: The three equal arcs represent eternity in their continuous moving form and indivisibility in their interweaving. The center forms a triangle, itself another symbol of the Trinity.

Triquetra

Triangle: Either a simple equilateral triangle or one with the all-seeing eye of God looking out of it.

Triangle

Water: A primary symbol related especially to baptism, with a wide range of meaning: cleansing, life-giving, chaos, death-dealing, womb and birth, rebirth, the river Jordan, the Red Sea, and the crystal fountains and rivers mentioned in the book of Revelation. Water is used in several of the rites of initiation and in various purification rites.

Wheat and Grapes: A chief natural symbol set related to the Eucharist, or Lord's Supper, from which bread and wine are made; but also signifying harvest, feasting, and plenty—the goodness of God's creation. In addition there are overtones of the gifts of Jesus Christ to his people. The gifts of creation, made by human hands offered in thanks to God, and received transformed by God's grace in Christ.

GLOSSARY OF
LITURGICAL TERMS

Advent (Latin, "coming"): A season of four Sundays which closes on December 24 and focuses on the coming of Jesus Christ, historically, experientially, and eschatologically. In fifth and sixth century Gaul it had six Sundays, and in other places five. Its permanent form derives from the reduction of the number to four in Rome. In Eastern Orthodoxy six weeks before Christmas are kept as a fast, although this is not a liturgical season. In the Western church the season is solemn but not as heavily penitential as Lent. Indeed, in much contemporary practice, emphasis on the joy of the coming of Messiah almost excludes a penitential tone.

Advent Wreath: A wreath containing candles that are lighted progressively on each Sunday of Advent. Because it arose as a domestic rather than an ecclesiastical practice, its use is not carefully prescribed. Thus, sometimes it has four colored candles that are exchanged for four white candles during the Christmas Season. More recently a fifth, larger candle (sometimes called the "Christ candle") is used at Christmas. No significance should be given to the four candles individually; their symbolism lies entirely in the progressive illumination, not in attributes (faith, hope, love, joy) or in beings (prophets, angels, shepherds, Magi) sometimes attached to them. For liturgical (as distinct from domestic) use, the candles generally follow the color of the season. Where churches no longer use rose rather than violet for the Third Sunday of Advent (and the Fourth of Lent) use of one rose (or pink) candle in the wreath is odd at best and probably confusing. The best rule is that the color of candles be the same as vestments for the day.

Alleluia, Burial of the: In liturgical traditions that regularly say or sing an "Alleluia" in the rite, this is dropped throughout Lent in deference to the solemnity of the season. Sometimes just prior to Lent, the Alleluia is symbolically "buried" with liturgical ceremony so that its return with great joy on Easter morning can be seen as a "resurrection."

All Saints Day: November 1, also known as All Hallows' Day; its eve gave us the term *Halloween*. In contemporary understanding, it celebrates the saintly status of all Christian people, known and unknown, not merely all officially canonized saints, as formerly. Originally, the feast was closely associated in the calendar with the resurrection (Syria, fifth century, Easter Friday; Rome, from 610, May 13); and in Eastern Orthodoxy it is observed in the Octave of Pentecost. In the West it was moved to November 1 in A.D. 835.

All Souls Day: Growing out of the medieval distinction between heaven and purgatory, November 1 was the day devoted to those already in bliss ("the saints") and November 2 to all other deceased Christians ("souls in purgatory"). Particularly in contemporary liturgical recovery by Protestants, the two occasions are conflated and November 1 celebrates Christ's saving work on behalf of all of the departed faithful.

Altar, Stripping and Washing of: The custom of removing from the Lord's table all linens and paraphernalia at the close of the service on Holy Thursday evening probably originated for wholly utilitarian reasons. Since Good Friday was the one day of the year on which Mass was not to be said (see **Mass of the Presanctified:**), and since giving the church a thorough cleaning just before Easter seemed fitting, the altar was stripped so its stonework could be scrubbed and polished and its linens laundered. Later pious minds saw in this action a reminder of the stripping of Jesus before his crucifixion. Where the practice is observed now, it is not for utilitarian purposes but for reasons that are allegorical or, perhaps, psychological (so the altar will have a markedly different appearance on Good Friday from that on Easter Day).

Annunciation [Feast of]: March 25, selected probably in the seventh century as being nine months prior to December 25. In some pious thought, however, it was said that Jesus died on March 25; therefore, that also must have been the day of his conception, so that the time of his incarnation could be perfect in its temporality as well as in its character.

Antiphon: See **Response.**

Ascension Day: See p. 223.

Ash Wednesday: See p. 115.

Baptism of the Lord: See p. 89.

Bible Sunday: In older calendars, the Second Sunday of Advent, since on this day the collect, derived from the first verse of the Epistle (Rom. 15:4), began, "Blessed Lord, who hast caused all Holy Scripture to be written for our learning. . . ." This occasion does not exist as such in contemporary lectionaries, but the historic circumstance explains why hymns and prayers about the Bible occur in the Advent sections of certain older hymnals and service books.

Candlemas: See **Presentation.**

Catechumen: A person receiving instruction in the faith (cf. "catechism"—that which is being learned). In the ancient church a three-year catechumenate prior to baptism was common; the rites accompanying transition to the status of candidate for baptism and then to that of a baptized Christian dictated the form of Lent.

Chrismon: Contracted form of "Christ's monogram," a decorative form of monogram (IHS, XP) and other symbols related to the person and work of Christ, typically hand-fabricated in materials of white and gold colors. In recent popular piety an evergreen tree is so decorated as an alternative to the secular form of Christmas tree, and in worship space may stand in juxtaposition to a tree of Adam—a deciduous tree devoid of foliage though decorated, perhaps, with apples—as a reminder of temptation and death in contrast to restoration and life. Such usage is, however, paraliturgical at best.

Christ the King [Feast of]: In the contemporary calendar, the Sunday prior to Advent. In earlier calendars, the last Sunday in October (Roman Catholic) or the last Sunday in August (Methodist).

Circumcision [Feast of]: See Holy Name of Jesus.

Colors, Liturgical: Before the Reformation, great flexibility in use of colors existed, often varying from one diocese to another. The rigidity imposed by the Council of Trent has now been overthrown, and within limits, variety is again allowed. Contemporary options include.

Advent: Violet, purple, or blue: except rose may be used on Advent 3.
Christmas Season and Baptism of Lord: White.
Sundays After Epiphany: Green.
Transfiguration: White.
Lent: Violet or purple; except rose may be used on Lent 4 (if also on Advent 3). Scarlet or red may be used throughout Holy Week. Black may be used on Ash Wednesday, Good Friday, and Holy Saturday until the Easter Vigil. No color at all may be used on Good Friday and Holy Saturday until the Vigil.
Easter: White, with gold optional for Easter Day.
Day of Pentecost: Red.
Trinity Sunday: White.
Sundays After Pentecost: Green.
Saints' Days: Red, if martyrs; except that the Confession of Saint Peter and the Conversion of Saint Paul (January 18 and 25) are white, as is the birth of John the Baptist (June 24), which is considered a festival of

the Lord, rather than of a martyr. White is used for other saints, including Saint John the Evangelist (December 27) and All Saints Day (November 1).

In some traditions the assigned color gives way to white, violet, or purple for funerals; it is unchanged for weddings, however. Red is commonly used for ordinations and other particular festivals of the church.

Corpus Christi: The Thursday after **Trinity Sunday** in the Roman Catholic calendar. Since 1264 it has been a day honoring the presence of Christ in the Eucharist; hence, the eucharistic bread is carried in public procession.

Easter Day: In the West, the first Sunday after the full moon on or after March 21 (as reckoned in ecclesiastical calendars, not necessarily as astronomically determined); but if this full moon falls on a Sunday, Easter is the Sunday following—hence, any time between March 22 and April 25, inclusive. The Eastern Orthodox follow the old Julian calendar which was displaced in the West by the Gregorian calendar. Therefore, Orthodox Easter only rarely coincides with Easter in the West. Vatican II encouraged a fixed date for Easter but only after agreement by all churches. Later the Vatican, in collaboration with the World Council of Churches, proposed as that date the Sunday after the second Saturday of April; but consensus has not yet been achieved, particularly on the part of the Eastern churches. The centrality of Easter in the calendar is evidenced by a regulation of Constantine that Easter Day be counted as New Year's Day in the civil calendar—a practice that was continued in France until 1656.

Ember Days (from Middle English, *yaber*, "a circuit"): The Wednesday, Friday, and Saturday following (1) Lent I, (2) Pentecost, (3) September 14 (Holy Cross Day), and (4) December 13. Historically these were days of prayer and fasting connected to agricultural cycles in the four seasons. The Saturdays were regarded as being particularly suitable for ordinations. In contemporary calendars, observance of Ember Days is optional, if they are included at all.

Epiphany (Greek, *epiphaneia*, "an appearance or manifestation"): January 6. It was originally an Eastern festival concerning both the incarnation and baptism of Jesus; in the West it came to commemorate instead the arrival of the Magi. Contemporary usage, with the Baptism of the Lord being observed on the Sunday following Epiphany, seeks to restore the Eastern perspective in the Western church.

Eve: The practice of celebrating festivals beginning on the evening of the prior calendar date springs from the Jewish heritage in which days are counted from sunset to sunset. Hence liturgical celebrations begin with vespers and may include a **vigil** such as that common at Christmas and being restored at Easter.

Exsultet (Exultet): The Easter proclamation sung (preferably by a deacon) at the **vigil** in conjunction with the stationing of the **paschal candle.** It is sometimes known as *Laus Cerei* ("praise of the candle"). It takes its more familiar Latin name from its opening words: "Rejoice, heavenly powers! Sing, choirs of angels! Exult, all creation around God's throne! Jesus Christ, our King, is risen!"

Fat Tuesday: See **Shrove Tuesday.**

Feast and Feria: Festival and nonfestival days, respectively. Confusion ensues from the fact that *feria* in Latin means "holiday," but in common liturgical usage it has taken on the opposite connotation.

First Day: The Lord's Day or Sunday. See pp. 17-18.

Forty Hours: The time between the commemoration of Jesus' entombment and his resurrection, marked by special acts of devotion—particularly the exposition of the Eucharistic bread in the Roman church, where by extension the Forty Hours' Devotion may also be used outside of the Easter Triduum.

Gaudete Sunday: The Third Sunday of Advent, named after the opening word of the traditional introit, Philippians 4:4 ("Rejoice in the Lord"). Since the Sunday was more joyous than the others of Advent, rose rather than violet was the formerly prescribed liturgical color in the Roman Catholic Church.

Good Friday: See pp. 189-90.

Good Shepherd Sunday: The Fourth Sunday of Easter on which, in all three years, the lectionary prescribes a portion of John 10 as the Gospel. In several former lectionary systems, the day was the Second Sunday After Easter Day.

Great Fifty Days: See pp. 108-10.

Green Thursday: An alternative name for Holy, or Maundy, Thursday, particularly in Germany. The title may have originated in a custom of giving green branches to penitents as an indication that their reconciliation was effected. It gave rise to the superstition that the eating of green vegetables on this day would have a salutary effect.

Holy Cross [Feast of]: September 14, called "The Triumph of the Cross" in the Roman Catholic calendar. The date was originally that for the consecration in A.D 335 of a basilica built in Jerusalem by Constantine at the site where his mother, Helena, presumably discovered the instrument of Jesus' crucifixion. It is a commemoration of the atonement approximately midway between Easter and the beginning of the next Lent.

Holy Innocents: December 28. The day commemorates the children of Bethlehem whose death (or "birth" into eternity, in the ancient way of speaking of martyrdom) is placed so closely to the observance of Jesus' birth as a special mark of honor. The next day immediately after December 25 honors Saint Stephen, who as the first martyr of the church has his "birthday" as close to the nativity of his Lord as possible. December 27 is given to Saint John who, as the disciple especially loved by Jesus, is given first place among non-martyrs following the birth of Jesus. Holy Innocents thus completes the sanctoral triduum (three days) of Christmas.

Holy Name of Jesus: January 1, the eighth day after the birth of Jesus, when he was circumcised and named (Luke 2:21; Lev. 12:3). It was formerly known as the Feast of Circumcision and has been changed in the Roman Catholic Calendar to the Solemnity of Mary, Mother of God. The liturgical observance of this date in relation to the story of Jesus' nativity is not to be confused with the secular observance of New Year's Day. See pp. 78, 258.

Holy Week: See pp. 159-60.

Hunger Cloth (German, *Hungertuch*): A cloth hung between the congregation and altar in the medieval church during Lent, or the latter part thereof. As Lenten discipline on food provided a "fast for the stomach," and the silencing of the organ on Good Friday produced a "fast for the ears," so the hunger cloth imposed a "fast for the eyes" so that the joy of Easter would be enhanced by the removal of all these forms of fasting.

Jesse Tree: A variation of the Chrismon Tree. During Advent various emblems are displayed depicting the Old Testament heritage of Messiah who is born of the house of Jesse, King David's father.

Jubilate Sunday: Formerly in the Roman Catholic calendar the Third Sunday After Easter Day; from the opening word of the introit, Psalm 66:1 (= 65:1, Vulgate). This psalm is now in part the responsorial psalm for the Sixth Sunday of Easter, in Year A only.

Judica Sunday: Formerly a title for the Fifth Sunday of Lent, named from the introit, Psalm 43:1 (= 42:1, Vulgate).

Kingdomtide: A season devoted to social concerns, recommended by the Federal Council of Churches in 1937, extending from the last Sunday of August until Advent. See p. 241.

Laetare Sunday: Formerly the Fourth Sunday of Lent, named for the opening word of the introit (Isa. 66:10). On this day the penitential character of Lent was relaxed somewhat, in token of which rose rather than violet vestments were used. It was also called "Refreshment Sunday" and "Mothering Sunday" in England, where it was a kind of precursor of Mother's Day in the United States.

Lazarus Sunday: In the ancient church, the Fifth Sunday of Lent when the Gospel reading was from John 11; restored in Year A under the three-year lectionary.

Lent: See p. 117.

Letter Days, Red and Black: In the post-Reformation liturgical calendar in England, major feasts and saints' days were indicated in red ink, while lesser observances were printed in black. Hence the popular names used to distinguish major and minor festivals.

Lord's Day: See pp. 17-18.

Low Sunday: A popular name for the Second Sunday of Easter, perhaps from a corruption of the opening word of the Latin sequence—*Laudes*. The technical name for the Sunday is *Dominica in Albis [deponendis/depositis]* because on this day the newly baptized wore for the last time the white garments given at the **vigil**.

Mass of the Presanctified: The liturgy particular to Good Friday (in Orthodoxy, Wednesdays and Fridays throughout Lent), in which the solemnity of the day precludes the joy of the eucharistic rite; hence when communion is distributed, it is from elements previously consecrated.

Maundy Thursday: The name is probably an English corruption of the theme of the Gospel reading traditional to the day (John 13:34) in which Jesus gives his new commandment (Latin, *mandatum novum*). In England the monarch enacts this by sharing royal wealth with the poor; this token gift money is there called "the maundy." (See also pp. 160–61.)

Michaelmas: September 29, the Feast of Saint Michael. The Anglican churches added to the day the commemoration of All Angels, though the angels are so honored on October 2 and November 8 in Catholicism and Orthodoxy, respectively. In the Roman calendar, however, the archangels Gabriel and Raphael share the day with Michael.

Mystagogy: The instruction of the faithful, particularly in the spiritual meaning of the liturgy after baptism, as distinct from catechesis before baptism. In the ancient church the **octave** of Easter was devoted to daily mystagogy for those initiated at the **vigil.**

New Fire: The flame from which the **paschal candle** is lighted at the Easter **Vigil.** So called because formerly it was required that the candle be lighted from a flame created by sparks from flint and steel, representing the fire of the Holy Spirit coming forth from the resurrection.

O Antiphons: Seven responses, rich in Old Testament allusions to Messiah's titles; used traditionally with the Magnificat at vespers just preceding Christmas—December 16–20 and 22–23, December 21 being the Feast of Saint Thomas with its own antiphon. The antiphons are the basis of the hymn "O Come, O Come Emmanuel," although few hymnals print all seven stanzas. For a contemporary version of the antiphons, see p. 62.

Octave: The eighth day after a feast, or the whole period of eight days, during which the joy of the feast is prolonged. While earlier calendars abounded with octaves, now no more than three are maintained—Christmas, Easter, and Pentecost.

Palm Sunday: See pp. 125–26.

Pasch: The ancient and most venerable name for the resurrection festival, preserved in the Romance languages but replaced in Saxon tongues by the name of the pagan goddess of spring fertility, Eastre. Contrary to common belief, *pasch* (*pascha* in Greek) is not derived from the Greek *paschein* ("to suffer"), nor is it related to the Latin equivalent *(passus)*. Rather, *Pasch* is derived from the Hebrew term *pesah* ("deliverance" or "passover"). Thus *Pasch* connects the church directly to the celebration of the exodus.

Paschal Candle: The candle lighted at the Paschal **Vigil** in token of the light of the risen Christ, and the corollary in the new exodus of the pillar of fire in the Hebrew exodus. Traditionally it is lighted throughout the **Great Fifty Days** and stands at a central place. Thereafter it stands at the font and is lighted at baptism, which the ancient church called "enlightenment." At funerals it is lighted and stands at the coffin in token of Christ's leading the baptized through the exodus of death. The candle should be the largest used liturgically. (In medieval England, the paschal candle and stand at Durham was seventy feet high and had to be lighted from above; at Salisbury in 1517 the candle itself was thirty-six feet high.) The candle is inscribed in red wax with a Greek cross, with the four numerals of the calendar year in its corners. An Alpha and an Omega above and below, or to each side, complete the insignia. Formerly five grains of incense were imbedded in the center and ends of the arms; this is no longer encouraged, as it arose from a misreading of a portion of the **Exsultet.**

Paschal Mystery: The whole range of meanings associated with the saving work of Jesus Christ and the church's participation therein; more narrowly, the saving power and benefits of Christ's death and resurrection.

Passion Sunday: See pp. 125–26.

Penitential Seasons: Advent and Lent, though the latter is the more solemn and therefore more marked liturgically, as by the disuse of certain music, for example. See **Alleluia, Burial of the.**

Pentecost (from Greek, *pentecosta*, "fifty"; and *pentecoste*, "fiftieth"): The fiftieth day after Passover and therefore after Easter, though the entire fifty-day period was given this designation in the ancient church. See p. 227.

Presentation, Feast of: February 2, celebrating the presentation of Jesus in the temple forty days after his birth (Luke 2:22). It has also been called the Feast of the Purification of Mary and Candlemas. Because of the word of Simeon about Messiah as "a light to the Gentiles" (Luke 2:32), the blessing of candles and a candlelight ceremony in connection with the Mass for the day became popular; hence, the name in England "the Candle Mass." See p. 258.

Purification, Feast of: See **Presentation.**

Quadragesima (Latin, "forty days"): Another name for Lent. Formerly the Sundays prior to Lent were referred to by similar names: Septuagesima (seventy), Sexagesima (sixty), and Quinquagesima (fifty), although of course these numbers were approximations of the number of days prior to Easter.

Quartodeciman Controversy (Latin, "fourteen"): Because the church celebrated the resurrection weekly on the **Lord's Day,** a division of opinion arose as to whether the annual celebration also must fall on a Sunday or whether in accordance with the date of the Jewish Passover festival it should occur on the fourteenth day of the month Nisan, regardless of the day of the week. The latter option, popular in Asia Minor in the second century, came to be heretical, and those who adhered to it were called the Quartodeciman party.

Response: A phrase sung by the congregation that gives specific focus to a sung or recited psalm, traditionally known as an **antiphon** and usually taken from the psalm.

Responsory: A brief dialogical or responsorial form of scripture used as a congregational reply to a specific reading, often from the prophets, in some instances set to music.

Rogation Days: In certain calendars the three days preceding **Ascension Day,** kept as times of prayer, and sometimes of fasting; characterized by the custom of walking in procession to bless the spring crops. The name is from the Latin *rogatio,* "a request or a prayer"; and sung litanies were particularly associated with the processions on these days.

Sabbath (Hebrew, *shabbath,* "intermission" or "rest"): The seventh day of the week in the Hebrew calendar used by early Christians oriented toward Judaism. For Jews it was an obligatory day of rest in commemoration of the Creation and the Exodus. Despite popular misuse, especially by the Puritans, the term is not appropriate for the **Lord's Day,** which is the first day of the week and was not a holiday prior to the Constantinian era. In the early centuries, the Lord's Day was characterized not by rest but by the eucharistic celebration of the presence of the risen Lord.

Saint John's Day: See **Holy Innocents.**

Saint Martin's Lent: See **Advent.**

Saint Stephen's Day: See **Holy Innocents.**

Sanctoral Cycle: See pp. 268-69.

Shrove Tuesday: The day before **Ash Wednesday,** so called in England because of the custom of the pre-Lenten shriving or granting absolution to those who made their confession to the priest. Also called "Fat Tuesday" (cf. French, *Mardi Gras*) from the custom of using up fat (particularly in fried confections or pancakes) in preparation for the Lenten fast.

Strepitus: (Latin, "a loud crash or clatter"): A harsh noise during the **Tenebrae** service, after the extinguishing of the candles, to call to mind the earthquake and Jesus' loud cry and death.

Tenebrae: (Latin, "darkness"): A rite of Holy Week, characterized by the progressive extinguishing of candles as the passion account is read. In its original medieval form, fifteen candles were placed on a triangular stand. On the Wednesday, Thursday, and Friday in Holy Week, seven candles were extinguished during the psalms of matins, and seven more during the psalms of lauds, immediately following. The fifteenth candle was hidden temporarily and then returned to the top of the triangular stand. (See also p. 170.)

Thomas Sunday: The Second Sunday of Easter **(octave),** so called because on this day the Johannine account of Jesus' appearance to Thomas is read in all three years. The occasion is not to be confused with the Feast of

Saint Thomas on December 21 in Protestant calendars as originally in the Roman calendar, but now July 3 in the latter.

-tide: a suffix indicating an extended period of time or liturgical season, as "Eastertide" (= **Great Fifty Days).** The designation is used far less now than previously and is not appropriate to Sundays in the Year (ordinary time). See pp. 241-42.

Transfiguration, [Feast of]: August 6 in traditional calendars; transferred to the Sunday before Lent in several current calendars. See pp. 97, 259.

Tre Ore: Italian designation for the three-hour service for Good Friday. While such a service was used in Cyril's plan for pilgrims in Jerusalem, this fourth-century practice is not the source of contemporary patterns, which arose in the seventeenth century in Peru. See p. 189.

Triduum: See pp. 107, 160.

Trinity Sunday: See pp. 236–37.

Veil: In some traditions it has been the custom to cover or veil the crucifix and statues throughout Lent or for the last two weeks of Lent as a means of creating a "fast for the eyes." (See **Hunger Cloth.**) These veils, usually in the appropriate liturgical color, were removed at the Paschal Vigil, or prior to the service on Easter morning.

Vigil (Latin, *vigilia*, "a watch"): The service held on the eve or early morning of great festivals. See **Eve.**

Visitation, [Feast of]: May 31 in current calendars, July 2 in older calendars. Commemorates the visit of Mary to her cousin, Elizabeth, as reported in Luke 1:39. See p. 259.

Watch Night: A vigil service, particularly among the Moravians and early Methodists. The former group employed it on New Year's Eve. John Wesley adapted a Puritan covenant service for such a service at the New Year; he also held vigils on Friday evenings nearest the full moon, as a means of reaching those who worked all day, and as an alternative to Friday evening drinking bouts. Despite the vigil character, neither the New Year covenant service nor other forms of Wesley vigils can be directly related to the keeping of vigil on festival occasions traditional to the church.

Week of Prayer for Christian Unity: Traditionally in the Roman calendar, January 18 was the Feast of Saint Peter's Chair and January 25 the Feast of the Conversion of Saint Paul. Because of the primacy accorded Peter in Catholicism and the dominance of Pauline theology among Protestants, the eight days embraced by these feasts were set aside as a time of prayer for the unity of the church. This has become an ecumenical occasion in the last quarter century. Ironically, January 18 is no longer given to Saint Peter in the new Catholic calendar (having been combined with a similar observance on February 22) but has been included in the Episcopal and Lutheran calendars as "The Confession of Saint Peter the Apostle."

Whitsunday: Another term for Pentecost. A contraction of "White Sunday"—not because of the liturgical color for the day, but from the fact that like the opening of the **Great Fifty Days,** the closing came to be a time of baptism at which candidates wore white robes.

World Communion Sunday: The first Sunday in October. A day of recent origin on which all congregations are urged to celebrate the Eucharist so that all Christians may receive communion on the same date. Of particular pertinence, of course, in those churches that lack a weekly eucharistic tradition.

Yew Sunday: An English title for the Sunday before Easter, since yew branches often were distributed, palms being unavailable.

11

ANNOTATED BIBLIOGRAPHY

A. General Books on the Christian Year

Adam, Adolf. *The Liturgical Year*. New York: Pueblo, 1981.
McArthur, A. A. *The Evolution of the Christian Year*. London: SCM, 1953.
Nocent, Adrian. *The Liturgical Year*. 4 vols. Collegeville, MN: Liturgical Press, 1977.
Talley, Thomas J. *The Origins of the Liturgical Year*. New York: Pueblo, 1986.

B. Denominational Worship Books

Anglican Church of Canada. *Book of Alternative Services*. Toronto: Anglican Book Centre, 1985.
Episcopal Church. *The Book of Common Prayer*. New York: Church Hymnal Corporation, 1977.
Lutheran Book of Worship. Minneapolis: Augsburg Fortress, 1978.
Presbyterian Church (U.S.A.). *Liturgical Year: Supplemental Liturgical Resources 7*. Louisville: Westminster/John Knox, 1992.
Book of Common Worship, published by the Presbyterian Church in Canada, 1991.
Roman Catholic Church. *Sunday Missal*. Editions published by various publishers in the United States and Canada.
United Church of Christ. *Book of Worship*. New York: Office for Church Life and Leadership, 1986.
The United Methodist Book of Worship. Nashville: The United Methodist Publishing House, 1992.

C. Resources Based on the Revised Common Lectionary

The Revised Common Lectionary. Consultation on Common Texts. Nashville: Abingdon, 1992. The basic book on the Revised Common Lectionary, including an extensive introduction giving the story of its development and the rationale on which the choice of readings is based.
Abingdon Preacher's Annual. Nashville: Abingdon. Offers examples of ways others approach lectionary-based preaching.
Bone, David L. and Mary J. Scifres. *The United Methodist Music and Worship Planner*. Nashville: Abingdon, 1992. Scripture readings are printed out, together with hymn, keyboard, anthem, and other musical suggestions for each Sunday.
Brown, Carolyn. *Forbid Them Not*. Nashville: Abingdon, 1992-94. 3 volumes (Years A, B, C) which provide insights for lectionary-based worship with children.
Church Music Handbook, published annually by Gemini Press, Box 603, Otis, MA 01253, suggests hymns related to the lectionary for each Sunday.
Crouch, Timothy J., Nancy B. Parks, Chris E. Visminas, and Mark R. Babb. *And Also With You*. Published 1992 by OSL Publications, 5246 Broadway, Cleveland, OH 44127-1500. 3 volumes (Years A, B, C) of comprehensive worship resources based on the lectionary.

Dozeman, Thomas, Kendall McCabe, and Marion Soards. *Preaching the Revised Common Lectionary*. Nashville: Abingdon, 1992–. A 12-volume series of commentaries that help pastors and worship leaders plan lectionary-based preaching, music, and liturgy.

Gathering: A Packet for Worship Planners, published three times yearly by the Unit for Worship, Mission, and Evangelism of The United Church of Canada, 85 St. Clair Avenue East, Toronto, ON M4T 1M8, Canada, provides lectionary-related liturgical and musical resources for each Sunday.

Hessel, Dieter T. *Social Themes of the Christian Year*. Philadelphia: Geneva Press, 1983. Social themes and implications for each day and season.

The Lectionary Bible. Nashville: Abingdon, 1992. Printed texts (NRSV) of all three annual cycles of the Revised Common Lectionary.

Lowry, Eugene. *Living with the Lectionary*. Nashville: Abingdon, 1992. Basic guidance for authentic biblical preaching.

O'Donnell, Michael J. *Lift Up Your Hearts*. Published 1989–1991 by OSL Publications, 5246 Broadway, Cleveland, OH 44127-1500. 3 volumes of Communion resources (Years A, B, and c), based on the lectionary.

Reformed Liturgy and Music, published quarterly by the Theology and Worship Ministry Unit of the Presbyterian Church (U.S.A.), 100 Witherspoon Street, Louisville, KY 40202-1396, includes suggested hymns, anthems, organ music, and other worship resources for each Sunday.

Tilson, Everett and Phyllis Cole. *Liturgies and Other Prayers for the Revised Common Lectionary*. Nashville: Abingdon, 1992–94. 3 volumes (Years A, B, C). Newly revised to correspond with the Revised Common Lectionary.

Troeger, Thomas and Carol Doran. *New Hymns for the Lectionary: To Glorify the Maker's Name*. New York: Oxford University Press, 1986. Forty-six original hymn texts and tunes designed for use with the lectionary.

Word Alive! weekly bulletin inserts (available from Cokesbury, P.O. Box 801, Nashville, TN 37202) that include the lessons and Psalter in the New Revised Standard Version.

Worship Arts, published six times a year by the Fellowship of United Methodists in Worship, Music and Other Arts, P. O. Box 24787, Nashville, TN 37202, includes hymn suggestions for each Sunday and seasonal liturgy and anthem ideas.

INDEX OF
SCRIPTURE READINGS

(Versification follows that of the *New Revised Standard Version*)

Genesis

1:1-5	Baptism of the Lord, B
1:1–2:4a	Trinity Sunday, A Easter Vigil, ABC
2:15-17; 3:1-7	Lent 1, A
2:18-24	Oct. 2-8, B
3:8-15	June 5-11, B
6:9-22; 7:24; 8:14-19	May 29-June 4, A
7:1-5, 11-18; 8:6-18; 9:8-13	Easter Vigil, ABC
9:8-17	Lent 1, B
11:1-9	Pentecost, C
12:1-4a	Lent 2, A
12:1-9	June 5-11, A
15:1-6	Aug. 7-13, C
15:1-12, 17-18	Lent 2, C
17:1-7, 15-16	Lent 2, B
18:1-10a	July 17-23, C
18:1-15, (21:1-7)	June 12-18, A
18:20-32	July 24-30, C
21:8-21	June 19-25, A
22:1-14	June 26-July 2, A
22:1-18	Easter Vigil, ABC
24:34-38, 42-49, 58-67	July 3-9, A
25:19-34	July 10-16, A
28:10-19a	July 17-23, A
29:15-28	July 24-30, A
32:22-31	July 31-Aug. 6, A Oct. 16-22, C
37:1-4, 12-28	Aug. 7-13, A
45:1-15	Aug. 14-20, A
45:3-11, 15	7 after Epiphany, C
50:15-21	Sept. 11-17, A

Exodus

1:8–2:10	Aug. 21-27, A
3:1-15	Aug. 28-Sept. 3, A
12:1-14	Sept. 4-10, A
12:1-4, (5-10), 11-14	Holy Thursday, ABC
14:10-31; 15:20-21	Easter Vigil, ABC
14:19-31	Sept. 11-17, A
15:1b-13, 17-18	Easter Vigil, ABC
15:1b-11, 20-21	Sept. 11-17, A
16:2-15	Sept. 18-24, A
16:2-4, 9-15	July 31-Aug. 6, B
17:1-7	Lent 3, A Sept. 25-Oct. 1, A
19:2-8a	June 12-18, A
20:1-17	Lent 3, B
20:1-4, 7-9, 12-20	Oct. 2-8, A
24:12-18	Transfiguration, A
32:1-14	October 9-15, A
32:7-14	Sept. 11-17, C
33:12-23	Oct. 16-22, A
34:29-35	Transfiguration, C

Leviticus

19:1-2, 9-18	7 after Epiphany, A
19:1-2, 15-18	Oct. 23-29, A

Numbers

6:22-27	Holy Name of Jesus, ABC
11:4-6, 10-16, 24-29	Sept. 25-Oct. 1, B
11:24-30	Pentecost, A
21:4-9	Lent 4, B
21:4b-9	Holy Cross Day, ABC

Deuteronomy

4:1-2, 6-9	Aug. 28-Sept. 3, B
5:12-15	May 29-June 4, B
6:1-9	Oct. 30-Nov. 5, B
8:7-18	Thanksgiving, A
11:18-21, 26-28	May 29-June 4, A
18:15-20	4 after Epiphany, B
26:1-11	Lent 1, C Thanksgiving, C
30:9-14	July 10-16, C
30:15-20	6 after Epiphany, A Sept. 4-10, C
34:1-12	Oct. 23-29, A

Joshua

3:7-17	Oct. 30-Nov. 5, A
5:9-12	Lent 4, C
24:1-2a, 14-18	Aug. 21-27, B
24:1-3a, 14-25	Nov. 6-12, A

Judges

4:1-7	Nov. 13-19, A

Ruth

1:1-18	Oct. 30-Nov. 5, B
3:1-5; 4:13-17	Nov. 6-12, B

I Samuel

1:4-20	Nov. 13-19, B
2:1-10	Visitation, ABC Nov. 13-19, B
2:18-20, 26	1 after Christmas, C
3:1-10, (11-20)	2 after Epiphany, B May 29-June 4, B
8:4-11, (12-15), 16-20, (11:14-15)	June 5-11, B
15:34–16:13	June 12-18, B
16:1-13	Lent 4, A
17:(1a, 4-11, 19-23), 32-49	June 19-25, B
17:57–18:5, (10-16)	June 19-25, B

II Samuel

1:1, 17-27	June 27-July 2, B
5:1-5, 9-10	July 3-9, B

Daniel

7:1-3, 15-18	All Saints, C
7:9-10, 13-14	Christ the King, B
12:1-3	Nov. 13-19, B

Hosea

1:2-10	July 24-30, C
2:14-20	8 after Epiphany, B
5:15–6:6	June 5-11, A
11:1-11	July 31-Aug. 6, C

Joel

2:1-2, 12-17	Ash Wednesday, ABC
2:21-27	Thanksgiving, B
2:23-32	Oct. 23-29, C

Amos

5:6-7, 10-15	Oct. 9-15, B
5:18-24	Nov. 6-12, A
6:1a, 4-7	Sept. 25-Oct. 1, C
7:7-15	July 10-16, B
7:7-17	July 10-16, C
8:1-12	July 17-23, C
8:4-7	Sept. 18-24, C

Jonah

3:1-5, 10	3 after Epiphany, B
3:10–4:11	Sept. 18-24, A

Micah

3:5-12	Oct. 30-Nov. 5, A
5:2-5a	Advent 4, C
6:1-8	4 after Epiphany, A

Habakkuk

1:1-4; 2:1-4	Oct. 2-8, C
	Oct. 30-Nov. 5, C

Zephaniah

1:7, 12-18	Nov. 13-19, A
3:14-20	Advent 3, C
	Easter Vigil, ABC

Haggai

1:15b–2:9	Nov. 6-12, C

Zechariah

9:9-12	July 3-9, A

Malachi

3:1-4	Advent 2, C
	Presentation, ABC
4:1-2a	Nov. 13-19, C

Wisdom of Solomon

1:13-15; 2:23-24	June 26-July 2, B
1:16–2:1, 12-22	Sept. 18-24, B
3:1-9	All Saints, B
6:12-20	Nov. 6-12, A
7:26–8:1	Sept. 11-17, B
10:15-21	2 after Christmas, ABC
12:13, 16-19	July 17-23, A

Sirach (Ecclesiasticus)

10:12-18	Aug. 28-Sept. 3, C
15:15-20	6 after Epiphany, A
24:1-12	2 after Christmas, ABC
27:4-7	8 after Epiphany, C
35:12-17	Oct. 23-29, C

Baruch

3:9-15, 3:32–4:4	Easter Vigil, ABC
5:1-9	Advent 2, C

Matthew

1:18-25	Advent 4, A
2:1-12	Epiphany, ABC
2:13-23	1 after Christmas, A
3:1-12	Advent 2, A
3:13-17	Baptism of the Lord, A
4:1-11	Lent 1, A
4:12-23	3 after Epiphany, A
5:1-12	4 after Epiphany, A
	All Saints, A
5:13-20	5 after Epiphany, A
5:21-37	6 after Epiphany, A
5:38-48	7 after Epiphany, A
6:1-6, 16-21	Ash Wednesday, ABC
6:24-34	8 after Epiphany, A
6:25-33	Thanksgiving, B
7:21-29	May 29-June 4, A
9:9-13, 18-26	June 5-11, A
9:35–10:8, (9-23)	June 12-18, A
10:24-39	June 19-25, A
10:40-42	June 26-July 2, A
11:2-11	Advent 3, A
11:16-19, 25-30	July 3-9, A
13:1-9, 18-23	July 10-16, A
13:24-30, 36-43	July 17-23, A
13:31-33, 44-52	July 24-30, A
14:13-21	July 31-Aug. 6, A
14:22-33	Aug. 7-13, A
15:(10-20), 21-28	Aug. 14-20, A
16:13-20	Aug. 21-27, A
16:21-28	Aug. 28-Sept. 3, A
17:1-9	Transfiguration, A
	Lent 2, A
18:15-20	Sept. 4-10, A
18:21-35	Sept. 11-17, A
20:1-16	Sept. 18-24, A
21:1-11	Passion/Palm, A
21:23-32	Sept. 25-Oct. 1, A
21:33-46	Oct. 2-8, A
22:1-14	Oct. 9-15, A
22:15-22	Oct. 16-22, A
22:34-46	Oct. 23-29, A
23:1-12	Oct. 30-Nov. 5, A
24:36-44	Advent 1, A
25:1-13	Nov. 6-12, A
25:14-30	Nov. 13-19, A
25:31-46	Christ the King, A
	New Year, ABC
26:14–27:66	Passion/Palm, A
27:57-66	Holy Saturday, ABC
28:1-10	Easter Vigil, A
	Easter, A
28:16-20	Trinity A

Mark

1:1-8	Advent 2, B
1:4-11	Baptism of the Lord, B
1:9-15	Lent 1, B
1:14-20	3 after Epiphany, B
1:21-28	4 after Epiphany, B
1:29-39	5 after Epiphany, B
1:40-45	6 after Epiphany, B
2:1-12	7 after Epiphany, B
2:13-22	8 after Epiphany, B
2:23–3:6	May 29-June 4, B
3:20-35	June 5-11, B
4:26-34	June 12-18, B
4:35-41	June 19-25, B
5:21-43	June 26-July 2, B
6:1-13	July 3-9, B
6:14-29	July 10-16, B
6:30-34, 53-56	July 17-23, B
7:1-8, 14-15, 21-23	Aug. 28-Sept. 3, B
7:24-37	Sept. 4-10, B
8:27-38	Sept. 11-17, B
8:31-38	Lent 2, B
9:2-9	Tranfiguration, B
	Lent 2, B
9:30-37	Sept. 18-24, B
9:38-50	Sept. 25-Oct. 1, B
10:2-16	Oct. 2-8, B
10:17-31	Oct. 9-15, B
10:35-45	Oct. 16-22, B
10:46-52	Oct. 23-29, B
11:1-11	Passion/Palm, B
12:28-34	Oct. 30-Nov. 5, B
12:38-44	Nov. 6-12, B
13:1-8	Nov. 13-19, B
13:24-37	Advent 1, B
14:1–15:47	Passion/Palm, B
16:1-8	Easter Vigil, B
	Easter, B

Luke

1:26-38	Advent 4, B
	Annunciation, ABC
1:39-55	Advent 4, C
1:39-57	Visitation, ABC
1:47-55	Advent 3, AB
	Advent 4, B

5:6b-8	Easter Evening, ABC
6:12-20	Epiphany 2, B
7:29-31	Epiphany 3, B
8:1-13	Epiphany 4, B
9:16-23	Epiphany 5, B
9:24-27	Epiphany 6, B
10:1-13	Lent 3, C
11:23-26	Holy Thursday, ABC
12:1-11	Epiphany 2, C
12:3b-13	Pentecost, A
12:12-31a	Epiphany 3, C
13:1-13	Epiphany 4, C
15:1-11	Epiphany 5, C
	Easter, B
15:12-20	Epiphany 6, C
15:19-26	Easter, C
15:35-38, 42-50	Epiphany 7, C
15:51-58	Epiphany 8, C

II Corinthians

1:18-22	Epiphany 7, B
3:1-6	Epiphany 8, B
3:12–4:2	Transfiguration, C
4:3-6	Transfiguration, B
4:5-12	May 29-June 4, B
4:13–5:1	June 5-11, B
5:6-10, (11-13), 14-17	June 12-18, B
5:16-21	Lent 4, C
5:20b–6:10	Ash Wednesday, ABC
6:1-13	June 19-25, B
8:7-15	June 26-July 2, B
9:6-15	Thanksgiving, A
12:2-10	July 3-9, B
13:11-13	Triniy, A

Galatians

1:1-12	May 29-June 4, C
1:11-24	June 5-11, C
2:15-21	June 12-18, C
3:23-29	June 19-25, C
4:4-7	1 after Christmas, B
	Holy Name, ABC
5:1, 13-25	June 26-July 2, C
6:(1-6), 7-16	July 3-9, C

Ephesians

1:3-14	2 after Christmas, ABC
	July 10-16, B
1:11-23	All Saints, C
1:15-23	Ascension, ABC
	Christ the King, A
2:1-10	Lent 4, B
2:11-22	July 17-23, B
3:1-12	Epiphany, ABC
3:14-21	July 24-30, B
4:1-16	July 31-Aug. 6, B
4:25–5:2	Aug. 7-13, B
5:8-14	Lent 4, A
5:15-20	Aug. 14-20, B
6:10-20	Aug. 21-27, B

Philippians

1:3-11	Advent 2, C
1:21-30	Sept. 18-24, A

2:1-13	Sept. 25-Oct. 1, A
2:5-11	Passion/Palm, ABC
2:5-13	Holy Name, ABC
3:4b-14	Lent 5, C
	Oct. 2-8, A
3:17–4:1	Lent 2, C
4:1-9	Oct. 9-15, A
4:4-7	Advent 3, C
4:4-9	Thanksgiving, C

Colossians

1:1-14	July 10-16, C
1:11-20	Christ the King, C
1:15-28	July 17-23, C
2:6-15, (16-19)	July 24-30, C
3:1-4	Easter, A
3:1-11	July 31-Aug. 6, C
3:12-17	1 after Christmas, C

I Thessalonians

1:1-10	Oct. 16-22, A
2:1-8	Oct. 23-29, A
2:9-13	Oct. 30-Nov. 5, A
3:9-13	Advent 1, C
4:13-18	Nov. 6-12, A
5:1-11	Nov. 13-19, A
5:16-24	Advent 3, B

II Thessalonians

1:1-4, 11-12	Oct. 30-Nov. 5, C
2:1-5, 13-17	Nov. 6-12, C
3:6-13	Nov. 13-19, C

I Timothy

1:12-17	Sept. 11-17, C
2:1-7	Sept. 18-24, C
	Thanksgiving, B
6:6-19	Sept. 25-Oct. 1, C

II Timothy

1:1-14	Oct. 2-8, C
2:8-15	Oct. 9-15, C
3:14–4:5	Oct. 16-22, C
4:6-8, 16-18	Oct. 23-29, C

Titus

2:11-14	Christmas Eve, ABC
3:4-7	Christmas Day, ABC

Philemon

1-21	Sept. 4-10, C

Hebrews

1:1-4, (5-12)	Christmas Day, ABC
1:1-4; 2:5-12	Oct. 2-8, B
2:10-18	1 after Christmas, A
2:14-18	Presentation, ABC
4:12-16	Oct. 9-15, B
4:14-16; 5:7-9	Good Friday, ABC
5:1-10	Oct. 16-22, B
5:5-10	Lent 5, B
7:23-28	Oct. 23-29, B
9:11-14	Oct. 30-Nov. 5, B
9:11-15	Monday in Holy Week, ABC

9:24-28	Nov. 6-12, B
10:4-10	Annunciation, ABC
10:5-10	Advent 4, C
10:11-14, (15-18), 19-25	Nov. 13-19, B
10:16-25	Good Friday, ABC
11:1-3, 8-16	Aug. 7-13, C
11:29–12:2	Aug. 14-20, C
12:1-3	Wednesday in Holy Week, ABC
12:18-29	Aug. 21-27, C
13:1-8, 15-16	Aug. 28-Sept. 3, C

James

1:17-27	Aug. 28-Sept. 3, B
2:1-10, (11-13), 14-17	Sept. 4-10, B
3:1-12	Sept. 11-17, B
3:13–4:3, 7-8a	Sept. 18-24, B
5:7-10	Advent 3, A
5:13-20	Sept. 25-Oct. 1, B

I Peter

1:3-9	Easter 2, A
1:17-23	Easter 3, A
2:2-10	Easter 5, A
2:19-25	Easter 4, A
3:13-22	Easter 6, A
3:18-22	Lent 1, B
4:1-8	Holy Saturday, ABC
4:12-14; 5:6-11	Easter 7, A

II Peter

1:16-21	Transfiguration, A
3:8-15a	Advent 2, B

I John

1:1–2:2	Easter 2, B
3:1-3	All Saints, A
3:1-7	Easter 3, B
3:16-24	Easter 4, B
4:7-21	Easter 5, B
5:1-6	Easter 6, B
5:9-13	Easter 7, B

Revelation

1:4-8	Easter 2, C
1:4b-8	Christ the King, B
5:11-14	Easter 3, C
7:9-17	Easter 4, C
	All Saints, A
21:1-6a	New Year, ABC
	All Saints, B
21:1-6	Easter 5, C
21:10; 21:22–22:5	Easter 6, C
22:12-14, 16-17, 20-21	Easter 7, C

INDEX OF PSALMS

(Numbering and versification follow that of the *New Revised Standard Version*)

46	Easter Vigil, ABC
	May 29-June 4, A
	Christ the King, C
47	Ascension, ABC
48	July 3-9, B
49:1-12	July 31-Aug. 6, C
50:1-6	Transfiguration, B
50:1-8, 22-23	Aug. 7-13, C
50:7-15	June 5-11, A
51:1-10	Sept. 11-17, C
51:1-12	Lent 5, B
	July 31-Aug. 6, B
51:1-17	Ash Wednesday, ABC
52	July 17-23, C
54	Sept. 18-24, B
62:5-12	Epiphany 3, B
63:1-8	Lent 3, C
65:(1-8), 9-13	July 10-16, A
65	Oct. 23-29, C
	Thanksgiving, A
66:1-9	July 3-9, C
66:1-12	Oct. 9-15, C
66:8-20	Easter 6, A
67	Easter 6, C
	Aug. 14-20, A
68:1-10, 32-35	Easter 7, A
69:7-10, (11-15), 16-18	June 19-25, A
70	Wednesday in Holy Week, ABC
	Nov. 6-12, A
71:1-6	Epiphany 4, C
	Aug. 21-27, C
71:1-14	Tuesday in Holy Week, ABC
72:1-7, 10-14	Epiphany, ABC
72:1-7, 18-19	Advent 2, A
77:1-2, 11-20	June 26-July 2, C
78:1-7	Nov. 6-12, A
78:1-4, 12-16	Sept. 25-Oct. 1, A
78:1-2, 34-38	Holy Cross, ABC
78:23-29	July 31-Aug. 6, B
79:1-9	Sept. 18-24, C
80:1-7	Advent 4, C
80:1-2, 8-19	Aug. 14-20, C
80:1-7, 17-19	Advent 1, B
	Advent 4, A
80:7-15	Oct. 2-8, A
81:1-10	May 29-June 4, B
81:1, 10-16	Aug. 28-Sept. 3, C
82	July 10-16, C
	Aug. 14-20, C
84:1-7	Oct. 23-29, C
84	Presentation, ABC
	Aug. 21-27, B
85:1-2, 8-13	Advent 2, B
85	July 24-30, C
85:8-13	July 10-16, B
	Aug. 7-13, A
86:1-10, 16-17	June 19-25, A
86:11-17	July 17-23, A
89:1-4, 15-18	June 26-July 2, A
89:1-4, 19-26	Advent 4, B
89:20-37	July 17-23, B
90:1-8, (9-11), 12	Nov. 13-19, A
90:1-6, 13-17	Oct. 23-29, A

90:12-17	Oct. 9-15, B
91:1-2, 9-16	Lent 1, C
91:1-6, 14-16	Sept. 25-Oct. 1, C
91:9-16	Oct. 16-22, B
92:1-4, 12-15	Epiphany 8, C
	June 12-18, B
93	Ascension, B
	Christ the King, B
95:1-7*a*	Christ the King, A
95	Lent 3, A
96:1-9, (10-13)	Oct. 16-22, A
96	Christmas Eve, ABC
	May 29-June 4, C
97	Christmas Day, ABC
	Easter 7, C
98:1-5	Holy Cross, ABC
98	Christmas Day, ABC
	Easter Vigil, ABC
	Easter 6, B
	Nov. 6-12, C
	Nov. 13-19, C
99	Transfiguration, AC
	Oct. 16-22, A
100	June 12-18, A
	Christ the King, A
	Thanksgiving, C
103:1-8	Aug. 21-27, C
103:(1-7), 8-13	Sept. 11-17, A
103:1-13, 22	Epiphany 8, B
104:1-9, 24, 35*c*	Oct. 16-22, B
104:24-34, 35*b*	Pentecost, ABC
105:1-6, 16-22, 45*b*	Aug. 7-13, A
105:1-11, 45*b*	July 24-30, A
105:1-6, 23-26, 45*c*	Aug. 28-Sept. 3, A
105:1-6, 37-45	Sept. 18-24, A
106:1-6, 19-23	Oct. 9-15, A
107:1-3, 17-22	Lent 4, B
107:1-3, 23-32	June 19-25, B
107:1-7, 33-37	Oct. 30-Nov. 5, A
107:1-9, 43	July 31-Aug. 6, C
110	Ascension, C
111	Epiphany 4, B
	Aug. 14-20, B
	Oct. 9-15, C
112:1-9, (10)	Epiphany 5, A
112	Aug. 28-Sept. 3, C
113	Visitation, ABC
	Sept. 18-24, C
114	Easter Vigil, ABC
	Easter Evening, ABC
	Sept. 11-17, A
116:1-9	Sept. 11-17, B
116:1-2, 12-19	Holy Thursday, ABC
	June 12-18, A
116:1-4, 12-19	Easter 3, A
118:1-2, 14-24	Easter, ABC
118:1-2, 19-29	Passion/Palm, ABC
118:14-29	Easter 2, C
119:1-8	Epiphany 6, A
	Oct. 30-Nov. 5, B
119:9-16	Lent 5, B
119:33-40	Epiphany 7, A
	Sept. 4-10, A
119:97-104	Oct. 16-22, C
119:105-112	July 10-16, A

ACKNOWLEDGMENTS

This page is hereby made a part of the copyright page.

The scripture citations and scripture indices (adapted) are from *The Revised Common Lectionary* © 1992 Consultation on Common Texts and are used by permission.

Material from *Seasons of the Gospel*, copyright © 1979 by Abingdon Press; *From Ashes to Fire*, copyright © 1979 by Abingdon Press; and *From Hope to Joy*, copyright © 1984 by Abingdon Press is scattered throughout the book. Used by permission.

Prayers marked BCP are taken or adapted from *The Book of Common Prayer* of The Episcopal Church (1979).

On page 56 the poem "At Last Night Is Ending" is from *Prayers, Poems, and Songs* by Huub Oosterhuis, copyright 1970 by Herder and Herder. Used by permission of Uitgeverij Ambo bv, Baarn, Holland.

The first translation of the O Antiphons on pages 62-63 is from *The Book of Worship*, copyright © 1965 by The United Methodist Publishing House.

The collect on page 67 is reprinted from *Service Book and Hymnal*, copyright 1978, by permission of Augsburg Publishing House.

The responsories on pages 153 and 156 are adapted from *Saint John's Abbey Prayer*, copyright by Saint John's Abbey, Collegeville, Minn.

The text "The Passion of Our Lord" on pages 170-75 is from *A Liturgical Interpretation in Narrative Form of the Passion of Jesus Christ* by John T. Townsend, copyright 1985 by the National Council of Christians and Jews. Used by permission.

Text for the Benedictus on page 177 is taken from *Prayers We Have in Common*, copyright © 1970, 1971, and 1975, International Consultation on English Texts.

The English translation of the *Exsultet* on pages 194-95 and the text of "Christ has died," used in each of the Great Thanksgivings, are from *The Roman Missal* © 1973, International Committee on English in the Liturgy, Inc. All rights reserved.

The lines by Charles Wesley on page 274 are from hymn number 155 in Wesley's *Hymn on the Lord's Supper*, published in 1745.

ECUMENICAL SERVICE:
THE SACRAMENT OF
THE LORD'S SUPPER

*T*his service was prepared by the Commission on Worship of the Consultation on Church Union and published with the approval of the Executive Committee. It may be used at any time for celebrations of the Lord's Supper in which several denominations are represented. The member churches of the Consultation on Church Union are: African Methodist Episcopal Church, African Methodist Episcopal Zion Church, Christian Church (Disciples of Christ), Christian Methodist Episcopal Church, The Episcopal Church, International Council of Community Churches, Presbyterian Church (U.S.A.), United Church of Christ, and The United Methodist Church.

Gathering

OPENING SENTENCES *One of the following:*

The grace, mercy, and peace of Jesus Christ be with you.
And also with you.

Alleluia, Christ is risen.
The Lord is risen indeed. Alleluia.

Other scriptural sentences of greeting may be used.

HYMN OF PRAISE*

PRAYER* *One of the following:*

Almighty God:
You are infinite, eternal, and unchangeable,
　　glorious in holiness, full of love and compassion,
　　abundant in grace and truth.
All your works praise you in all places of your dominion,
　　and your glory is revealed in Christ, our Savior.
Therefore, we praise you, Blessed and Holy Trinity,
　　One God, forever and ever. Amen.

Almighty God,
to you all hearts are open, all desires known,
    and from you no secrets are hid:
Cleanse the thoughts of our hearts
    by the inspiration of your Holy Spirit,
that we may perfectly love you,
    and worthily magnify your holy name,
through Christ our Lord. Amen.

Proclamation and Response

FIRST LESSON

ACT OF PRAISE* *A psalm, canticle, or hymn may follow the reading.*

SECOND LESSON

ACT OF PRAISE*

LESSON FROM THE GOSPELS*

SERMON

RESPONSES

    There may occur in response to proclamation any of the following:
    1) An altar call or invitation to Christian discipleship
    2) The reception of new members
    3) The ordination and installation of church officers
    4) The Sacrament of Baptism
    5) A call to action
    6) The reciting of a creed
    An act of confession and reconciliation such as the following may be used in response to the proclamation:

We confess that often we have failed to be an obedient church.
We have not done your will, we have broken your law,
    we have rebelled against your love,
    and we have not heard the cry of the needy.
Forgive us, we pray.
Free us for joyful obedience, through Jesus Christ our Lord.
Amen.

Anyone in Christ becomes a new person altogether;
the past is finished and gone,
    everything has become fresh and new.
Friends, believe the good news of the gospel:

In Jesus Christ, we are forgiven.

CONCERNS AND PRAYERS OF THE CHURCH*

The people are encouraged to express their own concerns, whether by stating them personally or communicating them to the leader before the service. The intercessions may take the form of one continuous prayer by the leader, biddings, or a litany.

Service of the Table

THE PEACE*

The peace of Christ be with you.
And also with you.

The ministers and people may stand and exchange signs and words of God's peace.

PRESENTING THE GIFTS

GREAT THANKSGIVING*

Lift up your hearts.
We lift them to the Lord.

Let us give thanks to the Lord our God.
It is right to give God thanks and praise.

The Preface

It is right and good to give you thanks, Almighty God,
    for you are the source of light and life.
You made us in your image and called us to new life in Jesus Christ.
In all times and places
    your people proclaim your glory in unending praise:

Local congregations and eucharistic communities are encouraged to make their own decisions about the content and style of the Preface, focusing on general themes stressing the creation, the season or day in the church year, or a local occasion. Proper prefaces for seasons of the church year are suggested as follows:

Advent

It is right and good to give you thanks, Almighty God.
You sent your servant John the Baptist to preach repentance
    and to prepare the way of our Lord Jesus Christ.
Therefore, in all times and places
    your people proclaim your glory in unending praise:

Christmas

It is right and good to give you thanks, Almighty God.
You gave us the gift of your Son Jesus,
    who is the light in this dark world and our only Savior.
Therefore, in all times and places
    your people proclaim your glory in unending praise:

Epiphany

It is right and good to give you thanks, Almighty God.
You have given us the Word made flesh,
and through our baptism we are blessed to share
    in the healing and reconciling love of Christ.
Therefore, in all times and places
    your people proclaim your glory in unending praise:

Lent

It is right and good to give you thanks, Almighty God.
You call us to cleanse our hearts
    and prepare with joy for the victory of the Lamb who is slain.
Therefore, in all times and places
    your people proclaim your glory in unending praise:

Easter

It is right and good to give you thanks, Almighty God.
You have brought forth our Lord Jesus from the grave.
By his death he has destroyed death,
    and by his rising to life again he has won for us everlasting life.
Therefore, in all times and places
    your people proclaim your glory in unending praise:

Pentecost

It is right and good to give you thanks, Almighty God.
You poured out the Holy Spirit upon the disciples,
    teaching them the truth of your Son Jesus,
    empowering your Church for its service,
    and uniting us as your holy people.
Therefore, in all times and places
    your people proclaim your glory in unending praise:

Following the Preface, the Great Thanksgiving continues:

**Holy, holy, holy Lord, God of power and might,
    heaven and earth are full of your glory.
Hosanna in the highest.
Blessed is the one who comes in the name of the Lord.
Hosanna in the highest.**

We remember with joy the grace by which you created all things
    and made us in your own image.
We rejoice that you called a people in covenant
    to be a light to the nations.
Yet we rebelled against your will.
In spite of the prophets and pastors sent forth to us,
    we continued to break your covenant.

In the fullness of time, you sent your only Son to save us.
Incarnate by the Holy Spirit,
   born of your favored one, Mary,
   sharing our life, he reconciled us to your love.
At the Jordan your Spirit descended upon him,
   anointing him to preach the good news of your reign.
He healed the sick and fed the hungry,
   manifesting the power of your compassion.
He sought out the lost and broke bread with sinners,
   witnessing the fullness of your grace.
We beheld his glory.

On the night before he died for us, Jesus took bread;
   giving thanks to you, he broke the bread
   and offered it to his disciples, saying:
"Take this and eat; this is my body which is given for you,
   do this in remembrance of me."
Taking a cup, again he gave thanks to you,
   shared the cup with his disciples and said:
"This is the cup of the new covenant in my blood.
Drink from this all of you.
This is poured out for you and for many,
   for the forgiveness of sins."

After the meal our Lord was arrested,
   abandoned by his followers and beaten.
He stood trial and was put to death on a cross.
Having emptied himself in the form of a servant,
   and being obedient even to death,
   he was raised from the dead
   and exalted as Lord of heaven and earth.
Through him you bestow the gift of your Spirit,
   uniting your Church, empowering its mission,
   and leading us into the new creation you have promised.

Gracious God, we celebrate with joy
   the redemption won for us in Jesus Christ.
Grant that in praise and thanksgiving
   we may be a living sacrifice, holy and acceptable in your sight,
   that our lives may proclaim the mystery of faith:

Christ has died; Christ is risen; Christ will come again.

Loving God, pour out your Holy Spirit upon us
   and upon these gifts,
   that they may be for us the body and blood
   of our Savior Jesus Christ.
Grant that we may be for the world the body of Christ,
   redeemed through his blood,

serving and reconciling all people to you.
Remember your Church, scattered upon the face of the earth;
    gather it in unity and preserve it in truth.
Remember the saints who have gone before us,
    especially _____ and _____.
        Here may occur special names.)
In communion with them and with all creation,
    we worship and glorify you always:

**Through your Son Jesus Christ;
with the Holy Spirit in your holy Church,
all glory and honor is yours, Almighty God,
now and forever.
Amen.**

THE LORD'S PRAYER*

BREAKING OF BREAD

The minister breaks the bread in silence or while saying:

The bread which we break,
is it not a sharing in the Body of Christ?

**Because there is one bread,
we who are many are one body,
for we all partake of the one bread.**

The wine which we drink,
is it not a sharing in the blood of Christ?

**The cup which we bless
is the communion in the blood of Christ.**

SHARING OF THE BREAD AND THE CUP

Closing

PRAYER* *One of the following:*

**Bountiful God,
we give thanks that you have refreshed us at your table
    by granting us the presence of Christ.
Strengthen our faith, increase our love for one another,
    and send us forth into the world in courage and peace,
    rejoicing in the power of the Holy Spirit. Amen.**

**God our help, we thank you for this supper
    shared in the Spirit with your servant Jesus,
    who makes us new and strong, who brings life eternal.
We praise you for giving us all good gifts
    and pledge ourselves to serve you,
    even as in Christ you have served us. Amen.**

HYMN*

DISMISSAL*

The grace of the Lord Jesus Christ,
and the love of God,
and the communion of the Holy Spirit
be with you all. **Amen.**

A deacon or layperson may dismiss the people with these words:

Go out into the world in peace, have courage;
hold on to what is good; return no one evil for evil;
strengthen the fainthearted; support the weak;
help the suffering; honor everyone;
love and serve God, rejoicing in the power of the Holy Spirit.